VIOLENCE IN DEVELOPING COUNTRIES

CHRISTOPHER CRAMER

Violence in Developing Countries

War, Memory, Progress

INDIANA UNIVERSITY PRESS
Bloomington and Indianapolis

First published in the United States by
Indiana University Press
601 North Morton Street
Bloomington, Indiana 47404-3797 USA

http://iupress.indiana.edu

Telephone orders   800-842-6796
Fax orders   812-855-7931
Orders by e-mail   iuporder@indiana.edu

The right of Christopher Cramer to be
identified as the author of this volume
has been asserted by him in accordance with
the Copyright, Designs and Patents Act 1988.

Cataloging information is available from the
Library of Congress.

ISBN 978-0-253-34923-1 (cl.)
ISBN 978-0-253-21928-2 (pbk.)

1 2 3 4 5 12 11 10 09 08 07

In Memory of John Cramer, 1920-2004

CONTENTS

x   *Contents*

ACKNOWLEDGEMENTS

In writing this book I have enjoyed support, help, encouragement, and inspiration from many people.

My thanks go to the School of Oriental and African Studies (SOAS) for giving me two terms of sabbatical leave in 2003, most of which I devoted to this project; and for giving me a further term of 'special leave' from teaching during 2005, which I used to complete and tidy up the book. SOAS is unusual in a number of ways, but especially in recent decades for providing a base for a rich brand of heterodox and historically-minded political economy. Colleagues and students have provided a valuable environment in which to work, and in which I have developed many of the ideas explored in this book. In particular, colleagues teaching on the MSc in Violence, Conflict and Development (VCD), and on courses on the Political Economy of Development, on Growth and Development, and on Economic Development in Africa, have been a source of practical and intellectual support. The students who have studied and made a success of the VCD programme since it began in 2000 have been a great source of ideas and sometimes of constructive criticism.

A number of readers and listeners have helped me to clarify points, add (and subtract) material, and, I hope, improve sections of the book—in a couple of cases the whole book. I am grateful to student, seminar, and conference audiences (and their organisers) that have heard and responded to versions of some of the chapters. These include the audience at the Centre des Etudes et de Recherches Internationales (CERI) in Paris in September 2004 where I gave a talk organised by Roland Marchal, whom I thank for inviting me; participants at the 'Identidades, Resistencias y Conflitos en África' workshop in Madrid in 2004 (especially Ana Raquel Ferrão); students at the CAPORDE summer school in 2004 organised by Ha-Joon Chang; Dave Anderson, Deborah Bryceson, Jocelyn Alexander and others at St Antony's, Oxford, in discussion of some of the material on Mozambique in this book; those who came to the session where I presented a version of Chapter 7 during the WIDER conference on Making Peace Work in June 2004 in Helsinki, organised by Tony Addison and others; and participants in the workshop on Peacebuilding and Post-War Aid in June 2005 in Bergen, where I especially thank Astri Suhrke and Ingrid Samset. David Birmingham, James Boyce, Terry Byres, Jonathan Di John, Matthew Kentridge, Zoë Marriage, Nicolas Pons-Vignon, Hugo Slim, Ardashir Vakil, Marcus Verhagen, and Peter Cramer all read and made helpful and acute comments on one or more chapters. They also helped in a more enduring way by keeping me enthused. And I thank especially Henry Bernstein and John Sender for reading the whole book, some sections of it more than once, with astonishingly generous care. They have made it a much better read than it would otherwise have been, though of course they cannot be blamed for the shortcomings that remain; no more can Michael Dwyer of Hurst & Co., the publishers, who has been wry, patient, and enthusiastic in supporting me from drafts to completion, via lengthy debates over the title and more. Two anonymous readers also provided useful comments on the overall manuscript.

Many influences shape an intellectual conscience. I can identify some of the more important inspirations that have had a clear bearing on my work on the issues discussed in this book, and I am accordingly very grateful: for the humour and intelligence of my mother, father, sisters and brother; in particular for the wisdom and scepticism (but never cynicism) of my father and for the profound inspiration of my brother Peter; for the friendship and conversation of Ardashir Vakil (especially but not only on and around the tennis court), Marcus Verhagen, Matthew Kentridge, and Jonathan Di John; for occasional encounters in the warscapes of Luanda, Maputo, and elsewhere with Ernesto Latchmoor; and for the exceptional intellectual company, as well as friendship, of John Sender.

I thank the following for granting copyright permission to reproduce figures used in Chapter 3: the CIDCM at the University of Maryland for permission to reproduce figure 3.1 from *Peace and Conflict 2003*; the World Health Organisation, Geneva, for permission to reproduce 'The Typology of Violence' from the *World Report on Violence and Health* (2003); and Cambridge University Press for permission to reproduce figure 5 from Fearon and Laitin (2003), 'Ethnicity, Insurgency and Civil War', *American Political Science Review*, 97, 1.

Also at a practical but at the same time at a far more important level I thank Cathy, Gabriel, Carlotta, and now Linnéa too, for love and for being a home and family, for putting up (just) with piles of paper about the house, and for tolerating and challenging strange ideas (as Carlotta says, civil war is not a super thing).

London, April 2006 C.M.C.

INTRODUCTION
A WHIFF OF ANGOLA

'Civil war is not a stupid thing, like a war between nations, the Italians fighting the English, or the Germans fighting the Russians, where I, a Sicilian sulphur miner, kill an English miner, and the Russian peasant shoots at the German peasant; a civil war is something more logical, a man starts shooting for the people and the things he loves, for the things he wants and against the people he hates; and no-one makes a mistake about choosing which side to be on...' (Ventura, a character in 'Antimony', in Leonardo Sciascia's *Sicilian Uncles*)[1]

World at war

Wars and violence abound. By one count, between 1989 and 2003 there were 117 active armed conflicts in seventy-nine places around the world. Of these, thirty-one were active in 2002. Another estimate claims there were nineteen major armed conflicts in eighteen places during 2003.[2] Although the incidence of armed conflict declined during the 1990s, there is still some empirical anxiety about the degree of global 'security'. So while some take heart, others are gloomier. The World Bank, for example, argued that the incidence of civil war increased substantially over the forty years to 2002 and that the rate of 'civil war onset' remained relatively stable through the Cold War and afterwards. Further, 'the net positive effect of the end of the Cold War on war duration seems to have been modest and transient.'[3]

Most wars since the end of the Second World War are regarded as internal, intra-state or civil wars. Other kinds of violent conflict do not easily fit the established categories of war between nations or civil wars: genocide in Rwanda, for example, or conflicts that appear to some observers to be 'non-state' conflicts. Moreover, physical violence—let alone 'structural' or 'symbolic' violence—is a feature of normal life for millions of people around the world. Countries like Brazil, India and South Africa are shot through with violence

1

in struggles over land and labour, in urban life and in the management of family life. Violence against girls and women is especially rife in countless schools, townships, villages and households throughout much of the world and is then turned into a pandemic of viciousness during violent conflicts such as those in Rwanda, Congo and Darfur in Sudan. Meanwhile, violence in a country like Iraq slips between categories: the state violence of Saddam Hussein's regime; the violence of the invasion in 2003 by an international coalition; and the protracted violence of the period since President Bush declared the war of 2003 was officially over.

There is a growing preoccupation with these phenomena of violence in the world, and particularly in the 'South' or the 'developing world'. Governments in advanced industrialised countries, together with the UN, the World Bank, the OECD and other international bodies, have increasingly strained to catch up with the realisation of just how pervasive violent conflict and other manifestations of violence are in much of the world. Non-governmental organisations (NGOs) have paid more attention to these issues too, and new organisations have emerged whose focus is exclusively on issues of violence, war and conflict resolution.[4] Public opinion (or sections of it) has also been preoccupied with portraying, reacting to and understanding violent conflict around the world. The news media, humanitarian agency staff, academics and activists all worry over the ethics and efficacy of international interventions in developing or middle-income countries, over the phenomena of military humanitarianism and the re-emergence of mercenaries in the guise of private military corporations or PMCs, over the problem of whether humanitarianism itself represents a form of imperialism, and then over the ethics of *not* intervening in places like Zimbabwe and Uzbekistan.

At times the attention of governments and of public opinion has seemed to lurch from one 'crisis' to another: from Bosnia to Somalia to Rwanda to Afghanistan to Iraq to Darfur. But behind this there has been sustained debate in academic disciplines about the nature of wars. Until recently textbooks on economic development had little to say about violence and war. Major works on development barely touched on the subject. However, this has begun to change: new editions of textbooks devote chapters to war; development journals carry more and more articles on violent conflict; postgraduate courses on the subject have proliferated.

This preoccupation can be traced, for example, in the discipline of economics. Since the late 1980s there has been a surge of interest among development economists in the phenomena of violent conflict, usually conceived in terms of 'civil wars'. Towards the end of the Cold War a handful of economists tried to work out the cost of US interventions in Nicaragua and elsewhere in Central America and of South African destabilisation in Angola, Mozambique and elsewhere in Southern Africa. These exercises initiated a proliferation of analytical models for assessing the costs of conflict. What followed was an increase in empirical groundwork, putting together datasets, and in analytical work, suggesting ways of understanding what happened to economies during conflict, what the economic causes of war might be and what the priorities for post-conflict reconstruction ought to be. Consequently there have been intense arguments over appropriate assumptions, models, evidence and explanations for violent conflict.

Much of the work produced in this period has been preoccupied with novelty. Much of it stresses novelty in the forms of violent conflict, suggesting, for example, an era of 'new wars'. But much of it also implies explanatory innovation. This book argues both that there remains much to understand and that there is much to retain from earlier insights into violence, war and social change, for many of the questions raised in these debates, and the questions this book addresses, are old questions. Why do wars happen? Are they best explained by motives or by more structural forces? Why are there so many wars, and so many other forms of violence and violent conflict now, when peace was one of the main promises of modernity? What are wars? What are they about and how may they be explained? Is it possible to make sense of war? Do some wars make more sense than others? Are all wars essentially identical or are they so diverse as to defy general explanations? How far have economic and political changes in the world been matched by a change in warfare, generating 'new wars' that are sharply distinct from 'old wars'? How is global violence related to processes of change at local, national, regional and international levels? Is capitalism a force for peace or for war?

On war

Overshadowing the analysis of war and the efforts to answer some of these questions is the figure of Carl von Clausewitz, who wrote that war is a 'remarkable trinity...composed of primordial violence, hatred and enmity, which are to be regarded as a blind natural force; of the play of chance and probability within which the cre-

ative spirit is free to roam; and of its element of subordination, as
an instrument of policy, which makes it subject to reason alone.' In
a fastidious classification Clausewitz allocated each of these 'dominant tendencies' to a different group of people. The passions of
primordial violence he attributed to 'the people'. Creativity, imagination, strategy, improvisation and adaptability are the preserve of
armies and their commanders. Reason and policy is the domain of
governments.

He went on to argue that no explanation of war that relies on
only one of these parts of the trinity would make sense. Only in
their combination could they provide an explanation for war.

> These three tendencies are like three different codes of law, deep-rooted
> in their subject and yet variable in their relationship to one another. A the-
> ory that ignores any one of them or seeks to fix an arbitrary relationship
> between them would conflict with reality to such an extent that for this rea-
> son alone it would be totally useless. Our task therefore is to develop a the-
> ory that maintains a balance between these three tendencies, like an object
> suspended between three magnets.[5]

Another marker in the history of attempts to answer the enduring
questions about war was the correspondence in 1932 between Einstein and Freud.[6] Einstein invited Freud to help him work out, in
the title given to the published correspondence, 'why war?': 'Is there
any way of delivering mankind from the menace of war?' Einstein,
like Clausewitz, tried to understand war in terms of different motivations for different classes of people. First, there was the 'craving
for power which characterises the governing class' in every nation.
This group was supported in its hunger for power by another
group, 'whose aspirations are on purely mercenary, economic
lines. I have especially in mind that small but determined group,
active in every nation, composed of individuals who, indifferent to
social considerations and restraints, regard warfare, the manufacture and sale of arms, simply as an occasion to advance their personal interests and enlarge their personal authority.' However, war
is only really possible because of the interplay of these two groups
with a third, more general human factor: 'Because man has within
him a lust for hatred and destruction. In normal times this passion
exists in a latent state, it emerges only in unusual circumstances;
but it is a comparatively easy task to call it into play and raise it to
the power of a collective psychosis.'*

* Einstein is careful here to stress that this human proclivity to destruction is not
confined to the lumpen masses: indeed, he argued that experience proved that it

Freud's answer graciously admires Einstein's own hunches but then does something a bit different. Like Clausewitz, Freud emphasises the interdependence of motives. He argues that all human motivations can be divided into two broad categories: those that conserve and unify and those that destroy and kill. 'These are, as you perceive, the well known opposites, Love and Hate, transformed into theoretical entities; they are, perhaps, another aspect of those eternal polarities, attraction and repulsion, which fall within your province.'

However, there is no neat distinction between these two categories such that just one is involved, say, in the promotion of violence and war.

It seems that an instinct of 'either category' can operate but rarely in isolation; it is always blended ('alloyed', as we say) with a certain dosage of its opposite, which modifies its aim or even, in certain circumstances, is a prime condition of its attainment. Thus the instinct of self-preservation is certainly of an erotic nature, but to gain its end this very instinct necessitates aggressive action. In the same way the love instinct, when directed to a specific object, calls for an admixture of the acquisitive instinct if it is to enter into effective possession of that object. It is the difficulty of isolating the two kinds of instinct in their manifestations that has so long prevented us from recognising them.

Attempts to analyse and explain war—like those of Clausewitz, Einstein and Freud—still matter. First, they show the compulsion to classify, forever jostling with the artificiality of virtually all analytical categories. This is a tension that runs through all recent debates too, although arguably Clausewitz and Freud, especially, were subtler than many nowadays are in appreciating the inseparability of motives. Second, there is the impossibility of mono-causal explanations and even of invariant combinations of causes. Third, there was in these earlier ideas a tension between rationality and passion.

These themes echo through recent and older arguments about violent conflict. There are plenty of examples where opinion is divided on the mix of rationality and passion, and on the attribu-

---

was the intelligentsia that was most susceptible to such disastrous collective suggestions. But both Einstein and Freud were departing from a long line of liberal thinking stretching back at least to Tom Paine, which argued that ordinary people are essentially peaceable but that small minorities who rule them prevent this from becoming obvious: only reduce the role of government or, in the economists' version, remove barriers to free trade, and international relations would be peaceful. See Howard (1978).

tion of motives or causes to specific types of individual or group. Did the Bush administration and its allies fight the war in Iraq *only* over oil? Or was it a just war fought on behalf of liberty (what Freud might have called an ideal instinct)? Was it chiefly a war fought in subordination to policy and politics, in the form of a diversion from domestic ills in the democratic United States? Are suicide bombings and the 'war on terror' fuelled mainly by the bitterness of the oppressed and by the beneficiaries of imperialist oppression, by petty power hunger, by exclusively material rewards, or by a celestial proxy war in which both sides claim 'god on our side'?

Does the trade in 'conflict diamonds' and many other commodities like timber, gemstones, oil and coltan represent the creativity of military organisations? Or does it reflect a clear-sighted means-ends pursuit of wealth by violence? Is there a rational logic to the atrocities of young militia members in Sierra Leone or Sri Lanka, and not just to the manoeuvring of political leaders? And can the genocidal campaign of Pol Pot in Cambodia or the *genocidaires* in Rwanda be reduced to rational policy with no room for passion? When General Queipo de Llano bawled obscenities through a loudspeaker on the balcony of a hotel in Malaga during the Spanish Civil War, exhorting people to rape Republican sympathisers, was he simply being a good, tactically creative Clausewitzian general?

Was there no primordial, inherent violence in the technology of the British bombardment of Canton with 'shell and shot' in the 'Arrow War' (or Second Opium War) in the 1860s, or indeed in the technology of 'shock and awe' when the US-led coalition bombed Baghdad in 2003? Certainly, both these campaigns needed to appeal to the darker hatreds in humanity that Clausewitz, Freud and Einstein all identified.* The Arrow War, for example, was justified in the British parliament and press partly by arousing resentment of Chinese xenophobia and by generating hatred of the 'monster', Commissioner Yeh of Canton, who was resisting the revision of the Treaty of Nanking. Does the 'notorious irrationality to which ratio-

---

* Technological creativity in the service of rational policy making masks other passions too. Carol Cohn (2004), reporting on a university centre for research on defence technology and arms control, relays the intensity of sexual fantasy and anxiety in the appliance of science to violence: 'Other lectures were filled with discussion of vertical erector launchers, thrust-to-weight ratios, soft lay downs, deep penetration, and the comparative advantages of protracted versus spasm attacks— or what one military adviser to the National Security Council has called "releasing 70 to 80 percent of our megatonnage in one orgasmic whump". There was serious concern about the need to harden our missiles and the need to "face it, the Russians are a little harder than we are."'

nal argument leads'—as W. G. Sebald put it—blur the categorical boundaries between rationality and passion?[7]

The great challenge, in trying to explain and make sense of violence and war, and their relationship to profound societal changes at local, national, regional and global levels, is to steer between mystifying and over-rationalising. 'To counterpose the eroticisation and romanticisation of violence by the same means or by forms equally mystical is a dead end', writes Michael Taussig. 'Yet to offer one or all of the standard rational explanations of the culture of terror is similarly pointless. For behind the search for profits, the need to control labour, the need to assuage frustration, and so on, lie intricately construed long-standing cultural logics of meaning— structures of feeling—whose basis lies in a symbolic world and not in one of rationalism.'[8] This book takes up this challenge, trying to dodge the beams of the border guards on the unhelpful boundary between passion and reason.

Arguments and organisation

In addressing these enduring questions about war and violence this book contends against two main types of understanding on offer. The first involves a view of wars in developing countries as deviant, as aberrations from a more normal world of liberal peace, best exemplified by Northern prosperity and stability. The seductions of this view are those of imagining a world of barbarism and contrasting it with an idealised image of bourgeois civilisation. Essentialist ideas of ethnicity, tribalism, identity and 'primordial animosity' work as codes for an understanding of how primitive these warring societies are, of how distant they are from the grace of 'our' enlightened modernity. The mystification works at two levels. First, this view barbarises developing-country violence, dressing it in exotic masks of difference and pre-modernity. Thus, deviance comes from a failure of development and a lack of modernity. Second, this view expresses a self-image of Western, or Northern, society, distinguishing it by its stability and peaceful order and offering it as a generous model of shared values to be adopted off the shelf by aspiring modernisers.

A second influential view of war entails a different mystifying. When a World Bank economist sneers at historians and anthropologists popping up to explain a new war in terms of ancient hatreds he is right in that many accounts of war ignore the rather more recent causes of conflict, and he is right to stress that they downplay the influence of economic factors. But he is wrong to assume that all violent conflict may be adequately understood in terms of the assumptions and logic of neo-classical economics. Briefly, neo-classical economics is built on the axiomatic belief that everything is best explained from the point of view of the individual and that individual behaviour is a function of choices rationally made in order to maximise utility. This choice-theoretic methodological individualism operates within what Michael Taussig calls 'the paradigm of scarcity'.[9] That is, scarcity dominates all individual calculation of self-interest, which in turn dominates social behaviour and outcomes. Often elegant, the scientific pretensions of neo-classical economics are often attractive to policy makers in need of clear answers on which to base policy decisions. In recent years neo-classical, or orthodox, economists have grown increasingly confident that they can explain all social phenomena in terms of the basic toolkit assembled from these axiomatic materials. This book argues that neo-classical economics can only provide misleading and reductionist explanations that, at best, account for only one dimension (and a dimension of varying significance) of violence and violent conflicts around the world.

Methodologically, in orthodox economics (and many other variants of social science) the search is on for 'event regularities'. These are patterns that emerge at the directly observable, usually quantifiable level and they take the form 'whenever x happens, then y happens'. More typically, they are couched in probability, so that 'whenever x happens, there is a particular degree of probability that y also happens.' When claims are made, they are usually probabilistic. Thus one model might claim that the data confirm there is a significant statistical correlation between the variables that make up a model. This might translate into a conclusion that there is a particular risk of civil war when the average number of years of education attained in a country, combined with the share of that country's wealth generated by mineral exports, is above a particular level. This method creates the temptation to predict: for example, if the dependence on primary commodities were to increase by a certain amount, then the risk of civil war would increase by so many percentage points.

For now, the main point is that this kind of explanation of violent conflict can only deal in certain types of evidence: quantifiable evidence that can be assumed to 'mean' similar things across different contexts, in different countries and over a given span of time captured in the dataset that is matched to the model. Theoretical debates about violent conflict are as much about what evidence may be admitted as about substantive claims. Some argue, for example, that it is naïve to develop explanations that draw on the claims of combatants in wars about the 'grievances' they are addressing through violence, and that the drier, apparently more objective facts of statistical data are more revealing of the truth. Others argue that you do have to listen to what people say, though with caution. It may be especially important to listen closely where the evidence from quantifiable data, when applied to deductive models of, say, collective action, does not 'fit' the reality of a specific case.

For example, in Colombia and El Salvador a renowned social science model of collective action, where individuals will not act collectively without direct material benefits to themselves, collapses under the weight of evidence about how the FARC guerrilla organisation in Colombia operates and about who voluntarily joined the FLMN during El Salvador's civil war in the 1980s and why. Clearly, then, if an analysis of violent conflict around the world is to be of any help, it will have to deal in different kinds of evidence. The trouble is that all kinds of evidence suffer problems of quality. Just as a historian must be alert to inflections of interest in oral or written testimony, so social scientists cannot claim that statistical evidence is free of unreliability or produced without preconceptions.

The two influential attitudes to violent conflict that are criticised here—neo-classical economics and a general liberal presumption about the barbarism of developing countries—converge in an assumption that war is 'development in reverse'. This is very misleading. It is an attitude without historical memory and it borders on the sentimental. It is an attitude known since the First World War as the liberal interpretation of war, an interpretation that regards all wars as exclusively negative. This book explores the gap between this idea of war as development in reverse and the perspective that allows historians to write of 'great modernising wars'.[10]

The first chapter is an essay on perspective. It explores the relationships between historical memory, violence and the awkward concept of progress. It argues that the liberal perspective on violence and war may only be sustained by a form of historical amnesia. Through a discussion of a range of ideas on violence—like those of Walter Benjamin, Hannah Arendt and Michel Foucault—and through a discussion of European historical themes Chapter 1 arrives at the conclusion that the liberal perspective, despite its attractions, is untenable. Other possible perspectives may be labelled the 'tragic view of history' and the 'melancholic view of history'. By arguing for a shift away from the liberal perspective on war and violence Chapter 1 provokes the discussion conducted through much of the rest of the book, for it then becomes possible, if paradoxical and extremely difficult, to argue that development is not possible without often-violent conflict, though the forms this takes vary hugely. A corollary of this is that violent conflict, however destructive, may contain dynamics that have the potential to help bring about progressive long-run change.

If analytical perspectives affect the way people understand violence, then this understanding is further shaped by the choice of frame analytically arranged around the things to be understood: frames are made of descriptive and analytical categories, such as the category of 'civil war' or even the category of war as sharply distinct from peace. Chapter 2 begins with some of the more straightforward questions about trends in violent conflict. Are there more wars or fewer wars since the end of the Cold War than during it? How clear is the trend? What kinds of violent conflict dominate these trends? Where do the conflicts tend to take place? Is there an obvious pattern in which armed conflicts are concentrated in the poorest countries? Do recent and current wars fit the label of 'new wars' and are they, consequently, clearly distinct in form, origin and consequence from 'old wars'?

Some fairly straightforward answers may be given to these questions. But trying to answer them opens up further rounds of uncertainty, empirical and analytical. Chapter 2 provides an extended discussion of the concept of 'civil war', arguing that it is an ungainly notion whose usage is partly habitual but which might also be ideologically and politically convenient. The new war versus old war distinction allows for an entertaining parlour game of trying to find the 'old' in so-called new wars and the 'new' in older wars. A more serious side of this is to argue against those proponents of the new war thesis who have suggested that wars nowadays are not 'about' anything or that they are 'apolitical'. An inappropriate distinction undermines our understanding both of historically more distant wars and of more recent and ongoing wars.

Questioning the usefulness of concentrating exclusively on categories of violent conflict defined by artificial definitional boundaries leads to an emphasis on the value of having in mind a spectrum or continuum of violence. It then becomes clearer just how pervasive violent conflict is throughout many poor and middle-income countries. This is just what might be expected by a melancholy perspective on development. This argument is the basis for a critical review, in Chapter 3, of a range of explanations for violent conflict in developing countries. Many of these views emerge from the liberal interpretation of war: many of them regard violence and war as pathological. The chapter discusses the main explanations that influence and emerge within development studies, development economics and the expanding field of study of conflict and development. The chapter begins by highlighting, briefly, the debates over the causes of war in Iraq in 2003 and the debates over the causes of or reasons for 'terrorism'. It then considers the argument that wars are driven by 'relative deprivation'—the widespread assumption that ethnic differences or sharp material inequalities cause violent conflicts, and the idea that environmental scarcity or degradation provokes war; those arguments that, by contrast, stress the 'resource curse' idea whereby natural resource abundance may lead to armed conflict; and the elegant models of neo-classical economics that build a theory of contemporary war from the fundamental behavioural axioms of methodological individualism and rational choice theory. Many of these explanations or models violate Clausewitz's advice that a theory that stresses one 'tendency' to the exclusion of others is likely to be useless.

A good way to test the usefulness of these explanations is to apply them to a single case: if they are good general explanations, which many claim to be, they ought to explain a particular case accurately. Chapter 4 explores the fit between influential explanations of contemporary conflict and the specific case of Angola, a case that appears in a number of other chapters as well. Angola has a prolonged history of violent conflict. Although there were wars and armed skirmishes in the region before the Portuguese disembarked there, for the purposes of this chapter the historical *durée* begins with the encounter between the Portuguese and local kingdoms in what came to be given colonial boundaries and called Angola. One argument in this chapter is that extended historical analysis is relevant to understanding a contemporary war—just as it is relevant to understanding patterns of non-war violence in a country like Brazil.

Angola can easily look like a perfect example of various monocausal explanations of war. The recent war between the MPLA government and the UNITA rebels might be mapped onto a broadly ethnic division of the country. The war, certainly through the 1990s, was dominated by oil on one side and diamonds on the other: it therefore looked like a classic 'resource war' or indeed a classic 'new war', having earlier been one of the major 'old' confrontations in the Cold War. The violence of the war makes it easy to take for granted that it was a war that put development on hold and in many ways represented development in reverse. Closer attention reveals enough doubts about these characterisations of the war to suggest the need for a revised explanation.

Chapters 5 and 6 develop the argument that there may be more than 'development in reverse' to the very real horrors of war in countries like Angola and non-war violence in Brazil, India or South Africa. The focus in Chapter 5 is on war finance and its links to institutional creativity in recent wars and in the historical experience of many now economically advanced countries. One of the dimensions by which 'new wars' might be distinguished from 'old wars' is their financing. Many recent and ongoing wars appear to be characterised almost exclusively by how they are paid for—in much the same way that during the Cold War all wars were understood almost exclusively in terms of a 'proxy war' between the United States and the Soviet Union. Wars in Angola and Congo appear to be wars over oil and diamonds, or over coltan and other mineral resources. In Afghanistan and Colombia narcotics production and trade shape warfare. Sometimes the natural resources in question, or criminal trade networks, appear to be what the wars themselves are 'about'. This economics of war signals, for some commentators, the decline of war: from something grand and political to a grubby matter of short-term profit or, as Churchill had it, from something cruel and glorious to something cruel and sordid.

Chapter 5 explores war finance in historical and comparative perspective. It points out that those engaging in warfare have necessarily had to be financially and economically creative. Today's predatory warlords have something in common with late medieval warmongers. The shady adepts of international arms, drugs, timber or gemstone markets can be traced through genealogical rhizomes to the financiers of the Thirty Years War in Europe in the seventeenth century, or of the English Civil Wars: war finance then could be almost as intricately woven into global financial and commodity markets as it is now.

A historical perspective suggests it is worth adjusting the questions and the timeframe within which they are asked. It may then be beneficial to consider whether contemporary war finance in developing countries contains the seeds of institutional and organisational, even political, development. Consequently, exploring the hypothesis that some contemporary wars might not represent a deterioration of war but yet another example of war as a potential crucible of progressive development might also have value.

Armed with contrasting ways of thinking about violence and historical change, with the shield of scepticism against unreliable evidence and inappropriate classification systems, and with the warnings from Angola about the importance of specificity and the fragility of general explanations, Chapter 6 nonetheless tries to show a common thread running through much contemporary global violence. The explanation is rooted in the confusions and contradictions of transitions to capitalism that occur 'late' in its history and in the conditions of an evolving capitalist world economy and international system.

Chapter 6 works with two images or analytical metaphors. One is the continuum of violence. The other is the double helix of violent conflict, in which a ribbon of late transition and primitive accumulation and a ribbon of advanced international capitalism twine around each other and are linked by crossbars of policies, markets, institutions and flows of people. As in other chapters, there is an explicit focus on historical experiences from earlier transitions to capitalism, particularly in England and in the United States, which suggests parallels between those experiences and contemporary experiences of late development. If the institutional turmoil of any major societal transformation is one link, the other is that such transition periods are characterised by conflict over the terms of accumulation of wealth. This book uses the concept of 'primitive accumulation' explicitly to stress the links between the material dimensions of contemporary violence and war and the history of the development of capitalism in pioneering countries like England. Furthermore, primitive accumulation has never been a purely national experience.

Wars end, more or less. Societies cross a fuzzy border from war into peace: the territory on either side of the border can look very similar. The immigration and assimilation process is commonly taken to involve 'post-conflict reconstruction'. Although this used to be ad hoc, nowadays the process has to a considerable degree been standardised internationally. Also the policies encouraged are often rather different from those applied in historical examples of post-conflict reconstruction, whether in the American South after the Civil War or in the aftermath of the Second World War in European countries and Japan. After experiences in Cambodia, El Salvador, Mozambique and other places the standard process is deemed a success when a country is stamped with multi-party elections (sufficiently free and fair), market liberalisation, privatisation and deregulation, and security reforms that start with disarmament and demobilisation. The list of priorities is long and burdensome. In recent post-conflict reconstruction experiences there have been continuities with earlier experiences but there have also been significant breaks with previous experiments.

Chapter 7 argues that this standardised post-conflict reconstruction process is based in part on a fantasy: a fantasy that developing countries emerging from war present a blank slate on which it is relatively easy to sketch the ideal of a free market society with a small state, an ideal that is supposed to correspond to how the advanced capitalist countries themselves developed. This fantasy misrepresents the past of now advanced countries. While the liberal interpretation of war often assumes that war is 'development in reverse', this chapter argues that the onset of peace can itself threaten development. The problem begins with the notion of a blank slate, which denies the complex economic, institutional and political realities of war and encourages a naïve denial of post-conflict politics as well. Chapter 7 develops this argument first by discussing the longer-term history of post-conflict reconstruction and then by concentrating on the details of war and peace in Mozambique. The chapter concludes by stressing the relevance of this argument to recent developments in Afghanistan and Iraq.

A concluding chapter draws together some of the threads discussed through the book. It claims that a historical political economy can offer some answers to the enduring questions: Why war?; What does war represent?; To what extent is a general explanation compatible with an appreciation of the uniqueness of every violent conflict? It attempts to answer the questions whether, and how, contemporary wars and non-war violence make sense. This last chapter also highlights some of the implications of the book's arguments for research and policy responses.

The first time I heard of Angola I never imagined it, or any place, could be like this. Now I seem to see Angola everywhere... Even in the streets of American cities, where crack gangs and corrupt politicians vie for power, or among the homeless families in the cities of Western Europe, there is a little whiff of Angola.[11]

1

VIOLENCE, MEMORY AND PROGRESS

The Angola Gun

It was a seminal misunderstanding. In the seventeenth century African warlords operating roughly within what is nowadays Angola called on the support of small bands of Portuguese musketeers to gain an advantage in battles with other African armies. The immediate purpose of these battles was to harvest slaves, who could then be traded for other commodities—like cloth, alcohol and, increasingly, guns—with European merchants and their middlemen. At this stage African leaders did not have great quantities of guns. Nor did they have the training systems and know-how to incorporate them fully into their armies. And it was not always obvious that guns added much value to warfare: the weapons infiltrating the societies of West Central Africa were rudimentary. So the judicious incorporation of European 'mercenaries' was a useful means of pepping up the competitiveness of local kings and warlords. Portuguese traders and militias, though, seemed to see things differently.[1] For them, crowds of Africans wielding bows and arrows and hurling or prodding with spears were willing cannon fodder in the Europeans' wars in parts of the continent.*

---

* Things can often look similar now. Throughout Africa Western adventurers and their governments hire and organise large numbers of Africans in pursuit of a civilising mission to bring the values of liberal democracy and good governance to a region they often like to think of as 'marginalised' from the rest of the world. For their part African government ministers, rulers, opposition leaders and so on seem to think it worth engaging these outsiders for the resources they bring to their own struggles for power. Degree-toting technical assistants and resident representatives at the local World Bank mission might have taken the place of swashbuckling *conquistadores* and dab hands with a flintlock musket, but the mutual misunderstanding and usefulness often seem to be there still.

15

Angola—like many other parts of Africa—was shaken by successive waves of violent conflict through the seventeenth century and beyond. Warfare was not novel, but it certainly took on new forms at that time, and the scale and intensity of conflict increased too. The main force driving violence inland from the coastal trading posts of Loango and Luanda was slavery. Portugal was discovering a wider world, opening up new trade routes, and opening the way for new forms of competition among European powers, generating new sources of products like sugar, which in turn created massive needs for cheap labour.* Angola, which has had a knack of producing some of the core internationally traded commodities (from slaves to coffee to oil and diamonds), was one of the places most dramatically drawn into an expanding world economy.

During much of the sixteenth, seventeenth and eighteenth centuries approximately fifty to sixty thousand people every year (0.25–0.5 per cent of the total population of the region) set out as captives trudging west towards the ports of Luanda, Loango and Benguela, where the 'floating tombs' that carried them to Brazil were docked.[2] Perhaps half this number died along on the way to the coastline. About the same number were likely seized but kept as slaves within Africa. Meanwhile, people had to contend with the risk of being abducted not to be sent as slaves to the Americas, but to fight in African armies.

The violence that produced this crop of slaves threatened lives in other ways too. Warfare involved predation by armed forces on local food production. Just as war in Ethiopia in the 1980s, and in Sudan then and into the twenty-first century, was the main cause of famine mortality, so the slaving violence of the seventeenth and eighteenth centuries created famines and spread smallpox and other diseases. The effects on the lives of individuals, families, kin groups and broader societies were far more complicated than the crude figures of the slave trade suggest.

---

* In *The Rings of Saturn* W. G. Sebald (1998) ruminates on 'the fact that many important museums, such as the Mauritshuis in The Hague or the Tate Gallery in London, were originally endowed by the sugar dynasties or were in some other way connected with the sugar trade. The capital amassed in the eighteenth and nineteenth centuries through various forms of slave economy is still in circulation…still bearing interest, increasing many times over and continually burgeoning anew. At times it seems to me, said de Jong [his interlocutor in a hotel in Suffolk] as if all works of art were coated with a sugar glaze or indeed made completely of sugar, like the model of the battle of Esztergom created by a confectioner to the Viennese court, which Empress Maria Theresa, so it is said, devoured in one of her recurrent bouts of melancholy' (p. 194).

Slavery itself was unremarkable in Africa. Angolan political economies of the time were organised around the power kings derived from amassing large numbers of dependants. Often this involved bestowing gifts on people, which obliged them to give up their offspring, or members of their own retinue, to the king as dependants. Trade with the Portuguese and later with other Europeans gave these kings access to more goods that could be distributed through this political economy of binding largesse, each distribution effectively ratcheting up the king's power base. Local kings resisted selling slaves to the Europeans, though they could justify handing over some people, precisely in terms of this political economy of dependence, in which the separation of goods and people was vague, Joseph Miller argues, but the obligation derived from accepting gifts was strong. However, they came under increasing pressure, both political and economic, to add their own dependants to the basket of goods (along with beeswax and ivory) in exchange for the alcohol and cloth the Europeans brought. Over time the logics of power and rivalry compelled local kingdoms to follow a course of increasing violence to secure sufficient flows of people-goods to maintain or increase their influence.

As the violence spread and intensified, so the way African societies were organised became increasingly dominated by commercial transactions and calculations rather than by the gift economy that prevailed before. Like most major changes in the way societies are organised, this development was accompanied by, hastened by and made by appalling human disruption and violence. Violence was part of the economy, not simply a brake on it. Violence and war were integrated into the appropriation and production process, as they often have been and still frequently are.*

Another way in which violence is folded into political economy is through the technology and means of violence, from ancient historical innovations through the development of guns to the invention of barbed wire, the introduction of the tank, the evolution of aerial bombardment, the mass production of landmines and the research and development work on 'star wars' systems. The technology of violence played a part, too, in the changing pattern of war and society in Angola between the seventeenth and nineteenth centuries, up to the eventual, rather belated conquest of the terri-

---

* At one contemporary end of the spectrum, violence is arguably a straightforward input in the production of a commodity called protection, sold by firms known as the Mafia (Gambetta, 1996).

tory by the Portuguese. As the gun began to feature more in local military encounters, and African gunsmiths picked up the craft of boring and repairing guns, the weapon of local choice came to be the 'Angola Gun'. This was a cheap, long-barrelled flintlock musket made in Britain. In fact the British dominated the arms market in the West Central African region for much of this period. They had edged ahead of their main competitors, the Dutch, from around 1690 onwards, and the trade expanded rapidly through the eighteenth century, although exports to Africa fluctuated with the upheavals of European and American politics, in the course of which there were periodic restrictions on arms exports.

The Angola Gun was something like the Bic razor of its time: cheap, hardly top of the range stuff and something disposable after two or three firings.[3] But it was still preferred by most Africans in the market for firearms over the even shoddier Portuguese and French brands. The British sold these guns directly at ports such as Loango, to the north of Luanda, but they also found indirect ways of entering the market, chiefly by exporting them to Lisbon from where they would be sold on to the African coast. Trade between the two great nations of Britain and Portugal—two maritime superpowers of the day—was immortalised in the polite example of cloth and port wine that decorated the abstractions of David Ricardo's famous theory of comparative advantage, the economic theory that has been used ever since to underpin arguments for free trade. But in the world in which Ricardo lived and thought the less pretty business of the arms trade, closely tied to the international slave trade, was also important. Mr S. Galton of the Birmingham gunsmith's firm of Farmer and Galton spoke for much of the Birmingham trade when events in Lisbon threatened the health of business. In 1755, when Lisbon was destroyed by an earthquake, Mr Galton wrote: 'The dreadful earthquake at Lisbon hath very affectingly alarmed the inhabitants of this town, a great quantity of our manufactory being sold there. We have been suspended between hope and fear for some time.'[4]

Other, more political ructions in the world also had repercussions for the export of firearms to Africa. The War of Austrian Succession (1741–8), the Seven Years War (1756–63) and the American War of Independence (1775–83) all disrupted the direct and indirect sales of British arms to Africa. A business could get licences to continue sales to Africa but the regulations—stemming from a fear that the weapons might end up in enemy hands—were strict enough for gun manufacturers to try hard to evade them.

During the Seven Years War Farmer and Galton packed up a consignment of guns for Africa and tried to export them from Liverpool marked as Birmingham ironmongery. The guns were seized by customs officials. Farmer and Galton's main defence in the legal wrangling that followed was that the cheap guns made for the African trade 'would not be considered as arms useful to England's enemies as they were not proved or bored'.[5] Others agreed on the poor quality of matériel made for export to Africa. Lord Shelburne in 1765 complained, 'What is shocking to humanity, above half of them from the manner they are finished in are sure to burst in the first hand that fires them.' And the author of a consultancy report written about sixty years later, called *Observations on the Manufacture of Firearms for Military Purposes, on the Number Supplied from Birmingham to British Government*, wrote, 'It will hardly be believed in the present day, had we not sufficient knowledge that it is the fact, that firearms, if we may so call them, were made, the barrels of which neither underwent, nor were intended to undergo, any proof whatever; that immense numbers of guns were made, with the knowledge and certainty, that if they were ever fired out of, they were certain to burst in the discharge. These guns were made for one market—that of the coast of Africa. These guns…were called sham musquets, Dutch guns etc. and were made the article of barter for human flesh.'[6] In fact there were quite subtle grades of quality in the guns made for Africa, between the truly basic, unproved Catch Trading guns (sold at below 7 shillings a piece in the late 1750s) and the well-made, properly finished Swivel Blunderbusses sold for up to 18 shillings a piece to West African slave merchants.

The Angola Gun is a good example. It was one of the cheaper guns made in Birmingham, and at around 7 shillings a gun was a simpler article than Plain Birding Guns (10s), Jamaica Guns with a Beech or Walnut stock (9s 6d), Danish Guns (12s 6d), Buccaneer Guns (9s 6d) or Spanish Guns (10s 6d). Nonetheless, Angola Guns seem to have been made with some care. One customer order, from 1754, asked that the 700 Angola muskets to be delivered must have 'very neat stout barrels, proofmarked and the nose of the barrels clear bored as far down as can be'.[7] Being a flintlock musket it was still better than the matchlock mechanism that had been used before up and down the West African coast.

These exotically historical slaving skirmishes in Angola, and their integration into circuits of world trade and manufacturing, are not really so far away and long ago. The travails of Birmingham gun makers in the seventeenth and eighteenth centuries are not so removed from those of present day arms manufacturers. Current arms producers, like those of earlier times, have close but occasionally awkward relations with governments. They are sometimes encouraged by government promotions and they are sometimes restricted by regulations. As with Farmer and Galton's efforts to conceal their Africa-bound guns by packaging them as simple iron-mongery, so nowadays there are ways and means of evading the reach of regulation. These include, for example, British firms licensing arms production in third countries, whence they can be exported to countries that are blacklisted as importers directly from the UK. Heckler and Koch—a subsidiary of British Aerospace based in Nottingham—in the late 1990s licensed production in Turkey of hundreds of thousands of infantry rifles ordered by the Turkish state arms producer MKEK. MKEK then exported massive quantities of rifles to Indonesia, to which Heckler and Koch in the UK would not have been allowed to export directly.[8] Another manoeuvre is to profit from the arms trade by brokerage rather than direct production for export. Thus there were allegations in the 1990s about the involvement of Mil-Tec, a company registered in the Isle of Man, in brokering arms sales to Rwanda. Mil-Tec was delivering arms to Rwanda before and after the imposition of a UN embargo on arms sales in 1994. The UK government, because it did not extend the embargo to cover Crown dependencies and the Isle of Man, did not prosecute Mil-Tec.[9]

Angola's history reverberates with continuity. In 1994 a freight ship called the *Nora Heeren* arrived in the port of Plymouth in England en route from Russia to Angola. Its cargo was labelled as 'agricultural equipment', but because the ship's crew did not have the correct papers the port authorities examined the ship. They found a huge consignment of arms worth about $100 million. Nonetheless, the ship was allowed to move on.[10] This took place when there was an international embargo on arms sales to Angola in the wake of the Bicesse Accord, one of a series of attempted peace deals to end the war in Angola, a war that finally fizzled out when the rebel leader Jonas Savimbi was killed in 2002.

Hundreds of years ago English gunsmiths used as legal argument the fact that they were only exporting shoddy goods to Africa, and the Angola Gun was one example of a piece of military hardware that was obsolete in terms of the European technological frontier and the market demands of the time. To this day arms producers and traders are adept at offloading old models, used goods and scrap weapons to poor country governments. Outside Luanda is a weapons graveyard. A first impression would be that it contains tanks and other equipment damaged in combat. In fact a lot of the arms seem to have arrived at the port of Luanda already obsolete and unworkable. There are other reports of arms supplies to Angola including 40-year-old tanks that are potentially more dangerous to their operators than to the enemy, recalling those 'Angola guns' that would burst in the hand of the firer.[11]

If firms often have to be agile in finding loopholes to escape regulations, they also often benefit from government promotion of their overseas sales and, like the mercenaries and *condottieri* of sixteenth- and seventeenth-century Europe, they are more interested in profits than in taking sides. In September 2001, for example, the British government promoted the Defence Systems and Equipment international (DSEi) trade fair in London's Docklands on the River Thames. Delegations of buyers came from both India and Pakistan, from Angola and Uganda (fighting on different sides in the Congolese war) and from other pairs of warring countries.

And if three hundred years ago guns were sent to Africa as barter for human flesh, sometimes nowadays armaments are still bartered literally, in countertrade deals, though for peculiar commodities. Mark Phythian, in *The Politics of British Arms Sales Since 1964*, tells of two examples. In one the Thatcher government in Britain in the 1980s sold Hawk fighter jets to Finland and accepted in part-payment a large consignment of Finlandia vodka and other goods, including metal spiral staircases. To offload these the government persuaded a London department store to hold a Friendly Finland Week, selling cut-price Finnish goods. In another even more bizarre example the US government sold high-tech military hardware to Thailand in part-exchange for thousands of crates of frozen chickens.[12]

Now and then...and then again

This book is about contemporary wars of the late twentieth and early twenty-first centuries. Most of these have taken place in poor or developing countries, like Angola. The story about slaving violence and the Angola Gun, with its more recent echoes and embellishments, contains many of the themes this book will explore: historical continuities, the global interconnections underpinning contemporary violence, the violence at the heart of societal transformations and the frequent violence of the West in its expansionary modernism. The book explores the possibility that violence and war are more central principles for understanding institutions, pol-

itics and economic development than is typically acknowledged.
This includes the claims that violence and war are often foundational and that they endure beyond the beginning of institutions or
particular social orders.

To begin to explain current war, historical depth matters. The
standard social science literature on contemporary violent conflict
takes far too superficial a historical view of these conflicts. History is
about more than parallels and echoes, and time tourism to the
exotic past. A historical perspective shifts the parameters in assessing the significance of phenomena like widespread violence and
war. Below it is argued that a historical perspective encourages a
'tragic' or 'melancholy' view of contemporary violence that cannot
emerge from the more ahistorical analyses that are more typical in
much of the social sciences. Arguably, an ahistorical attitude is also
written into the ideology of social institutions, and not just academic disciplines and research methods. As Foucault argued, 'historical contents alone allow us to see the dividing lines in the
confrontations and struggles that functional arrangements or sys-
tematic organisations are designed to mask.'[13]

The history of war in Angola is a kind of palimpsest of violence
and civilisations: layer upon layer of mingled local violence and
international, imperialist violence, of violence and social change,
of the spent cartridges of technological innovation in violence.
There are countless other palimpsests like this, each with its own
variation; and every contemporary conflict has behind and beneath
it layers of previous conflict that help explain the present. One
other example is the island of Zanzibar off the mainland of Tanzania. In the nineteenth century Zanzibar cornered the world market
in cloves, and it grows virtually every other spice; it also has a history
as a base for the slave trade. An Anglican church was built on the
site of a jojoba tree in the capital, now the Zanzibar town district
called Stone Town, which was used as a whipping post for recalcitrant slaves, after the slave market was closed in 1873. Outside is a
modern sculpture, a pit with five slave figures, in memorial to the
huge numbers of slaves that passed through this *entrepôt* island.

Everywhere in Zanzibar there are markers of history, exposed layers of the violence of one international order after another, Portuguese, Omani Arab, British and international capitalist. On a
corner of the shore in Stone Town is the Palace of Wonders, and
next to it an old fortress. Outside the Palace of Wonders, on the
steps leading to the entrance, are two Portuguese cannon, about 10
feet long, remnants from the capture of the island from the Portu-

guese by Omani Arabs in 1698. The fortress next door was built by the Arabs from the rubble of a Portuguese church they had torn down. The fortress held till the British turfed the Arabs out. Like the Arabs, who built a fortress where they had knocked down a church, the British Empire put down its own layer of civilisation. In the grassy field inside the fortress they created a women's tennis club.

Next door, inside the Palace of Wonders, there are various quaint relics. Downstairs is an old, 1960s Simca car, the 'first car used by the Afro-Shirazi Party Youth League'. Upstairs the main museum room holds a range of bits and bobs from the time when the explorer Henry Stanley based his expeditions in Stone Town. They include a book with an insert at the beginning commemorating 'The American Testimonial Banquet to Henry M. Stanley—In Recognition of his Heroic Achievements in the Cause of Humanity, Science and Civilisation' in London in 1890.*

When I visited the Palace of Wonders in early 2002 I managed to shrug off my guide and walked over to a far corner of the building. There was some activity going on and I wanted to see what it was. A large number of pictures were lying about inside waiting to be hung for an exhibition. At one end of the room I found a young man who worked for the education department of the US State Department. He was arranging a new exhibition of photographs of 'Ground Zero' to commemorate the 9/11 attacks. He said there was nothing political about this, but the exhibition seemed like a powerful assertion in East Africa, rubbing in the violent victimisation of American civilisation, after the attack on the embassy in Dar es Salaam, and in Zanzibar, the home of the Muslim opposition to the ruling party in Tanzania, and on the East African front of international conflict.

Embarrassing violence

'When we've finished with you, you'll be able to stand up and slaughter your enemies like civilised men.'[†]

---

* Hochschild (1999) discusses how Stanley, a *faux* American who was unusual in having fought on both sides during the American Civil War, led a series of exploratory expeditions in Central Africa, eventually helping King Leopold II of Belgium secure a colonial foothold around the River Congo. Stanley, recollecting in tranquillity, wrote that when mud and wet sapped the energy of his porters 'a dog-whip became their backs, restoring them to a sound...activity'; Hochschild imagines that 'people in the villages that the expedition marched through may well have mistaken it for another slave caravan' (p. 31).
† This is what Sean Connery's character, an ex-soldier and conman, tells a group of

This image—the projection of US values onto Muslim island off the coast of Africa—announces a society by its victimisation. The image might contain a warning but it also disowns the values of violence in the 9/11 attacks. Certainly there is a common and powerful idea that liberal modernity has outgrown aggressive violence. It is a superior society founded on shared values of participation, rationality and peaceable conflict resolution through democratic mechanisms. This idea affects the way people see wars around the world, for seeing those wars as a function of backwardness, of a democratic deficit, a lack of modernity, a failure to grasp the values of liberalism, is easy.

There is a rich intellectual argument rooted in the Enlightenment and in the mechanisms of capitalism that justifies the idea. If violence and war are irrational, then modernity proper has no truck with either, since modernity is rationalism. Capitalism may even be a means of peace. This argument—a political argument for capitalism—is discussed further in Chapter 6; but one source of the argument is Adam Smith's claims about the transforming effects of commerce upon social life in the English countryside. Smith described the transition from feudalism to capitalism in terms of the effect of commerce and manufactures on the rural aristocracy and its relations with the state and other classes. For expanding commerce and manufactures finally made it possible for these landlords to gratify 'the most childish, the meanest, and the most sordid of all vanities', i.e. their selfish need for baubles and trinkets. 'For a pair of diamond buckles perhaps, or for something as frivolous and useless, they exchanged the maintenance, or what is the same thing, the price of the maintenance of a thousand men for a year, and with it the whole weight and authority which it could give them.' While during feudalism the open country was a scene of 'violence, rapine and disorder', 'commerce and manufactures gradually introduced order and good government, and with them, the liberty and security of individuals...who had before lived almost in a continual state of war with their neighbours.'[14]

The implication of the argument is that human violence can at least be successfully repressed and at best even overcome. That would then leave incidents of violence as a reflection of dark zones insufficiently enlightened by liberal capitalist modernity; or as

tribal warriors in 'Kafiristan' in John Huston's film *The Man Who Would be King*, based on Kipling's book; 'By my reckoning it's the top right-hand corner of Afghanistan', says a character in the original story.

examples of rare disorders, pathological complaints, distortions of normality. Violence and war could be overcome, then, simply by introducing free markets and democratic institutions. But this is a dangerously mistaken argument that has infected the common-sense of the Western world. Violence and war have persisted in modernity: they come to be seen as embarrassing, since either liberal modernity cannot escape from violence, war and barbarism, or it is decidedly incomplete.[15]

If instances of modern Western violence cannot be excused as purely defensive, then they may be explicable as perversity and aberration. One of the sites on which this kind of argument has been waged, an argument between understandings of human violence and civilisation, is the Nazi Holocaust. There are plenty of arguments that stress the extraordinary exceptionalism of this event. Some, for example, argue that the roots of Nazism and the Holocaust lie in the *perversity* of Germany's trajectory to modernity; that Germany experienced a *distorted* path of development in which the rural pre-capitalist aristocracy—the Junkers—were not effectively brushed aside by the urban, industrial capitalist élite; and that this led to a kind of extended immaturity in German politics even as the country underwent the beginnings of its industrial modernisation. One commentator likened the Nazi Holocaust (and the 'genocidal conjuncture' in Cambodia and Rwanda) to a thermonuclear friction reaction, a rare event only manageable under an extremely peculiar combination of conditions.[16] In a well-known book Goldhagen explained how masses of rather normal Germans became 'Hitler's willing executioners', because Germany was extraordinarily different from anywhere else.[17]

It would be soothing if this were right. We could continue to study the Holocaust with arms-length rage, in much the same way that we often see other paroxysms of atrocity like the Rwandan genocide, easily filed under oddity or category error. Uncomfortably, though, this might be mistaken. For Hitler's willing executioners were typically extraordinary only in their ordinariness, in how disturbingly like the rest of us they were. Some of them were more willing than others, some flinched at what they still did, some survived as bystanders without directly perpetrating or criticising atrocity, many became just jobbing killers. Their motivations were complex, but these included peer pressure and the most frighteningly banal of traits, the ability to do what authority tells us is right.

This is what Christopher Browning argues, for example in his book *Ordinary Men*, on the atrocities performed by a German police battalion operating in Eastern Europe. Goldhagen argues that the Nazis simply allowed and encouraged Germans to do what they had always wanted to do, given an immanent and permanent anti-Semitism. Browning, by contrast, argues that Germany's political culture and its anti-Semitism were transformed by three or four decades of changes in education, public conversation, law and institutional reinforcements and, of course, especially by the twelve years of Nazi rule before 1945. The recent political events—including attempted socialist revolution, economic crisis, the rejection of the Versailles Treaty by German society after World War I and the eventual rise to power of what the narrator in Thomas Mann's *Doctor Faustus* calls 'the dictatorship of the scum of the earth'—had transformed German political culture; and the early years of war itself further changed people's motivations and reactions.

The importance of situational and institutional factors in explaining the behaviour (the range of behaviour) of ordinary Germans in the war does not detract from a history of anti-Semitism, but it does have different implications for the all too human possibilities of violence more generally. When Hannah Arendt watched the trial of Eichmann in Jerusalem and then wrote about the 'banality of evil', she did not mean that evil was boring, or that Eichmann was a banal individual, but rather that evil in general was nothing special, that what produced the Holocaust was essentially commonplace.*

It is difficult to accept that liberal Western society has shed violence, that its violence has been only perverse or defensive. Rather, extremes of violence, cruelty and barbarism have endured in the Western imagination through its modernisation. Recalling Clausewitz's remarkable trinity of war, one strand of which was made of 'primordial violence, hatred and enmity, which are to be regarded as a blind natural force', there is something about this enmity that defies the social sciences. Arguably a different kind of evidence has

---

* Arendt (1963). Todorov (2001) reaches related conclusions from a different angle, that of the story of aborted Holocaust in Bulgaria. Despite tightening anti-Jewish laws after Bulgaria joined the Axis in 1941 and despite deportations starting in 1943, the full-scale deportation of Jews was averted. There were political protests against the deportations, but astute political leadership, including that of the king, played a significant role: 'The people were opposed to the anti-Semitic measures, but a community is powerless without leaders, without those individuals within its midst who exercise public responsibility... All this was necessary for good to triumph, in a certain place and at a certain time; any break in the chain and their efforts might well have failed. It seems that, once introduced into public life, evil easily perpetuates itself, whereas good is always difficult, rare, and fragile. And yet possible.'

to complement the kinds of data with which the social sciences more comfortably work. Wartime atrocity has its corollary in the artistic imagination, where its mainspring is vented, processed and represented. Thomas Mann offers one insight into this range of imagination. His lament for the descent of Germany in the first half of the twentieth century, in his novel of genius and evil, *Doctor Faustus*, is at once a meditation on German specificity and an encounter with the universal. The book is a biography of a fictional composer, Adrian Leverkühn, narrated by Serenus Zeitblom. Zeitblom thinks of Germany's predicament as driven by psychology, specifically by the tragic psychology of the drive for a 'breakthrough' to modernity: a breakthrough 'out of an isolation of which we are painfully conscious, and which no vigorous reticulation into world economy has been able to break down since the founding of the Reich. The bitter thing is that the practical manifestation is an outbreak of war, though its true interpretation is longing, a thirst for unification.'[18] This is a moment characterised by something specially German, argues Zeitblom: 'the very definition of Germanism, of a psychology threatened with envelopment, the poison of isolation, provincial boorishness, neurosis, implicit Satanism...'

But at the same time Zeitblom joins the discussion of Germany's abominable modernisation to his greater, universal human theme of the relationship between genius and progress on the one hand, and insanity or evil on the other. The join is made in the parallel between German history and the subject of Zeitblom's biography, his friend the composer Leverkühn, who makes the Faustian deal. In Leverkühn's masterpiece, *The Apocalypse*, the biographer has to admit that he sees the link between aesthetic achievement and barbarism. As Zeitblom puts it: 'Here no one can follow me who has not as I have experienced in his very soul how near aestheticism and barbarism are to each other: aestheticism as the herald of barbarism.' The musical work he writes about sought 'to reveal in the language of music the most hidden things, the beast in man as well as his sublimest stirrings'. Surely, Zeitblom goes on, in a desperate effort to remain loyal to his friend while trying to be honest, the combination of the very new with the very primitive, of the innovative and the barbaric, 'lies in the nature of things: it rests, I might say, on the curvature of the world, which makes the last return unto the first.'

The beast in me

What is disturbing in Mann's idea is the suggestion of a boundary transgressed. For barbarism as an idea invokes an anxious border.

The border distinguishes 'us' from the barbarian; the border is meant to keep the barbarian different and separate.* The border drawn by the idea of barbarism is a classic mechanism of displacement. Mann's Zeitblom claims that the innovative modernist composer Leverkühn, in joining the primitive, base and basic with the sublimely sophisticated, is showing the enduring past, ineradicable by progress, revealing the most hidden things, the beast in man.

Barbarism is meant to be a territory over the border from civilisation. But barbarism and atrocity are never as foreign as we might want to think. It would be neater if they were, if atrocity was all about culturally inbred cruelty, machete wielding Rwandans, ethnically-driven gang-raping Serbs, inscrutably cruel Cambodians, scarily masked Liberians, mad Mullahs of the Taliban. Reporting the Rwandan genocide, much of the international press played effectively on Western base reflexes, representing the conflict exclusively in tribal/ethnic terms and encouraging readers to picture a paroxysm of viciousness in which Hutu *hoi polloi* carried out the genocide largely with rudimentary implements like machetes. Horrible death by machete happened. Yet much of the violence was meted out by rifles and rocket-propelled grenades (RPGs).[19] Sustained massacre was a modern military manoeuvre carried out with common or garden small arms; this weaponry was not locally fashioned farm equipment but made in the West; further, the outcome of civil war and genocidal vengeance in Rwanda mattered greatly to some Western governments, above all France, and depended also on the politics of the rest of the West at the time.

Hutu Power extremists in Rwanda used radio and newspapers to rally the population with calls to rape and kill, coaxed them with pledges of land and jobs, and scapegoated the Tutsi population spectacularly to deflect from their own political fragility and the economic decline of the country. But these are not culturally specific traits. They are not confined to age-old ethnic rivalry in Rwanda or primordial hatreds in the former Yugoslavia. In Britain in 1189/90 mobs swept through London and York murdering Jews.

---

* Foucault (2003), in his 1975/76 Collège de France lectures, distinguished between the savage and the barbarian. The savage is the natural man dreamed up by jurists or theorists of right, who existed before society; the savage is also 'that other natural man or ideal element dreamed up by economists: a man without a past or a history, who is motivated only by self-interest and who exchanges the product of his labour for another product' (p. 194). Once the savage enters into a social relation he ceases to be a savage. By contrast, the barbarian can only be defined and understood in relation to a civilisation outside which he lives.

In Germany the Nazi regime succeeded in cooking up the ghastliest of scapegoating emotions in support of its extermination of Jewish Germans, Poles and so on. In the Spanish Civil War in Andalusia (where civilisations have clashed and mingled over the centuries) the Francoist general Gonzalo Queipo de Llano broadcast invitations to the people of Seville to rape and to murder anyone associated with the Republicans, while Anarchists executed large numbers of Roman Catholic nuns and priests.*

The Spanish Civil War, of course, also provoked a famous commemoration of aerial barbarity in Picasso's *Guernica*. Aerial bombardment was a technique that was refined in the coming years. Towards the end of the Second World War the Allies carried out a campaign of mass bombardment of German cities whose momentum carried it beyond strategic rationale. Data amassed by the Allies show that the Royal Air Force alone dropped almost a million tonnes of bombs on enemy territory. Many of the 131 towns and cities attacked were almost entirely flattened. Some 600,000 German civilians died in the air raids and three and a half million homes were destroyed. It was an unnecessarily and ineffectively crude campaign: it did not do that much damage to German industrial production and it did not break German morale. The indulgence in destruction was given away by the naming of the campaign. For example, in 1943 when the RAF, with US air force support, set off on a series of raids intended to reduce the city of Hamburg to ashes, it was performing 'Operation Gomorrah'. And on 13 February 1945, as part of 'Operation Thunderclap', the Allies unleashed 1,478 tons of explosive and 1,182 tons of incendiary bombs on the strategically marginal, beautiful city of Dresden. The bombing and the firestorm that followed rubbed out the city completely—a trauma recorded in Kurt Vonnegut's *Slaughterhouse 5*.†

During the last years of the Vietnam War the United States' terror bombing campaign unloaded almost three times the tonnage of ordnance that was dropped on Germany during the Second World War.[20] Also, in 1961 the United States began applying defoliating

---

* See Eltringham (2004: 51–68), on the similarities and differences between the Nazi genocide against Jews in Germany and the Rwandan genocide in 1994; and on the uses of this comparison within Rwandan politics.

† Vonnegut introduces his book as a failure, inevitably so since it was written by a pillar of salt. The narrator has been thumbing the Bible for scenes of destruction, and is taken with Lot's wife, who, of course, was told not to look back on what had happened to the people and homes and land of Sodom and Gomorrah. 'But she did look back, and I love her for that, because it was so human.'

herbicides (primarily Agent Orange) in Vietnam, covering 1.7 million acres by 1967, and over a nine year period spraying 20 per cent of the South's jungles and 36 per cent of its mangrove swamps.

As Robert Fisk put it in *The Independent* the day after the World Trade Center attack, it was 'also about American missiles smashing into Palestinian homes and US helicopters firing missiles into a Lebanese ambulance in 1996 and American shells crashing into a village called Qana and about a Lebanese militia paid and uniformed by America's Israeli ally hacking and raping and murdering their way through refugee camps.'[21] As the narrator of *Slaughterhouse 5* would have it, 'so it goes.'

The two main ways that liberal Western society has found to deal with atrocity and violence have been to push them back across the border into barbarism and to hide them by amnesia. That the border between barbarism and civilisation is an awkward one is shown in the renown of, and response to, Robert Kaplan's post-Cold War call to anxiety: 'The Coming Anarchy: How Scarcity, Crime, Overpopulation and Disease are Rapidly Destroying the Social Fabric of our Planet'.[22] Kaplan's article was supposedly placed, on the orders of Bill Clinton, onto the desks of every US ambassador round the world. Kaplan's argument has been characterised by liberal and left critics as 'the New Barbarism Thesis'. The argument was developed from Kaplan's travels in West Africa and the former Yugoslavia. Scarcity, crime, overpopulation and disease accounted for the anarchic violence of West Africans and others around the world behaving like 'loose molecules' spinning out of control in a combustible social fluid.* A common tendency in trying to comprehend the break-up of Yugoslavia, too, was to emphasise the instinctive and ancient 'Balkan mentality' that was simply let loose once the artificial lid of communism was lifted. These stereotypes might unnerve us with their potential for spillovers—refugees, crime networks, disease spread and so on—but their power as images is, again, to keep Yugoslav or West African violence firmly at a foreign distance, not only to keep them far away in place but, combined with the rhetoric

---

* It is as if Kaplan had been reading and taking too literally Flann O'Brien's novel *The Third Policeman*, in which a policeman expounds the philosopher de Selby's molecule theory: if two things spend too much time in contact, molecules from the one swap with molecules from the other. The policeman himself can no longer ride his bicycle for danger of becoming more than 75 per cent bicycle himself. By analogy, Kaplan seems to envisage international contiguity as a feature of globalisation, potentially leading to too much West African chaos rubbing off on civilised Western society.

of simmering ancient hatreds beneath pressure-cooker lids, to cast them back in time too.

In rejecting the new barbarism thesis there are two common responses: to argue that all 'barbarism' is rational and to argue that barbarity is an enduring feature of liberal democracy. One liberal response is to try to close the gap between West Africa, say, and the rich West or North by trying to stamp out the very idea of barbarism. It is racist and crude. There is no barbarism and no anarchy. In the 'one world' of globalisation there is no barbarian other. Rather, it is possible to unite the West African or Balkan mentality with our own. Underneath the apparent chaos is a means-ends rationality. We can do this by showing that 'civil wars' make sense, that what look like senseless atrocities are simply the applications in a given predicament of the same rational choice behaviour that makes you or me behave the way we do. Violence, war and atrocity have functional uses, often seen to be directly material functions.[23]

One of the most interesting analyses of the war in Sierra Leone during the 1990s—an analysis organised explicitly as a rejection of New Barbarism—is Paul Richards's book *Fighting for the Rainforest*. Richards asks us to think a bit when we hear of atrocious acts of war such as the practice in Sierra Leone, by the youth of the Revolutionary United Front, of slicing peasant women's hands off. This looks like a good example of the easy disrespect for life and dignity, it looks like the indulgent cruelty of anarchy. It looks inexplicable: how could they? They could, Richards argues, because this made completely rational sense, in the sense in which rationality is typically thought of nowadays, that is, in straightforward terms of means serving ends. Young men could chop off poor farming-women's hands because this ensured that they would not be able to harvest their crops when the RUF rebels had passed, so the women could not help feed government militias, and these women and their dependants would have to do the rebels' bidding. Atrocity here is calculation pure and simple. When things fall apart, they still make sense, as rational barbarism. Once we have built this bridge across a cultural divide, and evaded the troll of the New Barbarian thesis, it is but a short hop and skip to some of the most bizarre ways of understanding contemporary civil wars, that is, in terms of orthodox economic theory.*

---

* Richards does not support this analytical jump, and argues that it represents a 'warlord fundamentalism' where we see contemporary wars exclusively in terms of

If the effort to bind perpetrators of cruelty to us with the adhesive of rationality is one way of rejecting the new barbarism thesis, there is still an alternative. Instead of insisting that there is no barbarism in the world today, we might have to see that there is barbarism both in distant war-torn countries and in our own rich countries, that there is barbarism in the civilisation that knits together the world.* This means—among other things—that while there is means-ends rationality and powerful economic motive in the life of rich countries, there are also other forms of rationality, and there are other motives than the narrowly economic. There is, also, barbarity. This is rather different as a way of understanding our society. It does not allow for much smugness about 'our values', though it does not have to lead to a denial of the massive progress achieved in advanced countries and the historically spectacular benefits of living there. Rather, it is a work-in-progress way of seeing the world. The pithiest instance of its intellectual roots was Walter Benjamin's saying: 'There is no document of civilisation that is not at the same time a document of barbarism.'[24]

The imagery of US and British military personnel in Iraq revelling in the torture of Iraqi captives dramatised the durability of this phrase of Benjamin's. In some of these postcards from post-conflict reconstruction a female US guard, Lynndie England, sexually taunts naked prisoners. In another, a picture of particular symbolic ambiguity, an Iraqi inmate stands on a box draped in a black robe with a black hood over his head, cruciate with arms out to his sides, with electric wires taped to his fingers and trailing off to a wall. In another, a prisoner cringes naked while Alsatians bark and strain at their leashes.† Human Rights Watch also criticised US treatment of

---

the economic motivations of individual warlords. See Chapter 3, below, for a discussion of orthodox economic theories of violent conflict.

* Foucault, in *Society Must be Defended*, tried to trace the idea that rationality was perched on top of fundamental relations of force and domination.

† An interview with a former British special services officer who had served in Iraq, published in *The Guardian* ('UK Forces Taught Torture Methods', 8 May 2004), suggested a political economy of barbarism. The ex-officer claimed that sexual and other humiliations are role-play techniques applied to special services soldiers to help them develop R2I, resistance to interrogation, but in carefully limited and monitored environments. Former special service soldiers rehired by private security contractors—a bubble sector in an era of ideological privatisation—had been training their employee interrogators in these techniques but the trainees had never themselves been on the receiving end. The interviewee argued that in the special forces training recruits develop an empathy that helps them acknowledge the suffering they cause when they themselves conduct interrogations; but that this

detainees at an air base at Bagram in Afghanistan: the United States had not repudiated reports documenting use of 'stress and duress' techniques for extracting information—keeping prisoners naked, forcing them to maintain uncomfortable positions, sleep deprivation, disorientation—which are prohibited in international law that outlaws physical injury and all forms of 'cruel, inhuman or degrading treatment'.[25] There were also reports that the United States had 'outsourced' or 'rendered' some prisoners to Morocco, Jordan and Egypt for questioning, countries where torture is commonly used. Meanwhile, detainees at Guantanamo Bay are denied legal rights.[26]

Still there are differing interpretations of the idea that barbarism is alive and well in liberal democracies or in the twenty-first-century global capitalist world. Eric Hobsbawm, in a lecture on 'Barbarism: A User's Guide' given as the Amnesty Lecture in 1994, argued that barbarism had made a comeback in Western civilisation.[27] After 150 years on the slide, it returned through the twentieth century to unwind the Enlightenment, i.e. the establishment of a universal set of rules and standards of moral behaviour, embodied in the institutions of states dedicated to the rational progress of humanity. Everywhere systems of social rules have been breaking down. Barbarisation proceeded through four main stages: the First World War, the worldwide crisis between 1917 and 1947, the Cold War, and 'the general breakdown of civilisation as we know it over large parts of the world in and since the 1980s'. Hobsbawm reports that one of the US medical men monitoring or conducting the radiation experiments undertaken by the United States on human beings, from shortly after World War II to the 1970s, protested to his superiors that there seemed to be 'a smell of Buchenwald' about them.*

---

empathy, and the restraint it creates, are lacking in the private sector security firm labour market. 'It was clear from discussions with US private contractors in Iraq that the prison guards were using R2I techniques, but they didn't know what they were doing.' On the other hand, when British soldiers were being tried in January 2005 for abuse of Iraqi prisoners, evidence presented to the court suggested they had been trained specifically in how to treat prisoners humanely.

* Another possibility is that some forms of barbarism are durable in spite of progress or, as Leszek Kolakowski (1990) puts it, that barbarism is indigenous. 'The sources of totalitarianism are largely European, and they may be traced, in their various forms, through the whole history of socialist utopias, nationalist ideologies, and theocratic tendencies. It turns out that Europe has not developed an immunity to its barbaric past, a past whose monstrous conquests we have seen with our own eyes.' A related argument is Baumann's (2002), that the Holocaust was a realisation of the Enlightenment project and its technologies, not a challenge to the

Yet in the window of Enlightenment rules and regulations that Hobsbawm allows, let us say between 1750 and 1914, there were many ongoing instances of excessive viciousness, among them those perpetrated in the American Civil War and in the Congo Free State. Sven Lindqvist took one phrase from Conrad's *Heart of Darkness* and drew from it the essence of nineteenth-century European barbarism-in-civilisation. That phrase was Kurtz's 'Exterminate all the brutes', not just a literary creation but horribly clear as a statement of much of the attitude underlying the civilising mission of colonialism, backed by a misapplication of evolutionary ideas. The heart of European darkness in the midst of the extraordinary expansion of the nineteenth-century world and imagination nowhere beat stronger than in Conrad's unnamed Congo: the Congo of brutal rubber extraction; the Congo that was King Leopold II of Belgium's personal and immense overseas fiefdom; the Congo where, later, the blowback of appalling colonial rule and of manipulated decolonisation helped feed the rise of President Mobutu; the Congo where, after a spell as Zaire, the vicious accumulation of profit from extracting coltan and other minerals replaced the frenzy of the rubber boom a century earlier; the Congo of three or more 'civil wars' at the start of the twenty-first century and of multiple Sub-Saharan African military and economic involvements.*

Lindqvist is driven by a quest for the ideological roots of the twentieth-century Holocaust in the European nineteenth century—a century of empire and Darwinism. But arguably there were earlier prefigurings of twentieth-century atrocity in the European literary imagination. For example, Montaigne in his essay 'On Barbarians' and Swift in the fourth book of *Gulliver's Travels* and in *A Modest Proposal* were reminding Europeans of their own ever-present proclivities to cruelty and excess. The *Modest Proposal* includes a fantasy of making ladies' gloves from the cured skins of cannibalised babies of the Irish poor (and summer boots for fine gentlemen). This is a fantasy that looks forward to what appears to have

Enlightenment; that 'the Holocaust was as much a product, as it was a failure, of modern civilization' (p. 71). On modernity's barbarism and its roots, as well as on its departure from Enlightenment hopes, see also Steiner (1974).

* Coltan, containing tantalite, is a heavy metal that is very heat-resistant. The bulk of this ore is found in Africa, most of it in Congo. The structure of the world market is not widely known, but the war in Congo has publicised the metal's significance in the world economy. Its uses include space rocket technology and the manufacture of mobile phones and computer game consoles.

been at least an occasional feature of Nazi Germany. A witness in
the Buchenwald Report, for example, 'says that Ilse Koch [the
'Bitch of Buchenwald'] was as proud of her handbag made of
human skin as "a South Sea Island woman would have been about
her cannibal trophies"'.[28] In *Gulliver's Travels* the Houyhnhnms
(horse-like creatures of rationality and peaceable sensibilities) meet
in a Grand Assembly, where there is just one, recurring debate: the
Yahoo question. Yahoos are uncouth, hirsute creatures that do not
wear clothes, fight constantly and bear a very close resemblance to
human beings. The Yahoo question that the Houyhnhnms discuss
is this: 'Whether the Yahoos should be exterminated from the Face
of the Earth.'[29] The Houyhnhnms have never resolved the problem
though they did once cull the Yahoos, killing older ones. So it goes.

As Rawson puts it, the point in Swift 'is to rub in the incriminat-
ing resemblance with our despised subgroup, not to highlight a
depraved contrast with primitive virtue.'[30] Not that Swift was an
advocate of genocide, nor were his own satirical fantasies a 'causal
factor' in the development towards the Holocaust and other genocidal horrors of the twentieth century. Rather, Swift is highlighting
a universal and ever-present depth of the human imagination and
having a go at the 'mighty softeners', whose equivalent nowadays
would be the more naïve proponents of the values of liberal market
democracy.

Kafka managed something similar in his story of technological
delight in the means of violence, *In the Penal Colony*. In this story an
explorer, a Gulliver of sorts, is shown a prison camp in which the
former commandant developed a contraption that executes the
prisoner slowly, torturously, by engraving on his body, with a device
called the Harrow, the commandment that the condemned man
had transgressed. The old commandant's acolyte, an officer, is the
last supporter of the apparatus in the colony and excitedly explains
to the explorer how it works, imploring him to put in a good word
with the new commandant for the exquisite and apparently
redemptive artistry of the execution, which gradually, over twelve
hours, revealed to the condemned the name of their guilt. When
the explorer—desperately clinging to the bystander's dispassionate
neutrality—finally refuses to help, the officer frees the condemned
man from the straps of the apparatus, resets the cogs of the Harrow,
and ties himself into it. The Harrow—pen as sword—is now ready
to inscribe on the officer 'Be Just'. But the apparatus fails, clangs
noisily into action and scratches messily and quickly into the body,
jabbing instead of writing.

The past is a foreign country—they do things violently there

Selective amnesia is another common way for societies to cope with the discomfort of cruelty, violence and barbarity. Power corrupts the past as well as its incumbents. Contemporary Western liberal society has two especially important historical blindspots concerning its own development; though some like Eric Hobsbawm argue that there is a more general and specifically modern loss of historical memory, a loss of awareness of the links between our present and the past.* One blindspot conceals the policies that typically were necessary to winch societies out of the mud and ruts of pre-capitalist poverty and technological stagnation. For every country that is now industrialised got there through the four-wheel drive mechanism of protection against free trade and with the differential lock device of state intervention preventing the wheels of production from spinning endlessly in the mud. The British, pioneers of the industrial revolution, were also ahead of the game in trade protection. For example, as early as 1700 the British wool industry succeeded in having the import of competitive Indian calicoes banned, unwittingly paving the way for the monopolisation of the home market by the Lancashire cotton industry that provided the beginnings of the industrial revolution in the second half of the eighteenth century. The United States, messianic nowadays in its

---

* Jameson (1983: 125) argued that contemporary capitalist society—with its planned obsolescence in consumption, its standardisation, its frenetic rhythms of fashion changes, its unparalleled penetration by the media—'has little by little begun to lose its capacity to retain its own past, has begun to live in a perpetual present and in a perpetual change that obliterates traditions of the kind which all earlier social formations have had in one way or another to preserve.' Noting that nobody bar a few crusty historians got the point in 1992 when the then French president, Mitterrand, made a sudden appearance in Sarajevo on 28 June, Hobsbawm (1994) argued: 'The historical memory was no longer alive.' Mitterrand was trying to dramatise the seriousness of the Bosnian crisis by timing his visit to mark the anniversary of the assassination of Archduke Franz Ferdinand of Austria-Hungary in 1914, which led swiftly to the outbreak of World War I. Hobsbawm's point was that the destruction of the past, the erasure of the mechanisms linking contemporary experience to that of earlier generations, was 'one of the most characteristic and eerie phenomena of the late twentieth century'. The apogee of this forgetting, perhaps, is post-war Germany. The whole of the work of the German writer W. G. Sebald is dedicated to the melancholy recovery of a past of cruelty and depraved violence. This encompassed the barbarism beneath empire and civilisational advance, as in his book *The Rings of Saturn*; the historical abominations repressed in the history of an individual, as in *Austerlitz*; and the direct confrontation with Germany's amnesia about its own barbarity and that perpetrated against it in the Allied bombing campaigns of the last years of the war, in *A Natural History of Destruction*.

advice to poor countries to pursue development through free trade, did nothing of the kind itself. Tariffs and other protective measures and import substitution policies were critical to America's success in catching up with and then overtaking Britain. There have been countless nuances and variations in industrial policy, but it is indisputable that every successful industrialisation has involved state intervention in production and trade to support private accumulation, technological change and organisational innovation. The denial of this past is perhaps less of a blindspot and more of a device of continued competition. It is hard not to agree that it represents what Ha-Joon Chang, reviving a phrase of the original economist of trade and industrial policy Friedrich List, calls 'kicking away the ladder'.[31]

The other historical blindspot of modern liberal society obscures the role of violence and brutality within the West's own origins and development. Early modern polities were founded, basically, by thugs, warlords and racketeers. The historian Sir Michael Howard points out, 'the entire apparatus of the state primarily came into being to enable princes to wage war.'[32] As Charles Tilly argues, organised crime was at the heart of the formation of all early modern states, and their racketeering leaders, once established, had the power to rewrite history to inscribe themselves as kings by divine right. The contemporary equivalent of the rhetoric of rule by divine right is rule in the name of universal values of liberalism, justice and democracy. The United States, for example, might have a quite fantastic capacity for violence in its immense military apparatus but is able still to project its violence as distinct from its values, from its civilisational identity, and thus simply as defensive, protective of the universal values it claims to embody. Hence the projection of the United States as pure, bewildered victim in the House of Wonders in Stone Town, Zanzibar in the wake of 9/11. But it is only from a slightly different angle that US military might and foreign policies sometimes seem to combine to look like Kafka's Harrow, forcefully impressing on recalcitrant nations the commandments of good governance, representative democracy and open markets that they have dared to disobey.

Yet the United States was founded in revolution, developed through slavery, expanded through war with Mexico and created in civil war. Its wealth was founded on violence against indigenous people and on the rapacity of robber barons. The Civil War was a crucible of both import-substitution policy and of American barbarism. The limited war aims of the start of the war evolved into a commitment to total war. Distinctions between soldiers and civilians as legitimate targets began to collapse, prefiguring US policy in Vietnam and prefiguring the so-called new wars of the late twentieth century. General William Tecumseh Sherman in 1861 deplored the wanton looting and destruction by his ill-trained troops: 'No curse could be greater than invasion by a volunteer army... No Goths or Vandals ever had less respect for the lives and properties of friends and foes...' But Sherman himself developed into one of the most ruthless of generals. He and others forged a harder view of war largely in the experiences of fighting Confederate guerrillas in Missouri, where the war degenerated more than anywhere else into egregious vengeance.[33]

There is nothing exceptional in this. In what has often seemed like an exceptionally gradual and peaceable transition to capitalist modernity, Britain, the truth is also one of change and development forged in violence. Barrington Moore argued long ago that civil war in England was probably a necessary cataclysm on which later gradualism was built. Even that so-called gradualism involved the viciousness of the enclosures, the brutal exploitation of labour in the mills of industrialisation and the violent capture of markets round the world. It is also easy in this example to see how the two features of the foundation of liberal capitalist society typically hidden from view—government intervention in the economy and the violent establishment and monopolisation of markets and of property rights—are joined. As Eric Hobsbawm put it:

The country which succeeded in concentrating other people's export markets, or even in monopolising the export markets of a large part of the world in a sufficiently brief period of time, could expand its export industries at a rate which made industrial revolution not only practicable for its entrepreneurs, but sometimes virtually compulsory. And this is what Britain succeeded in doing in the eighteenth century. Yet conquering markets by war and colonisation required not merely an economy capable of exploiting those markets, but also a government willing to wage war and colonise for the benefit of British manufacturers.[34]

State violence to establish a trading monopoly was never more emphatic than in the *Arrow* War or Second Opium War in the 1860s. The interests of nineteenth-century British merchants and the politicians of empire, backed by the wounded ideology of superiority (in the face of the supposed xenophobic put-downs of the 'monstrous' Commissioner Yeh of Canton), combined to cause a war whose immediate spark was a petty conflict over honour and the misrepresented rules of the game in the South China Sea.* Proponents of the democratic peace thesis—the argument that democracies do not go to war against each other and are inherently more peaceable than other polities—suggest implicitly that when democracies do go to war against non-democracies they do so reluctantly and defensively. Despite vigorous democratic opposition to the war in Britain, the government pressed on with its military adventure and chiefly on the basis of pursuing ideological, strategic, personal and economic interests rather than defending against Chinese aggression. Meanwhile, among the more vociferous opponents of the war was the champion of free trade, Richard Cobden; however, it was the creation and control of market imperfections and militarily-secured absolute advantage that won the political day, rather than the theoretical niceties of Ricardian comparative advantage. The war reinforced a triangle of financial flows. Opium produced in India was sold to China, creating a large source of revenue for the government in British India. Indian opium profits helped cover the fiscal bill in India (including the financing of military adventures in Afghanistan). They also aided the British purchase of US cotton for the Lancashire mills as well as the consumption of Chinese tea and silk in Britain. Chinese authorities had threatened to suppress the opium trade through a revision of the Treaty of Nanking: the effects on British imperialism, industrialisation and consumer utility would have been dramatic.

At the origin of all capitalist development was the process known as primitive accumulation, which, roughly, is the point at which the circulation of capital and increase in its value begins—a moment characterised by prising people away from their own means of production through non-economic coercion, expropriating land and so on (see Chapter 6). What matters to the discussion of a perspective on violence and historical change is that primitive accumulation, as Marx put it, is to political economy as original sin is to theology.

Sustaining, exporting and universalising the values and interests of liberal capitalist society has involved continued aggression by major powers ever since, in ways that are often well hidden from view. Later chapters—particularly Chapter 6—will expand on the argument that most if not all societies, very much including capitalist societies, emerge in conditions of conflict and violence and furthermore depend on this violence.

* Wong (1998) discusses the complexity and controversies surrounding the *Arrow* War, which was triggered by claims of a Chinese insult to the British flag, flown by what was pretty much a pirate ship called *The Arrow*.

'Angola Blues': history in a violent perspective

What kind of perspective on war and violence, then, should we adopt? Specifically, what perspective is appropriate for an understanding of the relationship between violence and civilisation, war and progress? The most normal is the liberal interpretation of war, which is the dominant, hegemonic perspective in the West. Nonetheless, it has competitors. One is the perspective that assumes there is no such thing as progress. Another is the romanticisation of violence as a principle of creativity. And another stems from a tragic view of history.

The liberal interpretation of war presumes that all war is exclusively negative. This has an entirely obvious appeal: war is negative, destructive, everywhere abominable. If it is exclusively negative, it cannot, therefore, be positively associated with any progressive development, any social improvement. This leaves little for the social scientist to do other than to show in detail how destructive war is. For example, economists in the First World War and development economists at the end of the twentieth century developed models for assessing the costs of war. Drawing up the economic costs of conflict is a useful exercise. It in turn might help to deter would-be warmongers from sparking conflicts; and it might help in a practical way by providing a rational means of working out how much support is required after a war, to 'reconstruct' and 'rehabilitate'. If from the perspective of the liberal interpretation of war it is acknowledged that a handful of people benefit during war, then these are seen either as purely brutal, wartime speculators, economic criminals, or as abstract beneficiaries of wartime distortions, whose ill-gotten gains need to be tempted back into a peacetime economy. From this perspective the World Bank stated in 2003 that 'war is development in reverse'.[35]

The other side of the liberal interpretation of war is, of course, the liberal interpretation of liberalism. If violence and war are only obstacles to progress, then progress from this point of view is something that must unfold without violence. Liberal society and its development contain violence in one sense, i.e. restricting and stifling it; but they do not contain violence in the sense of any positive involvement. And this is exactly the heart of liberal ideology: the idea that all good things go together. Democracy and peace go hand in hand; therefore democratisation must be 'a method for peace'. Democracy and good governance combine effortlessly with economic growth, each supporting the other. Acknowledging the importance of 'institutions', policy prescriptions of development agencies in the 1990s recommended that low-income countries, generally with 'weak states', introduce governance reforms to stabilise property rights, improve democracy and reduce corruption. The expectation was that institutions such as these, imbued with liberal values, would themselves bring about faster economic growth.* More 'perfect' markets work better and produce economic growth. And if there are awkward challenges, like inequality in distribution of wealth and income, then further growth (so long as it is sustained by free markets looking increasingly like the benchmark of perfect competition) will iron them out in good time. In liberal ideology violence in and by advanced, modern societies is an embarrassment. Modernisation was supposed to release us from violence and everything it invokes: the primitive, the uncivil, the barbaric.

There are varieties of liberalism, and one of the greatest discussions of violence and war, from this perspective, was written by Hannah Arendt in the 1960s. Influenced by the Second World War and by her observation of the trial of Eichmann in Jerusalem, Arendt was contemptuous of what she saw as the infantile romanticisation of violence by some intellectuals of the time, above all by Jean-Paul Sartre. Arendt could understand the source of the disturbing anti-imperialist rhetoric of Frantz Fanon's *The Wretched of the Earth,* which set out violence almost as a duty for people in colonised societies like French Algeria. But she could not abide Sartre's excited foreword to Fanon's book. In contrast to Sartre, and to some extent Fanon, who argued that power could be gained by violence, Arendt distinguished categorically between violence and power. For her, violence was the opposite of real power: violence was a reflection of powerlessness. The distinction between violent and non-violent action, she wrote, 'is that the former is exclusively bent on the destruction of the old and the latter chiefly concerned with the establishment of something new.'

Hannah Arendt's views are appealing. They are also surely unrealistic, resting on an idealistic or exclusively spiritual rather than political idea of power. Progress, including the development of liberal conceptions and institutions of justice and governance as well as the accomplishments of industrial society, has not evolved without violence. This violence, arguably, has been more than simply

---

* The historical fallacy of this good governance approach was to imagine that the advanced industrialised economies developed by first introducing stable property rights, establishing democracy, and eradicating corruption: this is wrong on every count. For a formal explanation of the good governance approach and its historical and statistical errors see Khan and Jomo (2004b).

defensive; it has often been active and even barbaric. The clue to this is that liberalism has not been developed as the rational and unanimously agreed implementation of self-evidently superior values and institutions. Every liberal and capitalist modern development has been pushed forward in the interests only of sections of society and against those of others. And as the philosopher Stuart Hampshire suggests, renewing a phrase of Heraclitus: justice *is* conflict.[36]

Liberalism is worth fighting for in many ways and many of its institutions have precisely been developed to try to restrain excess and brutality. However, the West has never fully pulled out the thread of violence, it has not escaped barbarism. This is something that Michel Foucault, Walter Benjamin and others have also argued: that not even modern liberalism could escape this human bond of violence. As a political theory liberalism disowns all forms of violence beyond individual self-defence or the legitimate monopoly of violence that the liberal-democratic state exercises. In his 1975/6 'Society must be Defended' series of lectures, Foucault argued that Western politics had been dominated by a discourse that covered up the memory of real war that in fact lay at the genesis of sovereignty. Foucault's project was to explore the idea—and to trace its history—that politics was the continuation of war by other means: that war was the principle by which society must be understood. By contrast with the idea that war was an enigma and a disruptive principle, Foucault explored the history of the idea that war provided a grid of intelligibility for the world of power relations. This would mean that the constructs of liberal society are really a kind of barbed wire or electric fence—they look relatively harmless as definitions of political space, but always contain threats of violence if we challenge them.*

---

* Foucault's was an explicitly historical argument and an argument for history. His critique of Hobbes, for example, is precisely that Hobbes's state of nature, characterised by a war of every man against every man and pitting equals against equals, was entirely fanciful as a basis on which to construct a theory of absolute monarchical sovereignty, in which people willingly exchange their independence for the stability pact offered by obedience to sovereign and absolute power. Foucault argues that precisely at the moment when states were establishing a centralised monopoly of violence, i.e. when war was becoming no longer a class privilege or a widespread social phenomenon, there arose an idea that very real and unequal wars were the foundations of societies and their power structures, and that the principles of war continued to define 'peacetime' institutions and political order. This idea first emerged in the work of the Diggers and Levellers in seventeenth-century England, part of whose critique of royal absolutism was based on a rejection of the legitimacy

Western and more or less liberal civilisation had violence at its foundation, in war, slavery, imperial adventure and primitive accumulation. It has been violent in its spread. And it continues to find barbarism hard to escape. One way of seeing this is shown at length later in this book, in Chapter 6: the way in which capitalism and consumer satisfaction in the West are closely entwined with atrocity in Africa, the Middle East, Asia and Latin America.* Against this background the abuses in Abu Ghraib prison and elsewhere in Iraq, by the security forces of the Coalition occupation force, are far from freak outliers of barbarism.

If we recover from amnesia and exoticism, another perspective on war and violence might be possible. Many of those who have most honestly faced up to the persistence of violence have ended up enthralled by it. This has even been so for clearly anti-violent thinkers. Walter Benjamin, for example, set out to find a way to break what he saw as the endless cycle of violence and counter-violence. It was Benjamin, remember, who poked at liberal sensibilities by writing that every document of civilisation was a document of barbarism. Yet he ended up entrapped by the problem he wanted to resolve. In his *Critique of Violence* Benjamin takes analytical corners on two wheels, veering perilously close to the right-wing glorification of violence of Schmitt and to the revolutionary,

---

of a political order founded in the Norman Conquest. (The Diggers and Levellers were just the sort of people against whom Hobbes was writing.) On English radical political theory in the sixteenth and seventeenth centuries see Wood and Wood (1997).

* Another is the zealous fortification of Europe against immigration and refugees. This is a regulation that encourages a new class of primitive accumulators in trafficking and in pitching illegal immigrants into drugs and sex industries. It is a regulation in which the raw material of prejudice (e.g., the *Dover Express* calling Kosovar and Kurdish refugees 'human sewage') is processed into refined legalese of EU agreements and new laws like the spread of liability to air companies, the Eurorail company and haulage operators for possible carriage of illegal entrants. See Harding (2000). Harding draws on Arendt's comment, in *The Origins of Totalitarianism*, that 'those whom the persecutor had singled out as the scum of the earth—Jews, Trotskyites etc.—actually were received as scum of the earth everywhere', to argue that modern refugees are 'shuttled along a continuum of abuse'. In other words, the discrimination and sometimes the brutal exploitation of, or violence against, people is in some measure handed along from the regimes where refugees are pushed out to the 'host' nations where they end up. There has also been an enduring space for extreme exploitation and barbaric conditions in the migrant labour market, e.g. in Britain, where conditions of migrant workers employed in floriculture in the southwest, in chicken packing in East Anglia, in the prostitution business, and in cockle picking in Morecambe Bay began to receive more press attention.

syndicalist romanticisation of violence in Sorel's *Réflexions sur la Violence*. Benjamin ends up putting his faith in a religiously sanctioned violence that would put an end to all other violence.[37]

Foucault never really answered his own question of whether war was the main principle for understanding society and politics. But he did introduce an eschatological turn, arguing that one of the implications of inverting Clausewitz is that the final decision can only come from war, that the last battle with real weapons would put an end to politics, and that this would suspend the exercise of power as continuous warfare. Others too have ended up enamoured of the power of violence as a principle of social creativity, either a liberating power or simply an eternal force in human nature that looks especially dominant if one loses faith in progress. Drieu de Rochelle wrote, in *Le Jeune Européen*, 'Nothing is ever accomplished without bloodshed...I look forward to a bloodbath.' Lenin in 1919 declared that terror was indispensable. Indeed, in the years between the two world wars, something of a 'gospel of violence' spread through segments of the European intelligentsia.[38]

Possibly this dramatic encounter with violence is peculiarly Western. At any rate, Beatrice Hanssen, in a series of essays reviving Foucault's and Benjamin's work on violence, argues that the line from Heraclitus ('war is the father of everything') onwards represents a particularly Western philosophical tradition: what she calls a 'thanatological legacy'. As she puts it, 'Western philosophy has been weighed down by a being-towards-death, often to the point of elevating violence's so-called interruptive, disjunctive force to a philosophical principle.' For some people the obsession is more than an idea; it has become a material fact: the thanatological tendency has been elevated by modern social organisation and technological change to a level in which the whole of modern society is characterised by a 'logic of exterminism'.[39]

A third perspective is offered by a tragic view of history: the view that Marx developed. It is an Enlightenment perspective in that it wholeheartedly accepts that there is human progress. But from this perspective every instance of progress in human society comes with a price of cruelty. There is no shirking the brutality of this price. The exploitation of some individuals by others, the viciousness underpinning Greek civilisation, or the welcome advance of North American society through the Americas, these were not small inconveniences: they were 'sickening to human feeling'. However, not only is progress possible in spite of brutality. Progress might not be possible without this brutality.[40] This does not have to lead to the necessity of full-scale, organised violent revolution in the name of progress. It does, however, entail acknowledging that all momentous transitions have been brutally disruptive; they have shattered the stability—perhaps a stagnant, backward stability but stability nonetheless—of 'tradition'. And a further implication of this perspective is that not every instance of war and violence has to be seen as exclusively or necessarily negative. In-spite of the very real awfulness and waste of war, there can be long-run consequences that are socially progressive.

Violence and war should not, then, be seen as oddities, distortions or distractions but should be regarded as closely connected to progress and development. The role of convict labour in the development of capitalism in the postbellum Southern states of the United States provides a good example. After the Civil War, and as the Southern economy changed from slave-based plantation agriculture to capitalist industrialisation and infrastructure expansion, black Americans were still subjected to oppression, segregation, lynching and both legal and non-legal methods of disenfranchisement.[41] Part of this social system was the penal system, according to which, until the 1920s, black southern Americans who broke laws were auctioned off to work as convict labour on railways and roads, in mines and forests and in a range of industries.[42] Eventually this private use of convict labour—the convict lease system—was reformed and replaced by state labour, in the chain gang. The convict lease and chain gang systems were certainly a barbaric means of securing cheap and 'unfree' labour for the reconstruction and development of the South. They were institutions sustained by 'the rawhide whip, iron shackle, sweat box, convict cage and bloodhound'.[43]

The brutality of these institutions has been persistent. One example is Angola, Louisiana. The Louisiana State Penitentiary northeast of Baton Rouge, known as Angola Farm, started out as a slave plantation. In 1880 a Confederate major who had won the private lease to run a prison in Baton Rouge bought up an 8,000 acre plantation called Angola, housing inmates there and putting them to work on levee construction on the Mississippi River. Over time the inmates came largely to work crops on the farm. In 1901 the state of Louisiana took control of Angola Farm and its inmates, and after a series of floods had destroyed crops and ruined neighbouring plantations the state bought up more land and expanded the farm prison to its current 18,000 acres. Nowadays, under a reformist prison governor, Angola is changing: the 5,100 inmates still work on the farm, for 4 cents an hour, and the past is commercialised in a museum. However, Angola's past is among the most notoriously brutal in US penal history. When the state nationalised it in 1901 it was largely in response to media reports of the mistreatment of prisoners. Despite periods of reform, the establishment did not shake off its cruelty. In 1952 thirty-one inmates cut their Achilles tendons in protest against brutality and the labour regime. And during the 1960s Angola became known as 'the bloodiest prison in the South' thanks to the rate of violence between inmates. It was in Angola in 1934 that the musicologists John and Alan Lomax came across Huddie Ledbetter, better known as the folk and blues musician Leadbelly. Among the songs he wrote was *Angola Blues (So Doggone Soon).**

But, as Alex Lichtenstein argues, this was not some peculiar leftover from the old South: rather, the convict labour system was at the cutting edge of the modernisation of the new South. Convict labour was concentrated in some of the most significant and rapidly growing sectors of the Southern economy in the second half of the nineteenth century: first in railways, then in extractive industries like lumber and turpentine, then in state-owned mines, farms and road maintenance teams. Forced labour in the postbellum Southern states of the United States was compatible with both the ideals and the facts of socio-economic progress, a fact that serves as a reminder 'of historical tendencies that much of the rest of the world has been made well aware of: that progress is not necessarily progressive for all peoples, and that the bearers of modernity frequently carry with them its antithesis.'[44] This reminder is carried over into the discussion, in this book, of recent and contemporary wars and violence. While these wars are typically seen as throwbacks or reversals, as the inverse and undoing of development, this book argues that they can sometimes be a central part of development.

This is a profoundly uncomfortable perspective. It is also a realistic perspective and one with complicated implications for the understanding of contemporary conflicts. Perhaps, though, it needs qualification. For there is a danger that a tragic view of history indulges violence. The tragic view of history is imbued with the same Enlightenment hopes as the liberal conscience that emerged through the eighteenth and nineteenth centuries, but is less amnesiac. Its strength is its awareness of paradoxes in historical change and of combinations of opposites (precisely a characteristic

---

* *Angola Blues* can be found on the CD *Titanic—The Library of Congress Recordings Vol. 4*, on Rounder Records (1994).

of some definitions of the tragic). The risk is that this approach leans towards romantic consolation, which may then be distorted to justify cruel actions. It would be easy enough to take this perspective and write off the sufferings of so many people in wars around the world, blithely putting the destruction down to the march of progress. At worst, it would be possible to end up an advocate of war as a policy bound to have long-run progressive consequences. At best, there is a risk of ignoring the possibilities for improving people's lives while minimising the costs. Real life, as Iris Murdoch wrote, is not tragic.[45] For the tragic, even as it confronts unutterable suffering, transforms it aesthetically. And while progress remains worth struggling for, the idea needs to be tempered by a sharper awareness that it will not erase the essential sources of suffering in society. Faith in progress can elevate the 'end' to a level where it is given the power to resolve and end all violence. Historical materialism is no foolproof protection against this kind of transcendental political imagination. Therefore, an alternative may be a *melancholy* perspective, one that accepts violence in the 'human condition', the likely links between violence and progress, and the possibilities of progress, while accepting too that any and all progress simply raises new conflicts and problems, that no amount of progress will erase conflict and violence.

Every Congo has its Conrads and Casements.* If progress and civilisation can never break free of barbarism, then at least the two are perpetually, unpredictably in conflict as well as joined at birth. This perspective is more hopeful than the implications of glib liberal triumphalism, than the idea that every action in every society is born of rational choice, and certainly than the idea that there was such a thing as a progressive civilisation but it is in terminal decline thanks to someone letting the barbarians through the gate. If our society is always torn between its potential for progress and its capacity for barbarism, then there will always be people alive to the dangers of barbarism who will throw up a challenge to them.

A melancholy view of history also generates the problem of a perspective of assessment: from what angle or distance do we judge

---

* Much of Conrad's novel is concretely historical. Adam Hochschild traces these roots of the novel in *King Leopold's Ghost*, which also tells of other critics of the Congo regime, including Roger Casement. Casement, who went on to report on the violence of the Putumayo rubber tapping labour regime in Peru (see Taussig, 2004), was eventually hanged for treason for his role in supporting Irish independence from Britain.

whether or not there is any progressive potential within a given war or violent conflict? Which criteria should we apply? This book argues that the criteria of immediate liberal assumptions are too limited. It also argues that the criteria of anti-globalisation pessimism are inappropriate, and that they revive many of the errors of dependency theory.

Finally, the discussion of the criteria for assessing the outcomes and paradoxical by-products of violent conflict raises the need for a set of distinctions between types of social violence. For even if we do adopt a tragic or a melancholy view of history, this does not mean that all types of violent conflict are equivalent in their historical significance. There is violence that is institutionalised and historically 'stuck'. In this case, violence is not breaking the rules of the game, it *is* the rule of the game, it is the norm. This was very much the case in feudal Europe, where, as Marc Bloch put it, violence became in the thirteenth century a class privilege, restricted in theory at least to the durable hatreds between noble families.[46] Even in later centuries, characterised in Europe by a ruling class defined as a warrior class, war was not so much the unusual continuation of politics by other means as the very meat of politics, particularly international relations. There is also violence that is negative and destructive, not just in the immediate and short-run sense but in a more lasting way. Then there is violence that is part and parcel of creating new institutions, which may or may not be progressive. And then there is violence that, however vile, is part of the establishment of new social and economic arrangements whose long-run consequences are progressive, or else helps provoke the creation of such new arrangements. Again, this book argues that most theories of contemporary violence and war assume that all instances of violent conflict are identical in their significance (apart from 'defensive' Western violence).

The questions people ask about violence and war are phrased by their preconceptions. Many common preconceptions and definitions need challenging, among them the idea that violent conflict in developing countries obviously represents a reversal of development. The next chapter explores another way of asking questions about common ways of understanding violence: i.e. questioning classification systems that distinguish between types of violent conflict and, indeed, between war and peace.

2

CATEGORIES, TRENDS AND EVIDENCE
OF VIOLENT CONFLICT

'Cold War? Hell, it was a Hot War!' (Robert McNamara in the film *The Fog of War*)

If analytical perspectives affect the way we understand violent conflict, so too do the frames chosen to surround and organise episodes of violence. Frames are boundaries around what is observed; they help in identifying patterns among the data. This chapter discusses some of these frames, which involve classification and distinction between phenomena. There may well be a mutually supportive relationship between perspectives and frames. For example, the liberal interpretation of war partly relies on isolating discrete events, such as 'civil war onset', and trying then to determine the special correlates of their exceptionalism. But such an approach may rest on a categorical *trompe l'œil*. A different classification—one that acknowledges a broad continuum of forms of violent conflict relevant in the study of development—may by contrast support an alternative, melancholy perspective on violence and development.

Since this chapter is concerned with patterns of violence in the contemporary world, particularly in developing countries, it naturally touches on questions of security. Since the end of the Cold War commentators have commonly asked if the world is a safer place. This question is often linked to the question of whether there are more or fewer wars than in the past, and then to related questions such as whether there has been a change in the kinds of war that take place. In the 1990s commentators swapped labels and claims: the End of History, the Deadly Peace, the Coming Anarchy, the Clash of Civilisations, New Wars. More recently, there have continued to be sharply contrasting assessments of the global predicament. While the Human Security Report 2005 (p.15) claims: "Since the end of the Cold War, armed conflicts around the world have declined dramatically", Hardt and Negri (2005,) argue not only that there·"are innumerable armed conflicts waged across the globe today", and that these are part of a "global civil war", but also that "war is becoming a general phenomenon, global and interminable". They argue, indeed, that war has been raised by technological developments to an "absolute, ontological level". The simple question about global security is asked in different ways. In the early years of the twenty-first century asking if the world was a safer place had also come to mean asking whether international military intervention in and occupation of Iraq and the overthrow of the Taliban in Afghanistan had reduced the threat of international terrorism. But the question of security begs other questions: Is the world more or less secure for whom? When do we know enough to claim to have discovered a clear trend? And what do people actually mean by the term security? For since the Cold War there has been an extension of the idea of security. One common approach in the past—to identify security with national military security—has been mated with the broadening of the meaning of 'development'. The union produced the increasingly widespread concept, with multiple and often unclear definitions, of 'human security'.* In this chapter the concern is chiefly with violent conflict as a common source of the insecurity of nations and individuals.

Quantitative analysis might provide some answers to sweeping questions about global security. One approach is to count up conflicts and see if the annual number has recently been rising, falling or constant. However, there is no one definitive answer. Although it is possible to learn a lot from quantitative analysis of the incidence of violent conflict, arguably even more is learnt by exploring some of the difficulties in addressing the question and some of the reasons why there can be different answers. This chapter shows some of the patterns that emerge from the main databases of violent conflict. It then opens up these further questions: When and on what grounds is an event (or process) defined as a war? How clear is the difference between a civil war and an international war? How clear is the distinction between a civil war and non-war political or social violence or even criminal violence?

---

* King and Murray (2001–2) note that the development and security establishments underwent a period of 'conceptual turmoil' in the 1990s and that this was one source of the human security concept. Emphasising the abundance of alternative definitions of human security, and noting that most of these reflect a shift in security concerns from national to individual levels, they propose their own definition: 'the number of years of future life spent outside a state of "generalized poverty"' (p. 585). See also www.humansecuritycentre.org.

Exploring these labelling complications in some detail may help to show why the answers to questions about global security and insecurity can vary. It may also have other uses. A categorical label—for example, 'civil war' or 'inter-state war'—frames those phenomena collected under the label. Definitional frames are often more than purely descriptive: they may shape *what* is viewed and *how* it is interpreted. For instance, the 'civil war' category often suggests a conflict almost entirely internal to a country or nation-state. But that suggestion may easily deflect attention from other dimensions of a conflict, from other ways of understanding and responding to that conflict, and from the similarities between civil wars and some other types of violence. Further, labels are indispensable analytical devices but they are selected to serve a purpose. Sometimes different purposes might be pursued but using the same labels and frames. The broad purpose of this book is to explore the relationships between economic development and violent conflict. That purpose, it argues, cannot be served effectively by examining only those phenomena that are included in the categories of 'war' or 'intermediate conflict', whether intra- or inter-state. It may be that restricting the analysis to civil wars, say, produces a misleading idea that violent conflict is a relatively rare phenomenon. Treating a wider range of phenomena may produce a different conclusion, i.e. that violent conflict of very diverse types is an extremely common, basically typical, feature of development experiences, including those social transformations that are regarded as successful.

The end of history or a deadly peace?

Tracing trends in the incidence and distribution of conflicts is a fraught exercise. What are the historical trends of conflict, especially over the past fifty years or so? Where are wars concentrated? Are wars mostly so-called civil wars or wars between countries? Are wars concentrated exclusively in the poorest countries? Is there something categorically 'new' about post-Cold War wars?

From a certain vantage point the outlook is bright. Figure 1 gives a clear image of the trend in violent conflict from the end of the Second World War up to the year 2002. One way of explaining the image is in terms of the Cold War and the apparent fact that the world had got the Cold War and its problems out of its system by the end of the twentieth century. It is a commonplace that the twentieth century was the most violent century yet, despite being one of staggering progress (including a phenomenal rate of technological change and rising incomes in the advanced capitalist countries, the

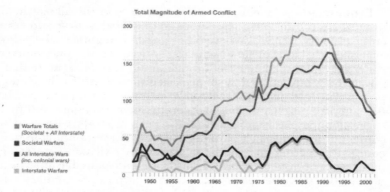

Figure 1. GLOBAL TRENDS IN VIOLENT CONFLICT, 1946–2002
Source: Marshall and Gurr (2003), Fig. 3.1.

overcoming of a number of vicious diseases and latterly the economic development of many poorer parts of the world, not least
the world's two most populous countries, China and India). But a
picture like that in Figure 1 offered hope that the twenty-first century might be a calmer, more peaceful era. Figure 1 is taken from a
report produced at the University of Maryland (USA) called *Peace
and Conflict 2003: A Global Survey of Armed Conflicts, Self-Determination
Movements, and Democracy*. Noting that the number and magnitude
of armed conflicts within and among states, as captured in the
graph, had lessened since the early 1990s by nearly half, that conflicts over self-determination were being settled more frequently,
and that democratic governments now outnumbered autocratic
governments by two to one, the report argued that if these trends
continued they would 'establish a world more peaceful than at any
time in the past century'.*

Even what the authors of the report call 'societal warfare'—wars
within countries, conceived as either 'political' or 'ethnic' conflict—

---

* As a warning against extrapolation from past trends, Darrell Huff (1973, p. 124),
in *How to Lie with Statistics*, quotes Mark Twain: 'In the space of one hundred and
seventy-six years the Lower Mississippi has shortened itself two hundred and forty-
two miles. That is an average of a trifle over one mile and a third per year. Therefore, any calm person…can see that in the Old Oölitic Silurian period, just a million years ago next November, the Lower Mississippi River was upward of one
million three hundred thousand miles long, and stuck out over the Gulf of Mexico
like a fishing-rod. And by the same token any person can see that seven hundred
and forty-two years from now the Lower Mississippi will be only a mile and three-
quarters long… There is something fascinating about science. One gets such
wholesale returns of conjecture out of such a trifling investment of fact.'

shows a precipitous falling away after 1992. These societal conflicts
had multiplied more consistently than other types of conflict in the
post-World War II period and had accounted for a growing proportion of all violent conflict in the world. This was so much the case
that a specialist in international relations called for a shift in the
way we think of war. Traditionally war was regarded mainly as a
confrontation between states. Ignoring plenty of exceptions, the
understanding of war crystallised around this notion—captured
classically in Clausewitz's saying about war being the continuation
of politics by other means. The analytical implication was that war
was something studied in the discipline of international relations.
However, Kalevi Holsti argued more or less that this way of seeing
war was the sediment of a bygone age. Instead we lived now in a
world of 'wars of the third kind'. These were wars within countries
and largely a matter of state weakness or collapse, chiefly in relatively poor countries.[1]

The University of Maryland project is one among a number that
maintain databases on war or armed conflict. Perhaps the two best
known are the Correlates of War (COW) project, housed in the
University of Michigan at Ann Arbor in the United States, and the
Conflict Data Project at the University of Uppsala (Sweden).
Another project is the Arbeitsgemeinschaft Kriegsursachenfors-
chung (AKUF)—Causes of War project—at the University of Hamburg in Germany. There are differences in scope, purpose and
definitions used in these projects. For example, the AKUF dataset
does not rely on a tally of deaths as a major conflict criterion, as
the other two do; rather, it judges conflicts through a measure of
continuity. It is broader in its coverage. While the AKUF and COW
projects were initiated with the purpose of establishing the causes
of war, the Uppsala dataset was begun especially with a view to studying conflict resolution patterns. Unlike the others, the Uppsala
dataset includes information on the 'type of incompatibility' between conflicting parties (e.g. territorial or over government).[2]

If, as Figure 1 suggests, there has been a similarly sheer drop in
the number and magnitude of wars between states and of societal
conflicts, the news really is good. This would suggest there is room
both for the kind of slowly spreading international peace that the
German philosopher Immanuel Kant (1724–1804) envisaged and
for internal stability and peace within countries.* The two might

---

* The argument that peace—as an enduring and defining feature of society—is a
  particularly modern concept, and one associated above all with Kant, is sketched
  by Howard (2001).

even reinforce one another. For if the less developed and more recently established nation-states could learn to resolve political conflicts without violence this would suggest increasingly that they 'shared the values' of the rich countries. And shared values, long before the phrase became a part of the rhetoric of international development aid agencies, constituted the core of Kant's idea of Perpetual Peace.

Kant was not known for snappy punditry. His treatise retained enough of his complex thinking to leave it, still, open to conflicting interpretations. However, its less contentious theme can be summarised fairly succinctly. If a lasting international peace were really possible, it could come about only if major states voluntarily signed up for a kind of club whose membership suggested 'like minded' principles were shared. The principles included not violating the sovereignty of other nation-states. The idea of the Kantian Peace has been absorbed not only into the institutions of the United Nations but also into a particular ideology of liberal democratic governance. According to this ideology, the only shared values upon which a voluntary restraint from international war may be built are those of liberal democracy, in the prevailing sense of government established by electoral representation. If, therefore, more of the nations of the world are adopting liberal democratic practices, this will clearly consolidate the foundations of a truly international and truly lasting peace. This is the hope offered by the exhilarating rush of the downward slope of both international and societal violent conflict depicted in Figure 1.

This same hope is exactly what propelled Francis Fukuyama early in the post-Cold War days to claim 'the End of History'—a kind of inversion of those gloomy placards declaring 'The End is Nigh'.[3] Fukuyama, and many others who welcomed his claims, saw the end of the Cold War as the final victory of liberal democracy in the war of ideologies. Evidence such as that in Figure 1 certainly helped both to shore up the optimism of observers like Fukuyama and to dispel the pessimism of some who insisted on seeing enduring difficulties in the world. For not everyone was convinced by post-Cold War optimism. The Carnegie Report on *Preventing Deadly Conflict*, for example, described the period after the Cold War as 'the Deadly Peace'.[4] Especially dramatic, Robert Kaplan countered the end of history with the 'Coming Anarchy'. Meanwhile, others too have seen sources of enduring violent conflict beyond the resolution of superpower rivalry—and the chief culprits tend to be developmental inequalities, ethnic hostilities and environmental or resource challenges, as well as, more recently, US hegemonic hubris. In the

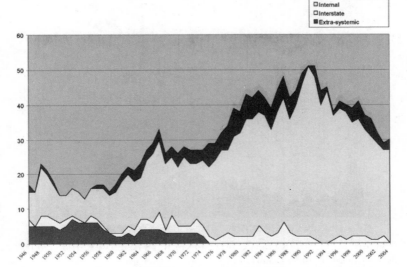

Figure 2. NUMBER OF ARMED CONFLICTS BY TYPE, 1946–2001
Source: Uppsala Conflict Database, www.pcr.uu.se/database.

contrast between the idea of the end of history or a successful post-Cold War peace and that of a deadly peace or an enduring insecurity, there are clearly questions of what evidence different interpretations draw on as well as how they interpret that evidence.

Twisting the lens a little changes the picture. Clearly there was still a peak of conflict—like a hysterical stock market bubble—shortly after the end of the Cold War, and then a sharp drop in the number of conflicts. But in the second half of the 1990s conflict recovered its composure, more or less levelling out at a number around that prevailing in the late 1970s. After 1999 there was another drop, followed by another small increase in 2004, when the Conflict Data Project at Uppsala recorded 27 'internal' armed conflicts and three 'internationalised internal conflicts', the latter including Iraq (see Figure 2). Past trends may not provide a reliable guide to the future, or even to the present, but the serrated course of conflict since the Second World War, as portrayed in Figure 2, suggests some interesting changes. While interstate wars overall declined in numbers, the incidence of 'internal' wars increased.

Conflicts continued to be distinguished throughout the 1946–2004 period as 'minor' conflicts, 'intermediate' conflicts and 'war'.

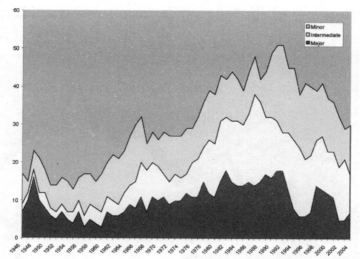

Figure 3. NUMBER OF ARMED CONFLICTS BY LEVEL, 1946–2001
Source: Uppsala Conflict Database, www.pcr.uu.se/database.

Figure 3 shows a gradual increase in the share of total armed conflicts that could be classed as intermediate. Finally, before the peak
in the incidence of armed conflict in the early 1990s there were
other peaks, for example, in 1948, 1966/67, and 1981–83. Following these peaks the number of conflicts settled each time around
an average plateau of violence higher than the previous one.

There are still other ways of characterising the trend in violent
conflict. If in recent years around one in six countries in the world
have been experiencing civil wars in any given year, this is a level
that was reached before the end of the Cold War. Rather than this
level of conflict being a 'product of the end of the Cold War', the
deadly shakeout of fundamental change in the international system,
it suggests rather a gradual accumulation of such conflicts since the
end of the Second World War. This trend does not, though, represent more conflicts breaking out over time but rather the way wars
end. The rate of civil war onset varied but showed no obvious trend
in the second half of the twentieth century. But the rate at which
these wars ended was slower. In other words, the world has not produced more and more civil wars, rather there has been a mounting
in-tray of unfinished wars. Thus James Fearon and David Laitin
argue, 'States in the international system have been subject to a

more or less constant risk of violent civil conflict over the period, but the conflicts they suffer have been difficult to end.'[5]

Looking at the figures over the span of time from the end of the Second World War, and at the different silhouettes of post-Cold War conflict in Figures 1 and 2, begins to open up a view of some of the major problems in understanding violent conflict. Holding up these slightly different panoramic snaps of conflict suggests the following kinds of question: What is the appropriate range to analyse? Should the focus be exclusively on post-1989 conflicts, or post-1946 conflicts, or should the span be even longer? Is there a solid basis in these aggregate data for any definitive statements about a 'deadly peace' or a 'world more peaceful than at any time in the past century'? The short answer is that there are too few observations on which to make a claim about a clear trend. That has become even more obvious since 11 September 2001, when analytical categories have been in turmoil. Finally, the contrasting images of what has happened to conflict since the end of the Cold War raise the questions of selection of evidence and definition of events: how do analysts decide what to include and what to exclude in a roster of violent conflict and how do they differentiate between the phenomena of violence?

When is a war not a war?

These are not trivial issues; for what begins as a set of necessary, if pernickety, quibbles about datasets, sources of data and the boundaries around analytical categories may open out into a richer discussion of the place of violence in the modern world and of how to try to understand it. This is an important theme in any analytical endeavour. Luigi Cavalli-Sforza discusses this problem of classification in relation to the question of racial diversity.[6] He shows how most efforts to classify the human population into races are doomed by arbitrary choices of definitions. Genetic and geographical reality is a series of continuities, while classification systems impose artificial discontinuities or boundaries. This is one reason why anthropologists have come up with wildly different tallies of human races—from three to more than a hundred.

Classifying is a compulsion of the curious. It is necessary if we are to try to understand almost anything. Without categorical distinctions and groupings the things people try to understand are typically too diverse to resolve into any clear patterns. The higher the degree of variation among related things, the greater the need for more sophisticated systems of classification. One of the most useful of these systems, for example, is Linnaeus's system for classifying plants. Most systems for classifying human beings are cruder—for example, the US census distinguishes between whites, blacks, native Americans, Asians and Hispanics, where the last category has virtually no biological meaning at all. Cavalli-Sforza argues that any proposal for an improved classification system can only end in failure: 'All systems lack clear and satisfactory criteria for classifying. The more we pay attention to questions of statistical adequacy, the more hopeless the effort becomes.'[7] Furthermore, there is a high degree of genetic variation even within small populations—say, a Pygmy camp in Central Africa or a village in the Pyrenees. 'Regardless of the type of genetic markers used', Cavalli-Sforza writes, 'the variation between two random individuals within any one population is 85 per cent as large as that between two individuals randomly selected from the world's population.'[8]

Genetic diversity is very nearly continuous. Nonetheless, one reason to continue pursuing the idea of a form of classification based on genetic difference is that genetic differences affect the chances of having specific diseases and responding similarly to the same drugs. However, the basis for such a classification system would probably be groups of between 5,000 and 500,000 individuals, which might yield a maximum number of genetically different groups in the world of around one million. The most straightforward implication is that classification systems are generally determined by some purpose—they are not 'natural' and they should always be questioned. Where the events or phenomena being organised are largely continuous, inventing or choosing categories involves fixing an artificial border around one group of events. Just as the imposition of borders is at the heart of much social and political conflict, so analytical borders are at the heart of much debate (and policy formulation) in the social and other sciences.

This is very much the case in the study of violent conflict. Here too what matters is whether or not a set of categories hides more than it reveals. The figures above show the compulsion to classify at work. Figure 1 distinguishes between societal warfare and interstate warfare, separating out a different category of independence wars. Figure 2 classes armed conflicts as interstate, extrastate, internal and internationalised internal. And figure 3 separates out war from intermediate and minor armed conflicts. These are just some of the classification systems applied to the study of violent conflict. Other systems include: the division between 'ethnic' and 'political' conflict; another division between 'ethnic/religious' and 'ideology/other' conflicts; the distribution of conflict in terms of the average level of per capita income of people in afflicted countries; and the distinction that became fashionable during the mid-1990s between so-called 'new' and 'old' wars.

— *The casualty threshold*

One of the most basic challenges is to decide which conflicts to include in a set of observations of violent conflict and which to exclude. Different choices affect the slopes and heights reached in ranges of conflict such as those in figures 1–3, and they also show how categorical boundaries are often arbitrary.* One source of variation between datasets on violent conflict is the choice of a 'threshold' that then determines whether or not a given episode is to be judged as a war. The number of 'battle-related deaths' in a conflict usually sets the threshold. This makes for differences, for example, between the observations included in figures 2 and 3 and those in the Correlates of War (COW) project that has been the main port of call for studies of data on conflict over the past thirty-odd years.[†] COW lists only 'code' an event as a war if there were more than 1,000 battle deaths in a single year. Figures 2 and 3 were taken from a project run jointly by the University of Uppsala in Sweden and the International Peace Research Institute (PRIO) in Oslo, Norway. Uppsala data have a lower threshold: any conflict with twenty-five battle deaths or more in a year is included. An intermediate conflict, in the Uppsala coding rules, is one in which a cumulative total of more than 1,000 battle deaths occurs but never more than 1,000 in a single year. These coding rules have significant effects. One implication is that Northern Ireland is excluded by the strictest Correlates of War rules, while in the Uppsala classification system, with its different boundaries, it is included as an 'intermediate conflict'.

The choice of where to set the threshold of deaths is arbitrary—it is a rough aid in conveying some idea of the scale or seriousness of an event. But the threshold might just as well be set at 700 as 1,200. The very high variance in the level of violence among civil wars

---

* Gurr *et al.* (2002) take their data from a list compiled at the Center for Systemic Peace, which includes 291 episodes of armed conflict in the 1946–99 period; Gleditsch *et al.* (2002) list 261 conflicts over precisely the same period.
† There is actually a larger difference between Uppsala trends and another dataset known as KOSIMO—even using the KOSIMO subset of war and 'violent crisis'. KOSIMO data are available at http://www.kosimo.de and are reported in Pfetsch and Rohloff (2000).

makes even clearer the problem of grouping all such conflicts as one set of events according to the battle-death coding rule. One study points out that in 123 post-World War II civil wars recorded in published sources, the average number of total deaths was more than 86,000, but that in almost half of them there were less than 13,000 battle deaths and in fourteen of them there were less than 1,500 battle deaths.[9]

An annual threshold (or a cumulative total) coding rule obscures the pattern of war in another way; for, as Nicholas Sambanis has pointed out, it fails to capture the intensity of a given civil war: it does not show whether the given number of battle deaths was a minuscule or substantial proportion of the total population.* Using the 1,000 battle death threshold skews any dataset on civil wars towards larger population countries: a conflict of equivalent intensity will lead to more absolute numbers of casualties in a much larger country than it will in a small country. Sambanis gives as an illustration of this problem the case of the Greco-Turkish war in Cyprus in 1963–4, which is omitted from most datasets on the basis that there were 'too few' deaths. The roughly 2,000 deaths in that war represented about 0.004 per cent of the total Cypriot population. 'A war with the same intensity in a country with 100 million inhabitants would have caused 400,000 deaths in two years and would be coded in all datasets.'[10] In other words, there is a case for a different classification system ruled by relative criteria rather than just absolute casualty numbers.

— *The battle death criterion*

The next problem with standard systems for classifying wars is the attachment to battle deaths as a major criterion. Again, this has varied both between and, over time, within datasets. The problem of whether to judge a conflict by battle deaths or total conflict-related deaths is perhaps especially tricky for so-called civil wars or societal conflicts. This problem leads, at one level, to slightly fuzzy statistics. Some studies include Cambodia 1976–7 while others have a break in Cambodian hostilities then—yet though there was little direct military confrontation during this period there were horrific massacres. At another level, once one includes conflict-related civilian deaths, to judge the inclusion or exclusion of a specific episode of

* This and the next section on the definition of civil wars owe a great debt to Nicholas Sambanis's (2002) careful study on the foundations of quantitative work on civil wars.

violent conflict there is then a question of whether relevant casualties are only 'direct' civilian deaths or whether it is appropriate (and to what extent) to include 'indirect' conflict-related deaths.

The most obvious example is famine. Between 1983 and 1985 there was famine in the provinces of Tigray and Northern Wollo in Ethiopia—one of the most famed of modern famines. Many observers explained it as a result of drought. There was drought and harvest failure in 1984, but in these areas famine had begun before the drought. Bad economic policies also provide part of the explanation. But above all this famine and the deaths and disease it caused were the result of war. The Ethiopian government conducted a counter-insurgency campaign in Tigray and northern Wollo throughout the first half of the 1980s. Both the timing of famine and the areas where it was most severe coincided with the pattern of military action. Counter-insurgency involved bombing markets in rebel-held areas; forcibly relocating people and restricting voluntary movement and trade; offensives against rebel strongholds in areas that produced agricultural surpluses; and manipulative negotiations with international humanitarian aid agencies, enabling the government to continue to deprive people in these areas of access to food.[11] Although it is difficult to separate those people who died from direct military causes (in bombardment, for example) from those dying as a result of military-caused famine, and to separate the latter from famine deaths elsewhere in the country due less to war and more to drought and policy failure, any reasonable assessment of the scale of casualties in the Ethiopian war of the 1980s must include deaths from war-created famine.

Then there is the Rwanda problem. In the genocidal outburst of 1994, by most estimates, civilians and militias killed between half a million and 800,000 people. But these were not battle deaths. So in some studies Rwanda 1994 is only counted as an intermediate conflict—there had been a civil war since rebels crossed into the country from Uganda in 1990 and the cumulative total was certainly above 1,000 battle deaths. Given the obvious magnitude of the massacres in Rwanda in 1994, and indeed the fact that they emerged in a context of a civil war, albeit perhaps one that had hitherto been a 'low intensity conflict', it does seem perverse to twist the data according to a battle death classification system.

What exactly is a civil war?

Those interested in violence in developing countries of late have been particularly concerned with the category of 'civil war'. Again, the key to a useful classification system and its set of definitions and distinctions is its ability to shape an enquiry into patterns and possible causes and responses. Often civil wars are grouped together into one category and studied separately from other conflicts. Yet there may be more variation within a group of civil wars than between some civil wars and other cases of violent social conflict (just the type of issue highlighted by Cavalli-Sforza, above). If the analytical category of civil wars obscures continuity between types of conflict then it may frustrate the development of understanding rather than encourage it. How, then, are civil wars defined? What order of diversity is there within the category of civil wars? And what kinds of overlap might there be between civil wars and other commonly used categories of conflict?

The border around the category of 'civil wars' is fenced with criteria. First, such conflicts must involve fighting between agents of or claimants to a state and organised non-state groups from within the same country but seeking to replace the government, to secure power in a region or even secession from the country, or to change government policy. Second, to be classed as a civil war a conflict of this type must produce enough deaths to cross the casualty threshold. Third, at least 100 of these battle deaths must be on the government side. The point of the last control post is to exclude state-led massacres where there is no organised or effective rebel opposition. The boundary may be marked by other coding rules. Some classification exercises will allow into the camp of civil wars those in which foreign troops are involved, so long as the other main criteria are satisfied; but others will treat a case like this as a distinct category—'internationalised internal wars'.

— Extra-systemic wars or civil wars?

The categorical territory of civil wars is contested in one other important respect: there is confusion in the quantitative literature on whether or not to include as civil wars those—like anti-colonial wars—that are otherwise labelled extra-systemic wars, i.e. wars between one group that is a member of an established set of states and one that is not.[12] As one paper put it, excluding the war between the French and the FLN in Algeria in the 1950s would logically mean excluding war in Chechnya as a civil war within Russia in the event that the Chechens finally win independence. The Mau Mau revolt against British colonial rule in Kenya in the 1950s was not included in the original Correlates of War dataset, because there were only 591 British casualties.[13] It has been included in more recent versions.

The euphemism 'the Troubles', for the conflict in Northern Ireland from 1968 to the peace agreement in 1998, captures some of the definitional ambiguity of that conflict. In thirty years of political conflict a cumulative total of more than 3,000 people (most of them civilians) died violent deaths related to the conflict. At the peak of intensity, in the first half of the 1970s, an average of around 270 people a year died in the conflict. The conflict involved local paramilitaries, the police and the British armed forces. It was an internal conflict over culture, 'identity', labour market and political discrimination. It was a colonial conflict, following the resolution of the earlier Irish Civil War and anti-colonial uprising in the independence of Ireland and the formation of Northern Ireland. And to the extent that the peace settlement endorses Northern Ireland as part of the United Kingdom, the Troubles were an internal, 'civil' conflict.[14]

— Confusion and clarity in statistical coding rules

Trying to resolve some of the debates about rules of entry, Nicholas Sambanis put together a definition of civil wars. Its nine criteria are as follows: (1) The war must take place within the territory of an internationally recognised state with a population of more than 500,000 (this population qualification is a specifically statistical rule to complement the choice of a relative casualty rate). (2) The parties to the conflict must be politically and militarily organised, with identifiable leadership and publicly stated objectives—this enables the exclusion of organised crime. (3) The government must be a principal combatant—or, at least, the party representing the government internationally and claiming government power must be involved as a combatant. (4) The main rebel group(s) must be locally represented and composed of local recruits, though there may be international involvement in the war. (5) The war is deemed to begin in the first year that the conflict causes 500–1,000 deaths and the war is only classed as a war if cumulative deaths over the next two years exceed 1,000. (6) The civil war must involve sustained violence, with no single year having fewer than twenty-five deaths and no three-year period having less than 500 conflict-related deaths. (7) The weaker party must be able at all times to inflict at least 100 deaths on the stronger party, though this criterion should be adjustable according to the overall intensity of the war. (8) The war ends if it is interrupted by a peace treaty, cease-fire or decisive military outcome producing two years or more of peace. Finally, (9) if new parties enter the war fighting over new issues, a new war is then begun. Even this definition leaves out the preference Sambanis has for a relative, per capita measure of the death threshold, given that virtually no work has yet been done on identifying a sensible level for this threshold. Note, too, that this definition breaks down the distinction between battle deaths and other conflict deaths.[15]

These are careful efforts to find a definitive idea of the contours of a civil war. If the aim is to understand civil wars, through statistical analysis of a large number of civil wars, then this is exactly the kind of cartographic effort that is necessary. At the very least, an agreed definition of a civil war might help to focus the analysis more sharply on what really is and is not known. At the moment, one of the reasons why these statistical analyses produce rather different findings, even when they use very similar explanatory variables, is precisely that the samples of civil war to which they apply the analysis differ. A model with a set of commonly tested explanatory variables—like per capita income, degree of inequality, degree of ethnic diversity, reliance on primary commodity resource exports and so on—generates different conclusions when let loose on a range of datasets differing in their definition rules for civil wars. Lining up pairs of datasets, Sambanis shows serious discrepancies between them. Some datasets differ even when they claim to be following the same rules. The differences encourage (or possibly reflect) diverging ideas of what factors really matter in the origins of civil wars. For example, a measure for the level of economic development, one factor that might be expected to influence the vulnerability of countries to civil war, seems far more significant in the context of some databases than in others. To give another example, with some definitions the statistics reveal a significant positive correlation between the level of democracy and the onset of civil wars; but using different civil war datasets leads to a negative correlation. In other words, in one model a greater amount of democracy and civil liberties increases the statistical risk of civil war while in another model it decreases the risk.*

---

* Sambanis tries to work out how robust are the main results from the literature 'explaining' civil wars by statistical association of the dependent variable, civil war, with independent, explanatory variables to changes in the coding of civil war. The 'barebones' explanatory model includes the level of development (measured by real per capita income or energy consumption per capita), the level of democracy (quantified in two of the various indices of democracy available), the level of eth-

If categorical boundaries are permeable and uncertain, one response certainly is to harden the definition in a bid to secure the border. But there are other possible responses. These include fragmenting the territory or radically redefining the map. Some of the problems in defining civil wars may be a clue to these alternatives. Therefore, it is worth mapping the marches a bit further. Arguably, there are three main problems revealed by doing so. First, does it make sense to think in terms of civil or intra-state wars if many, perhaps most or even all, of these conflicts are characterised to a large extent by the interdependence of the countries where they occur with other parts of the world? This interdependence may mean that it is more than just the presence of foreign troops that makes an 'internal' war an 'internationalised internal war'. Second, how much sense does it make to hive off, as utterly distinct, a conflict that qualifies as a civil war from large-scale social and political violence or communal violence (themselves awkward to define clearly) not directly involving the state? It is not clear that religious pogroms and clusters of rural conflict in India are 'non-political' or that state agencies and officials are not implicated in them. Nor is it clear that research into the causes of violence should assume that widespread violence in Brazil is totally distinct from some civil wars with battle death numbers probably lower than Brazilian homicide rates. And, third, are all civil wars equivalent? Given that the range of phenomena involved is spread out both spatially and temporally, there might be important sources of heterogeneity among these wars. Are all civil wars over a given time span analytically equivalent? For some people might argue that the causes of so-called civil wars in the 1950s or 1960s were rather different from those of the 1990s and that, therefore, treating a single dataset with one explanatory model does

---

nic heterogeneity (captured by the ethno-linguistic fractionalisation index, on which more in later chapters) and two further variables that anticipate the possible significance of population size and the Cold War. What matters in this exercise is not how significant any of the results of the statistical regressions of these variables on the dependent variable are, but how much variation there is between results when the alternative coding rules for civil war are used. While the development variables—income and energy per capita—point across datasets of civil war to a negative relationship between development and conflict, i.e. 'higher' levels of development 'reduce the risk' of civil war, there is still substantial variation in the size of the correlation coefficient, especially with the energy consumption variable. For the level of democracy, shifting between different datasets and their coding rules leads not only to variation in the size of the correlation coefficient between democracy and civil war but also, more disturbingly, to changes in the sign of the coefficient.

not make sense.[16] And are all relatively contemporaneous conflicts similar in their characteristics and causes? How alike were the causes generating war in Colombia, Rwanda, Chechnya, Sierra Leone, Bosnia and Algeria; or indeed, in Rwanda, Somalia, Angola and Liberia?

— The boundary between intra- and inter-state wars

The first problem, then, is the border between a civil war and an international war. The Spanish Civil War of 1936–9; war in Angola (from 1975 to 2002, or from 1961 to 2002); civil wars in El Salvador mainly in the 1980s, and in Nicaragua in the 1970s and 1980s; and wars in Liberia and Sierra Leone: these were all internationalised in their origins and conduct, but in different ways. So too were the Greek civil war of the 1940s and the Korean War in the 1950s.

In the Spanish Civil War it was partly very localised agendas that led to incidents like the assassination of the poet Federico Garcia Lorca near Granada in 1936.[17] At the national level there were multiple ideological, institutional and personal conflicts. Even at this level conflict was fragmented into further divisions. Orwell's *Homage to Catalonia*, for example, is a depressing account of the fissures among Republican groups.[18] But the way the war sucked in German Nazi bombers, Soviet weapons and the multinational volunteers of the International Brigades shows it was also part of a wider European struggle. This was the struggle between the equally European visions of liberal democracy, communism and fascism described in Mark Mazower's *Dark Continent: Europe's Twentieth Century*.[19]

The Sicilian writer Leonardo Sciascia also described this wider European conflict in his story 'Antimony', about a Sicilian sulphur miner recruited by Mussolini—as many Italians were—to fight for Franco's Nationalist army against the Republicans.* Through the war the Sicilian is gradually politicised and he starts to realise that he has joined up to fight on the wrong side. His political education begins with the conversations he has with another Sicilian, Ventura, who has only volunteered so that he can cross, if possible, to the

---

* The story is in Sciascia's book *Sicilian Uncles* (1988). Many Italians fought with General Queipo de Llano. At the start of the war Queipo de Llano led the assault that took Seville for Franco's Nationalists (although for years he had conspired against the monarchy). In the weeks after his troops took Malaga in February 1937 more than 4,000 supporters of the Popular Front were executed. Arthur Koestler, in *Dialogue with Death* (1942), wrote that there were 50,000 Italians in Queipo de Llano's army, three *banderas* of the Spanish Foreign Legion, and 15,000 'African tribesmen', with the remainder, about 10 per cent of the total, of Spanish nationality.

American Brigade (i.e. on the other, Republican side) and find a way to join his own family in America.

'And think about Sicily', said Ventura, 'think about the Sicily of the sulphur miners and the peasants who work on a day-to-day basis: think about the peasants' winter, when there's no work and the house is full of hungry children, and the women moving about the house, their legs swollen with dropsy, the donkey and the goat by the bed. I'd go mad, I would. And if one fine day the peasants and sulphur miners killed the Mayor, the Fascist Party secretary, Don Giuseppe Catalanotto, the sulphur-mine owner, and the prince of Castro, who owns the lands in fief—if this happened in my town, and your town began to rise as well, and if the same wind began to blow in all the towns of Sicily, you know what would happen? All the country gentlemen, who're Fascists, would join up with the priests, the Carabinieri and the police chiefs, and start to shoot the peasants and the sulphur miners, and the peasants and the sulphur miners would kill the priests, the Carabinieri and the gentlemen, there'd be no end to the killing, then the Germans would come and arrange a couple of bombardments that would make the Sicilians lose their longing for rebellion for ever, and the gentlemen would win.'

'It'll end up like that in Spain', I said.

'Thanks to us', said Ventura, 'because without the Italians and the Germans, the gentlemen would be dying like flies here...'

The significance of international military involvement can vary, from the German bombardment of Guernica to a CIA 'assist' in El Salvador or Guatemala, or the covert but more full-blown US support to the Nicaraguan Contras, to the neighbourly spillover of soldiers and political meddling from Liberia into Sierra Leone, or the frantic Cold War partnerships lining up in 1975 behind rival claimants to power prior to independence in Angola. It is not, therefore, obvious how well-defined a borderline there is between civil war and 'internationalised internal war'.

A different approach is Eric Hobsbawm's, in which the linkages—the continuity of characteristics, as it were—between wars override categorical distinctions.[20] From this perspective, not only was the whole of the twentieth century one of almost unbroken war, it was arguably a single era of world war. Hobsbawm sees a single thirty years' war from 1914 to 1945, with a breather between the withdrawal of the Japanese from the Soviet East in 1922 and their attack on Manchuria (China) in 1931, followed by the Cold War and then by a more complex period in which US armed forces have been involved in various ways in a range of places throughout the world. The Cold War qualifies as a period of world war for two reasons: first, because many conflicts around the world during this period were in some sense 'proxy wars'—i.e. a displacement of superpower confrontation onto the fringe theatres of war in Central America, Asia and Sub-Saharan Africa; and second, because the Cold War was a war by the seventeenth-century English political philosopher Thomas Hobbes's definition of war as consisting 'not in battle only or the act of fighting, but in a tract of time wherein the will to contend by battle is sufficiently known'. Hobbes's definition of war causes a little categorical havoc: it disturbs the peace of earnest debate on where to set the battle death threshold before deciding that a conflict is a violent conflict.

Hobbes's definition also complicates the question of what quantitative studies call 'onset of war', i.e. when wars begin. One of the characteristics of many modern wars is that they do not have clear-cut beginnings and ends. This is one of the sources of the argument that the categorical distinction between war and peace—one of the more reliable analytical distinctions, one might have hoped—has often been blurred. Exploding categories is an exercise that can be taken quite far: the French philosopher Baudrillard, for example, played with the idea that the Gulf War in 1991 was so much a 'postmodern war' that it did not happen.* More immediately interesting was the start of the 2003 war in Iraq. The principally US and British Coalition of the Willing had imposed a deadline for Iraqi full compliance with disarmament demands and then announced that the war would start, if the deadline were not met, with 'shock and awe' bombardment. On 20 March 2003 TV news announcers were toeing the line that the war had not begun, even though during the previous night there had been aerial 'precision bombardment' of targets in Baghdad aimed at eliminating the Iraqi leadership. Furthermore, judging the start of this war was difficult against a background of twelve years of, often, daily bombardment of parts of Iraq under the auspices of UN enforcement of no-fly zones. In the days leading up to 20 March there were reports of an intensification of this activity, though, again, military and political sources in the United States and Britain denied this was related to the coming war.

An excellent example of how the struggle of ideologies and for power continued after the Second World War, of how Hobsbawm's

---

* Baudrillard (1995) made two main arguments: first, there was no face to face military encounter, no duel, but rather the wholly asymmetric execution of a pre-conceived plan; and, second, US warplane crews (and Western TV publics) experienced war through the 'virtual' imagery of radar and computer graphics without directly envisaging Iraqi people themselves.

century of a single world war worked itself out during and beyond
the Cold War, is conflict in Congo. Beneath the surface of early
twenty-first-century war lie decades of President Mobutu's rule; and
beneath them previous conflicts. Congo, though, has never stood a
chance as an 'internal' war. From the late 1990s onwards there were
several conflicts inside the country—involving separate rebel groups
barely, if at all, co-ordinated in their resistance to central authority.
The latest round of conflicts ostensibly began with the spillover of
genocide and war in Rwanda. When the rebel Rwandan Patriotic
Front (RPF) overthrew the genocidal government, it provoked an
exodus of refugees and escaping *genocidaire* leaders across the border into what was still then called Zaire. Ever since, the RPF has
directly and indirectly pursued this rump of the previous regime,
forming alliances (and breaking them) with national level Congolese politicians and rebels, sponsoring a rebel group within Congo
based among the Banyamulenge people (historically, or ethnically,
related to the Tutsis of Rwanda), and organising the mining and export (through Rwanda) of the coltan—a heavy, heat-resistant metal—
whose biggest global source is in the Kivu provinces in eastern
Congo. The Ugandan state and army have also directly and indirectly been involved in rebellions in Congo. And these Congolese
wars have drawn in other African countries on different sides,
including Zimbabwe and Angola supporting the Kinshasa-based
government. Initially the spillover of Rwandan war into Congo
helped Laurent Kabila, a Congolese politician and entrepreneur
who had been living in exile in Tanzania for decades, to launch his
own push to overthrow Mobutu Sese Seko in Kinshasa.

Mobutu had taken power (in a coup in 1965) in the early years of
Congolese independence after the nightmare of Belgian colonial
rule. He had only been able to do so with determined support from
the United States, which had taken against the elected Prime Minister, Patrice Lumumba. During the early 1960s politics and violence
in Congo/Zaire were drawn into the wider ideological struggles of
the world. Historians have continued to unearth evidence of US
and Belgian roles in the assassination of Lumumba.[21] Meanwhile,
another historical document describes the shambles of war and the
internationalisation of Congolese conflict at that time: Che Guevara's diary of his incognito role in trying to motivate and organise
rebellion in the Kivus details, amongst other things, the staggering
ineptitude of the rebellion's main leader, Laurent Kabila.[22]

Congolese conflict, though, illustrates other ways beyond direct
military involvement, in which the category of civil war is fraught by

internationalisation. For at the very least, in part many such wars are 'about' the integration into the rest of the world of countries like Congo. The 'national' in internal wars is complicated by integration into markets, not just for arms or soldiers but also for commodities.[23] It is hard to accept the tag of an internal war when these wars are inseparable from the world markets, for example, for diamonds, oil, heroin, coltan. Furthermore, to treat these wars as exclusively internal is very difficult when many of the sources of conflict arise from the conditions of dramatic social change that prevail during a country's 'development', and when this development—however hesitant, slow or disruptive—is at the same time a process of increasing interdependence with the rest of the world.

The final sense in which the category of intra-state conflict is analytically fragile concerns regionalisation of war. The great majority of such conflicts these days take place within, and are part of, what have been called 'regional conflict complexes'. For example, to understand war in Sierra Leone without understanding the war in Liberia is impossible. Nor is it possible to explain conflict in Afghanistan without drawing in Pakistan, India, Tajikistan and others, let alone a history of US and Russian involvement and, before that, British influence. Conflict spills across national borders easily and in various ways—through encouragement by one country of rebellion in a neighbouring country, through direct incursion, through mimetic or demonstration effects, through interlinked markets for weapons or commodities and money, through shared political allegiances among groups with an ethnic identity overlapping two countries and so on. Regional conflict complexes include West Africa (drawing in Liberia, Sierra Leone, Nigeria, Côte d'Ivoire and others), Central Africa (Uganda, Rwanda, Burundi, Zimbabwe, Angola, Congo), the Middle East (Israel/Palestine, Iraq, Turkey and others) and Southern/Central Europe (around the break-up of the former Yugoslavia) and Central Asia.

— *The boundary between civil war and 'communal violence'*

If one zone of the territory of civil war is bounded artificially from international war, elsewhere it is closed off from communal violence or widespread violent conflict within a country's borders that does not meet the criteria for inclusion as a civil war. Aside from the fact that poor data might 'unfairly' exclude a given conflict as falling below the threshold of casualties, there are violent conflicts within countries that, while they do not overtly involve the state, can at times seem very similar to civil war. Brazil, India and South

Africa illustrate this. India has often been lauded as the world's largest democracy and its democratic institutions, including a free press, have been cited as a major reason why the country has conquered famine. India is also an extremely violent society with fuzzy divisions along a spectrum of violence. Uppsala data for 1989–2000 list conflicts in Kashmir, Punjab, Assam, Manipur, Nagaland and Tripura. Sambanis's list of civil wars from 1945 onwards includes three Indian civil wars—in 1965, from 1984 to 1994 and from 1989 to 1994. All three are defined as 'ethnic/religious'. The kinds of violent conflict included in these lists have involved relatively clear 'incompatibilities' over territory (i.e. for secession or local autonomy) or for regional government control. However, there is arguably no great distinction between these conflicts and two other kinds of violent conflict within India.

One of these involves the various inter-communal pogroms of the kind that have burst out in major urban areas, intermittently throughout the twentieth century and more recently during the 1990s and into the twenty-first century. Paroxysms of anti-Muslim violence have, for example, erupted in Gujarat in 1992, extending to Bombay and the massive, rapidly growing city of Surat, and again in 2002.[24] The scale of killing in both cases was substantial.[25] The main distinction between these pogroms and a civil war would, however, be in terms of the level of organisation of the main perpetrators and the fact that they did not present a challenge to the state. Thus, recalling one precise definition of civil war above, the violent parties are not obviously 'politically and militarily organised, with identifiable leadership and publicly stated objectives'— though this criterion was introduced to exclude organised crime rather than the organisation of pogroms in which there is little obvious military organisation or, often, identifiable leadership. Nonetheless, there is usually more political organisation and mobilisation for violence than meets the eye, and the objectives are usually made extremely public. The state is usually, in these cases, not a 'principal combatant'. Nonetheless, state officials and agencies are often implicated.[26] What is clear is that the weaker party in such conditions is typically not able to inflict at least 100 casualties on the stronger party. This does give a clear sense of the difference between a civil war and a pogrom, i.e. there is a far greater asymmetry of violence in a pogrom. Thus perhaps it is fair to say this is different from civil war. Yet if we are interested in collecting and subtly grading conflicts and understanding their sources, we might be wary of overdoing the distinction: these pogroms represent the

venting of political conflict within a country, in which there is a
high level of violence and in which elements of the state are typically involved, if secretly or indirectly. Moreover, if the objective is
to understand the links between policy, development issues and violent conflict, then both this kind of violence and more classic civil
wars must be studied together.

The other type of conflict not generally regarded as an Indian
civil war but from some perspectives very close to civil war conditions is found in Bihar (India's second largest state). For many years
there has been widespread social and political violence here, much
of it turning on the roles of two particular social groups or classes:
large landowners and the Dalits or 'untouchables'. Violence against
Dalits is common, but there has also been more organised violence
by Dalit groups or at the very least purporting to be on their behalf.
The Maoist insurgent groups known as the Naxalites have taken up
the Dalit cause, mobilising them, organising violent attacks in their
name, and sparking reprisals by the private armies of landlords.*
Locally an arms industry has evolved from the simple manufacture
of rudimentary and unreliable firearms to production of more
sophisticated weaponry. There is evidence that state institutions,
like the police, are effectively biased towards the landlord cause in
this conflict. The scale of violence varies but press reports suggest,
for example, that more than 400 people were killed in confrontations in 1997 between one private landowner militia, the Ranvir
Sena (banned in 1995), and the underground armed movement of
the Communist Party of India (Marxist-Leninist) or CPI (M-L).[†] As

---

* The Naxalites (originally based in Naxalbari in West Bengal) developed in the
  1970s a commitment to 'forcible protest against the social order relating to holding of property and sharing of social benefits' (see Human Rights Watch, 1999).
  The Naxalites were crushed in West Bengal but nowadays have a substantial following in parts of Bihar and the southern state of Andhra Pradesh; many have moved
  into electoral politics. Electoral politics have themselves been violent: on the one
  hand there has been coercive manipulation of the vote; on the other some groups
  have tried to enforce boycotts of elections by violence (see, e.g. 'Feudalism fuels
  election day massacre in Bihar', *Asia Times online*, 22 September 1999: http://
  www.atimes.com/ind-pak/AI22Df01.html). On the background to the conflict, see
  also Chandran and Gupta (2002).
† According to the Human Rights Watch analysis, the Ranvir Sena was founded in
  1994 and first made international headlines in July 1996 following an attack on
  Bathani Tola in Bhojpur district, Bihar, that killed nineteen villagers. The conflict
  was a retaliation for killings by the CPI (M-L) in the same district. The conflict had
  begun when the CPI (M-L) organised agricultural labourers to demand the statu-
  tory daily minimum wage, encouraging workers to refuse to work for less and to
  start a labour boycott on hundreds of acres of commercial farm land.

Atul Kohli put it: 'Political killings have become so common in Bihar over the last decade that...they no longer make news... As the killings have continued, private caste armies have proliferated. The rise of "warlordism" has generated new types of violence.'[27]

Violence runs throughout much of Indian rural and urban society, as it does in fact through most developing countries. Violence in these countries sometimes takes the form of overt and indisputable warfare, sometimes it is less obviously classifiable as such, and sometimes it appears to be highly dispersed, fragmented if pervasive, and is most easily categorised as 'social violence' or criminal violence rather than political violent conflict. A country like Colombia shows this well. Colombia has an extraordinary history of combining a stable state with sustained economic growth on the one hand and persistent civil war and non-war violence on the other. By some estimates more people are killed in non-war violence in Colombia than in the festering civil war.* Other examples include Brazil† and South Africa. The scale of such violence is hard to determine. By most definitions it is entirely reasonable to exclude Brazil from any set of civil wars. Yet the scale of violence, its political dimensions and the involvement of elements of the state suggest

---

* Colombia's homicide rate is the highest recorded anywhere in the world: the Seventh United Nations Survey of Crime Trends and Operations of Criminal Justice Systems cites a figure reported by Colombian authorities of 26,355 homicides in 2000, which represents a rate of 62.74 per 100,000 inhabitants. In India the reported rate was only 3.72 in 1999, but this reflected an actual number of 37,170 reported homicides. The only two countries that reported data suggesting homicide rates anything like as high as that in Colombia were, in this survey, South Africa (51.39 per 100,000, down from 60.08 in 1998) and Venezuela (33.15 per 100,000 in 2000, up from 19.61 in 1998). These figures, and even more so any comparison between them, should be treated with great caution, for reasons discussed below.

† The film *City of God* conveys brilliantly the historical dynamic and intertwining of urban gang violence with the development of the city of Rio de Janeiro and the politics of how the city has evolved. Human Rights Watch publications and reports record prison violence and police violence; for example, one report details the incentives, including promotions or bonuses for 'acts of bravery', that appear to encourage police murders of suspects that are then cited as acts of courageous self-defence. On frontier violence and the clash of property rights, see Alston, Libecap and Mueller (1997). Human Rights Watch (1991) notes, for example, that the regional office of the Pastoral Land Commission in Conceição do Araguaia registered from 1982–9 a total of 774 death threats, 834 rural workers arrested or detained, 558 rural workers injured or beaten, 2,514 *posseiro* [or squatter] families expelled, 704 farms burned or destroyed and 2,735 workers kept in conditions of slavery in the diocese of Conceição do Araguaia (p. 72). And on the pervasive violent conditions of life for the poor of the northeast, see Scheper-Hughes (1992).

that violence in Brazil is in many ways worth studying under the same broad heading as civil wars elsewhere.

— *The heterogeneity of civil wars*

The point is neither to explode all distinctions nor to argue that all so-called social violence and all civil wars are identical. Rather, the point is to suggest that the categories commonly used in the analysis of violent conflict encompass different circumstances and realities and hence can easily mislead. The reality is more of a continuum of violence, with overlapping phenomena. The point is also made by asking whether some forms of non-civil war violent conflict—for example in India—are closer to some civil wars than these civil wars are to other conflicts classed as civil wars. For there is arguably at least as great a diversity within the category of civil wars as between civil wars and other examples of violent political conflict.

One of the most obvious handles on this diversity is given by recorded casualty levels. Above it was shown that there is a high degree of variance around the mean number of 'civil war' casualties. Table 1 gives rough estimates of the number of deaths in the ten most deadly conflicts of the 1990s: most of these were classed as civil wars, though Rwanda in 1994, as we know, is often defined differently and the Gulf War in 1991 was an international war. The table shows the extreme difficulty in arriving at any agreed or accurate estimate of the number of war-related deaths. It also shows a wide possible range, from a lowest estimate of 4,300 deaths in the Gulf War to possibly close to a million victims of the Rwandan genocide (leaving aside the slow-burning homicides by purposely infecting women with HIV through rape).[28] Some of these numbers might be compared with the number of homicides per year in South Africa, which were on average 24,150 over the non-civil war period of 1996–2000; or with Russia, where there were 31,140 homicides recorded in 1999 (these do not include war-related deaths in Chechnya).

There may be an argument for more refined systems of classification that better capture the full spectrum of violent conflict and that include examples such as these.

— *Violence and the level of development*

Indeed, to return to the broad question of trends in violent conflict, the level of development is rather important. It is often assumed that the bulk of violent conflict—at least in terms of civil

Table 1. TEN MOST DEADLY CONFLICTS OF THE 1990S,
ESTIMATES FROM MAJOR PUBLISHED SOURCES

Conflict		*Estimated range of deaths*
Rwanda	1994	500,000–1,000,000
Angola	1992–4	100,000–500,000
Somalia	1991–9	48,000–300,000
Bosnia	1992–5	35,000–250,000
Liberia	1991–6	25,000–200,000
Burundi	1993	30,000–200,000
Chechnya	1994–6	30,000–90,000
Tajikistan	1992–9	20,000–120,000
Algeria	1992–9	30,000–100,000
Gulf War	1990–1	4,300–100,000

Source: Murray *et al.* (2002).

wars—takes place in the poorest countries. Violence then can be seen as a function of backwardness. Chapter 1 discussed the way this impression fits the liberal idea of violence as a thing of the past, where the past is something overcome in advanced societies, something buried by development. There are other angles to this impression. Micro-level theories of war, or what could be called individualist, rational choice explanations of war, regard the poor as prone to violence simply as a function of cost-benefit decisions. Where the poor have little alternative, there is little to be lost in fighting. Similarly, many statistical analyses of large numbers of wars and the coincidence of war with a range of other possibly explanatory factors or variables also stress poverty as a prelude to war. The level of development is a variable that is identified in many models as bearing a close correlation with the incidence of violent conflict or civil war. However, clearly there is violent conflict, including some fairly straightforward cases of 'civil war', in countries that are not the poorest, that is, in middle-income countries. Even in these instances violent conflict might not occur only where there is a lack of development, or a period of extended economic stagnation, but precisely in the thick of change, economic growth, development and social upheaval.

For now, it is worth noting that in the University of Maryland survey of armed conflicts referred to earlier in this chapter, Ted Gurr and his associates map the distribution of global conflicts onto a division of the world's economies into five groups or quintiles, the highest quintile representing the richest fifth of the world's countries. According to the data and definitions they use, the pattern of

conflict in the post-Second World War period is not straightforward. Generally, the fourth and fifth quintile groups, i.e. the richest
two fifths of the world's countries, experienced less conflict on
their soil than poorer societies, though the prevalence of conflict in
these countries was pretty much the same as in the middle quintile
group in the mid-1940s, through some of the 1970s and again at the
end of the twentieth century. The middle quintile group of countries often had as much violent conflict as the poorest and second
poorest fifth of countries. It is interesting, for example, that from
the end of the Second World War till 1963, from 1966 to 1970 and
for a while in the mid-1980s the magnitude of war was greater in the
middle quintile than in the poorest quintile.

New wars?

Much violence in developing countries like Brazil, India and South
Africa resembles civil war conflict in that it has a degree of organisation, it generates a high level of casualties, it reflects dramatic fissures in society, and the institutions of the state are implicated in
one way or another. By the same token, many civil wars have dis-
played in recent years characteristics of non-war violence. If the
modes and causes of contemporary warfare often resemble non-
war violence—for example, if these wars are defined as 'apolitical'
or 'criminal'—this is one more way in which the analytical category
of the civil war is unreliable and problematic. Thus Hans Magnus
Enzensberger argues, in *Civil War,* that for the participants in post-
Cold War conflicts 'no goal, no plan, no idea binds them together
other than the strategy...of plunder, death and destruction.'[29]
Those who have been drawn to the view that modern wars are more
and more like non-war violence have coined a categorical distinction between 'new wars' and 'old wars'.

Mary Kaldor highlights several features of these new wars, said to
be distinct from old wars in their mode of warfare, in their causes
and in their financing.[30] These changes are recent—for example,
the new war category is especially used to label the wars of Yugoslavia's disintegration and wars in Somalia and in West Africa. And the
changes in warfare are associated with 'globalisation'. Thus the new
wars live parasitically off the global webs of interdependence in markets, particularly those webs of illicit markets that have thrived in
an era of greater communication and weaker regulation. But the
most distinctive feature of so-called new wars is often said to be that
they are apolitical. 'Violence has freed itself from ideology', writes

Enzensberger, and contemporary wars, a form of 'political retro-virus', are 'about nothing at all'. Warlords of the new wars are re-garded as lacking any political programme: they are simply scaled-up organised criminals; they do not need to win hearts and minds of local populations but rather prey upon them, while manipulat-ing foreign humanitarian aid flows, to sustain their warfare and to accumulate wealth. The neat distinctions of old wars, for example between combatants and civilians, break down: now war targets civilians as much as it targets military personnel.

The historical dimension of changing war addressed by the new and old war classification is valid. One of the problems with the big category of civil wars, for example, was that it implied equivalence across time among a large variety of such wars. Yet the way war is fought does change. Not least, the technology of war changes. In recent years technological change has made it easier for very young boys and girls to carry and work the equipment of killing, strength-ening a trend towards the prevalence of youth wars.* From this view-point, then, the new wars of the 1990s and the early twenty-first century would simply be the latest notch in a constantly evolving trend.

Yet this distinction between new and old wars may obscure more than it reveals. Some elements of the category of new wars may be more sharply 'new' than others, and may hold true for more con-temporary wars than do other elements of the definition. Since the end of the Cold War the financing of so-called civil wars has chan-ged somewhat. Cold War rivalry regulated wars in developing coun-tries: either it made some countries no-go areas for warfare or it facilitated and influenced warfare, for example through direct military aid and through general and fungible financial support. Governments and rebel groups that might once have hoped realis-tically to be able to pay for a war by folding their war aims into Cold War tensions have since the end of the 1980s had to change their strategy. In many cases this has meant that commodity markets have come to play a more significant role in the conduct and scale of wars—hence the interest in 'conflict diamonds', conflicts lubri-cated by oil revenues, the links between illegal logging and conflict, and the role of cocaine or heroin in the financing of wars in Colom-

---

* Technological change has pushed war in contrary directions: on the one hand it has made war cheaper and simpler and in a way more childish; on the other hand advanced industrial countries have been developing aerial bombardment, aiming to minimise civilian casualties, but at immense expense. This latter dimension of technological change is partly what lies behind Baudrillard's commentary on the 'virtual reality' of the Gulf War.

bia and Afghanistan. Thus where once a developing country conflict might have been shaped by ideological allegiance, nowadays
often a similar conflict will be dominated by the characteristics of
production and marketing of a given commodity.[31] However, this
does not mean these wars are apolitical. Also, the significance of
changes in funding sources of violence should not deflect attention
from those conflicts (as well as those instances of possibly repressed
conflict) that continue to rely on heavy international government
political support—not least in Israel/Palestine.

There are important ways, though, in which it is difficult to identify sharp discontinuities in the realities of warfare.[32] First, if contemporary conflicts somehow reflect globalisation, far greater precision
is needed to identify how this is so, given that so-called civil wars
have virtually always, at the very least since the early twentieth century, reflected the influence of international capitalist interdependence. Second, there is little basis for arguing that contemporary
conflicts are apolitical. They might not shine with the same armour
of Cold War political projects and their politics often are profoundly
illiberal, but political they normally are. And third, the shifty warlords, multiple agendas, wars within wars and rebellious greed for
booty or 'instant taxation' are hardly novel.

Congo in the early 1960s was the big crisis of the day. Belgian
colonial rule ended abruptly in 1960. Moise Tshombe organised a
secessionist movement in the mineral rich province of Katanga.
The Prime Minister, Patrice Lumumba, secured the presence of a
UN force to help protect the country's unity. After Lumumba also
asked the Soviet Union for help, he was ousted by the President,
Joseph Kasavubu, and the army commander-in-chief, Joseph Mobutu.
Lumumba was assassinated—a job planned by the CIA—and the
UN Secretary-General, Dag Hammarskjöld, died in a plane crash
that has always been regarded as suspicious. In 1963 a series of
rebellions began in different parts of this immense territory—one
of the leaders being Laurent Kabila. These rebellions were only
loosely connected and the divisions between their leaders (as well as
among the leaders of each) mixed doctrinal political differences
with personal rivalries. The US government became sufficiently
worried to intervene, for example, by encouraging the formation
of mercenary military units and by diverting USAID money secretly
to fund bomber planes and helicopters to be sent to resist the
ostensibly left-wing rebellions. A range of African governments were
drawn into the conflict.

This was how Che Guevara came to be in eastern Congo in 1965,
working for Kabila's rebels to organise a rebellion but working in

disguise and under a *nom de guerre*. Guevara's diary *The African Dream* details many of the features that are said to characterise post-Cold War, so-called new wars: the chaos, the wars within wars, the frailty of ideology on the ground, the hostility of much of the local rural population, senseless violence and the fact that soldiers typically focus on immediate rewards rather than greater goals. In one apparently successful ambush, after 'the first moments of stupor, the brilliant victors realised that the greatest prize was on top of the lorry: namely, bottles of beer and whisky. Mbili tried to get the food loaded and to destroy the drink, but it was impossible. In a few hours all the fighters were drunk, under the astonished and reproving gaze of our men who were not allowed a drop... On the way back, a drunken Captain Zakarias ran into a peasant and finished him off with a few shots, claiming that he had been a spy.'[33] Guevara came to think of Kabila's military formations as 'a rubbish heap in which everything rotted away, as a result of the disorganisation and lack of leadership we have already complained about so often in these notes.'[34] And he was disappointed by the envoys of those leaders whom he did respect, saying they were 'swindling the revolution'.

There was considerable continuity in the characteristics of violent conflict in Congo/Zaire from the early 1960s to the 2000s. This is true more broadly of contemporary conflicts. There is a mass of evidence that classic Cold War conflicts contained much that was decidedly apolitical in terms of a definition of politics by grand Cold War programmes: grubby looting, extreme violence, multiple motives and interests. There is a strong possibility that the new versus old war distinction is as much a matter of a changed projection by Western academics as a shift in underlying reality, as much a change in perspective and frame as in what is actually happening.

For there are rather deeper continuities in the unappealing side of conflict too, which suggest that proponents of the new wars thesis, in dramatising the criminality and apolitical dimensions of contemporary wars, tend to romanticise 'old wars'. The American Civil War contained many features that were very 'new war'. This was nowhere more the case than in Missouri, where conflict deteriorated into vicious internecine violence between freebooting Unionist 'Jayhawker' counterinsurgency groups and the infamous Confederate guerrilla warlords William Quantrill, 'Bloody Bill' Anderson and George Todd, not to mention their followers Jesse and Frank James and Cole and Jim Younger. Short-term exploitation of the instability of war also sometimes threatened to dominate the whole

war. In the South, for example, a Georgia newspaper complained
of the 'conscienceless set of vampires...at home warring upon their
indigent families.' Others referred to a 'band of harpies preying on
the vitals of the Confederacy'; while in July 1862 the Richmond
Examiner judged that 'native Southern merchants have outdone
Yankees and Jews... The whole South stinks with the lust of extortion.' Nonetheless, in the American Civil War as in other, more
recent wars, the fact that short-term economic gains often dominate the actions and motives of participants does not mean that
these are what the war is 'about'.[35]

There have always been features of war that fit the description of
'new wars'. Likewise, many of these new wars contain traces of what
are presumably the characteristics of old wars: direct support from
other governments to either the government or rebel forces; general foreign development aid, whose obvious fungibility allows governments to pursue military activities in their own or in other
countries; political programmes; and so on. One conclusion is that
proponents of the new war/old war categorical distinction dramatise certain features at the expense of others, in diametrically opposed projections onto contemporary and previous wars.

Proxy war or civil war

Category labels are often political and they often at least suggest a
selective set of attributes and determinants of the things or events
that are, or are not, included. A number of wars that tend nowadays
to be classed as 'civil wars' unquestioningly were, during the 1980s,
regarded very differently by many, especially on the left. A good
example was Mozambique's post-independence war that ended in
1992, which, like others, was commonly labelled a 'proxy war'. This
label was coined in acknowledgement of the way in which this war
had, in fact, many of its origins and sources of sustenance outside
Mozambique. First, the rebel group Renamo was created by the
counterinsurgency forces of the Rhodesian government, which
used Renamo as a means of undermining the leftwing Frelimo government in Mozambique that was giving refuge and support inside
Mozambique to Robert Mugabe's ZANU-PF guerrillas. Then Renamo was adopted by the apartheid government in South Africa and
built up as one of its principal agents of destabilisation of governments throughout Southern Africa, the governments in particular
of what were then known as the Frontline States. Beyond this, Renamo
attracted the encouraging ideological and financial attentions of

other governments and groups further afield—including the United States of the Reagan Doctrine era and conservative individuals and groups there and in Britain and Germany. There was never any doubt that Renamo was nurtured and sponsored by foreign groups, and once their support faded Renamo showed that as a rebel force it could not really keep going on its own. Yet Renamo clearly had quite strong political support, partly because it appealed to local religious and/or customary sensibilities and partly because it drew on a reaction amongst many people against the policies of the Frelimo government (and against that government's perceived Southern bias)—a fact that has been very hard to swallow for many commentators but that was reflected in election results in the decade after the peace settlement of the early 1990s. Its support has been particularly strong in the more populous centre and north of the country.

There was a controversy over the nature and sources of this Mozambican war.[36] What this controversy shows is that the choice of categories and classification labels is itself often a political act. The choice of a descriptive label often implies a preference for particular explanations of a conflict. The proxy war category contained only part of the truth and deflected debate and analysis from the very real internal sources of conflict in Mozambique, Angola, Nicaragua and Afghanistan, the most renowned of these wars. And in exactly the same way there is a risk that the civil war category subtly proscribes some analytical dimensions of conflicts in the Congo, Sri Lanka and elsewhere—just as calling the war in Spain in the late 1930s a civil war easily suppresses the argument that this was really what E. H. Carr called the first battle of the Second World War.

Evidence of violence

There is one final point that, because it affects the robustness of categorical boundaries as well as many other aspects of the analysis of violent conflict, is worth highlighting in this chapter: the evidence on the incidence of, intensity of, and trends in violent conflict is typically unreliable. To find reliable data for social science research in most fields is hard enough, and especially so in poorer countries. Violence compounds the problem. Tattered and untrustworthy data affect the accumulation of case study material on individual countries, and compromise even more endeavours to make comparisons between cases.

There are two main ways in which data on violence are accumulated: official records and news reports (including eyewitness reports

and reports of official announcements, e.g. of the number of combatants killed by each side in a battle). There are often problems
with the official recording of violence, especially but not only in
wartime. In wartime health information systems and, particularly,
civil registration systems that would record deaths and their causes
often break down. For example, Bosnia and Herzegovina reported
registration data on causes of death to the World Health Organisation till 1991 but stopped after the war there began.[37]

Moreover, there are complications of interest as well as practical
constraints that undermine reliable data collection involving political violence, armed conflict or even some forms of inter-personal
or 'social' violence. Medical Research Council research in South
Africa, for example, uses the metaphor of an 'iceberg of sexual violence and coercion': rapes reported to and recorded by the police
represent only the tip protruding above the social surface.[38] In
some countries there is evidence that even where rapes are reported to police authorities they are not recorded unless bribes are
paid. When people claim there has been an increase, or decrease,
in the incidence of something like rape it is hard to know whether
or how far the recorded change reflects a real underlying change as
opposed to an increase, or decrease, in the proportion of rapes
reported and recorded.

There are also problems in comparing data on violence across
countries—again, partly because different countries may have more,
or less, accurate and full reporting systems or even cultures and
incentives of reporting. An example is international data on homicides. The Home Office *Statistical Bulletin* in Britain from time to
time compares criminal justice statistics across a range of mainly
European countries plus Australia, Canada, Japan, New Zealand,
South Africa and the United States. Notes to the tables in the bulletin show divergent reporting rules. Scotland, by contrast with England and Wales and Northern Ireland, includes all deaths initially
reported as homicide to the police. Estonia excludes assault leading to death. The Netherlands excludes euthanasia, which is included in most countries' statistics. Russian data include attempted
homicide. Sweden includes help with suicide—again, most countries do not include this. The United Nations Drug Control Programme (UNDCP) collects statistics on crimes, including homicides,
around the world. The UNDCP acknowledges a range of reporting
problems—including errors accumulating in the police recording
process, crimes reported to but not recorded by police, crimes
occurring without being either reported or recorded, variations

between countries in definitions of particular crimes, variations in levels of reporting and traditions of policing, and variations in the accessibility of the police (relating to the number of police stations, the road network, the spread of telephones etc.).[39]

As the authors of a report on war and public health, published in the *British Medical Journal*, point out, most published analyses of deaths from conflict have relied on press reports of eyewitness accounts and of official pronouncements from conflict contestants. Both sources are clearly subject to error and political manipulation.[40] Recall Atul Kohli's comment that political killings have become so common in Bihar in recent years that they no longer make the news. Think too of events like the bombing of a market in Baghdad in the Iraq war of 2003. This attack made the news, but it made contested news: there was doubt—and some of that doubt was itself politically motivated—about the veracity of the claims made by Iraqi news broadcasts about the number of casualties.* And in 2004 there were arguments over the levels of violent mortality in Iraq *since* the formal end of war there.† Another researcher, trying to review the links between unequal land distribution and outbreaks of violent conflict, argues that to assess the relative merits of competing arguments is difficult when they rely on 'the grossly inaccurate data set provided by the *World Handbook of Political and Social Indicators*'.[41] It is not just that this dataset underestimates the incidence of political violence in various countries, but, more significantly, that 'a more accurate reporting would alter both the rankings between countries and the magnitude of the intervals between country scores, thereby substantially altering quantitative analyses utilising this data set.' Thus, says Brockett, 'the *Handbook* reports deaths in Honduras during the mid-1970s as twice as num-

---

* As noted in Chapter 1, the war in Iraq in 2003, at least in its first weeks, took the politics of violence and power to new levels: a war in which one side sought to project power (through shock and awe rhetoric, if not tactics) ostensibly without causing casualties; and a war in which the contested evidence of casualties at times suggested a war in which all casualties were inflicted on one's own side! British and American soldiers died in 'friendly fire' incidents while it was insinuated that Iraqi civilians were killed in homes and marketplaces by cynically political missile attacks by Iraqis masquerading as Coalition of the Willing attacks.

† Roberts *et al.* (2004) report findings from cluster surveys and hospital records allowing for a comparison of mortality rates and causes in the 14.6 months before the March 2003 invasion of Iraq and the 17.8 months after the invasion up to their research. These highly contested (by US and, even more, British government officials) findings suggested that about 100,000 'excess deaths' or more had happened in the post-invasion period, with violence and coalition forces air strikes accounting for most of these.

erous as in either El Salvador or Guatemala! In reality, Honduras would rank fourth with Guatemala far ahead for all five.' Remote rural deaths are less likely to attract news coverage than urban assassinations. Brockett also gives an example of variation in news coverage tied to particular interests. In 1975 a 'bananagate' scandal involving a US multinational's allegedly corrupt ties to the president of Honduras led to unprecedented coverage of Honduran affairs in the *New York Times*, including a mention of six people killed at a peasant training centre in June of that year. Similar incidents prior to the scandal had gone unremarked.

Conclusions: war is the continuation of violence by other means

This chapter began by asking straightforward enough questions about the frequency and distribution of war. The answers were less straightforward. One of the reasons was that standard labels or categories used to classify violence and violent conflicts are unwieldy. A category involves a definition (and criteria by which events are judged to 'fit' that definition). On the one hand these definitions are extremely useful. The definitions, and the classification systems they support, have as their purpose the clarification of a complex and diverse world. On the other hand the process of clarifying through classification systems and categorical distinctions necessarily involves simplifying the world. Again, this is not necessarily a bad thing. However, the simplification can be misleading. It arises because the definitions involved work like borders separating artificially or at least crudely phenomena that might be rather closely related.

Questioning classification systems that work with definitions of war, civil war and other violence helps to illuminate some features of recent and contemporary violent conflict within and between societies. One of the issues raised was the argument that the term 'civil war' might be obsolete: it might be less appropriate in a world characterised by global but highly uneven capitalism. Another, larger argument is that the definitions and categories often used in the study of violent conflict hide realities that do not consist of discontinuous, discrete phenomena—inter-state wars, civil wars etc. It is more useful to begin by thinking in terms of a spectrum of violence: a continuum along which events easily shade into one another and the grand categories mark rather artificial breaks.

One implication of thinking in these terms might be a need to explode all such categorical distinctions on grounds of their artificiality. This has been tried—by some it is viewed as intellectual terrorism, by others as exciting, provocative and useful. Examples include, arguably, Hans Magnus Enzensberger's argument that the whole world is in a state of civil war: civil war 'has moved into the metropolis. Its mutations are part of everyday life in our cities, not just in Lima and Johannesburg, in Bombay and in Rio, but in Paris and Berlin, in Detroit and Birmingham, in Milan and Hamburg.'[42] And one might argue, if one agreed with some of the more dramatic conceptions of globalisation, that as the world becomes a single social entity so all wars represent civil wars within that world. But a more important implication of a critical reflection on classification systems is the need to encourage new and more refined ones.

A basic approach would arrange episodes of violent conflict that may be related, in some way, to 'development', along a spectrum of scale, from large-scale international wars, civil wars and genocide at one end, through pogroms, sustained state violence and widespread urban and/or rural violence, to intra-household violence and political assassinations at another end. Three other examples highlight ways of thinking about a continuum of violence. First, the World Health Organisation has developed a matrix of violence that distinguishes between self-directed violence, inter-personal violence and collective violence (and further disaggregates each category) and between types of violence for each category: i.e. physical, sexual or psychological violence, or 'deprivation/neglect' (see Figure 4).[43] The purpose of the matrix is to enable the study of the manifold consequences of violence for public health.

Second, Tilly proposes a matrix of collective violence whose purpose is to help in the analysis of varieties of political mechanism involved in generating such violence.[44] This matrix combines one scale assessing the degree of 'salience of violence' in collective encounters with another scale measuring the degree of coordination. In this 'salience-coordination space' a war or some forms of terrorism would occupy, for example, an area reserved for 'coordinated destruction', highly coordinated and with an extreme salience of short-run damage; the area of 'scattered attacks' would, by contrast, include generally non-violent types of interaction in the course of which, nonetheless, some participants 'respond to obstacles, challenges, or restraints by means of damaging acts; examples include sabotage, clandestine attacks on symbolic objects or places...'[45]

Finally, the category 'political assassinations' or political killings has been used sometimes in quantitative studies attempting to predict the circumstances under which economic growth will be slower or faster.[46] However, without knowing more about what might be called the composition of killing—i.e. the basic question of who is killing whom and how this itself might be changing—it may be hard to know how political killings relate to economic growth rates. Anderson, in an unusual study that looks beyond the numbers of killings, identifies a trend in which there is a change in the socio-economic or class characteristics of who is doing (or ordering) the killing and who is being killed, in a way that does illuminate changes in Thai society that affect long-run economic growth and structural change.[47]

More subtle classifications of violence, along these lines, may make for a richer analysis of linkages between development and violence than can be generated by exclusive focus on one, awkward category such as 'civil war'. In demonstrating the diversity and prevalence of violence in developing countries—and not only in developing countries—a continuum of violence further undermines the influence of the liberal interpretation of war on development thinking and justifies a melancholy perspective on violence, development and history. With this in mind, the next chapter reviews some of the most influential recent explanations of the patterns of violence, especially so-called civil wars, that have been framed by prevailing classification systems and influenced by common analytical perspectives.

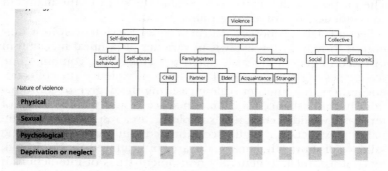

Figure 4. WORLD HEALTH ORGANISATION TYPOLOGY
OF VIOLENCE

Source: WHO (2002).

3

DEVIANT CONDITIONS

The why of war

'Croesus had a craving to extend his territories, but there were two other reasons for his attack on Cappadocia: namely his trust in the oracle and his desire to punish Cyrus for his treatment of Astyages.' (Herodotus, *The Histories*)

Chapter 1 argued for a specific interpretation of the relationship between violence and economic development, influenced by a melancholy view of history. Such a view, as Chapter 2 showed, is complemented and encouraged by an empirical approach that adopts the instrument of a continuum of violence. This chapter reviews the most common types of explanation of contemporary global violence that draw links between violence and development. Most of these contrast with the approach suggested in the first two chapters in that they are rooted in the liberal interpretation of war and of development, a perspective sustained partly through the framing devices (conceptual and empirical) they adopt. They tend to regard violence and war as a product of the pathology of underdevelopment. And where global violence involves advanced capitalist countries, the typical view from the liberal perspective is that this violence is defensive, a legitimate barricade against the incursions of barbarism. The chapter focuses chiefly on studies of so-called civil war in developing countries. However, it begins by highlighting briefly the debates over the explanations for the war in Iraq (in 2003) and for 'terrorism'.

— *War in Iraq*

Early in 2003 there were televised debates and a multitude of newspaper and magazine articles contesting the answer to a simple question: what was the imminent war in Iraq about? All sorts of answer seemed possible, even plausible. The debates have carried on since the end of the war was declared. A few predominant explanations were commonly presented as mutually exclusive alternatives. The three main explanations revolved around oil, international (above all, US) security and the characteristics of Saddam Hussein's regime in Iraq.

Thus it has been argued that the underlying cause of the war was the need in the United States for a hegemonic control over a stable supply and predictable prices of oil. Iraq has the world's second largest known oil reserves, after Saudi Arabia. The Saudi royal regime is considered by many to be increasingly unstable and, therefore, the future of its alliance with the United States is perhaps uncertain. The search for stable supplies of oil had, arguably, already been a preoccupation of US foreign policy for some years—taking in US involvement in places such as Angola and Colombia.*

Others argued that the main source of the war was the pursuit of international security against terrorist threats to Western and especially US interests and people. This explanation sets the Iraq war in the context of wider Middle Eastern politics and frames the war as a sequel to the post-9/11 war in Afghanistan that overthrew the Taliban but failed to extinguish the threat posed by al-Qaeda. Hence, political leaders in the United States and Britain argued insistently both that Iraq had produced or imported, and then secreted, 'weapons of mass destruction' and that Iraq had 'links' to al-Qaeda.[†] Despite the lack of any subsequent evidence of these weapons of mass destruction, or of clear links proving Iraqi willingness to support al-Qaeda, this explanation continued to be offered by some politicians and analysts. Note that this also ties in with a vogue for explaining contemporary wars in religious terms, or at the very least in terms of differences between distinct 'civilisations'.[1]

There were also certain more psychological conjectures about the origins of the war that were linked to this security explanation. On the one hand many regarded the war as a kind of lashing out in

---

* If the main reason for war on Iraq was oil and the 'war on terror' a distraction from this, then similarly the 'war on drugs' in the US Plan Colombia has been interpreted as a distraction from oil interests.

† One indication of the commitment to projecting this fear of terrorism as a motivation for supporting war against Iraq was the subtle interaction of a child's letter to the British Prime Minister and the reply from the Prime Minister's office. The original letter complained that the child (my son) disagreed with the war and asked for clarification on the justification for the war; the reply claimed to understand why the child was 'frightened', not something the child in question had mentioned in his letter. On the politics of fear see Robin (2004).

revenge, and warning, against the perpetrators of the 9/11 attacks in the United States, a national exercise in venting fear and rage that was reflected in the astonishingly high popularity ratings for President Bush (Bush the Younger or, as Saddam Hussein called him, the Idiot Son) and Donald Rumsfeld, the US Secretary of Defence. On the other hand there was some speculation about possible psychological mechanisms at play.*

Meanwhile, the other main reason put forward for the war was the need to unseat a dictatorship: in other words, this was a humanitarian and just war. This is the kind of war that represents the unfinished business of a global Kantian peace. It was what some political scientists call a dyadic conflict, pitting two systemically different societies against each other: one liberal democracy and one corporatist dictatorship.[2] For these political scientists democracy is a more peaceable organisation of society than any other.† As time goes by and democracy spreads, it would be expected that at first, because of a rising number of dyads around the world, there would be more and more international wars; but then as democracy came to dominate national political systems, there would be fewer and fewer wars till the overall Kantian peace was secured by the universal installation of the 'shared values' of democracy. The source of dyadic incompatibility in this case was the violation by the Ba'athist Party government in Iraq of international law. In fact, this war was something of a parody of the recent trend towards seeing war as criminal. On the one hand the US government justified the war by citing Saddam Hussein's crimes, against international law and against humanity. On the other hand many lawyers have argued that the United States and its coalition partners were themselves breaking the rules of international law in defying the UN Security Council.‡

---

* For example: 'Bob Woodward reports that there was a "subtle rivalry" between Rumsfeld and the elder Bush dating back to their time serving together as young Republican Congressmen in the 1960s' (Callinicos, 2003: 46).

† This was not exactly the preoccupation of Herodotus, who argued simply that democracies make better war-makers: 'Thus Athens went from strength to strength, and proved, if proof were needed, how noble a thing equality before the law is, not in one respect only, but in all; for while they were oppressed by tyrants, they had no better success in war than any of their neighbours, yet, once the yoke was flung off, they proved the finest fighters in the world' (2003: 340).

‡ The legal contortionists trying to bend definitions and even justify use of torture by the Coalition of the Willing, and the evidence of prisoner abuse in Iraq by US and British guards, have taken further shine off the claims that this was a humanitarian war.

There were, of course, other explanations of the justification for, objectives of and causes of the war.* However, the debate raises a few more general issues that run through most discussions of the causes of wars between and within countries. This chapter reviews a particular set of explanations for many contemporary violent conflicts in developing countries.

First, the debate remains precisely that: it has not been clearly resolved. This is partly a matter of evidence—there remain dimensions of the origins of the conflict that are poorly established in openly available facts. It is partly also a matter of perspective, or the selection of evidence—depending on one's point of view one can usually find at least some evidence for one particular explanation of a war over and above others. Second, proposed theories of war often do separate into explanations or theories based on material reward; those based on ideas about the role of difference as a source of conflict; and those based on ideology and norms. Put differently, some explanations of war favour economic reasons while others favour more ideological or political ones. Third, explanations of war often like to claim one major factor or variable as the predominant cause of conflict. By contrast the war in Iraq in 2003 was made possible by a complex combination of facts or developments, and these included more or less structural factors and rather more contingent twists.

— *Explaining terror*

Related questions have been asked about why some people undertake terrorist activities; particularly, what is the explanation for suicide bombers? 'The war against terrorism will be won by eliminating poverty' ran the headline of a newspaper interview with James Wolfensohn, president of the World Bank, shortly after the attacks on the Pentagon and the Twin Towers.[3] Asked what he thought the sources of terrorism were, Mr Wolfensohn replied: 'Poverty and inequality. Failure to understand this means closing our eyes to the origin of the resentment of the poor against the North.' Elsewhere he suggested that the poor and poorly educated were the most likely perpetrators of the kind of terror activities that have been common during the Second Palestinian *Intifada*.

Not everyone within the World Bank would agree with these statements, or at any rate with everything Mr Wolfensohn had to say

---

* For arguments that explain the war in imperialist terms and that refuse to rely on mono-causal explanations but prefer to stress the inseparability of ideological, strategic and economic interests see, e.g., Callinicos (2003) and Harvey (2003).

about the socio-economic correlates of terrorist proclivities. Some researchers based at the Bank were arguing in the late 1990s and early 2000s that inequality was more or less irrelevant to civil wars and that social resentments barely mattered; rather, what mattered to civil wars, which were seen as akin to criminal gang behaviour, was a set of opportunities for violence. Poverty is important, according to this argument, because it reduces the opportunity cost of violence, but this must be combined with the promise of direct material benefits, e.g. in the form of loot. So some observers have pointed to reports that Saddam Hussein offered a bounty to the families of individuals offering themselves as suicide bombers.

Various other academics and senior public figures have supported the idea that aid to reduce poverty and increase education is the best way of erasing the risk of terrorism. Others disagree. For example, a paper presented at a World Bank conference suggested that any 'connection between poverty, education and terrorism is indirect, complicated and probably quite weak. Instead of viewing terrorism as a direct response to low market opportunities or ignorance, we think it is more accurately viewed as a response to political conditions and long-standing feelings (either perceived or real) of indignity and frustration that have little to do with economics.'[4] The evidence in that paper—that in Lebanon in the late 1980s and early 1990s having a living standard above the poverty line or secondary school or higher education was positively associated with participation in Hezbollah terrorism—is supported by research on participants in the Palestinian *Intifada*.

Root and branch—family trees in theories of conflict

Against this push and shove to assert one more or less exclusive 'causal factor', one of the conclusions of a review of some of the main alternative explanations of contemporary wars is the simple argument that like most social phenomena wars or violent conflicts only ever have *many* causes. The historian Marc Bloch wrote a small book called *The Historian's Craft*, in which he discussed the problems of causation. Bloch distinguished between very general causes or 'conditions' (which outlasted the particular events they lay behind) and differentiating, more immediate generative causes. For example, if a man falls over a cliff is this because of a misstep, or is it because of gravity or geology? In the contemporary study of violent conflicts, predominantly in developing countries, this distinction is typically translated into the difference between 'root causes' and 'proximate causes' or triggers. For Bloch there were two additional points. First, there is always a *choice* among possible causes and this selection will depend on one's perspective. Thus, different inquiries into the causes of a disease epidemic will select and prioritise according to whether they are led by biologists or social scientists. Second, there are always multiple causes rather than mono-causes.

Bloch also distinguished between causes and motivations. 'To read certain books of history, one might think of mankind made up entirely of logical wills whose reasons for acting would never hold the slightest mystery for them… We should seriously misrepresent the problems of causes in history if we always and everywhere reduced them to a problem of motive.'[5] He cautioned historians to be ever sceptical of the 'pretended psychological truths of common sense'. Bloch's distinctions are useful in trying to pick a way through the competing explanations of the causes of contemporary wars. It will become clear in this chapter that there are influential explanations that do prioritise logical motives, and that there are certainly explanations that argue for mono-causes.

The need for explanations of violent conflict that allow for a more subtle arrangement of types and levels of causation emerges from a review of standard interpretations of recent wars. This chapter shows that there is still a lack of evidence and that there are still contested explanations of the causes of war. And there is still often a gap between the claims of theory and the facts of violence. As Tolstoy wrote: 'The deeper we delve in search of these causes the more of them do we discover; and each separate cause or whole series of causes appears to us equally valid in itself and equally unsound by its insignificance in comparison with the size of the event.'[6] This is why it is important always to bring an analytical discussion of violence and war back to the description of suffering and the infliction of pain, to the brutality of killing. There are plenty of theories of war that stop short of analysing *violence*.[7]

This continuing 'problem of causes' is partly a question of method and of data, in other words a matter of how explanations are constructed and supported. A few features of the analytical debates that are reviewed in this chapter need highlighting. There are two main ways to study the problem of causes in war: to develop individual case studies and to extract and compare categorised features of a large number of wars, generating statistical analyses. The usual complaints are that case studies are overly descriptive, they do not confirm any general theoretical constancy and the more detailed they are the less useful they are for the rest of the world; and that quantitative studies, by contrast, lose their connection to reality in stripping wars of their specific contexts and ignoring the processes out of which war emerges from a typically conflictual 'peace'. Nonetheless, the trend of late has been to conduct quantitative tests of hypotheses about the causes, or at the very least the correlates, of war. This trend is partly driven by technological possibilities—computers can perform ever more complex statistical tests of larger and larger datasets and can, for example, make possible the large-scale trawling of media archives for reports on violent conflict that would take years for individual researchers to do. Yet the studies of war that are reviewed through the rest of this chapter are typically compromised by tainted data.

As Chapter 2 showed, the data on violence and war are often unreliable. The same goes for many of the other variables that are commonly used in quantitative models—variables such as those capturing inequality, or average income levels, or political rights, or ethnic diversity, or unemployment. Even with the data that are available, quantitative and statistical studies have failed to prove the existence of any event regularity, any empirical pattern connecting quantifiable indicators in repeated and predictable patterns. Although there are very good reasons for believing that such event regularities, even with a clear probabilistic character, rarely occur in the real world of social phenomena, many people continue to have high expectations of confirming their common existence.

Then there is the enduring tension between types of evidence that are regarded as admissible, and the types of explanation with which they are associated. Thus many theories will stress the role of subjective factors: for example, 'relative deprivation theory' is all about perception, and many more recent studies emphasise that perceived inequality or grievance is as relevant as objective conditions. Other theories are only really interested in 'objective' factors, often thought to be those that are quantifiable (directly or by indirect proxies). These types of explanation are particularly scornful—for good or ill—of 'narratives of grievance': i.e. just because someone tells you they are fighting to overturn injustice does not necessarily mean this *is* why they are fighting. It is fairly obvious that where we are faced with perceptions we are relying on delicate judgements about the veracity, reliability and significance of qualitative information and about the appropriate sources of this information. But if this undermines the robustness and reliability of particular kinds of explanation, it is equally true that most statistical research into conflict is just as tainted by empirical fragility.[8]

It will also become clear that similar 'causes' and conditions can have rather different outcomes. As William Reno asks, why did similar conditions in southern Somalia and in the still unrecognised 'state' of Somaliland produce very different outcomes in social organisation, coercion and international integration, just as, despite many shared conditions, political developments have differed markedly between Chechnya and Ingushetia, or between different regions of Georgia?[9] This kind of question, the method of contrastive exploration, is a useful procedure for picking between different levels of causation. Another example, the role of inequality, is discussed in detail in this chapter. The fact that equally dramatic degrees of income inequality can be associated with very different political developments across countries somewhat confounds the effort to prove an empirical law of the kind: whenever inequality is so high then the following will happen. Just as the same causes can have different effects, so similar effects or phenomena can have different causes. The conditions leading towards civil war in Somalia might not provide a tracing that then maps perfectly onto origins of war in El Salvador, Chechnya or Sierra Leone.

The search for substantial causal factors in common across a range of conflicts is still valid. As Suganami suggests, the best that we can do is try to identify broad 'family resemblances' rather than hard and fast event regularities.[10] Furthermore, in each period of history wars have important ties to the way in which societies are organised in that period. Chapter 6 of this book argues that important features of contemporary society, in particular the way in which capitalism and power are spread through the world and the varieties of experience of late development, are at the heart of contemporary conflicts without providing any glib template from which we can read off obvious forecasts.

The other main theme of this chapter is that although the various explanations of war reviewed are different—in fact they are often presented explicitly as in dispute with one another—they do have something in common. Most of them are characterised by a quest for a deviant condition that increases the risk of war. Thus war is regarded as some kind of congenital disorder, often emerging in conditions of 'distorted' development. While one argument or theory may claim that market distortions are critical causes of war, another will claim that some other form of distorted development is to blame. The aberration from 'normality' may lie, for example, in extreme levels of income inequality; it may be a highly particular degree of ethnic fractionalisation; or it may be an unusual coincidence of primary commodity dependence with particular demographic and economic characteristics that then unleashes an otherwise dormant social violence. Lurking beneath all of these arguments is an implicit assumption, the counterfactual fantasy of a nice and smooth form of capitalist development. This is the liberal perspective challenged throughout this book.

This chapter does not perform a comprehensive review of all the recent contending explanations of war and violence in developing countries, but it does outline their main features and discusses in a little more critical detail two in particular: the inequality explanation and the neo-classical economic explanation.

Categories of explanation

Chapter 2 discussed various ways to classify incidents of violent conflict. Similarly, there are various ways of organising explanations of violent conflict. The purpose is the same—to manage what can otherwise be an overwhelming diversity. There is no universally agreed way of doing this. One way to classify explanations or theories of conflict is by intellectual discipline: security studies, international relations, political science, economics, environmental studies, anthropology etc. However, there is another way to group them. For behind every theory of war is a set of assumptions. These assumptions are usually implicit, they are very basic, and they are fundamentally subjective. Two examples of how people have proposed this kind of classification system make particular sense in terms of the themes raised in this book from Chapter 1 onwards. One idea is to distinguish between 'affective', emotional sources of collective violence and rational reasons. Another is to arrange explanations according to 'behaviour theories', 'ideas theories' and 'relations theories'.

— Affective versus rational explanations

An example of the emotional/rational categorisation is Eckstein's argument that all theories of collective violence differed after a fundamental 'branch point', some following a branch of thinking emphasising 'contingency theory' and the rest growing off the bough of 'inherency theory'.[11] For Eckstein, contingency theory holds that the normal state of social affairs is peaceable, but that extraordinary upheavals can provoke affective, irrational outbursts. The mechanism that unleashes such outbursts is the 'frustration-aggression nexus'—but the key is that the mechanism only operates if there is a confluence of a range of facilitating, quasi-accidental, i.e.

contingent factors. The most renowned theory of this type is Gurr's theory of relative deprivation as the origin of conflict.[12] If people feel a discrepancy between what they have and what they expect to be able to have, this will trigger the frustration-aggression nexus. But that nexus would only generate collective violence of one kind or another if there were a propitious combination of facilitating factors. The relevant factors could be grouped together as either 'justification'—from ideology or a social habit of culturally learned violence—or 'balance' in the allocation of coercive capabilities between the state and others.

From a different angle the psychologist James Gilligan argues that individual and collective violence are affective outbursts, the last resort of cornered people, and that they are caused above all by shame.[13]

A consensus on the causes and prevention of violence has been emerging over the past few decades among investigators of this subject from virtually every branch of the behavioural sciences. All specialties, independent of each other, have identified a pathogen that seems to be a necessary but not sufficient cause of violent behaviour, just as specifically as exposure to the tubercle bacillus is necessary but not sufficient for the development of tuberculosis. The difference is that in the case of violence the pathogen is an emotion, not a microbe—namely, the experience of overwhelming shame and humiliation. And just as people's vulnerability to tuberculosis is influenced by the state of their body's defence mechanisms, so their vulnerability to violence is influenced by the state of their psychological defence mechanisms.

Gilligan's theory of shame-induced violence emerged from his interviews with violent inmates in US prisons. Aside from the argument about the role of shame, the imagery of disease and emotional immunology echo the arguments of political scientists and others about the abnormality of violence and war. For Gilligan violence is something you are unlucky to catch; catching violence is a matter of the confluence of what is done to you and your own lack of a healthy immune system (which requires defences of guilt, or sources of self-esteem such as education or wealth).

Along the other branch of Eckstein's analytical tree versions of inherency theory unfurl. This type of theory begins with an assumption that human beings are naturally, inherently disposed to violence as much as towards peace and that actual collective violence represents the outcome of a rational selection of violence as simply one option along a continuum of possible political actions. The possibility of violence is always present in the perpetual jockeying for power among interest groups—what trips the switch to turn on the option of violence and war is the right mix of costs and benefits. Here, again, factors like the coercive balance come into play, though in this type of theory they are rather more than contingent, they play a more centrally determining role given the underlying disposition to violence.

Eckstein suggested that the dominant representative of this type of theory was Tilly's collective action explanations of violence in early modern Europe.[14] More recently, the sweeping confidence of neo-classical economists in the applicability of their precepts and logic across all the social sciences has generated another example of this kind of theory. Neo-classical economic theories of violent conflict, which are discussed in detail later in this chapter, propose that social phenomena like civil wars can by explained fully in terms of the apparatus of individual maximising 'agents' making rational choices and that, where the signals of costs and benefits suggest that utility is maximised by violence, violence will ensue.

Each type of theory—each secondary branch and twig of the tree of 'root causes' of violence—picks up on a different dimension of development. Relative deprivation stories suggest that development matters because it throws 'traditional' practices, mores and organisation into disarray, generates expectations and hence ups the ante of relative deprivation, and fails to produce early enough the political institutions for coping with the resultant welling up of frustration. Collective action theories—at least those close to Tilly's variant—stress the way that economic and social development reshapes the organisation of power and, indeed, the technology of violence. As states form they tend to make demands on subject populations who, naturally enough, either want a greater stake in central authority or resist these demands—at times with force. The emphasis, then, is on group relations and on how economic and technical change provokes realignments in the organisation of power relations, with potential implications for violent conflict.

— *Ideas, behaviour and relations explanations*

A second scheme for distinguishing among theories of violence has been proposed more recently by Tilly himself.[15] This categorisation divides theories of violence into ideas theories, behaviour theories and relational theories. 'Ideas people' stress beliefs, concepts, rules and values; 'behaviour people' stress the autonomy of motives, impulses and opportunities; and 'relations people' stress the role of transactions, as well as generally insisting on collective processes having properties irreducibly distinct from individual propensities. 'In this view, restraining violence depends less on destroying bad ideas, eliminating opportunities, or suppressing impulses than on transforming relations among persons and groups.'[16] Gilligan's theory of violence and shame fits mainly into the behaviour type of explanation. Understanding conflict in the former Yugoslavia in terms of entrenched ethnic animosity is essentially an 'ideas' explanation. And seeing the Korean War in terms of an international 'East-West' conflict imposed on what was fundamentally a domestic conflict (i.e. a conflict principally over the challenge of late development rather than straightforwardly between North and South Korea) is a 'relations' explanation.*

Both these schemes for classifying theories and approaches are useful. However, the offshoots and foliage overlap and intertwine, so that to which major branch a particular explanation belongs is not always obvious. An explanation like Samuel Huntington's well-known 'clash of civilizations' theory, for example, fits clearly into the 'ideas' category.[17] Conflicts between or within countries result from a confrontation of belief systems, sets of values, institutional 'rules of the game'. One could see violent conflict along a physical, historical and social frontier like that in Amazonian Brazil, over land access, precisely as a product of a clash of different values and beliefs about land use: particularly, between communal versus individual property rights. Yet behavioural impulses and motive and opportunity also play a role in this frontier violence. Where laws are unclear and their enforcement sporadic, different types of individual—large landowner, migrant labourer etc.—have clear opportunities to exercise some measure of choice to improve their well-being by grabbing apparently available land. And Brazilian frontier violence also has clearly collective and relational dimensions: historically shaped relations between indigenous communities and others, between the state and capitalists, between poor landless Brazilians and large and often absentee landowners.

To put it differently, where a particular set of social rules, rights and obligations is being established—for example, private property

---

* For this kind of explanation of the Korean war see Halliday and Cumings (1988). They argue that the Korean war was essentially the same as the Vietnam war or the civil war in China—'a civil war fought between two domestic forces: a revolutionary nationalist movement, which had its roots in tough anti-colonial struggle, and a conservative movement tied to the *status quo*, especially to an unequal land system. What was different in Korea was the form and timing of outside intervention' (p. 10).

rights—different beliefs, values and ideas come into play in what is predominantly a class encounter, a meeting of groups of people with more or less clearly defined interests. Clustering explanations according to their fundamental assumptions does help in identifying what kinds of theory they are and in spotting internal contradictions. However, for a particular theory or explanation to draw on different strands of thinking, even on different assumptions, is not necessarily a bad thing. What matters is that the relationship between types of causal mechanism is made clear.

Culture clash

'Cleisthenes...then changed the number of Athenian tribes from four to ten, and abolished the old names.' (Herodotus, *The Histories*, p. 335)

— Ethnicity or religion

The military historian John Keegan wrote in the *Daily Telegraph* that war in Bosnia in the 1990s represented 'a primitive tribal conflict only anthropologists can understand'.[18] Others have offered similar opinions about conflicts elsewhere throughout the world, from Sri Lanka to Rwanda and Burundi to Indonesia to the Chiapas rebellion in Mexico, even to Northern Ireland. Ethnic cleansing was one of the terrors of the post-Cold War period, though many forgot that virtually every contemporary democracy was built on its own ethnic cleansing or national consolidation exercise, including Anglo-Saxon violence against the Celts and settler North American expulsion of and violence against Amerindians.[19] Ethnicity offers an easy handle on what makes a group of people distinctive, it suggests their homogeneity and so suggests the habitual allegiance that might pass for a solution to what social scientists call 'the collective action problem', i.e. what gets people to act as a group rather than to free ride in their own individual interest and hope that others will do the hard work for them. Ethnicity also suggests an unbroken and long history—the term often goes with an idea of primordialism: you are born with an ethnic identity that is an ancient and unavoidable fact. This interpretation of ethnicity is usually described as an 'essentialist' understanding of collective identity. It is easy to apply the argument, for example, to conflicts in various parts of sub-Saharan Africa, where it is also stressed frequently that the borders of internationally recognised nation-states are entirely artificial creations of colonial invention. These historically artificial polities threw together awkward collections of ethnic groups.*

The argument that contemporary conflicts reflect ancient tribal or ethnic incompatibilities is similar to the argument that conflicts are driven predominantly by religion. The anthropologist Jack Goody argued that in fact wars typically regarded as ethnic are really religious. Thus in Bosnia ethnicity was a euphemism for religious conflict in a society where Bosnians, Serbs, Croats and Muslims speak the same language. He cites Michael Sells arguing: 'Those organising the persecution identified themselves through explicit religious symbols, such as the three-fingered hand gestures representing the Christian Trinity, the images of sacred figures of Serbian religious mythology on their uniform insignia, the songs they memorised and forced their victims to sing, the priest's ring they kissed before and after their acts of persecution, and the formal religious ceremonies.'†

Eric Hobsbawm claimed that history after 1917 was to be that of wars of religion. He cited one of the French officers who pioneered the barbarism of French-Algerian counter-insurgency policy in the 1950s saying: 'There is no true war but religious war.' Confrontations in the twentieth century were between God and the Devil, and any such confrontation contains a tendency to barbarism. This is because there is in such a conflict only one outcome: total victory and/or total defeat. This zero-sum game, this totality of the end, comes to justify *any means* to protect against the victory of the Devil. So the Cold War transformed the civilised competition, cunning diplomacy and great game of the nineteenth century into the apocalyptic conflict of Good against Evil.[20]

Another version of this argument, the idea that religion or religious tendencies make wars 'total wars' and lead to extremes of brutality, can be found in Canetti's *Crowds and Power*. Amid the ninety odd pages Canetti devotes to classifying crowd types is the invisible

---

* While there is an obvious truth to the argument that the modern national boundaries of Africa are in some sense 'unnatural', it tends to be made rather lazily: for it is not clear what benchmark of natural nationality really exists in most of the world. European nation-states are themselves the product of historical politics and conflict rather than pure geographical entities or ethnic going concerns.

† Goody (2001). As he points out, Catholic Croats were often equally brutal in pursuit of what at times was a project to expel Muslims and share Bosnia between the Orthodox Serbs and Catholic Croats, 'a programme Tudjman described as "Europeanization". For their part, some Muslims sought to establish an Islamic Republic, and the later recruitment of mujaheddin fighters from Afghanistan to aid the Bosniak cause gave some colour to this notion.'

crowd. One of the most obvious and significant types of the invisible crowd is the crowd of the dead, which divides typically into a double crowd. An example of the contemporary political significance of this idea is the importance in political struggles in Argentina and Chile of invoking that invisible crowd called *Los Desaparecidos*, the Disappeared. Canetti has a passage on Islam and war, in which he writes: 'The bi-partition of the crowd in Islam is unconditional', meaning the partition of everyone who has ever lived, at the Last Judgement, into the faithful and the unbelieving: this is an organising principle that makes social conflict into either/or conflict, all or nothing rather than a divisible conflict where compromise and restraint might be possible. He goes on: 'The war of religion is a sacred duty and thus, though in a less comprehensive form, the double crowd of the Last Judgement is prefigured in every earthly battle.'[21]

One of the most unnerving examples of Christianity being used as a mobilising weapon to overcome fear and to drive people into battle is St Bernard of Clairvaux's justification for his preaching of the Second Crusade in the twelfth century. Replying to criticism after the disastrous crusade, Bernard drew on the virtuous perseverance of the Israelites who, in one Old Testament story, take defeats on the collective chin and keep going back into battle.

The weaker they are in battle, however, the more superior they prove to be in faith. What then would have been the reaction of the crusaders if I had encouraged them once more to attack, and if they had succumbed once more? What if they had heard me tell them for a third time to embark again on the journey and on the labour in which they had failed repeatedly? And yet the Israelites, ignoring the two earlier failures, prepare for a third battle, and are victorious.[22]

Arguments that ethnic or religious identity contributes the predominant causal factor to contemporary violent conflicts are also analytically close to the widely known argument of Samuel Huntington that the world is defined by a series of clashes between civilisations. It is well documented, for example, that the military adventurism of the George W. Bush administration is shaped in part by the influence of fundamentalist American Christians, goaded on by national fear in the wake of 9/11.[23] Huntington globalised the issue by arguing that the world has been and will be characterised by a series of civilisational fissures, a kind of grinding together of civilisational tectonic plates that inevitably throws up serrated ranges of violence. 'In this new world the most pervasive, important, and dangerous conflicts will not be between social classes...but between peoples belonging to different cultural entities... And the most dangerous cultural conflicts are those along the fault lines of civilisations.'[24]

Various forms of collective identity do play important organisational roles in the production of violent conflict. By calling on historical memory (mythical or otherwise) and on cultural markers of loyalty and values they lend a depth to political experience. Arguably this depth is instrumental in bridging the gap between many reasons for political conflict and the brute facts of violence. They enable individuals to see themselves as heroic (when they may well be acting at the same time out of petty rivalries). Religion especially can up the ante of viciousness, making conflicts indivisible and, as orthodox economics might have it, redefining the scope of utility to make death part of the calculative utility function. Also, collective identity—and though this is unfashionable with many contemporary intellectuals this includes class—can impose a burden of obligation on individuals as well as redefining risk, utility and the meaning of violence. Moreover, religious belief in the context of political and armed conflict may be a simple organisational instrument when, otherwise, there is an asymmetry of armaments. This is the way one member of al-Qassam (the military brigades of Hamas in Palestine) explained it to an interviewer: 'We do not have tanks or rockets, but we have something superior—our exploding Islamic human bombs. In place of a nuclear arsenal, we are proud of our arsenal of believers.'[25]

Furthermore, a source of collective identity like shared religion or ethnicity can rearrange the emotions invested in social relations—so that hierarchies, differences and tensions within a given group are erased in a shared opposition to some external group: immigrants or hosts, another ethnic or religious group and so on. For these reasons, independently of any possible autonomous, spontaneous and direct effect of ethnic or religious difference, 'identity politics' is an attractive mobilising instrument for would-be warmongers. Nationalism has had similar powers as a source of mobilisation and a spur to go to extreme lengths, including violence and death.[26]

This mobilisational advantage of collective identity is partially independent of the actual content of religiosity or ethnic attachment or any other collectivity, and is not just functionally tied to violent outcomes. For the same mobilisational advantage can be used in very different ways and the values of religion or ethnicity or class can be used to mobilise people against violence or at the very least to restrain violence.* Thus within Islam there has been a long debate both on the interpretation of *jihad* and on the relative place of peace and *jihad*.† That debate on the interpretation and implications of the concept of *jihad* continues is obvious from international conflicts over politics, war and terrorism within Islam. And this debate is mirrored by an equally unresolved debate on just war within Christianity.

The appeal of ethnic loyalty or religious identity has also possibly acquired an increasing social and political value in recent years, reflected in the vogue for studies of identity politics, from the weakening or even repression of other forms of social ties. In Yugoslavia administrative and economic policy reforms from the mid-1960s onwards, and the way these were interpreted and exploited by politicians, unravelled federal cohesion. Reforms unpicked connections—such as railway and postal infrastructure and financial flows—between the republics, pitching them into an enormously wasteful lack of coordination, for example of investment, exports and imports or of the division of labour within the federation. The reforms also unravelled the thread of common trade unions that had tied factory workers in different republics together. There was a kind of centrally planned atomisation of Yugoslav society, in which individual production units were thrown onto their own organisational mettle and discouraged from collective bargaining or other linkages. At the same time, the economic consequences of policy choices became more and more depressing and what had begun to look like an economic success in the Balkans developed into a deepening crisis. Ambitious republican politicians took advantage of this predicament and were left only with the ties of religion and ethnic mythology to mobilise fearful and deprived populations.[27]

---

* As David Turton (1997) puts it, ethnicity has a darker side, it can be used to move people to atrocious acts of violence, but it also has a broader and more positive significance in human social life.
† See Peters (1996). Said (1997) distinguishes three main schools. The new classical school takes a more cautious line and regards *jihad* as a defensive possibility; the radical militants, since the 1920s, extended the morality of holy war to include a wider range of military actions and to include circumstances in which Muslims could start a war; the Islamic reformation school interprets *jihad* mainly in terms of a moral rather than military conflict, chiefly a holy war on inequality and injustice and poverty—much like the proliferation in secular international politics of injunctions to fight a 'war on poverty' etc. Many stress the original meaning of *jihad* as 'effort' and its emphasis on an inward moral struggle of the individual.

— *Measuring ethnic diversity*

Ethnic and religious identity can matter, clearly, in the generation of violent conflict. But there is nothing automatic about it. Difficulties arise when academics and others treat these types of collective identity lazily—as the fashion for identity politics encourages them to—and then make grand generalisations about the association of religion or ethnicity and war (or ethnicity and anything else, like economic growth rates, for example). And this is the case with most adherents of essentialist approaches, for example, to ethnicity.

Some of the most extraordinary and rigid versions of this essentialising and generalising about ethnicity have appeared in the introduction of ethnicity into orthodox economic models. Working out the basis for ethnic difference is fraught. Sometimes people mean a racial or genetic difference, at other times all they have to go on is a difference in language. In all but the most superficial of traits the continuity of genetic patterns overwhelms the crude and arbitrary imposition of categorical discontinuities.* It is not surprising, then, that efforts to find event regularities in large statistical comparisons, linking a given degree of ethnic diversity or polarisation to outcomes such as the rate of economic growth or the incidence of civil war, are doomed.

Nonetheless, there have been many attempts to find such a pattern of regularity. The key to this is to use a quantitative index measuring ethnic fractionalisation in a range of populations (the populations in question are normally countries but can be, for example, cities within a country). Statistical tests are performed on the data from an index of ethnic fractionalisation and their association with data observed for other variables. Then, couched in probability, conclusions are offered about the relationship between, say, fractionalisation and civil war.

There is a standard way of doing this, based on an index developed initially on the basis of work done by Soviet geographers that has led to something called the ethno-linguistic fractionalisation index or ELF. The ELF index measures the probability that two ran-

---

* This is not surprising when it is seen that many ethnic groups are, first, relatively recent and, second, the products not of natural enclaves deep in forests or high in mountains but of historical developments: for example, the Ovimbundu of the Central Highlands in Angola—like many ethnic groups around the world—are effectively the product of a period of migration of disparate groups of people away from the depredations of the violence associated with the slave trade (see Miller, 1988). Also, 'Israelis' and 'Palestinians' are genetically identical.

dom individuals in a population are from different ethnic groups. Formally, this is written:

$$ELF = 1 - \sum_{i=1}^{i=n}(x_i/N)^2$$

where x_i is the number of people in the ith group, N is the total population and n is the number of ethno-linguistic groups in the country or relevant population. There are variations on this formula, but the basic idea remains similar and the purpose is typically to identify some special 'score' for ethnicity—it might be a particularly high score for diversity or fractionalisation or it might be a striking polarisation between two groups—that might then be strongly correlated with the historical incidence, or probabilistic risk, of civil war. Various claims are then made. For example, although some claim that a high score, that is, a high degree of diversity, makes for more conflict, a more common argument of late has been that a particularly strong degree of *polarisation* is associated more with statistical vulnerability to civil war (these datasets are applied to civil war data rather than including wars between developing countries, for example, such as the Eritrea/Ethiopia war of the 1990s).

The rationale used to explain the statistical finding (and possibly the assumption on which the test was set up in the first place) draws on the simple theory of collective action. Thus there may well be reasons in lots of societies to rebel against a government but there are costs and challenges involved in persuading people to join the fight. These coordination costs will be much higher where there is ethnic diversity, but where there is polarisation there is a large group of people with common cultural beliefs and ties of loyalty who will be relatively easy to coordinate against, presumably, the ethnic group represented by the incumbent government. Diversity presents high coordination costs because of mistrust between peoples, and perhaps because of straightforward communication problems since ethnic groups often speak different languages.*

* The other reasoning behind the use of the ELF variable in rational choice economic models of conflict is what seems a slightly lazy translation of the ideas in what Jack Hirshleifer (1988) calls 'bioeconomics'. 'The premise of bioeconomics is that our preferences have themselves evolved to serve economic functions in a very broad sense: those preferences were selected that promoted survival in a world of scarcity and competition.' Thus social preferences, including xenophobic ethnic nationalism, might have started from kinship relations and the ethnic organisation of the idea that survival depends on looking after number one but that some degree of cooperation might help, so long as it is with closely related people. However, for Hirshleifer there is a far broader 'affiliative instinct' that can have a powerful hold over people's loyalties and actions even when individuals are assigned quite arbitrarily (by which he means not genetically) to groups; indeed, citizens of

The underlying observations for each country or population are less precise and consistent than might be implied by the mathematical formula itself and by the confidence of claims for its predictive powers. Moreover, there is no sound basis for 'scientific' measurements of ethnic diversity that hold equally well across a wide range of societies. A more important problem is that there is no reason to trust that a given score for ethnic diversity will have the same social meaning and political significance in different countries. The ELF index is used as an independent variable in models trying to explain a dependent variable such as the incidence of civil war. However, ethnicity is not a discrete social category with internal consistency and predictable, mechanistic functions and implications. It is not independent as a political variable. Rather it is bound up with a large range of other factors that vary across contexts. Therefore, the organisational significance of ethnicity and ethnic diversity or polarisation should be expected to vary across time and space. A further fallacy is the idea that ethnicity has identical precedence as the key to collective action, allegiance, animosities and obligations in every society. That idea erases all possible significance of religion, class, political ideology or nationalism.

All these difficulties are illustrated by the example of Afghanistan. Conrad Schetter points out that, contrary to the common view that ethnic groups have existed since time immemorial, most Afghan ethnic groups were twentieth-century creations.

> Driven by the scientific endeavour to classify people according to cultural customs, ethnologists invented an entire series of ethnic groups: Nuristani, Pashai, Aimaq, Tajik or Farsiwan. The segments of the population for whom they were invented are often not even familiar with such labels, much less aware of any common identity. In addition there is a lack of viable criteria to determine who is Uzbek, Hazara or Pashtun. For example, those who maintain that Pashtuns speak Pashtu and are Sunni Muslims err, since there are also Shiite Pashtuns in the Qandahar region and Pashtuns from Kabul often do not speak a word of Pashtu.[28]

A German survey from the 1980s claims there are about fifty different groups in the country, while a Soviet Russian study from the

---

great and highly diverse nations like the United States are likely to be 'as patriotic and self-sacrificial as citizens of tiny states like Andorra or Luxembourg'. Thus, even a bioeconomic explanation of war, introducing collective action as the evolutionary rationalisation of individualist calculations, would not predict any particular determinative role for ethnicity, or for religion, but would give some credibility to the formation of various 'arbitrary' systems of assigning group membership.

mid-1960s found some 200.[29] Nonetheless, ethnicity does serve as a basis for political mobilisation in Afghanistan, in the Balkans and elsewhere. Its role, though, cannot be read from summary (and often misleading) statistics but can only be gleaned from detailed historical-political analysis.

It is not surprising, then, that there is not even any consensus among those statistical studies that do accept the basis of the ethno-linguistic fractionalisation index. The evidence of James Fearon and David Laitin suggests there is virtually no association of this kind at all, particularly when one looks also at the level of income as another variable. Figure 5 below comes from their paper and shows the results of their descriptive statistics. For a given level of ethnic diversity/polarisation, as income rises the 'risk' of civil war declines dramatically. But if the level of income is held constant, then the lines show how minimal the change in risk of conflict is when the degree of ethnic diversity is changed.

No empirical law ties ethnicity to collective violence. The very fact that so many *different* forms of collective identity can have such

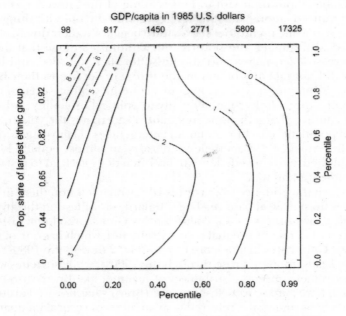

Figure 5. CIVIL WAR ONSETS/100 COUNTRY-YEARS
Source: Fearon and Laitin (2003).

powerful effects on people's behaviour does suggest that social groups are extremely important starting points in any analysis of conflict, and that conflict probably cannot be explained solely from individualist perspectives. What matters to how a given source of collective identity works on individuals and to how deftly it can be exploited by political leaders is largely a matter of specific histories rather than fixed and eternal properties.

Inequality

One of the very oldest ideas about collective violence is that it springs from social and economic inequality. 'We maintain that if a state is to avoid the greatest plague of all—I mean civil war, though civil disintegration would be a better term—extreme poverty and wealth must not be allowed to arise in any section of the citizen-body, because both lead to both these disasters.'[30] In 1562 Montaigne met a small group of Brazilian Indians (the subject of his essay 'On Cannibals') and asked them what they found most remarkable about their visit to France. One of the answers was they 'had noticed among us some men gorged to the full with things of every sort while their other halves were beggars at their doors, emaciated with hunger and poverty. They found it strange that these poverty-stricken halves [*sic*] should suffer such injustice, and that they did not take the others by the throat or set fire to their houses.'[31] Contemporary development economics often sustains this idea of a direct link from inequality to political instability and violent conflict. 'Large income inequality exacerbates the vulnerability of populations to humanitarian emergencies', claims one review of the evidence.[32] Nonetheless, there is an almost equally long-established awareness that inequality often does *not* lead to instability, violence and war.

Even if the evidence were trustworthy, which it is not, there probably is no statistical pattern. The standard way of testing this hypothesis is by using the Gini coefficient. A Gini score closer to zero represents a relatively equal country (Finland, which has one of the lowest Gini scores, had a score of around 0.2 during the 1980s and early 1990s, though it rose through the 1990s), while societies with an extremely uneven distribution of income, like Brazil or South Africa, have Gini scores closer to one (Brazil's has hovered around 0.6). This is sometimes referred to as an index of vertical inequality: the distribution of incomes, from lowest to highest, is measured across all individuals (at any rate, this is estimated from surveys of a representative sample of the total population) and resolved into a Gini coefficient.* Whether in bivariate analysis that tests the simple correlation between income distribution and some measure of violence or war, or in more complex multivariate tests, there is no generally accepted pattern.

The box charts in Figures 6.1 and 6.2 make this clear. A sample of developing countries for which there are *relatively* good distributional data is separated into those that have experienced civil war and those that have not. Figure 6.1 describes the evidence for the post-Cold War period while Figure 6.2 shows the data over the period back to 1944. The 'yes' group (those that have had civil wars in the period observed) and the 'no' group are then lined up according to their range of income distribution or Gini measurements on the vertical axis. Most of the countries in each group are clustered in the box, though the extended lines and markers capture a fuller coverage of their range of income distributions. If it were straightforward, if for example higher income inequality went

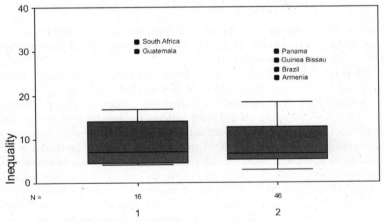

1 = Conflict; 2= No Conflict

Conflict Source: Wallensteen & Sollenberg (1998,2000)
Inequality Source: Deininger & Squire (1996)

Figure 6.1 POST-1989 CIVIL CONFLICT

* The Gini coefficient represents a ratio derived from the Lorenz curve, a curve that bends away from a hypothetical line of perfect equality in income distribution: data that produce Lorenz curves are taken from household surveys.

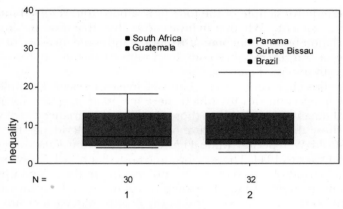

1 = Conflict ; 2 = No Conflict

Conflict Source: Sambanis (2000)

Inequality Source: Deininger & Squire (1996)

Figure 6.2 CIVIL CONFLICT 1944–2000

with a clearer incidence of civil war, then the yes box and its anten-
nae would sit markedly higher in the chart than the no group. Yet
there is a remarkable overlap.

Chapter 2 has already explored the difficulties with datasets on
civil war and shown that different lists of civil wars can produce—
in quantitative comparisons—contrasting findings. The problem,
though, is worse than that. Comparisons of the data on inequality
across a range of countries are almost useless. This is in spite of a
succession of improvements in the collection of large datasets on
distributional data. Most of the problems come about because the
surveys conducted in different countries are often measuring different things and, when they are trying to measure the same thing,
they often do so with varying degrees of precision. For example,
prior to the war and genocide in Rwanda the country was often
regarded as a country with a low Gini coefficient. However, Rwanda
had been growing far more unequal than Gini estimates suggested.[34]

Statistical work in the social sciences, particularly but not only
where this involves developing countries, is like trying to remove
splinters with an oven glove. Recent research into economic inequality in Latin America confirms the dangers of building causal arguments on inequality data. Székely and Hilgert analysed household
survey data from eighteen Latin American countries to explore the

basis for economists' efforts to find a clear pattern relating inequality to economic growth. They found that rankings among these countries in terms of conventional inequality indicators were illusory. Scores were driven by variations in the characteristics of the data and their treatment. Hence our 'ideas about the effect of inequality on economic growth are also driven by quality and coverage differences in household surveys and by the way in which the data is [*sic*] treated.'*

Accepting the crudeness of the evidence, the images in Figures 6.1 and 6.2 may nonetheless suggest another way of thinking about the implications of inequality. First, some of the outlying countries in the sample—those that stand out from the box-crowd by their exceptional inequality—have certainly been characterised by high levels of social and political violence even if not necessarily by civil war as normally defined. Again, breaking down the artificial boundaries around continuous phenomena of violence may be worthwhile. To take four examples, all with high Gini coefficients: South Africa, Guatemala, Brazil and Guinea-Bissau have all experienced political turmoil and high levels of violence.† South Africa by some measures has been through a civil war. Guinea-Bissau has had a brief civil war in recent years. Guatemala has an atrocious record of repression, war and external intervention in aid of repressive regimes. Brazil has not had civil war, though it has had a period of military rule. Second, clearly countries with roughly equivalent levels of inequality in income distribution can have different outcomes in terms of homicide rates, vulnerability to *coups d'état*, or whether or not they are shredded by war. In other and very simple words, the political implications of economic inequality vary though they can often be violent.

Therefore, it is worth spending more time investigating what affects this variation. That involves asking what lies behind and generates the quantifiable observations of inequality; what are the conditions (such as rates of economic growth and forms of institutional arrangement) within which a measured expenditure, income, or wealth, distribution exists; and what mechanisms exist that counter any possible tendency for inequality to provoke conflict and vio-

---

* Székely and Hilgert (1999: 1). The problem is not confined to developing countries. One recent study showed that swapping the inequality dataset used led to dramatic changes in the ranking of OECD countries by distribution: see Brandolini and Atkinson (2001).

† Between 1997 and 2000, for example, there were an average of 23,742 homicides recorded each year in South Africa; see Barclay and Tavares (2003, Table 1.1).

lence. Questions like these return the inquiry to collective experiences of inequality, which may include but by no means have to
mean strongly perceived ethnic experiences of inequality.

Tilly's book *Durable Inequality* proposes a set of mechanisms that
work more or less everywhere to sustain over long periods of time
what he calls 'categorical inequality'.[35] This framework highlights
inequality between social pairings—citizens and non-citizens, men
and women, black and white, Anglican and Catholic in pre-emanci-
pation England, large landowners and peasants, and so on. The focus
of the book is largely on the way these kinds of categorical inequality endure in spite of their obvious unfairness. The key, for Tilly, lies
in four social mechanisms: exploitation, adaptation, emulation and
opportunity hoarding. 'Because exploitation and opportunity hoarding often involve an effective means of control over members of
excluded and subordinated categories, because emulation natural-
ises distinctions by making them ubiquitous, and because adaptation ties even exploited groups to the structure of exploitation,
most categorical inequality stays in place without sustained, overt
struggle.'[36] The fundamental mechanism is exploitation.*

In this analysis of social relations, inequality between categorical
pairings is sustained by social mechanisms: exploitation is at its
core; where there is exploitation there is typically opportunity
hoarding by one group (of access to jobs, of control of certain markets, of political position etc.); emulation spreads categorical
inequality through various branches of a society and internationally; and adaptation ensures that even the disadvantaged develop
footholds of survival and acquiescence in the system.† In this approach, exclusion is not simply a negative, an absence, but a directly relational factor that is at the same time a form of inclusion in
a given social system.‡ Where the state takes a direct interest in creating and supporting categorical inequality, as is common, it adds a
coercive element that further fixes the paired inequality. Redressing
this inequality is only possible through sustained political action

---

* Tilly (1999: 10) defines exploitation as a mechanism that operates 'when powerful, connected people command resources from which they draw significantly
increased returns by coordinating the effort of outsiders whom they exclude from
the full value added by that effort.'

† Wright (1999) characterises Tilly's theory of durable inequality as, first, essentially
a functionalist theory (organised around the primacy of a problem-in-need-of-a-
solution mechanism) and, second, far closer to Marxist theory than Tilly's own
claim of providing a bridge between Marx and Weber.

‡ This echoes Joan Robinson's (1962) comment that it is better to be exploited than
not to be exploited at all.

and in circumstances where the benefits accruing to the beneficiaries from exploitation and/or opportunity hoarding fade and the
costs of maintaining the system rise. Examples include the rising
cost of discrimination against British Roman Catholics during
international wars, when legal restrictions prevented the army from
recruiting Irish Catholic soldiers; and the rising cost to South African capitalists of apartheid. For the most part, the 'histories of land-
lord-tenant relations, religious inequalities, and social movements
indicate...that organisers generally have a difficult time stimulating
shared awareness of oppression and determination to resist, that
even with intense organising efforts they fail except in special structural circumstances.'[37]

Albert Hirschman traced some similar ideas about the conditions in which inequality might be challenged but did so within the
context of economic and social change, or development. Hirschman's reflections of the workings of a 'tunnel effect' were prompted
specifically by two episodes of violent political conflict in the late
1960s and early 1970s: the Biafra war in Nigeria and the civil war in
Pakistan leading to the independence of Bangladesh.* Observing
that both these 'development disasters' followed periods of developmental surges rather than the protracted stagnation so commonly associated nowadays with civil wars, Hirschman argued for
the existence of a social mechanism that could suppress relative
deprivation, the frustration-aggression nexus, or, more plainly, envy.
As development proceeded, some people's fortunes improved while
others were left behind, and thus inequality increased. But the
expectations of those left behind might be raised rather than overwhelmed by bitterness, and thus there might well be a tolerance for
inequality. Greater inequality gave information about social and
economic change that could be interpreted as a signal of hope even
for those not immediately benefiting from development. However,
this tunnel effect must be qualified. First, it would not last indefinitely. Second, the suspension of envy would be unlikely to operate
where the opportunities provided by economic development were,
or were believed to be, monopolised by certain groups.† Third, bene-

---

* The image of the tunnel comes from Hirschman's analogy with a tunnel traffic
  jam, legally confined to one lane but initially stirred into hope by movement in the
  other lane, while eventually if the logjam only seemed to be clearing in one lane
  some drivers would illegally cross into that lane.
† 'If in segmented societies, economic advance becomes identified with one particular ethnic or language group or with the members of one particular religion or
  region, then those who are left out and behind are unlikely to experience the tun-

ficiaries of change are not always complacent about inequality: if the tunnel effect wore off and sections of the middle classes supported a redistributive agenda, this might provide the classic conditions of revolutionary coalition building.*

As with ethnicity, so again a brief discussion of inequality and conflict shows how isolating one explanatory factor and trying to foist on it a law of empirical regularity is a non-starter. But also as with ethnicity, inequality is still relevant to an explanation of violent conflict. Its role is not easily predictable and only works through the specific political, institutional and economic relationships that lie behind somewhat blurry measures of distribution. Furthermore, though, there are clues to an explanation of at least some experiences of violent conflict to be found in linking the subjects of this and the previous sub-section. Arguably, sustained and substantial inequality requires a frame of collective identity—not necessarily religious or ethnic but possibly including these formats.

Resource scarcity

The idea that conflict has environmental sources is also an old and emotive idea. Just as with other explanations of conflict that give an unwarranted priority to a particular variable, there are all manner of empirical problems—not least with the evidence for phenomena like desertification or the scientific basis for concepts like the 'carrying capacity' of land. In conjuring up projections into the future, the soothsayers of environmental conflict sometimes explicitly invoke the ideas of Thomas Malthus. Indeed, prophets of environmental clashes tend to draw on the combined (if misinterpreted) inspirations of Malthus and Hobbes. 'It is Thomas Malthus, the philosopher of demographic doomsday, who is now the prophet of West Africa's future. And West Africa's future, eventually, will also be that of most of the rest of the world,' wrote Kaplan.[38]

As Kaplan put it: 'One must understand environmental scarcity, cultural and racial clash, geographic destiny and the transformation of war. The order in which I have named these is not accidental. Each concept except the first relies partly on the one or ones

---

nel effect: they will be convinced almost from the start of the process that the advancing group is achieving an unfair exploitative advantage over them' (Hirschman, 1981: 49).

* See also Wolf (1969) on the need—for peasant revolutions—for a combination of a peasantry politically mobilised and the mobilising power of small outside groups.

before it...' This set-up, in which there may be multiple causes of conflict but they begin with the environment, is common to a number of authors and draws, above all, on the arguments of Homer-Dixon, which are organised in a framework that begins with this assumption about the environment as *ur*-cause. The then German environment minister, Angela Merkel, claimed that 'the greenhouse effect, desertification and increasing scarcity of water are likely to cause violent conflicts.'[39] Two things are conflated here—environmental degradation and environmental scarcity—which are treated by many researchers as distinct. There is also a focus on water, which is a particular source of fevered projections. US intelligence services reportedly estimated in the mid-1980s that there were at least ten places in the world where war might break out over dwindling shared water.[40] Those who emphasise water scarcity and point to the fact that many societies depend for freshwater on flows that pass through, and so under control of, neighbouring countries have coined the phrase 'water wars' to highlight this particular variant on the larger theme of the 'greenwar thesis'.

Critics have pointed out a number of flaws in the empirical basis for explanations of a link from environmental scarcity/degradation to violent conflict within or between countries. These flaws range from the weak evidence on degradation to what one critic calls the use of the future as evidence, or the effort to convince by emphasising the *potential* for conflict, even where there is little or no evidence that water scarcity or environmental degradation has in the past been the principal cause of conflicts.* Others point out

---

* Gleditsch (1998) lists nine weaknesses in Homer-Dixon's empirical analysis: (1) the confusion of scarcity and degradation; (2) the use of vague definitions whose polemical value outstrips their social science content—e.g. the term 'environmental security' is as vague as 'sustainable development'; (3) overlooking important variables, or at least unaccountably relegating to the sidelines variables such as economic, cultural and political factors; (4) designing untestable and, therefore, unfalsifiable models, that is, putting together unwieldy models whose interactions are too complex and whose variables are often too imprecise to allow for statistical testing; (5) the lack of a control group—thus, Homer-Dixon and associates pick out case studies where there has been conflict and look for environmental correlates but do not examine non-conflict cases where the same environmental factors might be at work; (6) reverse causality, whereby people confuse the effect of conflict on the environment with environmental causes of conflict; (7) using the future as evidence; (8) confusing inter-state and intra-state conflicts and using analyses developed for one type of conflict to account for and predict conflict in the other type, without questioning the validity of doing so; and (9) the lack of specification of or distinction between levels of analysis, such as systemic, national, dyadic etc.

that emphasising water scarcity in a particular location—e.g. the Middle East—ignores 'virtual water', i.e. the access to water embodied in imports of goods produced elsewhere with water as a major input.

Conflict between Israel and Palestine is a good example. Israeli policy in particular targets coercion against Palestinian resources (though as well as natural resources like water and land this includes control of labour as well). Water is a particularly scarce and critical resource throughout the region. The Israeli Prime Minister Levi Eshkol acknowledged this in 1967, before the Six Day War, saying water was 'a question of survival for Israel' and that Israel would therefore 'use all means necessary to secure that the water continues to flow'. Yet to conflate this significance of water, and its role in conflict, with the cause of conflict is wrong. During violent conflicts there is typically wrangling over resources—it is part of economic warfare. But there is little support in the literature on water in the Middle East for the argument that water has been a leading cause of political conflict.*

Scarcity in the form of famine is also sometimes regarded as a source of violent conflict: however, most of the literature on famines acknowledges that famines are more often a consequence than a cause of warfare. Most famines in Africa during the twentieth century, for example, were the direct or indirect product of political conflict and war. Similarly, there is no clear reason why environmental degradation has to lead to violent conflict: degradation has sparked social and technical innovation and adaptive responses as much as conflict, if not more. Thus environmental scarcity and/or degradation are at the very most likely to be secondary causes of violent conflict.

Some work on land scarcity in Rwanda before the 1994 genocide illustrates this secondary role. Catherine André and Jean-Philippe Platteau collected information in the early 1990s on the pressure of rising population on land allocation and use and on social tensions related to this pressure.[41] They argue change took place at a breakneck pace that paved the way for later violence. There were ten-

---

* Zeitoun (2004), for example, identifies a conflict/cooperation paradox in Israel-Palestine relations, in that there is both conflict, sometimes violent (but no water war), and cooperation over water; he argues that the complexity of the issue is what pushes many people by default into polarised dramatisations of hydro-conflict. Similarly, Allan (2002) argues that although the Middle East effectively ran out of water resources to meet its strategic needs in 1970, 'international relations over water have, if anything, become less tense since then' (p. 255).

sions within families over land allocation. There were legal conflicts. And an informal land market developed in spite of the national land law that forbade such market transactions: people who could not survive on tiny plots sold or rented out to those with the where-withal to accumulate larger holdings. They also emphasise that the response to absorb population growth was constrained by policy choices, given a history of encouraging extensive expansion rather than agricultural intensification. André and Platteau are adamant that extreme scarcity of land and lack of non-agricultural employ-ment resources did not cause the civil war, which was triggered off by macro-political forces cynically playing upon ethnic divisions to maintain power. 'Yet, there can be no doubt that the strained situa-tion engendered by economic scarcities goes a long way towards explaining why violence spread so quickly and so devastatingly...'

Institutions incapable of containing conflict, combined with ac-cumulating localised and highly personal rivalries and envies, echo René Girard's theory of human violence. For Girard, an object itself and its scarcity or plenitude is not a cause of conflict: to argue this is a romantic delusion. Rather, an object can only become party to a violent conflict to the extent that it is a product of the relations between two individuals (or groups). Relations between people are typically driven by the mechanism of mimesis. Mimetic rivalry arises because one person, in pursuit of identification with the chosen model, wants not just to be like that model but also to appropriate the model's attributes and, then, possessions. The model will over time be alert to this and erect protective boundaries. Violence natu-rally resolves this tension, unless contained by institutional mecha-nisms. For Girard, then, scarcity or degradation of the object in question is almost neither here nor there.[42]

Distinguishing between divisible (or reproducible) goods and non-divisible—or between more/less goods and all/nothing goods—might refine this idea.[43] For where identification through mimesis can take place by *also having* rather than by *having instead*, by catch-ing up rather than simply by wresting from, then the scope for vio-lence presumably will lessen if not fade altogether. Nonetheless, the point is the argument that scarcity and violence are a product of social relations rather than inherent in the relative abundance of a particular good, object or resource. Barbara Ehrenreich, too, is sceptical of theories that prioritise scarcity as the source of vio-lence. Developing her argument that humans are in thrall to vio-lence not because of our ancient history as hunters but because of our primordial experience as prey, she also argues:

The...problem with the standard account is its assumption that people will not fight...unless there are vital material resources...at stake. This view slights the widespread conflicts over 'goods' which service little function except as badges of prestige and warrior prowess: scalps and skulls; severed heads, hands, penises and other portable body parts; captives for rituals of human sacrifice. Just as prehistoric humans probably killed animals for reasons other than hunger, they no doubt killed one another for purposes other than gain...[44]

The Rwanda example, particularly if seen through the prism of Girard's ideas of mimetic rivalry (and, indeed, of scapegoating), generates two factors that will tie in well with the discussion in Chapter 6. First, when the paroxysm of viciousness came in Rwanda, in 1994, it took the form of a largely ethnic genocide within the context of an ongoing civil war. Much but not all of the violence was focused on Tutsis, some of it on other Hutus, but there was a powerful element of displacement, of projecting onto the scapegoat Tutsis a pervasive collection of political and petty, localised and broader tensions. It is important not just to find objective indicators of horizontal inequality between collective identity groups but also to explore the relationship between intra-group political and material tensions and the characteristics of inter-group relationships. Second, explanations of collective violent conflict need to draw links between the social and the highly localised and interpersonal (which are also social). Private passions, envy and conflicts are a hugely important feature of all major civil wars or intra-society conflicts.[45]

Resource abundance

In the land of the wise horse-like Houyhnhnms, in *Gulliver's Travels*, there live the Yahoos, uncouth creatures that resemble human beings, except that they don't wear clothes and are more hirsute. In some fields in this country

there are certain shining stones of several colours, whereof the Yahoos are violently fond; and when part of these stones is fixed in the earth, as it sometimes happeneth, they will dig with their claws for whole days to get them out, then carry them away and hide them by heaps in their kennels...[he] further assured me, which I also observed myself, that, in the fields where the shining stones abound, the fiercest and most frequent battles are fought, occasioned by perpetual inroads on the neighbouring Yahoos.[46]

If the evidence of a causal role for resource scarcity or degradation is generally unconvincing, a rather different class of explanation for violent conflict has lately proposed that resource abundance is one of the main causal factors. The 'resource curse' argument is accepted by many people simply because of the dramatic association between countries with huge natural resource wealth and warfare. The standard examples are Angola, seen as a play-off between oil and diamonds, Sierra Leone with its timber and diamonds, and Congo with its copper, gold, coltan (columbite-tantalite) and other precious minerals.

The theory of the resource curse is often explained in terms of 'political Dutch Disease'. This is an analogy with the standard economic concept of Dutch Disease, from which not only the Netherlands but also countries such as Nigeria and Britain (with North Sea oil) are supposed to have suffered. Dutch Disease affects countries that experience a surge in earnings from enclave sectors like natural gas (the Netherlands) and oil by undermining the international competitiveness of other sectors of the economy. The transmission mechanism is exchange rate movement. A windfall of oil or gas revenue pushes up the value of a country's exchange rate relative to other countries. This makes non-oil exports more expensive internationally than previously. Persistent loss of competitiveness, combined with the relatively limited linkages from the oil sector to other economic activities, then provokes de-industrialisation. There is plenty of debate in the economic literature about this concept: some argue that de-industrialisation is caused by other, more fundamental factors, and that the Dutch Disease effect can be circumvented by effective economic policy.[47] A good example would be Venezuela from 1940 to 1975: during this period oil revenue expanded rapidly but this was combined with the encouragement of non-oil sectors and manufacturing too grew strongly. More recently there has been a change in the economic, and political, fortunes of Venezuela.* The manufacturing sector has stumbled into something of a developmental *cul-de-sac* and the political settlement has been increasingly fraught. Oil itself cannot be to blame for either trend.

* To put it differently, at least for a substantial period Venezuela managed effectively to combine a Ricardian strategy of integrating into the world economy by exploiting its comparative advantage in oil production with a Kaldorian strategy of integration through structural change and industrialisation exploiting the greater economies of scale and scope and the greater productivity gains generally available in manufacturing. For this simple distinction between strategies of international economic integration see Schwartz (1994). On the political economy of Venezuela see Di John (2004a).

The political strain of Dutch Disease is more vague and is said to work through different mechanisms. Rent windfalls from oil, gas or diamonds allow state beneficiaries to misallocate resources and to ignore political challenges or the economic challenges that historically have led to the formation of more democratically accountable states. First, energy and resources are allocated to the business of jostling for position to get hands on the rent. Second, because of oil revenue, for example, the state has little need to take seriously the task of widening the tax base. The state can fund its conceits out of oil revenue rather than sustaining itself by taxation. Yet taxation and the struggles over tax have, historically, been the key to the politics and slow formation of states. Taxation has also often been the key to conflict—both to its origin and to its funding—but in resource cursed economies conflicts and war finance tend to have more to do with contested rent. Partly because of this lack of need to cultivate a wider tax base and partly because of the enclave characteristics of the resource sector, the state also avoids having to cope with an expanding set of bureaucratic, material and political interests generated by economic activity (outside the enclave). Such states are typically rife with 'bad governance': and when they do need to raise revenue from sources other than rent they tend to tax in a predatory way. Meanwhile, the allure of rent means they are prone to political and armed challenges that, given their frail and indulgent governance, they are poorly equipped to rebut, even if they can throw substantial sums at the problem. For these reasons, resource abundant economies may be especially prone to political instability and violent conflict.

Evidence for this developmental affliction is unclear. Some researchers have found that statistically the incidence of civil war rises with a country's dependence on natural resource exports. In some versions of this research, resource abundance is taken to mean any economy whose economic activity is dominated by primary commodity exports. Other versions focus more narrowly on high value minerals and a handful of other rent-intensive primary commodities.[48] What this book has shown to be a familiar indeterminacy in this kind of statistical enquiry is a strong feature of this resource issue too. Thus one study claims that a country with a heavy mineral dependency is, other things being equal, forty-six times more likely to have a civil war than a country with no mineral exports. Yet a different survey of the evidence only comes to the conclusion that the incidence of civil wars in oil and gas exporters is not much greater at all than for other natural resource exporters.[49]

This survey, by Michael Ross, looks at different types of resource dependence and looks also at the effect of per capita income. First, without taking account of income levels and just focusing on the resource question, civil wars in the sample happen slightly less often than the average in those counties depending on oil and gas, on other minerals but excluding gemstones, on food crop exports, and on non-food agricultural exports. Second, if countries are grouped simultaneously according to resource dependence and income level, then resource dependent economies do seem to be more prone to conflict. But this is so for all types of resource concentration, including food and non-food agricultural exports. Poor countries whose economic activities are dominated by mineral exports do not seem any more prone to civil wars than non-mineral dependent, natural resource exporting poor countries. And given that poor countries tend by definition to be dominated by primary commodity production and exports (economic development basically being a process of structural change involving the rising share in economic activity of manufacturing and services and the *relative* decline of primary commodities), this then explains very little about which developing countries experience violent conflict (and when) and which do not.

Table 2 is another way to query the existence of the resource curse ailment. The table lines up a range of countries that experienced 'complex humanitarian emergencies' in the early 1990s in terms of their estimated intensity (the number of casualties) and their mineral dependence. Of these twenty-two countries only seven could be called mineral dominant economies. And though it only gives a rough guide, the table suggests the non-mineral dominant countries (especially Rwanda and Burundi) suffered higher casualty numbers than the mineral economies (with the exception of Angola).

The Angolan example makes it clear that mineral rich but generally poor economies certainly can be associated with massive destruction. Another example is Congo, which in recent years has experienced such levels of violence that it has been estimated to be the worst humanitarian destruction since the Second World War. Yet resource wealth has been less significant in other conflicts, for example in Somalia, where if anything conflict ended and a less predatory political formation emerged in the better endowed north rather than in the south, which remained in thrall to predatory competition.

Underpinning the argument that resource abundance is an ailment likely to lead to conflict is an unspoken evasion of the politi-

Table 2. WAR CASUALTIES IN HUMANITARIAN EMERGENCIES
(1992–4) IN MINERAL DOMINANT ECONOMIES AND
NON-MINERAL DOMINANT ECONOMIES

	Mineral/fuel exports, 1980 (% total exports)	Number of casualties
Mineral-dominant economies		
Angola	90+	100,000
Liberia	45	20,000–50,000
Afghanistan	40	6,000
Peru	64	3,100
Algeria	98	2,000–3,000
Iraq	98	2,000
Azerbaijan	90+	2,000–7,000
Non-mineral dominant economies		
Rwanda	4	200,000–500,000
Burundi	0	100,000
Mozambique	7	100,000
Bosnia-Herzegovina	n/a	10,000–30,000
Croatia	10	10,000
Sudan	2	6,000
Somalia	0	6,000
Tajikistan	10	4,000–30,000
Sri Lanka	15	4,000
Turkey	8	4,000
Colombia	3	3,500
South Africa	11	3,000–4,000
Georgia	n/a	2,000
Guatemala	6	2,000
Myanmar	11	2,000

Source: Di John (2002).

cal realities in countries with mineral wealth. The argument assumes away society in order to trace a restricted (and by itself very plausible) logic. Further, the resource curse argument assumes simply that the state, or some private sector cronies, has been assigned property rights or ownership over income streams from mineral deposits, rather than exploring how rights are created and assigned.* And the state is assumed to be a simple 'thing', a monolith with self-serving interests. States do not spring into life fully constituted, predatory or otherwise, but emerge and change and are sites of conflict between multiple interests. What matters, then, is how this

* I am indebted to Jonathan Di John for this point.

Resource abundance 123

conflict develops at different stages and in different places and which set(s) of interests get the upper hand over the state.

The management of mineral wealth and exports, even in enclave production, creates administrative bodies and material (and political) interests. Building military forces similarly produces new interest groups—and it is far from obvious either that the military fuses seamlessly with the state or that the military is itself an internally consistent body of interests. The same is true of the sets of interests that build up around the interaction with foreign donors.*

So, to assume that all countries whose economies are structurally dominated at a given point in time by mineral exports are likely to follow identical paths of political development and violent conflict seems to miss the point about the organisation of power and the legitimation of property rights and other institutions.† War can be both a product of challenges to legitimacy and a means of pursuit of legitimacy. Tyrants, Plato wrote, are 'always stirring up some war or other, in order that people may require a leader'.‡ As Di John puts it: 'It is not clear, *a priori*, why mineral-dominant economies generate a more unjust or illegitimate distribution of rights and income than non-mineral dominant economies.'[50]

Sierra Leone illustrates this argument, that there is nothing innate in natural resource plenitude that imposes an ineluctable logic of violence. Rather than politics and violent conflict unfolding within the controlling context of resources, resources came to play a prominent role in the 1991–2002 war in Sierra Leone in and because of the context of the country's political and economic history. The particular history of post-independence Sierra Leone destroyed

* Indeed, when donors speak of the importance of 'national ownership' of aid and policies to the effectiveness of that aid and those policies, typically they mean ownership and power of particular sections of the state and their allies outside formal state structures; for some donors this basically means the Ministry of Finance but for others it can involve a broader set of interests.
† The resource curse argument cannot explain, for example, why the Sudanese government has followed the logic of a nationalist-religious ideology to the point where this has undermined the prospects for exploiting oil rent. As William Reno puts it: 'Khartoum's rulers fail to make the most basic programmatic and ideological compromises and equivocations grasped by rulers of oil rich Angola, Uzbekistan, Kazakhstan and elsewhere to appease foreign business partners and officials in powerful states', in 'Resources and the Future of Violent Conflict in Sierra Leone' (2002).
‡ This is a version of the old saw that nothing unites people like a war against a common enemy. It is also possibly a partial explanation of the enthusiasm of George W. Bush for war against Iraq, given the questionable legitimacy achieved in the election results of 2000. See also Harvey (2003: 12–16).

other, non-mineral, economic activities, thereby increasing the relative value of natural resources and shunting these resources closer
to the heart of Sierra Leone's politics.

The interaction in Sierra Leone of youth politics, economic policy and performance, and political strategies by a group of leaders
increasingly drawn to the control of diamond markets helped produce the conditions for warfare.* But migrants to the diamond districts that financed war were not just 'feckless proto-criminals in
search of quick wealth...these footloose youths are simply trying to
find waged work, where to remain in a rural community risks the
arbitrary labour demands of the chiefly classes.'[51] Meanwhile, there
were many other factors involved, not least the role of an IMF macroeconomic stabilisation package, which included a sharp currency
devaluation combined with capital account liberalisation. Not sur-
prisingly, this allowed and encouraged a sudden transfer of capital
savings out of the country that further weakened the economy and
radically shifted the relative power of different material interest
groups in the country.[52]

Homo economicus goes to war

'About these matters there is no scientific basis on which to form any calcu-
lable probability whatever. We simply do not know!' (J. M. Keynes, in 1937,
commenting on the prospects for a European war)[53]

The two contrasting arguments about resources and conflict, one
about scarcity and the other about abundance, capture two basic
ideas about the material dimensions of what drives political violence and conflict. One stresses desperation and inequity; the other
calculation and opportunity. In recent years the debate on causes
of war was channelled towards a focus on these two as opposites
defining the whole of war: greed versus grievance. It was proposed
that one of these apparently neatly discrete drives must account
wholly for the incidence of war. This distinction, between greed or
grievance, loot or justice, emerged out of neo-classical economic
theories and predictive models of violent conflict. And this thinking, in turn, is representative of a tremendously influential trend in

---

* On the complex history of youth politics in Sierra Leone see Abdullah and Muana
(1998). The tensions within youth groups—e.g. between overtly political youth
groups and frequently violent gangs—mirror those in South African townships
and elsewhere: for the history of Johannesburg gangs and youth politics see Glaser
(2000).

the social sciences—what some have called 'economics imperialism', in which a certain brand of economic theory colonises other
social sciences. *Economic Imperialism*

— *The theory*

Economics imperialism represents for supporters and critics alike
the confidence among neo-classical economists in their ability to
explain an increasingly wide range of social experiences in terms of
the axioms and logic of this form of economics. In other words,
with the assumption of methodological individualism, i.e. that the
individual is the analytical starting point for all social behaviour
and, therefore, explanation, and that of rational choice in service
of maximising individual self-interest (utility, profit), it might be
possible to explain clearly virtually everything that otherwise is inar-
ticulately garbled in the efforts of historians, sociologists, political
theorists, non-neo-classical economists (often called heterodox economists) and so on. Marriage, crime, institutional developments,
racially discriminatory labour market practices, how many children
people have, membership of community associations and so on:
these things may be explained not partially but completely as responses to signals from often imperfect markets. Neo-classical economics used to be criticised because it could not capture in its models
the reality of politics and power. However, nowadays neo-classical
economists claim the discipline can in fact account for power: that
rather than only focusing on peaceful exchange it can explain 'the
dark side of the force'.

   The most elegant example of this thinking as it applies to violent
conflict is the theoretical work of Jack Hirshleifer, whose tongue is
only partly in cheek when he writes of the intellectual continent of
violence and conflict on which economists have alighted relatively
recently:

As we come to explore this continent, economists will encounter a number
of native tribes—historians, sociologists, psychologists, philosophers etc.—
who, in their various intellectually primitive ways, have preceded us in
reconnoitering the dark side of human activity. Once we economists get
involved, quite properly we'll of course be brushing aside these a-theoreti-
cal aborigines.[54]

The footnote to this quote explains: 'When these researchers do
good work, they're doing economics!' Doing economics involves
starting by recognising that people face a choice between producing and appropriating. If the opportunity cost of appropriative

activity (the value of what is foregone by not appropriating) is low then violence will ensue; put differently, actors choose conflict where this is more profitable at the margin than exchange. Others argue, similarly, that if the payoff to conflict outweighs the calculated risk then more time will be allocated to war.*

What matters then is the particular combination of factors that add up to make for a profitable or utility maximising conflict (at least, those that add up to make an expectation based on available information that conflict will maximise individual self-interest for enough people). There are two obvious circumstances that might tip the balance in favour of conflict: one is poverty and the other is the lure of a windfall profit, the conflict dividend. The poor are no more or less inherently prone to violence than anyone else. However, the poor choose violence more often than the better off because they have a comparative advantage in violence. This is what they do most efficiently, i.e. at least cost, because the opportunity cost of violence is relatively low. Poor people do not forego much by selecting violence, precisely because there is little else on offer for them anyway. So, where there are lots of poor people with few opportunities for peaceable employment there is a greater likelihood that they will make for an aggregate choice of collective violence. At least, there is a greater likelihood that a conflict entrepreneur (this is a widespread phrase whose usage is far from restricted to economists) will be able to hire in a free labour market sufficient war employees to produce a competitive war effort. There is an interesting assumption in this idea, but one that is generally not made explicit. Given that war often involves not only killing and maiming but being killed or maimed, one thing rather possibly foregone in war is life. Thus it must be assumed that poverty is so gruelling that the opportunity cost of being killed is very low. The poor engage in war because life is cheap.†

---

* For a fuller discussion of neo-classical economic theories of war see Cramer (2002).

† One indicator of the value put on life might be suicide statistics. A very rough idea may be gleaned from data discussed in WHO (2003). Although this does not disaggregate within countries, the report's statistical annex shows that suicide rates (per 100,000 of the population) are lower in low and middle income African societies (6.7 per 100,000) than the world average of 14.5; that in the Americas region the rate of 10.6 in high income countries is higher than in low and middle income countries (6.3); that the most suicide intensive regions are Europe and the Western Pacific but that the lowest recorded suicide rates are in the Eastern Mediterranean region. In short, the data show marked differences across regions and no obvious pattern pinning suicide on the poorest countries where economic opportunities are fewer.

If there is little to lose by choosing violence, then there must also be some incentive to choose violence. This too is simply a matter of economic gain. Economic gain may be interpreted rather differently in neo-classical economic models of war, according to how and at what stage issues of collective action—the fact that war is a group activity—come into theoretical play. In some models collective or social behaviour comes in right at the start. Hirshleifer, for example, draws on the 'bioeconomics' that, he argues, is the missing link that completes economic theory.[55] This is a form of social Darwinism that suggests humans have an 'affiliative instinct' whose origin lies in kinship and ethnicity but that is so entrenched as a hereditary trait that it will latch onto the most vague and unpromising programmes of solidarity, including ideology. The roots of this affiliative instinct, which is inseparable from hostility to other groups (xenophobia), lie in individual self-preservation and the essentially economic business of ensuring reproductive success. In other models describing why people go to war economic gain is a rather more immediate concern that solves the collective action problem. In these versions, instant taxation (loot) ensures that people will engage in collective action in spite of the powerful individual impulses and thought processes that run counter to any affiliative instinct. Here it is presumed that individuals will not want to engage in a risky activity that will at best generate an outcome (produce a good) from which other individuals cannot be excluded even if they do not participate in its production or pay for its delivery. In other words, justice and equality and a better life are public goods and the selfish gene encourages us to be free riders, to sit back and enjoy these without contributing to their availability, if we can help it. At the same time, it is possible that one mechanism of affiliative bonding can help resolve this collective action problem (which is also a problem of the cost of coordinating a rebellion). This mechanism is ethnicity, commonly captured in the ethno-linguistic fractionalisation index (ELF) introduced earlier in the chapter.

That is the theory, stripped of nuance. The toolbox of neo-classical economics makes it possible to construct more sophisticated models: for example, identifying the conditions affecting the slope and shape of the 'conflict success function' that may be plotted in a diagram and mapping the effect of increasing returns to scale in conflict. 'Mutually inconsistent opportunity sets' between two groups, or players, may be mapped according to the degree of edge that one player might have, for example on account of being the incumbent in power, to predict the influences on behavioural decisions.

Nonetheless, the core theoretical approach remains the same, resting on the idea that when individuals make rational choices they do
so as people who are not merely virtuous creatures of liberalism but
perfectly capable of brutishness, coercion, exploitation and violence.

   It is a theory that holds considerable appeal for many people but
one that equally provokes revulsion in others. It appeals because it
appears to offer a proper theory rather than just a gut feeling. It
seems to eschew a simple identification of one variable—inequality,
say—in favour of a set of factors and conditions whose delicate
interaction will affect whether or not a war actually takes place. It is
a theory that has helped analysts of conflict in developing countries
escape from the mesmerising hold of Cold War rivalry, which had
encouraged in many people a rather trite understanding of such
conflicts. And it is an unsqueamish theory: it tries to capture the
greed and the role of the resources that rather obviously play a central role in many conflicts. It would be even more appealing, perhaps, if there were good empirical evidence supporting its claims.

   Building an empirical model of the economic rationale that adds
up to war—putting together a model that can test the theory against
reality—is extremely difficult. As in many examples of social science exploration, it is often not possible directly to measure or
quantify a factor identified in a theory as significant. If the theory
predicts, say, that greed (more precisely, the opportunities for
indulging greed) is more important than grievance in causing war,
the problem is how to test this idea. A common approach is to try to
quantify such possibly causal factors, to enable statistical analysis of
a collection of observations across a large and hopefully representative sample of, in this case, wars. Quantifying grievance, or greed,
or in a slightly more refined example quantifying the coordination
costs of rebellion, cannot be done directly. Therefore, modellers
have to find quantifiable proxies, indirect measures to stand in for
the actual theoretical postulate. Data can then be amassed on these
quantifiable variables across the sample and some results or findings produced. If there are weaknesses in the use of proxy variables
and if there is convincing evidence of wars developing according to
rather different influences from those predicted in the model,
then the models are unreliable guides to reality and policy.

   Models of civil war built with the tools of neo-classical economic
analysis and with the materials of rational choice assumptions are,
arguably, shambolic. First, the proxies have only a tenuous link to
the theoretical variables they are meant to stand for and, as a result,
may equally well represent rather different factors and explana-

tions. Second, there is good evidence that the genuine problems identified in these models, particularly the collective action problems, are resolved in ways that not only lie beyond the models but actually undermine their foundations. Third, pretensions of predictive precision in these models are misleading: there are no convincing statistical regularities produced in these models.

— Greed versus grievance?

Among the most intriguing and pioneering of these models are those developed by Paul Collier. Collier has generated a succession of variations on the theme, and overall the models describe a consistent analytical picture.[56] The most widely digested version is the greed versus grievance model of civil war, built with three empirical proxies for greed and four for grievance and then tested against available data for a sample of countries.[57] Greed may be reflected in the following variables: the dependence of the economy on primary commodity exports (the ratio of primary commodity export revenue to total GDP); the proportion of young males in the total population; and average years of schooling. The productive labour force of civil war is provided mainly by young men. Where there is a preponderance of young men in a society, where these young men have few opportunities for employment (reflected then in a low average number of years of schooling, since it is thought that education is correlated with employment opportunities), and where there are plenty of opportunities for instant gratification or economic gain by looting primary commodities (loot being the poor man's rent), then the opportunity is ripe for the exercise of the greed motive. Alternatively, according to the model and its rationale, perhaps grievance drives civil war. If so, then there must be good proxies for this too. Grievances might well increase if the economy is stagnant and this is reflected in the variable of the growth rate in the five years prior to the outbreak of civil wars. Next, repression might be measured through, for example, indices of civil rights. A further presumed source of grievance that could provoke war is inequality, quantified in the Gini coefficient. Finally on this side of the ledger of motives, there may be ethnic grievances or animosity, whose social complexity may be snared in the ELF variable. In an earlier model, ELF measured more explicitly the coordination costs of rebellion—on the assumption that if a group of conflict entrepreneurs wished to launch a rebellion they would stand a greater chance of success if they would not face too complex a challenge of mobilising people (the challenge is simplified where a large enough group share ethnic loyalty and speak the same language).*

When the data were collected for these variables, the contrasting hypotheses could be tested. The tests suggested that the statistical incidence of civil war was significantly higher not in those countries characterised by obvious evidence of bitter grievance but in those where greed could let rip more efficiently, i.e. where the opportunity cost of civil war was minimal. The explanation for the findings is exactly in line with the neo-classical theory already sketched. Grievances are real enough, but they cannot produce sufficient violence to clear the market for conflict. Conflict might succeed in producing public goods such as equality, stability, general economic growth and so on, but because these are non-excludable there is every incentive to free ride on the violence of others;† if enough people think like this, conflict will not reach a scale sufficient to produce war or at any rate sufficient to produce a successful rebellion. Yet the logic of greed overcomes this market imperfection and, therefore, does produce enough conflict if the opportunities are there. There is no need to be concerned by the properties of public goods where individuals can reap a private return to their investment in violence. Further, other obstacles to conflict are overcome. For example, there is no particular need to trust the rhetorical promises of leaders that they will deliver a bright new dawn of equal land and income distribution, fair and democratic government, human rights guarantees and so on: instead individuals can do their own instant redistribution and protect their own security and interests by engaging in violence, wartime rape and looting.

---

* The earlier model expressed the likelihood of civil war thus: $U_w = \{p(D).T; M; C\}$. This means that the utility of rebellion (U_w) is a function of the right-hand side variables, namely: p, the probability of victory; D, potential defence spending by the government; T, the windfall gain upon victory; M, the expected duration of the conflict; and C, the coordination costs of rebellion. This cost-benefit analysis may be intuitively performed by would-be rebels—for example by Nelson Mandela and the ANC leadership agonising over whether or not to move towards armed struggle against apartheid in South Africa. But the analysis may be done retrospectively with some precision, perhaps. Nonetheless, variables like potential defence expenditure and the coordination costs of rebellion are impossible to quantify directly, so they require proxy variables like the ethno-linguistic fractionalisation index for coordination costs or, in this model, inequality as one of the proxies for potential defence spending, given the assumption that where inequality is high there will be an élite willing to be taxed to the hilt to fund a temporary military effort designed to protect the *status quo*. Collier and Hoeffler (1996).

† Enjoyment of a public good (cleaner air, defence, street lighting etc.) cannot be exclusive to an individual.

In *The Periodic Table* Primo Levi finds in one of his tales:

...that one must distrust the almost-the-same...the practically identical, the approximate, the or-even, all surrogates, and all patchwork. The differences can be small, but they can lead to radically different consequences, like a railroad's switch points; the chemist's trade consists in good part in being aware of these differences, knowing them close up, and foreseeing their effects. And not only the chemist's trade.[58]

When the models of civil war are subjected to closer inspection, Levi's advice seems salutary. The use of empirical surrogates for theoretical hunches is patchwork through and through. Thus, it is not clear that the proxy is capturing the thing it is meant to stand for in the abstract model. For example, preponderance in exports of primary commodities might indicate the availability of lootable goods and so make violence more profitable at the margin than the dreary grind of underemployment and poverty. But in doing this it might just as well be a proxy for failed policy, missing economic dynamism, a probable shortage of consumer goods and imports and widespread grievance or dissatisfaction with this predicament. Similarly, a low average for years of schooling might represent the lack of decent opportunities for (non-conflictual) gainful employment and therefore reveal a low opportunity cost of conflict: however, it might just as well reflect or be directly a source of social anger.* Each proxy used in these models is strapped to the underlying theory by assumptions and logic that are questionable on both logical and empirical grounds.

— *Collective action*

Neo-classical economic theories of violent conflict make a serious attempt to take account of the collective action and mobilisation problems that are a feature of all group endeavours such as warfare. Arguably, though, these theories and their empirical models do not give a good account at all of how these problems are addressed in particular places at particular times. The models have very little to do with the behaviour, for example, of the *kapetanios* and their followers in the mountains of Greece during the Second World War

---

* As Stewart (2000) argues, it is not just the quantity of education that matters to socially conflictual outcomes but its distribution given categorical inequalities drawn up along lines of collective identities; thus 'unequal educational access was prevalent from colonial times in Rwanda, Burundi, and until the Khmer revolution, in Cambodia. In post-colonial Burundi there were deliberate attempts to limit educational access by the Hutu, while educated Hutu were targeted for killing in the 1970s.' (p. 9)

and the Greek civil war that followed. There were some incidents of looting but hardly large scale looting of high value commodities or entrepreneurial management of rent-intensive natural resources. This was not the criminal gang-like organisation suggested in neo-classical theories of civil war. Nor was the life in the mountains a particularly superior alternative to agricultural or urban opportunities, except perhaps on grounds that surpass the narrowly economic, grounds like excitement, freedom from traditional drudgery and gerontocracy, and idealism. Similarly, the models look gawky when put aside the reality of the Korean War. The lives of the Korean guerrillas living underground and in mountain caves offered precious little scope for economic advancement in the short run and were extremely harsh, even before the US-led UN force bombed dams that were the basis of irrigation systems sustaining the rice fields basic to peasant subsistence, and before the US mass bombing of much of the country.[59] Meanwhile, the limited available evidence from Lebanon and Palestine suggests that young terrorists (or guerrillas) and suicide bombers do not conform to the idea of the comparative advantage in violence among the poor and ill educated. Rather, this evidence suggests that these young men (typically) are not the poorest or worst educated. One study conducted in Palestine of the volunteers for suicide bombings claims, 'None of them were uneducated, desperately poor, simple minded or depressed. Many were middle class and, unless they were fugitives, held paying jobs. More than half of them were refugees from what is now Israel. Two were the sons of millionaires.'[60]

To obtain much information on the organisation of militias and rebel organisations, or on the lives of their fighters and workers, is often rather difficult. But the research on years of violent conflict in Colombia shows how badly these neo-classical economic models can fit reality.* For the organisation and behaviour of rebel groups, especially the Fuerzas Armadas Revolucionarias de Colombia (FARC), shows that neat economic motives cannot explain the membership and sustainability of these organisations. Collective action and principal-agent challenges are not resolved simply by allowing individuals to loot. Nor is there an ethnic or religious division that determines individuals' collective behaviour. For a young man from the countryside, with few employment opportunities, joining the FARC is not a straightforward labour market substitute for farming or agricultural wage labour. The FARC does not pay its soldiers or

---

* This material on Colombia draws heavily on Francisco Gutiérrez Sanín (2003).

cadres and they are explicitly forbidden to take booty from their attacks. Yet most recruitment is reportedly voluntary and there is little defection to the paramilitary groups that do pay their troops. Meanwhile, the time horizon of the FARC's programme for social change is extremely long—there is no promise to recruits of imminent gratification of material or ideological goals. And life for the FARC recruit is harsh: an onerous moral code prevails, family ties are cut, and the high personal risks involved in membership are reflected in a poor statistical record in military encounters with government forces and anti-rebel paramilitaries. Bureaucratic regulation appears to prevail over individual interests and this organisational relationship is sustained by strong normative controls.

Without a doubt there are material, economic factors at the core of the history of the FARC, its organisational development and expansion and its recent activities, which rather obviously depend on the management of commodity markets, chiefly illegal markets like coca cultivation and cocaine production and export. The FARC is obviously criminal in another way, specialising in kidnap extortion. Colombia accounts for more than half of the kidnappings in the world each year, and the FARC is the sector leader in this activity. The transformation of the FARC from a group pursuing something of a fantasy war, what Gutiérrez Sanín calls guerrillas without war, to a group involved in an enduring war owes a lot to changes in the production structure of the Colombian countryside that included a decline in the relative price of coffee and the development of the coca sector. However, this does not fully account for the change (the organisational take-off of the FARC), or indeed for the origins of the organisation. In other words, with a strictly and neo-classical individualist economic explanation a number of puzzles remain: why the FARC began and how it scaled up, why people join, and how it manages to remain competitive vis-à-vis other groups in Colombia. The answer has to be that the material cannot be hived off surgically from historical experience, powerful norms and ideas. Further, the answer has to focus on a mixture of organisational and recruitment devices and of individual motives, a mixture, indeed, of motives within individuals and a combination of individual motives with historical causes.*

* Moreover, where the neo-classical economic explanation proposes a Ricardian idea that the poor have a comparative advantage in violence the Colombian experience suggests that more Kaldorian factors like learning-by-doing in violent 'firms' account for increasing returns to scale and for the longevity and success of groups like the FARC. Very similar conclusions arise from a study of the 'puzzle' of collec-

— Either/or?

Finally, there are two further weaknesses in the neo-classical eco-nomic explanations of contemporary violent conflicts: one is con-ceptual and the other empirical. Conceptually, some of these explanations turn on a sharp distinction between greed and griev-ance. Proponents of this perspective might protest that this distinc-tion was an accident of an effort to persuade and popularise and that the models are usually rather subtler than this. They have a point. But this crude distinction does capture a more general fail-ing of analytical frameworks that separate out factors as discrete that in fact are not independent of one another. So it does make sense to focus briefly on the greed versus grievance distinction. First, there may be a marriage of convenience in war between motiva-tions of greed and of grievance. While some leaders and soldiers may be essentially greedy, their prospects for satisfying greed de-pend on the participation of many others driven by grievance, resentment and rage or desperation. Second, grievance may be at the origin of many people's interest in fighting a war but then may elide with greed as opportunities become available. Third, greed and grievance may be internally related, inseparable motivations. Greed may in other words be a product of grievance and might not exist without that grievance. And the grievance, in turn, is likely to be relational and rooted, for example, in envy or in a Girardian mimetic rivalry. The psychoanalyst Melanie Klein, for example, in her essay *Envy and Gratitude*, made exactly this argument that greed and grievance are inextricably linked.[61] If there is anything to this or the previous two points, then it is absurd to try to prise apart moti-ves like this, set them up as opposites and then choose between them to point to the exclusive or dominant determinant of civil war.

The empirical point is that, however elegant the theory may be, it remains speculative until proven realistic; yet the statistical models have not generated convincing regularities. As with the other explanations of conflict discussed earlier in this chapter, there are contested findings, problems with reliability of data for the vari-ables, suspicions of selection bias in the 'representative' samples to which the statistical tests are applied, and problems with the cate-gorisation on which these samples are constructed. Even without

---

tive insurgent action in El Salvador during the civil war, where voluntary support for the rebels was substantial even though the costs were high and the apparent benefits (especially selective benefits to participants, not liable to free riding by others) were very low. See E. J. Wood (2003).

all the critical discussion above, it would be hard to trust in reported findings when, as Chapter 2 showed, fairly minor adjustments in the coding rules for inclusion in the sample of 'civil wars'
can have quite dramatic effects on statistical results. The findings of
the models are sensitive not just to which countries are included in
the samples but to the variables used in the model. For both reasons, Fearon and Laitin's investigation, for example, produces results very much at odds with Collier's. Their results suggest that
primary commodity dependence does not predict (or, more accurately, post-dict) the incidence of civil war. The modelling and statistical techniques applied in Collier's models, probit and tobit
analyses, are particularly prone to selection bias, that is, to results
being driven by the sample of countries thrown into the statistical
pot in the first place. (And it is impossible to tell much about the
degree of significance of correlations in these tests of association
between the independent variables and a categorical yes/no dependent variable.) Thus the claim to predictive precision is spuri-
ous. Looked at differently, if the aim is retrospectively to predict
civil wars among the overall sample the model gets roughly half of
the twenty-seven countries that actually had civil wars right and half
wrong—like tossing a coin. Further, it is worth asking how legitimate it is in this kind of exercise to load the sample with relatively
rich countries with a long history of having earlier worked through
civil wars, institutional change, the establishment of capitalism and
prolonged economic growth and structural change. It is not
entirely clear how fair it is to include in a sample trying to predict
civil war and its absence between 1960 and 1992 countries such as:
Australia, Austria, Britain, Canada, Denmark, Finland, France, Germany, Iceland, Ireland, Italy, Japan, Malta, the Netherlands, New
Zealand, Norway, Spain, Sweden, Switzerland and the USA (twenty
of the total sample of 98—more than a fifth of the sample—are
OECD countries). The dice are loaded.

Conclusion

In snatching at some apparently obvious feature of at least some
wars, the explanations discussed in this chapter fall into a number
of conceptual and empirical fallacies when generalising about the
causes of violent conflict. It is particularly clear that the quest for
statistical event regularities, even with the proviso of probabilistic
significance, is misguided. This suggests, first and very simply, that
any explanation of war must acknowledge the diversity of violent

conflict: the diversity of its causes and motivations and the diversity
of its conduct and organisation. Perhaps there can be no theory of
war. Perhaps, though, it is still worthwhile trying to suggest theoretical explanations but only if these take a different form. The expectations of theory may have to be scaled back to match the diversity
of conflict and the likelihood that there are *no* clear event regularities. This would also mean rejecting the standard methods of statistical comparison, in favour of a gradual accumulation of more pared
down but detailed sets of comparisons and contrasts. The purpose
of a different methodology would still be to search for an explanation rather than an agglomeration of unrelated incidents rich in
detail but devoid of significance. The purpose would be to tease out
analytical and policy implications and family resemblances as a
basis for a policy response that would admit its limitations and
would not prescribe a single off-the-shelf remedy for a wide range
of problems.

Another challenge for a theory of violent conflict is how to deal
with violence and power; for the explanations reviewed in this
chapter do remarkably little to take account of this. Game theory
tries to model competition and power but produces something like
a desiccated lemon by the foot of a tree: the juice and flavour of
power having been driven off, there are only the dry membranes of
rationality left. Some economic theory tries to bring power and violence into theory. This can involve pointing out that if individuals
are driven by rational choice and the maximisation of self-interest
that may include opting for violent means. Or it may involve the
description of power as a 'positional good', one whose positive consumption by one person necessarily involves its 'negative consumption' by someone else: power may then be treated with the same
toolkit used to assess markets for other goods, with minor adjustments. However, none of these approaches effectively accounts for
the hold that *power* has over people or the way in which power and
its pursuit go beyond the economic and involve a rationality beyond economic rationality. These models and perspectives seem
rather paltry, for example, alongside Jean Améry's writing on Nazism,
power and torture. Améry sees the 'practice of persecuting, tortur-
ing and exterminating an arbitrarily chosen adversary', writes
Sebald, 'not as a lamentable but incidental feature of totalitarian
rule but, unreservedly, as its essential expression. He remembers
"serious, tense faces…concentrated in murderous self-realization.
With heart and soul they went about their business, and the name
of it was power, domination over spirit and flesh, an orgy of

unchecked self-expansion". To Améry, the world devised and realised by German Fascism was the world of torture in which "man
exists only by ruining the other person who stands before him".[62]

The explanations of conflict discussed in this chapter differ in
many ways but it is worth once more highlighting some of their similarities. Roland Marchal and Christine Messiant, for example,
argue that there is a typically unrecognised link between the new
wars theory, new barbarism anxieties and neo-classical economic
theories of conflict. They are linked by the ideology of liberal
democracy.[63] It is precisely this, they argue, that leads the proponents of all these explanations to ignore the realities of power. And
it is this liberal ideology that leads its adherents to ignore what
Mark Duffield calls 'emerging political complexes', characterised
by decidedly illiberal politics. This may offer a clue to something
else that is generally missing from the standard explanations of
violent conflict in low and middle income countries: profound societal change. Chapters 5 and 6 take this up, arguing that these conflicts must be understood in terms of such change and that this
change cannot be apprehended without a historical perspective
scorned by some economists and without going beyond methodological individualism.

What these explanations also have in common is a commitment
to the idea of violent conflict as perversity, aberration, deformity
and abnormality. A rare score for ethno-linguistic fractionalisation,
like some rogue gene surviving through genetic drift, exposes some
countries to a high risk of civil war. War breaks out when development goes wrong and young men are unemployed. Instead of a
smooth process of structural change and movement towards perfect markets development sometimes goes off the rails and proceeds with distorted markets. Development might unfold nicely
except that in certain delicate conjunctures of demography, policy
and geography some precise carrying capacity of the land is vio-
lated, provoking mayhem. If a country is stuck at a precise point on
a non-monotonic curve relating primary commodity or natural
resource concentration to civil war, and especially if this is combined with the affliction of low educational attainment figures, that
country's grip on stability and peace will most likely slip. The argument of this book is that there is a strong connection between this
perspective on the perversity of violent conflict and the ideology of
liberalism. Further, this ideology leads to a misleading and limited
understanding of violent conflict. Drawing on the discussion and

evidence of previous chapters, Chapters 5 and 6 develop further the argument proposed in Chapters 1 and 2. First, though, Chapter 4 illustrates the analytical discussion of this chapter in the context of protracted violence in Angola.

4

ANGOLA AND THE THEORY OF WAR

Beginnings and ends

The death of Jonas Savimbi in February 2002 seemed to snuff out decades of war in Angola. It did not wipe out the many sources of intense political and personal conflict, nor did it bring an instant end to violence, but the way in which one of the world's longest wars fizzled out after he was hunted down and killed, and his bullet-riddled body broadcast on TV and in press photographs, reflects a broader theme. Although Savimbi was not a one-man cause of war, he was a one-man embodiment of contingency. Had Savimbi not existed, it is quite possible war would have continued into the twenty-first century; but it is also possible that things would have gone differently. War might have begun but been shorter. It might have been a different war, with different outcomes. War might even have fizzled out before it reached the appalling proportions it quickly assumed at independence in 1975.

21 February 2002 might be a fairly clear ending, but Angola's war had several beginnings.[1] It started in 1975, at the country's independence from Portugal, with a battle essentially between Cubans and South Africans south of Luanda. The Cuban force backing the Movimento Para a Libertação de Angola (MPLA) pushed back the column of South Africans supporting Jonas Savimbi's União Nacional para a Independência Total de Angola (UNITA), allowing the MPLA to claim Luanda at the 11 November independence day and forcing the South Africans to retreat across the border in the south and to rethink their military strategy.

However, war really began in 1961, in two rebellions: one in the capital, Luanda, and one in the northern countryside. These uprisings formed a sort of start to the armed struggle against Portuguese colonialism, initially carried out by two rival groups, the MPLA and the Frente Nacional de Libertação de Angola (FNLA). There were

139

other beginnings too. One was later, in 1966, when UNITA was created after Jonas Savimbi had split from the FNLA. One was earlier,
in 1960, when violence broke out in the northeastern cotton growing area, a precursor to the rural uprising of the following year in
coffee and cotton growing areas. Another, a re-ignition, was in 1992
when Savimbi refused to accept electoral defeat and returned to
war. To see how any of these multiple beginnings makes sense is
hard without some knowledge of the history of how the Angolan
economy was organised, how the society was managed politically,
and what kinds of social groups had developed contrasting political
positions.

During the late 1950s and at the start of the 1960s the politics of
opposition to Portuguese colonial rule was settling into a rivalry
between two groups, the MPLA and the FNLA. Personality clashes,
ideological differences, cultural distinctions and stoking by regional
and international backers drove a widening wedge between these
two movements. Both fretted over the question of armed struggle,
arguing internally and hoping that, in a context of decolonisation
throughout much of Africa, they would be able to negotiate with
the Portuguese. Violence as strategy emerged from prolonged debate, and did so as both movements—based outside the country, in
neighbouring Congo/Zaire and Congo-Brazzaville—caught up
with events inside Angola; and it emerged partly through the working of a mimetic mechanism. In 1960 leaders of the MPLA and the
União das Populações de Angola (the group that became the FNLA)
went to Tunis to attend the Second All-African Peoples Conference. The Algerian war was being fought at an intense pitch. Franz
Fanon was at the conference and—together with other delegates—
called on colonised Africans to take up direct action. The MPLA
hesitated. The UPA was keener to begin a war for independence.[2]
In early 1961, while the leaders of the two movements were still for-
mulating strategies, Angola burst into violence.

In February, in a bid to free political prisoners, a band of men
attacked the jail in Luanda. Portuguese settlers there unleashed
their anxieties in reprisals through the *musseques* (slums) of the city.
Portuguese security forces created a precedent for urban violence
by doling out firearms to white vigilante groups, who went on a calculated rampage.* The MPLA claimed the jail attack as theirs,

---

* As Birmingham (1992: 36) puts it: 'Frustrated poor white immigrants took the
  opportunity to wreak vengeance on any upwardly mobile blacks who might
  threaten their aspirations to social and economic advance. Violence was directed

absorbing it into its own political mythology and finally committing itself to military strategy.

The following month violent conflict erupted in the northern coffee growing regions. The spark was a fight that broke out on a coffee plantation over a claim by workers for payment of wage arrears. The violence that followed pitted northern Angolans from the area—Bakongo—against Portuguese settlers but also against migrant workers, mainly Ovimbundu people from the *planalto,* the central highland plateau, who had been drafted in by their thousands for years during the coffee boom after the Second World War. This rural uprising is one of the least well known but largest of anti-colonial uprisings.* Estimates of the number of deaths, over eight months, vary from 8,000 to 50,000.[3] Holden Roberto, the leader of the northern-based UPA/FNLA, at first denied any connection with this violence but soon claimed his movement had directed the attacks.

As the two main nationalist movements developed a more coherent strategy of liberation war they had to find ways of funding this and securing supply lines and political allies. Although there were Marxist intellectuals in the MPLA who had developed their ideas in the networks of diasporic disaffection and through links with underground Portuguese communists, there was not a fully formed ideological platform. The need to find arms nudged these groups into the arms of international sponsors. Meanwhile, outsiders with an interest in the Angolan conflict dithered over which group best reflected their ideological expectations. The FLN in Algeria at first backed the FNLA, but later switched its support to the MPLA. The Organisation of African Unity gave sole recognition to the FNLA and then also changed its mind. The Soviet Union took some time to throw its weight behind the MPLA, as did Cuba. The United States—mainly thanks to its close relations with Mobutu's Zaire—first (covertly) backed the FNLA and rejected UNITA but over time opted to back UNITA too.

---

predominantly against school leavers, townsmen in Western dress, Portuguese speakers, and against the literate and the employed. Anyone who might remotely be thought of as a nationalist leader, or even supporter, was hauled out of bed and murdered in the street.'

* Comparisons are sometimes drawn with the Mau Mau uprising in Kenya in the 1950s: Mau Mau killed thirty-two white settlers and tens of thousands of Africans; the British imprisoned thousands and herded around a million people into concentration camps; colonial military forces killed many; and the British state hanged more than one thousand convicted insurgents (Anderson, 2005).

The liberation war dragged on through the 1960s and early 1970s, complicated by violence between the FNLA and MPLA and then by the emergence of UNITA.* Salazar's regime in Portugal clung to empire, though its commitment to wars in Africa generated mounting discontent at home. After Salazar's stroke Marcello Caetano carried on this policy. In April 1974 pent up opposition within the military and within radical underground movements finally exploded in the Revolution of the Carnations in Lisbon. The Salazarist *Estado Novo* was overthrown and the new administration quickly gave up the ghost of empire.

In January 1975 the three rival nationalist movements met with government officials in Portugal and signed the Alvor Agreement, which committed them to a ceasefire and to elections in November of that year. The agreement barely held at all. Soon the three groups were at each other again and as independence neared the fight was on for control of Luanda. The FNLA crumbled rather quickly and the main contest developed between the MPLA and UNITA, and their respective backers.

After the Cuban-South African encounter south of Luanda and the MPLA's successful assumption of power in Luanda, war in Angola settled into a protracted Cold War stalemate, miring the country in violence, poverty and landmines. At the end of the 1980s there was one last Cold War conflagration. The Battle of Cuito Cuanavale was perhaps the largest conventional battle in Africa since independence. In keeping with much of the war this battle had no obvious victor. However, it did produce a decisive humiliation of the South African army, which was forced to retreat.[4] The battle of Cuito Cuanavale was followed by a negotiated deal securing the withdrawal of Cuban troops and the independence of Namibia from South Africa. That deal paved the way for a ceasefire in Angola itself, a programme to demobilise MPLA and UNITA troops, and a plan to hold parliamentary and presidential elections in 1992. In fact, though, the end of South African covert aid to UNITA was the beginning of the transformation of the war rather than its end.

* UNITA was created in 1966. Its founders, including Savimbi, were disaffected by the exclusiveness of the FNLA leadership and sought instead to create a movement targeting the Southern/Central highlands, though there was only a weak social basis for nationalism in the Ovimbundu speaking highlands. To some extent this changed during the later years of the anti-colonial war, when political mobilisation could take advantage of people's experiences of the Portuguese forced villagisation strategy. Meanwhile, the UNITA leadership had its origins in the Congregationalist mission activities and schools on the *planalto*. See Birmingham (1992).

Angola's peace initiative of 1992 was a classic case of international half-heartedness. In the enthusiasm for electoral peace and the easy assumption that because the Cold War was over then the war in Angola must now be baseless, too little attention was paid to the fact that demobilisation and disarmament were faltering.[5] Elections went ahead and were deemed more or less free and fair by UN observers. Savimbi demurred, since the results gave a slim victory to the MPLA and to its leader and presidential candidate, José Eduardo dos Santos. Savimbi left Luanda to organise a new war. The reaction in Luanda was instant. Echoing the Portuguese arming of white vigilantes in 1961, the authorities armed civilian groups there. The battle of Luanda in 1992 was intense: apart from attacks on UNITA offices and arrests of UNITA leaders still in town, there was a pogrom against perceived UNITA sympathisers in the *musseques*, most of whom were Ovimbundu.

There was another attempt to make peace. The Lusaka Accord was signed in 1994. Even though some UNITA leaders did take up positions in the national assembly, providing the first parliamentary opposition to the MPLA, the peace faltered. War escalated again but over time the MPLA achieved a substantial military advantage, culminating in the intelligence and capacity that let them hunt down Savimbi in February 2002. Despite a project to round up the guns that had been handed out to civilians at the start of the battle of Luanda in 1992, weapons were still circulating in the slums and suburbs.* There were claims that the *Ninjas*—commando troops who had been fighting in Angola's contribution to the wars in Congo—were being redeployed in the *musseques* of Luanda. The political parties and international donors imagined holding elections in 2004; this target then slid to 2005/6.

The rest of this chapter explores how neatly Angola fits some of the main theoretical explanations for war that were reviewed in the previous chapter. The chapter views the war through a crystal whose angled planes are those of common explanations of war: the 'new war' analysis, the role of natural resources, the role of ethnicity and that of inequality. The characteristics of Angola's history of conflict offer both confirmation and challenges to the various explanations of the causes of conflict sketched out in the previous

---

* In mid-2003, after an official roundup of arms in the reception areas where UNITA troops and families were demobilised, three to four million small arms and light weapons were estimated to be in civilian hands. See the All-Party Parliamentary Group for Angola (2003); and Porto and Parsons (2003).

chapter. Angola's history also raises two further questions. One is that put by Buijtenhuis: have wars changed or is it that we have changed the way we understand them?[6] The other is whether it is possible to find a convincing general theory of war or whether instead every war is *sui generis.*

Was Angola's conflict a 'new war'?

There is a yes and no answer to this question. For at one level the Angolan conflict, at least during the 1990s and up until it appeared to fizzle out with Jonas Savimbi's death in 2002, was a clear case of a new war. The conflict during this period was devoid of ideology—at least if we mean by that a recognisable, twentieth-century struggle of modernist political projects. There seemed to be no difference in many fundamentals of ideology between the MPLA and UNITA: both were reconciled to the rhetoric, at least, of capitalism and the market economy. The MPLA government dragged its feet on reforms proposed by the World Bank and IMF, but not out of any convincing commitment to an alternative developmental strategy. Some Angolans argue that there is no parliamentary opposition even after the absorption into the national assembly of UNITA delegates: rather, UNITA and MPLA bosses have simply become partners in profitable crime. Clearly, also, the war in Angola thrived on linkages to international 'networks', both those woven around the trade in diamonds and those built up to sustain interests within the global oil sector.

After the end of the Cold War financial imperatives forced a change in the way war was conducted in Angola. The MPLA and UNITA were thrown back on their own wits. Rather than relying on international military aid, they had to fund war through markets and were horribly effective. The MPLA had used oil revenue before as part of its war economy. And UNITA had been preparing for new war by increasing its financial self-sufficiency in the late 1980s. Despite this continuity, the post-1992 phases of war were clearly different. Commodity markets rather than international solidarity or geopolitical strategy sustained war and created new material and political interests within Angola. Mercenaries replaced large Cuban and South African military contingents.

Blurred distinctions between peoples, armies and governments were also a feature of war in Angola. There have been repeated reports of members of the government armed forces selling weapons to UNITA officials.* An astonishing image of networks sustaining war in Angola is that drawn in Global Witness's *All the President's Men* report, which highlights evidence of criss-crossing interests between private entrepreneurs and French and other national governments, between these interests and officials in the Angolan government, and between interests in banking, oil and arms sectors. One example that shows how these webs of accumulation not only fuelled the war in Angola but also fuelled mighty inefficiency in the war effort (and in fact appears to show a complete disregard for military efficiency or a political project to win the war) concerns the trade in obsolete arms; for at least some of the matériel piled up in the arms junkyards outside Luanda was apparently already dysfunctional on arrival in Angola, the useless silt left after deals in which all traders appear to have gained. Arms supplies to Angola have included forty-year-old tanks that might be more dangerous to their operators than to an enemy. Over-priced invoices and hefty commissions ensured that plenty of Angolans and others have done well out of supplying the matériel of war to Angola.[7]

Angola's is also a new war, perhaps, in that enormous numbers of non-combatants have died, been seriously injured, uprooted and traumatised in the course of the conflict. The UN estimated that during the 1992–4 fighting, one of the fiercest periods of war in the country, some 300,000 people died war-related deaths, including battle deaths and deaths from aerial bombardment, from starvation under siege, from landmines and from disease and malnutrition caused by war.[8] Human Rights Watch estimated in late 2003 that some 900,000 Angolans were still internally displaced.[9]

At another level, though, Angola challenges the new war thesis and suggests enduring continuities of conflict: the new is not so new and the old carries over into the new. The atrocities of war in the 1970s and 1980s already had a very 'new war' stamp on them. UNITA rebels kidnapped thousands from the highlands and took

---

* Lévy (2004) describes the co-existence of a group of diggers under the guard of a UNITA detachment at a diamond mine in Lunda Norte with, two or three kilometres away, an MPLA mining brigade watching over their own diggers. 'That's the final paradox of this war. They fight each other, and with an incredible perseverance, wherever there's nothing but poverty, desert, villages plundered over and over, dead cities, lifeless landscapes. But wherever there are riches, in the horn of plenty that the Lundas are, a non-war is imposed, a gentlemen's agreement, and, effectively, another kind of sharing, which contains perhaps the only logic of this war' (p. 25).

them south to form an internal colony of forced labour. They destroyed plough oxen, and ate or destroyed seeds, as well as spilling landmines onto rural paths, all to bring the economy to its knees. The MPLA adopted similarly brutal policies towards rural civilians, driving them from their homes to prevent UNITA from finding and cultivating any social base. Soldiers frequently looted food convoys. There was massive internal population displacement and civilian human suffering. In short, Angola's was a complex humanitarian emergency long before the term was coined.

The Cold War gave the conflict a buff of ideological difference. However, Cold War ideology always ran rather shallow through Angolan society—where the social preconditions for nationalism and for other twentieth-century ideologies barely existed. Instead, arguably the war in Angola has always been, as it were, a war of position. In other words, what drove allegiance and commitment to conflict—at least among élites—was a desperate struggle for social position, with expectations and resentments born chiefly out of historical and material formations of social identities. (Struggles for position in terms of histories of Creole society, *assimilados*, and the battle over *echt* Africanness are discussed further below.)* Further, to the extent that a localised political imagery in the Ovimbundu highlands, drawing on oral history and attitudes to witchcraft but reshaped by Christianisation in the nineteenth century, had always played a part in the political appeal of UNITA, this was undisturbed by the end of the Cold War.[10]

Furthermore, *within* each of the three main movements involved in the anti-colonial war there was rivalry and conflict, in which political position or stance mingled with competition over positions within the movement, and over leadership and privilege. All three movements developed centralised, illiberal and anti-democratic leadership structures and organisation.[11] Even the 'new war' phenomenon of warring parties co-operating and fighting simultaneously is not new: one well-known example involved UNITA,

---

* Although the term 'war of position' has a long history of usage in military and political history, e.g. by Gramsci, here it is used more in the sense of intense positional competition, a war for position in (hierarchical) society. In Hirsch's (1976) terms, economic growth—but we might equally in this case say economic, social and political change—creates social scarcity of particular goods whose supply is restricted and whose consumption is charged with the thrill of exclusiveness. Positional competition involves competition for positional goods—those for which one person's, or group's, consumption necessarily involves another person's, or group's, loss (or 'negative consumption').

during the anti-colonial war, collaborating with the Portuguese secret police, PIDE. This collaboration was the product of UNITA's rivalry with the MPLA and FNLA and was formalised in 'Operation Timber'.[12]

Once the MPLA had taken power and throughout the post-independence war these trends continued. The MPLA's socialist ideology—especially after the defeat of an attempted coup in 1977 and repression of MPLA critics—was for the most part sham.[13] Leaders and their friends led lifestyles wholly at odds with ideological precepts and legal restrictions that affected most of the population. Private and public interests overlapped long before the end of the Cold War: the most obvious examples relating to the oil sector. The Marxist-Leninist MPLA encouraged joint oil exploration and production with international firms, especially with US firms whose government would not recognise the MPLA. The combination of food and consumer goods shortages, official fixed prices and oil money made for a fabulous parallel economy where, again, ideological, public and private distinctions blurred. In Luanda a concrete mausoleum for Agostinho Neto, the country's first president, encapsulates the mixture of overblown ideas, corruption and incompetence that characterised MPLA hubris—in the form of a space rocket. This grandiose project, at vast expense and with Soviet aid, was never completed.

Angola's war also has always been associated with international linkages, political and economic. The oil and diamond interests are only the most recent of these major commodity links to the origins and course of violent conflict. The idea that something new called 'globalisation' is causing the war is ridiculous. International interdependence is not new in Angola. Nor is it a simple matter of the most recent, post-Cold War phases of war being different and especially 'globalised'. Angola's peculiar linkages to the world economy—and the way these relate to warfare—stretch back through the Cold War, the colonial period and some 500 years of violent conflict. Duffield argues that new wars are tied to a new phase of globalisation characterised by a shift in the nature of international capitalism: where once capitalism was expansionary and inclusive, now it is consolidating in core capitalist countries and exclusive of the rest of the world. This is a misleading distinction to impose on Angola. For from the early days of merchant capital, the slave trade and the international sugar and coffee business, right up to present day oil and diamonds, capitalism has taken a brutal interest in Angola. Capitalism itself has not been purely inclusive or exclusive at any moment in this history. How far linkages have spread beyond these obvious points of international integration has tended to be driven not by any essential features of capitalism but by particular policies followed by external and internal political forces. Reno argues that 'the commercialisation of diplomacy and strategic interests in relationships between non-African and African states is occasionally portrayed as a novel feature accompanying the expansion of the global economy', but that in fact this is a very old practice, harking back to the mid-nineteenth century; and that the MPLA government has shown a considerable capacity to 'manipulate the conditions of their own bureaucratic weakness'.[14]

Finally, in the early twenty-first century national states continue to be important in deciding the fate of Angola. The state in Angola itself remains the key to social position, political power and economic privilege. And other state interests influence war and society. National state political concerns have affected the limits on UN intervention in Angola; and state interests and competition (influenced by particular private lobbying power as they always have been) affect the limitations on regulation of the diamond business and also affect the closely interlinked markets for oil and arms. The 'Angolagate' scandal in France, around government and Elf Aquitaine operations in Angola, is one example. And as Reno shows, US assistance to Angola's government goes well beyond state-to-state diplomatic measures and includes use of the Africa Growth and Opportunity Act, equity financing schemes run by the Commerce Department, Treasury and Department of Transportation, commercial guarantees by the quasi-official Overseas Private Investment Corporation (OPIC), and the Export-Import Bank, as well as the fruits of US influence in the World Bank's Multilateral Investment Guarantee Agency (MIGA). In the weeks before the war in Iraq in 2003 Angola found itself clearly included in the interplay of international states. Angola had the rotating chair of the UN Security Council and was under pressure from both France and the United States to vote one way or the other on any upcoming UN Resolution on military intervention in Iraq. The wails of dilatory protest that came from the Angolan foreign ministry really reflected a canny awareness of the country's bargaining position and of the fact that the French and Americans had a longer-term rivalrous interest in Angolan offshore oilfields.

Nor do tales of intricate international arms deals, involving the evasion of sanctions, forgery of end-user certificates, and the sale of obsolete weaponry, reveal a new world of degenerate warfare.

These details have precursors. Very similar things happened, for example, in the Spanish Civil War, when end-user certificates were invented to monitor international arms flows. International Non-Intervention policy forced the Republicans and the Nationalists in Spain, and their international backers, to develop deft methods of secret arms supplies. Hypocrisy, venality, betrayal and lack of ideological purity characterise most of this history. Economic imperatives often seemed to outweigh political loyalties. The grandest swindling of the Republicans came at the hands of Stalin's Soviet Union. Not only did the Soviets sell the Spanish Republicans absurdly old weaponry, but they also used sleight of multiple exchange rates to cheat them on prices.* The supply of poor quality, old stock weaponry also echoes the report of the cheap and nasty Angola guns. And the fact that some Angolans have exploited the secrecy of arms deals to make private fortunes also fits an old tradition.[15]

Is war in Angola caused by commodities?

Angola is in many ways the ultimate primary commodity economy. Its economy was based first on slaves, then on coffee, then on diamonds and, increasingly over the past thirty years, on oil. It is blindingly obvious that high value commodities have a massive effect on conflict in Angola. Control over diamond fields enabled UNITA to continue war after Cold War patronage faded away at the end of the 1980s, and the MPLA political and military engine kept turning over thanks to oil revenue. Certainly the possibility of peace is awkward for some of Angola's rulers: with peace comes more well-intentioned international meddling, lighting up the fantastic levels of corruption and the degree of control by the families tied mainly to the fuel cell of power in Futungo de Belos, the presidential palace.

However, it is possible that the flash of oil money and the glare of diamonds really have blinded people analytically. Do resources determine outcomes by themselves? If so, why do all countries with

* See Howson (1998: 151). Many of the rifles, machine guns and artillery supplied to Spain by the Soviets were obsolete. For example, the Russians supplied more than 13,000 Swiss-designed Vetterli rifles that had been made in Brescia in 1871, sold to Turkey and probably captured by Russia in the Russo-Turkish war of 1877. They came with 185 rounds of ammunition each, which were not interchangeable with the cartridges of other rifles supplied. 'When this supply of ammunition ran out, which it would do after a day or two, all these rifles would have to be thrown away… In short, of the 58,183 rifles sent from the USSR in 1936, nearly 26,000 were ancient museum pieces with hardly any ammunition and another 6,000, also much used, had only half their required supply.' (ibid.: 139)

oil, diamonds etc. not experience the same kind of conflict? Commodity theories of war—both those leading with environmental degradation and scarcity and those in which resource abundance drives war—end up fetishising commodities. In the process they depoliticise conflict.

A more realistic analysis of Angolan conflict would examine the direction of causality more closely and would explore the social relations that shape the role that commodities play in politics and in conflict. First, oil and diamonds had little to do with the beginnings of the contemporary war in Angola in the 1960s. Mineral production was still modest at that stage and political conflict, particularly the start of the liberation war, erupted out of different histories of urban tension, rural repression and rebellion (particularly the 1961 uprising in the north-west), and nationalist politics. In fact, in some ways war and economic policy after independence created a *new* dependence on mineral resource exports. The economy had been undergoing significant structural change in the late colonial period, with one of the most rapid manufacturing booms experienced anywhere in Sub-Saharan Africa in the late 1960s and early 1970s. Manufacturing accounted for 25 per cent of GDP just before independence, and posted annual rates of growth of output of 6.9 per cent in 1972 and 14.3 per cent in 1973.[16] All that changed after independence. 'As war progressed, and the economy dramatically deteriorated, with sharp falls in agricultural and industrial production, oil output increased and oil revenue came to represent almost all of Angola's currency earning and the bulk of state income.'[17] The direction of causality seems almost the reverse of that presumed by the resource curse literature.

Nonetheless, rapidly increasing oil revenue certainly allowed the MPLA to wage one of the most expensive wars in Africa, sustaining large armed forces and huge arms imports. SIPRI estimates put the 1999 Angolan military expenditure, for example, at $2,419 million (in constant, 1998 US dollars), equivalent to 21.2 per cent of GDP

Table 3. STRUCTURE OF ANGOLAN EXPORTS, 1962 (% of total)

Agricultural origin	65.7
Industrial products of agricultural origin	5.2
Mineral extraction	17.9
Fishery production	5.5
Animal husbandry	1.2
Miscellaneous	4.5

Source: Guimarães (2001), p. 18.

(though, again, data on military expenditure and on GDP in Angola are extremely untrustworthy).[18]

The specific properties and production requirements of these commodities—slaves, coffee, oil and diamonds across the past five centuries—have helped define the particular characteristics of war. However, second, rather than beginning and ending with the commodity itself, it is important to explore the social relations that surrounded, built up around and helped determine policy towards particular commodities.* The true role of oil, for example, cannot be appreciated without seeing how the development of the oil industry has been entwined with a much older history of the formation of a Creole élite and slightly more recent emergence of so-called 'new *assimilados*' chiefly in Luanda. For these social groups were first encouraged to take leadership roles in Angolan society, then were humiliated by the twentieth-century *Estado Novo* period of colonial rule and a huge Portuguese settler influx, and later still formed the basis of MPLA rule and the evolution of a *nomenklatura* intent on preserving social position, political power and immense wealth.

Finally, resource scarcity and poverty in rural areas more recently have definitely helped to reproduce warfare, generating people to fight for the MPLA and UNITA and to sustain military operations with logistical work. However, environmental degradation and resource scarcity are not the true starting point of this sequence. And while it is clearly true that joining military forces is one of the only ways in which poor young men and boys, particularly, can survive, it is not enough simply to state that the poor have a 'comparative advantage in violence' or a 'low opportunity cost of violence'. War and political conflict have created scarcity, and have pushed people into military camps, towns and resettlement villages and refugee camps where many have joined but many more appear to have been forced to join militias. It is not merely a case of relative opportunities or the balance of costs and benefits, for these suggest a large measure of calculative rationality and choice. Rather, it is a matter, for most people, of coercive relations: of being press-ganged into military or sexual service of the MPLA and UNITA (see below).

---

* A good way to understand how the social organisation and political ramifications of a given commodity can vary is to explore contrasts in historical experience: an excellent example is Yashar's (1997) contrast between the twentieth-century political trajectories of Guatemala and Costa Rica, and their roots in the different economic and social organisation of coffee production and trade.

— Coffee and cotton

In the 1960s it was not the glamour of diamond or oil rents that drew Angolans into violent conflict, but the way the colonial regime had organised production of coffee and cotton and the changes this wrought on African societies. The growth of agricultural wage labour and cash-crop farming brought radical disruptions to pre-colonial production systems. Some were coerced into growing coffee in the north-west; some were forced to migrate, especially from the *planalto* to the coffee farms to the north; and some were forced to labour on cotton plantations. Contract cotton farming was the source of the first violent anti-colonial activity, in Baixa do Cassanje, in 1960.

The most dramatic changes in the countryside came with the post-Second World War coffee boom. By the early 1970s Angola would become the third or fourth largest exporter of coffee in the world. Coffee production was concentrated in the north-west, in the region of the old Bakongo kingdom. This location and its particular political history were to influence the future of political conflict in Angola. For this history tied many Bakongo people into the economy, language and society of the Belgian Congo. The region was to be the base for the formation and political orientation of the FNLA.

Coffee exports increased from 40 per cent of the volume of agricultural exports in 1948 to 88.3 per cent by 1967, and from 30.9 per cent of total value of exports in 1948 to 51.9 per cent in 1967. The Portuguese colonial regime chose to organise coffee production partly through small-scale Bakongo farming but also by encouraging huge land expropriation and settlement by Portuguese immigrants and by corralling migrant labour from the Ovimbundu highlands in the centre and south of the country to meet labour demand on settler coffee plantations (and to undercut local wage rates). The largest estates employed as many as 11,000 workers. Colonial *policy* aimed at reducing labour costs in coffee production, rather than primordial ethnic identities, was at the root of disputes between northerners and those from the *planalto*—as well as between Angolans and white settlers.

— Diamonds

According to one argument, primary commodities and above all natural resources cause wars, or at the very least sustain them, and this is reflected in evidence that warring parties prefer continued war to peace, even to victory. Victory is not the point when a profitable war may be carried on. However, the easy functionalism of this line, that the army does not want peace because peace would dissipate rent, is belied in Angola by the hunting down of Savimbi and the swift end to the war after his death. The killing of Savimbi was not accidental: it was the climax of months of planning and military activity. What this suggests is that at the very least two sets of interests coexist in a situation like Angola's. On the one hand war is convenient; it makes space for the control of markets. On the other, some of those making war are intent on military and political victory. Even if one were to reduce all objectives to the economic, there are conflicts of interest between those with different time horizons—those that prefer to take advantage of the profit opportunities enabled by war and those that aim to secure a flow of profit from longer term stability and power. Looking a little more closely at the political economy of diamonds in Angola helps to show how complex is the relationship between war, profit and power.

Diamonds were first found in Angola in 1912. As the industry grew, diamonds became the main export until they were overtaken during the post-Second World War coffee boom and later by oil. There is a dramatic difference between diamonds and oil, which has affected the roles of the two commodities in the war. In Angola there are primary diamond deposits, which require large-scale industrial mining; but there are also alluvial diamonds that can be mined with rudimentary technology and without skilled labour. This is rather different from oil whose production requires technological sophistication and large sunk costs and relatively concentrated amounts of skilled labour.

There are three points about the Angolan diamond economy and its part in the war that bear on the purpose of this chapter. First, the timing of interactions between war, peace and the shaping of interests in the diamond sector challenges the idea that opportunities in the diamondiferous area of the Lundas caused war. Second, the recent institutional and organisational history of diamonds—the ways the state and UNITA sought to manage diamonds—has implications for the relevance of the 'new war' thesis. Third, the way that production and trade in diamonds have been organised undermines the easy assumption that wartime alluvial diamond mining 'caused' war by offering opportunities for an easy living for young men compared with the poverty they would otherwise suffer. Mere correlations between the presence of diamonds and the fact of war do not explain the war.

During the 1980s the Lundas were increasingly lawless and unstable. Under cover of UNITA incursions and in the interstices of UNITA and government control there was a rise in informal diamond mining by small-time miners or *garimpeiros*. UNITA itself was taking an increasing interest in the area, possibly in a bid to reduce its dependence on US and South African aid.

However, the big change came not with war but with peace and then with the new phase of war after the 1992 peace collapsed. During the period from the signing of the Bicesse peace agreement and ceasefire in 1991 to the renewal of war in October 1992, *garimpeiro* diamond mining expanded rapidly. One estimate put the number of *garimpeiros* active in mid-1992 at between thirty and forty thousand. The promise of peace also meant demobilisation of troops, at least some of them. After Bicesse there were large numbers of MPLA ex-soldiers schooled in violence. Many of these ex-soldiers came to play a significant role in the diamond sector through the 1990s (and beyond) as founders or employees of mining groups or domestic security companies.

When war restarted in October 1992, after the debacle of the elections and the battle of Luanda, it took a different form. Cold War finance had dried up. This imposed new strategic imperatives on UNITA, which now had to give greater priority to controlling the diamond fields in order to generate the financial wherewithal of war. The new environment of war also affected the government. The Cuban soldiers had gone and Soviet aid was a thing of the past. Oil revenue and oil-backed loans were the principal source of war finance, along with inflationary finance. And the MPLA sought to substitute imports of commercial soldiery for the troops of solidarity. Angola became one of the first places where the new mercenaries—like Executive Outcomes—played a central role. Executive Outcomes was hired by the Angolan government though it included staff whose knowledge of Angola owed more to earlier South African military support for UNITA.

Reorganised war led to the rise of new interest groups. For example, FAA officers undertook joint venture operations with outfits like Executive Outcomes. This educated army officers in the ways of entrepreneurialism. They took cuts on arms deals. They began to realise the financial returns to controlling diamond territory. They began to achieve military successes against UNITA in the Lundas. And they found opportunities for some autonomy from the central state. Serving officers interacted with demobbed officers and rank and file soldiers who were also active in the area.

Meanwhile, UNITA was also taking diamond rent far more seriously than during the 1980s. There are conflicting estimates of how much UNITA made from diamonds in the 1990s, but its cumulative revenue between 1992 and 1998 was probably $2–3.5 billion. This was far larger than the scale of external assistance before 1992: William Minter estimated that Reagan-era US aid to UNITA peaked around $40–60 million a year between 1989 and 1991.[19] To some extent the business of profit distracted people from war. For example, serving and former FAA officers running supply businesses in the Lundas would trade openly with UNITA diamond bosses, selling and exchanging goods across a river that was also a frontline. And diamonds mined by UNITA, during a period when these were internationally banned by sanctions, were often 'laundered' when they passed through officially registered trading groups and emerged as government-approved exports.

This new environment was also a new site of political conflict and negotiation and of institutional change. It is interesting to consider the relationship between these interest groups and the state (and UNITA as a political organisation) in terms of the triangle of 'guns, lawyers and merchants' discussed in Chapter 5. There was no clear monopoly of violence. There were lawyer-like interventions in the form of regulatory adventures and initiatives. And there was an uneasy relationship between the diamond (and security) merchants and the state.

At times the state has tried to crack down on *garimpeiro* mining, declaring it illegal and rounding up miners and labour contractors. At other times since the early 1990s the state has openly tolerated *garimpeiros*, appearing to realise that by doing so the state can, for example, acknowledge the need to distribute something of a peace dividend to those involved. When the state has sought to regulate the diamond sector, military-commercial individuals and groups in the sector (mine bosses, gatekeepers to *garimpeiro* mining, or security firm bosses) have tried both to dodge and duck the regulatory impositions and also to go along with them and even to secure greater influence within the state. Also during the 1990s the government adopted a new policy towards the regulation of the diamond sector: it allowed greater competition, issuing licences to traders and mining concerns; and it allowed Endiama to form various joint ventures with foreign companies. The government was simply making the fiscal best of reality: it could not fully control mining activities in alluvial diamonds but it could legalise the previously illegal and then tax it, as well as opening up multiple opportu-

nities for its own favoured sons and daughters.[20] Taxing diamond
activities is just one of the ways in which the Angolan state has in
recent years been experimenting with taxation beyond oil. Another
is the activities of the 'fiscal police', who have been trying to capture revenue from the myriad unofficial economic activities in and
around Luanda.

Meanwhile, UNITA was also experimenting in organisational
innovation as it sought to secure its future through diamond revenue, before it was squeezed out by FAA successes. UNITA managed
the diamond fields in three ways: by engaging in direct production
and labour control; by selling licences to diamond buyers to operate in areas under its control; and by taxing independent mining
operators that it tolerated in its zones.[21] UNITA operated under
international constraints, in the form of sanctions that were meant
to work through the insistence on end-user certificates for the
international arms market and on certificates-of-origin for diamonds. Evading sanctions tends to be interpreted as evidence of
the criminality of war and the crafty illegality of warlords. Another
way to see it is as a form of soft technology that parodies the evasion
of intellectual property controls and patents elsewhere in the world
and as revealing an organisational nouse for negotiating the challenges of internal conflict and international integration. For these
are challenges that are the bread and butter of late capitalist development everywhere, in one way or another.

When a developing country evades intellectual property rights
established through patent law by international pharmaceutical
companies, e.g. by importing or manufacturing generic HIV/AIDS
anti-retroviral drugs, many people cheer their resourcefulness in
the face of iniquitous practices by multinationals. When a government or an organisation like UNITA evades international controls
on arms transfers or trade in diamonds, the global media express
shock. However, rather than pausing at the level of moral and political revulsion, it may be worth identifying commonalities between
these evasions. For there are implications for the potential of accumulation and development in UNITA's—and the government's—
organisational management of diamonds and the war economy.
Successful developing countries have developed and absorbed
hard technology, e.g. in manufacturing, and they have also had to
adapt and create soft technology, which is a matter of organisational innovation in the face of internal and international competitive challenges. This has been part and parcel of most wars. And
just as vicious pre-capitalist primitive accumulation has always pre-

ceded proper capitalist development, so the development of organisational know-how for managing the production and trade of commodities may be a valuable precursor to future developments of economic management in other sectors in Angola.* It is only a liberal fantasy of development and political economy that prevents this from being obvious.

Finally, the *garimpeiro* bonanza under control of military groups looks like an excellent case of war offering better opportunities to unemployed young men (and hence might have played a role in 'causing' the war, at least its post-1992 phase). Given that *garimpeiro* mining by independent groups and individuals had gradually been increasing through the late 1980s and that it exploded precisely during the brief 1991–2 peace, what actually happened much of the time was that war took over and made life in some ways harder for young males *already* engaged in existing mining activities rather than offering new opportunities. And insofar as the wartime diamond business did offer new opportunities and income streams it was largely for people who were rather far from being the poor: ex-officers, serving soldiers, rebel leaders, local big men, international players, the president's daughter and so on. *Garimpeiro* mining was happening to some extent before the new phase of war and in spite of it. Working as a *garimpeiro* in an outfit controlled by military groups—or by any larger commercial concern, for that matter—is not wonderful gold rush employment. These kinds of business are not renowned for their excellent employment benefits, labour rights and wage rates.

— Oil

'Control of the country's oil resources is the ultimate prize of the Angolan war', claimed one recent book.[22] Oil in Angola has been the government's main means, increasingly, of sustaining war. Its role in war finance has increased as Soviet aid and soft loans evaporated and as the rate of discoveries has brought more and more offshore oil on-stream. The oil business in Angola is also a classic case of corrupt governance. To some extent, given the way the economy is both dominated by oil and cannot be divorced from power, it

* For example, the *chaebol* in South Korea, and the organisation of 'intermediate assets' allocated by the state to support their expansion and guide their investments, emerged in the political economy of the Korean War and, after that, political coalitions built on the management of scarce resources to generate economic independence in the face of extreme security threats. See Amsden (2001), Woo-Cumings (1998), and Doner, Ritchie and Slater (2005).

must be fair to say that oil is a reason for war, again especially for the post-Cold War phase of war.

Oil as a means of war is tied directly to arms procurement. Oil revenue is the basis of budgetary expenditure on the military—according to the IMF the government spent around $1.2bn per year on the military during late 1990s.[23] Large flows of oil income have for years been spirited away before reaching the official budget figures and these have also been used to fund secret arms deals. Oil revenue is used as collateral to secure commercial loans that are used for buying arms, when the state is unable to get concessionary finance because of its poor credit rating. And the MPLA government has given companies involved in the arms trade an equity stake in the new deepwater oilfield blocks that have been opened up in the past few years. International oil market conditions—just like international cotton price movements during the American Civil War—affected the military balance in the Angolan war. Thus UNITA military successes in early 1999 followed a period of decline in international oil prices in 1998. This was mitigated by the government's success in securing a commercial loan against future oil revenues, by the signature bonus payments by oil multinationals to the government in exchange for offshore exploration licences, and then by a recovery in oil prices. These improvements in government finances were directly linked to major purchases of military hardware.[24]

The system would not function without multinational oil companies. One Texan oil company worker once told me, commenting on the capacity levels of Sonangol, 'Those guys don't know their ass from a tin whistle.' Although Sonangol has evolved in recent years into a company with a stronger skills base, the production of oil is still predominantly run by multinationals. Chevron, Petrofina, Texaco and Elf have been the main players. During the 1990s there was a high rate of discovery in large deepwater fields further offshore. BP-Amoco, Exxon and Elf won the bids for the first three blocks auctioned by the government at the end of the 1990s: between them they paid more than $900 million in bonuses.

These companies deal with Sonangol, which also has a direct joint venture share in some operations. It also has joint ventures with foreign partners and Angolans that make up much of the supply sector servicing oil needs: providing helicopters and boats, support bases, seismic studies, civil construction and drilling. These service activities make up the limited but real direct linkages from oil to the rest of the economy. Otherwise, Angolan offshore oil, employing only 10,000 Angolans directly, is very much an enclave economic activity. However, there is still scope for oil to have powerful linkage effects on the rest of the economy, through government revenue and expenditure. The actual linkages thus far have been governed not by natural laws of economics but by the politics of a social enclave, a Creole élite cut off from much of Angolan society by its own history, by being soaked in oil revenue and power, by war, and by the limited spread through the country of education and print newspaper.

Oil has smoothed the rise of an élite with gargantuan wealth. The rise of a rentocracy certainly suggests that oil must have become a prize worth war and political illegitimacy, even if it was not the original cause of war. Oil income has shored up a class consolidated around rent, corruption and rapid turnover businesses rather than longer-term, riskier investments. At the heart of the system is the presidential compound of Futungo. There has, for example, been pressure on international companies to make contributions to the Eduardo dos Santos Foundation, FESA, a charitable foundation that also acts as a branding exercise for presidential power.[25] The government has been creative in developing a financial system parallel to the official budgetary system. Grudgingly the government agreed to produce a 'diagnostic study' of the oil business, intended to force greater transparency on the state, but this was dogged by delays.* Oil multinationals have been complicit in secrecy. When BP announced in 2002 that it would declare payments made to the Angolan government no other companies followed suit; and Sonangol issued insinuations about the consequences for future relations

---

* The diagnostic study idea was a reaction to the inability of IMF and World Bank economists to trace financial flows. Global Witness (2002: 45) quotes a World Bank official: 'Successive IMF/WB missions during the last few years worked with data supplied by the authorities and found large unexplained outlays equivalent to between one third and one half of total reported fiscal revenues. Unfortunately, these problems have not yet been resolved, and the staff of the IMF is awaiting explanation of the disposition of about $1.4 billion in fiscal revenues and external loans in 2001. These calculations are solely derived from government data. The information on current payments made by oil companies is still scant, since some companies claim confidentiality clauses and no framework has been established for an ongoing reporting of oil-related payments.' In mid-2003 the government did publish the executive summary and initial report of the diagnostic study (as a Ministry of Finance document compiled by the management consultants and accountancy firm KPMG): the published report details the many contortions of financial flows, bank accounts, multiple exchange rates and complex institutional mechanisms, though it is restrained in its discussion of the implications and of actual diversion of funds.

with BP. But it is also important to note that the Angolan state is not a monolith of venality. Budget statements regularly decry the state of off-budget spending and lack of transparency, though to no avail. And to the extent that secretive financial networks and international relationships have been part of the effort to finance war (and not only to secure personal wealth), this fits a very old historical tradition of wartime financial innovation, even if it does not fit neatly the expectations of good governance held dear in development agencies.

Angola's war cannot be 'read off' from a table of the country's structural dependence on natural resources. For the war began and developed its extraordinary momentum during the 1960s, a period when oil and diamonds were less dominant. First, war and economic mismanagement—along with the recent waves of discovery—have created oil dependency rather than the other way around. Secondly, during the late colonial period—precisely when war was getting under way—there was extraordinarily rapid diversification. Manufacturing in Angola grew by 11 per cent a year in real terms during 1960–73, faster than in the rest of Africa.

Angola began spewing oil in 1955, in the onshore Kwanza basin. In the 1960s offshore oilfields were discovered off the coast of the tiny enclave of Cabinda. Production there began in 1968 and by 1973 oil exports were earning more than coffee. Expansion accelerated later in two waves. From 1983 to the end of the 1990s production expanded sixfold. And in the past few years the new deepwater oilfields further out to sea have created a fever of expectations. Some observers expect Angola to overtake Nigeria as Africa's largest oil producer by 2015. The government has been earning more

Table 4. MAIN ANGOLAN EXPORT COMMODITIES, 1966

Product	Value (US$ million)	Percentage
Coffee	107.2	48.1
Diamonds	39.4	17.6
Fish products	14.1	5.8
Sisal	10.5	4.7
Iron ore	4.7	2.0
Timber	4.3	2.0
Maize	4.1	2.0
Cotton fibre	3.7	1.7
Other	34.8	16.1
Total	222.8	100

than $1 billion a year from oil in recent years. Non-oil tax revenue in the late 1990s was only around 7 per cent of GDP. 'In 1997, crude oil accounted for 90 per cent of exports, diamonds for 7 per cent, refined petroleum for 2 per cent, and all other products, including gas, for 1 per cent.'[26] Oil accounted for as much as 58 per cent of GDP in 1996.

Is Angola's conflict caused by ethnicity or inequality?

Angola is a fantastically unequal society. War itself has aggravated inequality in income levels as incomes from thriving business sectors like oil, diamonds and trading became concentrated in relatively few pockets while immense numbers of people were cast to the very edge of survival (and obviously many were pushed further into starvation, disease and military related mortality). Reliable income distributional data are not available.* Social indicators, to the extent that these are reliable, suggest horrendous levels of poverty. UNICEF estimated under-five mortality of 292 per 1,000—two thirds higher than the Sub-Saharan African average.[27]

Meanwhile, ethnicity has certainly been a factor in the country's political history. Some commentators have emphasised ethnic divisions as the basis of the competing projects of the three (and then two) warring parties.[28] Malaquias argues that the MPLA, UNITA and FNLA 'represented almost exclusively the Mbundu, Ovimbundu, and Bacongo [*sic*] ethnic groups respectively'; that ethnic tensions were there before the war and before colonialism; and that they were there at the end. The 'main rationale for creating UNITA was primarily ethnic'. The 'fundamental cause' of war is ethnic division.[29] Certainly, the FNLA never really escaped from a narrowly Bakongo base. Indeed, aside from the authoritarian leadership of Holden Roberto, this ethnic narrowness was one of the reasons why significant numbers—including Jonas Savimbi—left the movement. UNITA has often been associated with an Ovimbundu social support base, while the MPLA drew support from the Mbundu areas around Luanda as well as from *mestiços* in the capital.

However, in terms of causing the conflict this is a misleading account. Inequality mattered in Angola in terms of the specific his-

* One urban poverty study carried out in 1995 (INE, 1996) and cited in Hodges (2001) found that monthly expenditure by the richest decile of urban households surveyed was twelve times more than that of households in the poorest decile, compared with the ninefold difference in equivalent spending found in a 1990 Luanda survey.

tory of institutionalised categorical inequalities between groups
(white, Creole, *assimilado*, black African) rather than in terms of
the vertical income range among individuals that is measured by
the Gini coefficient. Ethnicity was not by itself a very powerful
determinant of conflict and the conflict did not take the form of
ethnic cleansing, despite the ethnic targeting of Ovimbundu in the
battle for Luanda in late 1992. Ethnic identity was not an evenly distributed source of mobilisation. Apart from the Bakongo, 'there
did not exist in Angola in 1974 any strong ethnic tradition. One
could not speak of the Mbundu or the Ovimbundu as "corporate
groups"'.[30] Economic expansion and structural change in the late
colonial period, by provoking greater social differentiation, had
undermined the simplicity of three grand ethnic blocs in the country, and there was increasing diversification of interests within
'ethno-linguistic groups'. Moreover, the war has involved massive
population movements and urbanisation, and people's collective
identities have shifted; in the burgeoning cities there seems to be
evidence that ethnicity matters less and less. Meanwhile, the results
of the 1992 elections suggest quite strong cross-ethnic support for
the MPLA.[31]

UNITA clearly is limited to its base in the *planalto*. In the 1992
elections it won the vote only in Benguela, Bié and Huambo provinces. Yet UNITA does not have unanimous support in Ovimbundu
areas. Many Ovimbundu fight for the government armed forces (as
they did in the colonial army). Even the idea of a homogeneous
group called the Ovimbundu with shared traditions and conver-
gent interests based on a common culture is mythical. The Ovimbundu population is not a primordial cultural monolith but is an
aggregation out of the twenty-two chiefdoms formed in the seventeenth century on and around the *planalto*, and often mixing peoples who had lived there for many generations with migrants from
the slaving wars elsewhere and with the Jaga who invaded from the
northeast.[32]

Ethnic differences have mattered but only insofar as they overlapped with other sources of differing material interest and ideological formation, including specific circuits of economic activity
and distinct domains of denominational mission influence divided
between Presbyterians, Methodists and Baptists.* Altogether, unequal

* There is an important element of 'contingency' here tied to the specifics of Portuguese colonialism and the limited mission activity of the Catholic Church, especially outside Luanda. For the history of merging material interest, mission

distribution of social position, economic wealth and social, economic and political opportunities across groups with varying degrees and forms of collective identity was extremely important causal factors in the origins of war in Angola. This was all the more so because these groups were directly linked by relations of power in political or economic terms. One example is that of coffee production, which bred resentments between expropriated Bakongo peasants and Portuguese settlers, and between migrant Ovimbundu labourers and coffee farm owners. But the most dramatic and enduring source of political rivalry developed around the historical relations between the Luanda Creole, *assimilado* and *mestiço* society and 'black African' Angola. From the earliest days of the anti-colonial struggle, through to the later conflict between the MPLA and UNITA, issues of legitimate claims to 'Angolanness' and 'Africanness' were intensely divisive. Ultimately this became the organising principle around which contests for position in Angolan society developed. This is hardly surprising given a long-standing association of the coastal Creoles not only with monopolising the benefits of early capitalist society but also with direct complicity in the slave trade and the raids on the Angolan hinterland, and given the colonial institutional gradations of privilege according to Portuguese, *assimilado*, or indigenous identity coding. Thus inequality does seem to have been causally important, but only if seen in terms of Tilly's categorical pairings: Creoles/hinterland Africans, settlers/farmers, northern landowners/migrant coffee labourers; and if one notes that these pairings have class foundations rather than emerging out of free-floating or primordially entrenched 'identity politics'. Neither ethnicity nor inequality was causally significant as an 'independent variable'. With different treatment, in terms of specific histories of distributional relations and struggles intertwined with complex patterns of collective identity, a more plausible basis for an account of the origins of and characteristics of war in Angola emerges.

Coordination, mobilisation and competition: collective action in Angola

All parties to conflict have used various means to try to meet the competitive and collective action challenges faced by any political and military organisation. Political leaders drew on a history of

---

schooling and collective identity within different regions of Angola, see Clarence-Smith (1980), Heimer (1979), Birmingham (1992) and Heywood (2000).

protest to mobilise support and bid for competitive legitimacy
against colonial administration and against rival nationalist movements. Thus the MPLA used the legend of Queen Nzinga and
called on the resistance by Dembos warriors to Portuguese military incursions after the Treaty of Berlin and the late-nineteenth-
century colonial pacification campaigns; the FNLA peddled the
restoration of the glorious Kongo kingdom, though this compromised aspirations to pan-Angolan nationalism;* and UNITA
appealed to the memory of the Bailundo rebellion (against the
Portuguese and against *mestiço* merchants) in 1902.

Modernist ideology was used by all three but not extremely effectively. UNITA was indecisive, putting together in the 1960s a collage
that seemed largely driven by an opportunistic need to forge a way
between the other two movements while still receiving international and African support. Savimbi criticised Soviet revisionism
and socialist imperialism, claimed to be anti-communist, praised
Maoism, and ended up backed by, first, covert US aid and, then, by
apartheid South Africa. A more powerful mobilising ideology for
UNITA has been that of race. Throughout the history of the conflict UNITA railed against the littoral mixed race élite, arguing that
it does not represent 'Africans'.[33] It also made genuine efforts to act
like a state in regions it controlled, mainly in the 1980s. It set up
schools and scholarship programmes and built up something of a
network of health provision and food distribution, even while it
built a reputation for witchcraft and brutality. It is fair to claim that
UNITA was not simply apolitical but was what Mark Duffield calls
'an emerging political complex', but the character of this itself
changed over time.

Above all UNITA and the MPLA have relied, for military repro-
duction, on force: on kidnapping and press-ganging recruits. Karl
Maier refers, for example, to UNITA's 'rigid mind control, the total
obedience of its members to *O Mais Velho* (The Eldest One)'.[34]
Maier himself suggests this obeisance might come from the history
of the *planalto*. 'Maybe its methods come from the tyranny which
reigned in the central highlands in the seventeenth century when
the militaristic Jaga people came down from the north-east and
established modern chieftaincies in places like Bailundo, Bié,
Huambo, Andulo and Caconda. Their method of recruitment was

* It seems that Holden Roberto dropped the FNLA's attachment to a separate Kongo
state after developing contacts with other nationalist leaders, such as Nkrumah,
Lumumba and Kaunda, at the All African Peoples Conference in Accra in 1958.

to kidnap children from neighbouring villages and train them as soldiers. Often they would force the youngsters to attack their own villages or even to kill members of their family to ensure loyalty to the Jaga cause.'

On the basis of his own interviews in 1989 and reporting a handful of other primary research endeavours, Minter argued that forced recruitment had become an increasingly central part of UNITA's strategy during the 1980s. More recent evidence suggests this trend became more intense in the 1990s, after South African assistance had ended. UNITA used perhaps 11,000 child soldiers in the 1998–2002 phase of warfare.* Further, we know that life in UNITA territory for most people, including these children, was extremely tough. Human Rights Watch interviews with former child soldiers reported stress, constant sickness, frequent bouts of malaria and so on.† There were strict command structures in UNITA, with brutal punishments that included taking part in the execution of young deserters.

Each clear, abstract theory or possible explanatory 'independent variable' looks at first to have solid historical content in the Angolan conflict. Yet the closer we get to that historical content, the more these theories and variables appear to quiver like mirages and then evaporate. Perhaps there can be no general theory of war, at least not one that ignores specificity as many recent theories, complete with large cross-country statistical testing, risk doing. If a context-sensitive general theory is possible, it would have to take account of one factor ignored by the current stock of theories. Contemporary wars are rooted in the transition to capitalism. One implication is that even if the 'new wars' thesis is often simplistic and misleading, it does rest on an important insight: that war has always evolved to reflect and help shape specific historical contexts. From this perspective also, the distinction between greed and grievance

---

* Human Rights Watch (2003) cites the Cape Town definition of a child soldier— 'any person under 18 years of age who is part of any kind of regular or irregular armed force or armed group in any capacity, including but not limited to cooks, porters, messengers and those accompanying such groups, other than purely as family members.'

† Another very old characteristic of war. Bollet (2001) reports—among other things— the opinion that not a single Confederate soldier had a fully formed stool during the entire war. Diarrhoea, scurvy and pellagra were endemic.

is a false one: greed and grievance are too closely related to be separable, they are jointly relevant but both need to be understood within the political economy of dramatic social change, which is normally very slow and also produces moments of traumatic, uprooting disturbance. There is another way to put this. Statistical tests and economic models that emphasise the role of primary commodities and/or natural resources in affecting the incidence of violent conflict are fumbling towards something more meaningful. Violent conflicts, as well as widespread non-war violence, in recent decades have been concentrated in poor and middle-income developing countries, which tend by definition to be structurally dominated by primary commodities. These societies are undergoing phenomenally disruptive traumas of change, which—in its many dimensions—makes them more prone to violence.

The historical analysis sketched above suggests that individual behavioural impulses and the sets of opportunities faced by individuals making some form of choice matter;[35] and that ideas, beliefs, memories and traditions matter too; but that, fundamentally, an effective explanation of the causes and characteristics of war in Angola can only be derived from a relational analysis (and an analysis of collective as well as, and probably more than, individual relations). Similarly, the relative deprivation felt by many Angolans was aggravated (perhaps especially for those who were *not* the most deprived) by colonial upheavals and institutionalised class and social identity differences; but there was not just an 'affective', irrational outburst of violent expression of frustrations. Instead, relative deprivation (the chief representative of 'contingency theory') took shape within the long-run history of social groups vying for power and position, to hoard opportunities and lay claim to particular structural places or levels in society, to be exploiters rather than exploited. There was reason in this constantly renegotiated, conflictual history, but this cannot be reduced to the individual interest rationality of neo-classical economics.

Such a perspective allows for the following conclusions. First, where some see greed, arguably primitive accumulation and brute survival are more appropriate characterisations. Some individuals (Angolan and non-Angolan) have been and continue to be extremely greedy in this conflict. However, more important are the social relations formed over centuries and influenced by political and economic changes generating sources of power and wealth and threatening older sources of power or livelihood. Second, where some see choice, it might be better to stress coercion of different orders: coercion in press-ganging into armed forces, the force of material pressures to survive, the impositions of historically institutionalised cultures of obedience, and so on.[36] Third, where some highlight the causal role of resources, this perspective emphasises that of relations. Power in Angola, since the arrival of the Portuguese and the beginning of the slave trade, has depended on the interaction of local organisation of power and manipulation of production and trade.[37] Fourth, where some studies score ethno-linguistic fragmentation or Gini coefficients, this perspective redirects analysis towards policies, politics, history and culture. It is not a quantifiable score for ethnic fragmentation or income inequality that mechanically determines outcomes, but the specific historical relevance of ethnicity, class etc., all of which are relational rather than just structural, and all of which are affected by and affect evolving local cultures. Fifth, contingency and individual character have to be part of any explanatory model. If oil and diamonds 'caused' war in Angola, it is somewhat odd that the war should have ended so abruptly with the death of Savimbi. Sixth, war in Angola emerged from and was sustained by a knitting together of the warp of large structural factors and ideological conflicts with the weft of pettiness, localised envy, small scale beginnings on colonial farms, personal rivalries in political movements and so on. Seventh, Angola is unique: for example, the resolution of collective action challenges by UNITA was different from that by the FARC in Colombia, the FMLN in El Salvador or the RUF in Sierra Leone.[38]

A World Bank press release derides the tendency for 'some historian' to come along and trace the roots of a new conflict back 'to the fourteenth century'. But to understand war in Angola is not easy without going back, at the very least, to the late fifteenth century when the Portuguese landed on the coast. Experiences of slavery, the way Europeans sought to co-opt rulers or fomented rivalry within kingdoms, the emergence of a Creole stratum of society, and remarkable early adventures in nationalism led by Queen Nzinga in the seventeenth century: these were all significant influences on the emergence of violent anti-colonial revolt and nationalist divisions in Angola in the twentieth century, as of course were more recent political and economic developments. Through the late twentieth century there was conflict between nationalists and the Portuguese colonial administration and between rival nationalist organisations. It is rather difficult to explain this without examining the emergence of political formations in Angola: formations of common material experience, of at least a common agenda of

interests, of experiences of physical movement, education and economic organisation and indeed of culture. Furthermore, violence
is typically not spontaneous. Violence was cranked up in Angolan
politics precisely by a slow series of developments, including shifts
of strategy within anti-colonial organisations after prolonged debate, a downswing in the coffee economy, the awakening interest of
the rest of the world in Angolan political conflict, personal styles
and rivalries, the escalating call and response of Angolan protest
and settler viciousness, and so on. And, of course, violence had
been an ever-present feature and learned practice of that prolonged colonial encounter, from the violence of slave production,
through colonial conquest of the hinterland, to forced labour regimes and the repressive presence of the Portuguese secret police.

Source: AROEE database, 2002.

5

HOW TO PAY FOR A WAR

'Apart from normal tribute, the whole Persian empire is divided into regions for the purpose of furnishing supplies for the king and his army...'
(Herodotus, *The Histories*, p. 84)

Nostalgia for wars past

One way of classifying wars is to distinguish between 'new wars' and
'old wars'. There is, in this kind of distinction, a whiff of nostalgia
for old wars. The idea that contemporary wars—especially those
regarded as intra-state or civil wars—are apolitical, are 'about nothing at all', is a lament for wars that were 'about something', where
that something is usually understood as a particular version of
'ideological conflict'. The basic complaint is that there has been a
deterioration of warfare. War just isn't what it used to be. This complaint is quite widespread and runs through all the literature that
criminalises contemporary conflict, seeing wars around the world
as essentially little more than warlord banditry. It is the lament of
commentators like Bernard-Henry Lévy: 'For a long time, wars
used to have meaning... Those days are over.'[1]

The argument that war has degenerated takes different forms.
Eric Hobsbawm suggests a similar complaint when he argues that
recent wars represent history going backwards, undoing the civilised rules of the Enlightenment in a return of barbaric ill-mannered
conflict. Yet while Hobsbawm argues that very recent conflicts
do indeed represent a new stage in the reversal of civilisation, he
regards this stage as produced by a kind of degenerative history
beginning around the time of the First World War. First, barbarisation, the undoing of the rules of civilisation manifest in the conduct of war, has proceeded through stages starting in the First
World War itself. Even when wars had some 'meaning' and were
shaped by religious or ersatz religious eschatology (as in the Cold

170

War and in nationalist conflicts), war was un-writing the rulebook.
Second, the most recent phase of barbarisation is a product, not
just of this ongoing trend, but of 'the collapse of political order as
represented by functioning states…and the crumbling of the old
frameworks of social relations over a large part of the world'.[2] And
there is an older heritage to the nostalgia for meaning in earlier
wars: in 1935 Ernest Hemingway lamented the contemporary wars
of his day: 'They wrote in the old days that it is sweet and fitting to
die for one's country. But in modern war there is nothing sweet nor
fitting in your dying. You will die like a dog for no good reason.'[*]

This apparent meaninglessness of war is often associated with the
financing of contemporary conflicts, and especially with the various
commodities whose production and trade generate the income to
support a war effort in many places: diamonds, timber, oil, gemstones,
narcotics and so on. If war once meant something—religious or
ideological, for example—it has now, goes the argument, been
reduced to a petty scramble for riches. Something similar affects
analyses of international violent conflicts: thus, for many, the war in
Iraq in 2003 was almost exclusively a war fought for and because of
oil, in contrast to the ideological conflict of the Cold War.[†] The
notion of a poorer sort of war is linked, in the literature on violent
conflict in developing countries, to the argument that 'war is development in reverse', an argument that is itself tied to what the
Retort authors call the 'deep mystification' of commodities.[3]

And if wars in developing countries are now senseless (at any
rate, if they are thought in the West to be senseless), this may also
be because the places where they take place and the people that
take part in and are victims of them have fallen off the radar of the
West. Paradoxically assigning some meaning to modern wars, Lévy,
for example, explains them as the inward-turned rage of societies

---

[*] Hemingway (2004: 304). And Churchill wrote: 'War, which was cruel and glorious,
has become cruel and sordid.' Lévy (2004: 123–8) traces two traditions of nostalgia
for bygone war. One is aesthetic, pining for wars of direct and 'real' human contact
in combat, a style of war undone by technology, of which the First Gulf War (1991)
and the war in Kosovo (1999) were nothing but the most recent development. The
other nostalgia is for wars with meaning, for wars that had stakes. However, Martin
Shaw's (2003: 23–6) concept of 'degenerate war'—in which the development of
the technology of violence combines with strategic expansions of the 'enemy' to
include civilians, from around the time of the First World War onwards, to produce
a genocidal tendency in modern war—eschews nostalgia.

[†] Given the nexus of oil interests in the Bush administration in the United States
and their very obvious direct material benefits, as the Retort collective point out
(2005), spinning a conspiracy theory to make this case is not necessary.

forgotten by, or excluded from the world of a global economy.* Similarly, Duffield argues the 'new wars' are in part a reaction against marginalisation: that they arise in a context in which global capitalism has changed from being expansionary and inclusive to a state of contraction and exclusion.[4]

Commodities, rent and the financing of violence

Perhaps, though, there is an alphabet and grammar that can make contemporary violent conflict legible. This chapter makes an exploratory argument: that contemporary violence and war are rich with meanings, and that one kind of meaning may be understood precisely in terms of the history of how wars are financed.[†] War finance has historically been critical to the development of institutions that have become central to modern liberal democratic societies. Violent conflict and the soft technology of institutions and social organisation in conflict have been as important to the trajectories of modern societies as the hard technology of arms and warfare provisions has been to the productive evolution of modern economies. Modern societies, in part, may be the unintended consequence of the business of war. The argument of this and the next chapter is that characteristics of contemporary violent conflicts that are often regarded as signs of the pathological meaninglessness or the undoing of development are in fact dramatic examples of processes that have been, historically and logically, at the very heart of modernisation, development and the transition to capitalism.

— Commodities

One way to explore this idea is by looking at how organisations pay for wars, in contemporary wars and in a historical perspective. For a notable feature of many recent wars (but not all) is that they are paid for by control of the production or trade of special kinds of

---

* 'Say there is a community that, in the tragedy of its misery, sees added to that misery the misery of being alone, forgotten by everyone, erased from the great global projects, crossed off the maps of the soft-hearted politicians and their compassionate systems. Can't you imagine a kind of backlash, then? A wave of rage and revolt?' (Lévy, 2004: 69).

† There are many other ways in which violence in developing countries in the late twentieth and early twenty-first centuries has 'meaning': developmental, political, personal, even spiritual. These multiple meanings are not the chief concern of this book, but they have been explored well by some anthropologists and others: see, for example, Richards (2005), Aijmer and Abbink (2000), Scheper-Hughes and Bourgois (2004), Besteman (1999), Kriger (1991), Sanín (2003), E. J. Wood (2003).

commodity. Among the culprit commodities, diamonds finance war in Sierra Leone; timber, drug and gemstone trades all help fund violent conflict around the borders of Burma/Myanmar; the cocaine commodity chain, from leaf to refined powder, sustains conflict in Colombia and violence in Brazilian cities; poppy cultivation and trade—along with manipulation of regional cross-border smuggling of a range of consumer goods—have been central to the organisation and financing of war in Afghanistan.

A special form of gum arabic whose main source is Sudan has played a role in the Sudanese conflict, along with the tantalising presence of large oil reserves in the south of the country. In the wake of terrorist attacks against US interests in the Middle East in the 1990s, in 1997 the US government banned all imports from Sudan, claiming the Sudanese government was a conniving host to terrorists. However, the Coca-Cola Corporation and other US firms pressed for and won an exemption from this sanction for imports of gum arabic on grounds of special need. The extract from the Sudanese gum tree stops soft drinks like cola from solidifying in refrigeration storage. It is also used to help newspaper print stick to the paper without smearing, and as a thickener and emulsifier in the food and pharmaceuticals industries. Continuing to allow this trade provided an important source of foreign exchange for the Sudanese government, helping it to continue its war against the southern-based rebel movements.* However, this was actually the *main* Sudanese export to the United States, so exempting it from the import ban undermined the US policy of starving the Sudanese government's access to foreign exchange.[5]

Financing war by producing or trading illegal commodities or abusing monopoly control over other high value commodities is not restricted to rebels or warlords. Governments, too, indulge in this activity to fund wars. For example, US government officials have found evidence of cocaine in Colombian government planes, suggesting individuals in a government meant to be aiding the US 'war on drugs' were at the same time profiting from the drugs trade. But the classic commodity-sustained and financed war is Angola. At least in the post-Cold War phase of war in Angola the conflict was usually presented internationally as a contest between oil and diamonds: the government paid for the war by siphoning off massive oil revenue (and by borrowing commercially against future oil revenue) to sustain a huge army and expensive foreign military advice

* Sudan earned about $54 million from gum arabic exports in 1995, for example.

and technology, while the UNITA opposition paid for its continued rebellion by controlling production and export from much of the country's diamond producing areas.

— Rent

The special characteristic of the most notorious conflict commodities is their high value and the scope for rents. There is also scope for rent in other commodity markets. Rent is difficult to define. It is a category with different coding rules. The definition of classical political economy, going back to Ricardo and Marx, ties it more specifically to land rent than other definitions. Modern economic definitions vary but often refer to profit over and above normal, or competitive profits, however these are defined. For others, rent is taken to refer simply to all forms of income that are created or sustained by non-market interventions.* The often astonishingly high profits that can be won from selling some commodities conveys the idea that their value is extremely high relative to their production costs; but the key is that governments or other actors intervene in markets to restrict or to protect restriction of competition.

High rent commodities often include valuable natural resources like oil deposits. International oil prices, for example, are not purely a product of supply and demand or the interplay of unrelated, dispersed market participants, but are influenced by the management of coordinated interventions by OPEC. But rent can arise in other circumstances. For example, where a commodity is declared illegal this is likely to increase the income stream to those that manage to succeed in the market, i.e. in shaping and controlling the market. If heroin were legalised, for example, much of the attraction in producing it would fade as its production became increasingly common and competitive, pushing down prices: certainly, it would be harder to make the immense profits that are currently made.

* There are several, sometimes contradictory definitions of rent in economics dictionaries and textbooks, among which there are perhaps two main definitions. In one, rent is the income, from one use of an asset, over and above that which would flow from the next best use of this asset. In the other, as in this chapter, rent is income derived from non-market interventions: e.g. government intervention to transfer use rights between beneficiaries or to create or maintain a monopoly market structure (e.g. the government licensing of a monopoly marketing board for gum arabic in Sudan). This latter meaning is relevant to the idea of 'rent-seeking', where people try to use political influence to secure such interventions. On this usage of the term, see Khan (2000). However, the key in this chapter is that non-market interventions need not be governmental: violence is one other means, often effective, of capturing or maintaining income flows.

Another example is columbite-tantalite ore, a very heavy and heat-resistant metal, one of the main sources of which is found in the eastern Kivu districts of the Congo. The rarity of this ore immediately raises its value. Columbite-tantalite ore, or coltan as it is often called, might not be as well known as diamonds or oil but it also plays a central and prized role in the contemporary global economy. It is used in spacecraft. It is also an important input in the production of both mobile phones and games consoles. Control of the mining, transporting and export of this ore within the Kivus is at the heart of battles for supremacy in the Kivus between rebel and government forces, and has drawn in the Rwandan government that backs one of the rebel movements based in eastern Congo and taxes the coltan business. Just as with oil in Angola and diamonds there and elsewhere, the double involvement in these commodities of local producers and traders with international corporations is intriguing and commonly under-emphasised. This joint involvement is taken up in greater detail in Chapter 6, but it is worth stressing here that funding a war through commodity exploitation requires access to the commodity in question and access to and relationships with market makers in the advanced capitalist countries.[6] War finance of this kind is far from excluded from international capitalism.

Successful war finance through manipulation of high rent commodities often depends on the creation or exploitation of clandestine networks that evade government controls, international sanctions or international regulations. This is the case, for example, with efforts to smuggle diamonds out of conflict zones and to succeed in selling them on the world market where they may have to avoid identification schemes branding them as 'conflict diamonds'; and more obviously so with the heroin and cocaine trades. These clandestine activities are partly what tars commodity war finance with the brush of criminality.

Beyond this, though, once systems of production and trade of drugs or blood diamonds, or illegal timber logging, or military manipulation of cashew nut trade in the Casamance region of Senegal, or smuggling of stolen cars or recycling of small arms and cocaine and so on are set up, like war itself they have a way of developing their own momentum. They can become so attractive to their beneficiaries—the war entrepreneurs or violence entrepreneurs—that they can appear to lose interest in either winning or losing the war. This certainly makes it more difficult to bring conflicts to an end, especially if both sides in a conflict appear to be focused on the benefits of wartime accumulation. For in this case war is a system that regulates the ways in which economic surpluses are generated and appropriated, more than a direct conflict between two opponents.

— Means and ends

These situations may confirm Foucault's idea about violence—in *Society Must be Defended*—that it levels the hedge between means and ends. The means becomes the end and at that point there is no difference between means and ends. Alternatively, the distinction is not extinguished but the relationship is simply reversed: the means of war—war finance—become the end and the end—prosecuting the war—becomes the means of securing access to rent. Given that there are normally multiple ends and objectives in wars, even where this does occur, i.e. where war finance mechanisms become confused with war aims, the phenomenon is unlikely to define fully the nature of a given conflict. Possibly, at an abstract, *a priori* level, the objective of accumulating rent provokes people to want to start a war. However, this is not necessarily the case and would only be an effective explanation of war if there were no other plausible causes. It is also an argument or assumption that presumes all participants in a war are reducible to 'two players', the so-called warring parties, that can be seen neatly as individuals making individual and coherent and consistent choices. In reality, for some individuals within a war the accumulation of rent from war finance or from wartime market conditions may be or become the principal goal; while for some others the goals of profit maximisation might actually conflict with wartime instability (if their commercial farms or manufacturing firms or rural trading businesses are disrupted by violence); for others still, the war and victory may be or remain more important than wartime accumulation.

Not only the proponents of the 'new war' thesis emphasise the centrality of these types of war finance. Chapter 3 discussed the analysis that claims an empirical association between dependence on primary commodities and the statistical risk of 'civil war', and then *explains* war in terms of this dependence on primary commodities. The argument runs that a high proportion of primary commodity exports in total economic activity (or GDP) stands for, acts as a proxy for, an incentive to pursue policies of 'instant taxation', i.e. looting. Given certain other conditions—such as a preponderance of ill-educated young men in the population—it is then argued that the opportunities for starting a rebellion are often irresistible. To put it crudely: where there's a way, it is assumed there is always a will to go to war.

So it is quite common to argue that commodity based or re-source based war finance methods account for the causes of war as well as its source of sustenance; and that these methods of war finance define wars themselves as criminal, apolitical and ideologically disappointing to Western sensibilities. Arguably, this is an extension of, or a projection of, a more general value judgement made about developing country economies and their political organisation, which are often characterised by 'rent-seeking' and 'corruption' that are then seen not only as morally unappealing but also as economically inefficient and ruinous. For a long time there has been a voluminous literature in development economics on this question of rent-seeking activities and their alleged implications for economic development. The basic argument is that rent-seeking involves allocating resources to the chase for easy money, rent, rather than to efficient and productive activities in competitive market conditions. It is also argued that the greater the degree of state intervention in and management of an economy, the more the scope for this wasteful use of energy and resources. And rent-seeking is typically associated with poor overall economic performance.

— Rent and development

This is just one of the dimensions of the argument that has been dominant since the early 1980s that state intervention is generally 'a bad thing', leading to economic inefficiency and slower growth, in rich and poorer countries. The emphasis has been on scaling back the state, pursuing privatisation and deregulation policies that are supposed to inject entrepreneurial enthusiasm and the benefits of competitive markets into economies, generating greater efficiency and faster growth. Development, from this perspective, is seen as a movement from highly imperfect or 'distorted' market structures towards more competitive markets, heading in the ultimate direction of perfect competition.[7] This kind of economic thinking can then be applied to war. The result is the theory that war is essentially the *ne plus ultra* of rent-seeking. As Jack Hirshleifer puts it, 'rent-seeking, in its usual connotation of maneuvering [*sic*] for licenses and monopoly privileges, is to conflict as milkwater is to blood, sweat, and tears.'[8] This is in line with the definition of rent as income secured by non-market interventions, in this case through violence.

However, this book departs from the standard economic literature in questioning the assumption that rent creation and rent-seeking, and in this case violence and war, are necessarily exclu-

sively bad for development. Non-market interventions in economies, including those that create or seek to capture rents, have
been a typical feature of successfully developing countries just as
they have been a feature of failed development transformations. In
more successful development cases the rents have been associated
with productive expansion rather than stagnation. Likewise, war,
violence and coercion of one form or another have been common
features of successful transformations as of failed ones. This suggests two implications. First, that it is worth exploring the creativity
of war finance, or the creation of rent through violence. Second,
that these wartime activities should be assessed in terms not only of
their immediate characteristics and effects but also of their possible
longer-term consequences. To take up both of these implications
involves a more historical approach than is common in the literature on contemporary or 'new' wars.

Paying for war has taken many different forms: it has included
predation on local populations, taxation, feudal levies of people
and material resources, ransoming cities, borrowing domestically
and abroad, creating currencies, printing money (i.e. paying for
war through inflation), trying to pay for war by manipulating the
flows of income associated with greater production for the war
effort, mercantilist conquest of new markets and trading networks,
relying on foreign military and financial aid (in the form of grants
or low-interest loans) and capturing income flows from production
and trade and then diverting these to the war effort. Changing
technological demands of warfare have also had effects on the compulsion to find new funding sources. For example, at one time
European statelets could conduct their almost perpetual wars by
relying chiefly on fairly small mercenary forces; but as warfare changed and became a larger scale enterprise these emerging states had
to mobilise domestic military forces and then had to find ways of
paying for the increasingly expensive business of war.

Much of the institutional apparatus of modern government and
economic management has its origins in this compulsion to finance wars. For example, taxation institutions in England and elsewhere were more or less created to mobilise war finances. The
Prussian monarchy's chief tax collection agency came into being as
the General War Commissariat. And the first federal income tax in
American history was enacted in August 1861, largely as a measure
to reassure the financial markets that the Northern government
would have enough money to pay interest on bonds sold as a first

means of paying for the Civil War.* In short, the monopolisation of the means of violence by emergent (and, later, fully-fledged) states depended on the mobilisation of tax and other revenue and the monopolisation of currencies; these in turn depended on an effective monopoly of violence. If the financing of late-twentieth- and early-twenty-first-century wars and violence is potentially linked to a trajectory of societal transformation or longer-term social and economic development, then there may be clues to this potential in the history of war finance. In other words, this history may provide part of the alphabet and grammar that makes this violence legible.

War finance and state formation in Europe

In medieval and early modern Europe war was a way of life for the ruling classes. War was institutionalised; it simply was 'the rules of the game'.[9] Kings waged wars within their own countries and against others. They had to face internal rebellions which were largely sparked by the pressure of tax demands on the peasantry that were increased to pay for external wars. Kings had to manage relationships with a nobility for whom violence of one sort or another was a way of life. In the early Middle Ages, as was noted in Chapter 1, violence was a kind of class privilege for the upper classes, exempting them to some degree from the efforts of central rulers to establish order.

The major powers in the sixteenth and seventeenth centuries were almost constantly at war, battling for survival and supremacy. By one estimate there was major warfare in something like ninety-six years of the sixteenth century and ninety-four of the seventeenth. There was a climax of sorts in the Thirty Years War of 1618–48 that drew in most states in Central and Northern Europe. The Treaty of Westphalia in 1648 consolidated a kind of peace that at

---

* Larry Neal argues, 'The development of macroeconomics as a separate sub-discipline within economics can be traced precisely to the efforts of government officials and advisors to determine the economic base available for the logistical support required for a winning military effort. We can think of William Petty in seventeenth-century England, concerned about the appropriate economic policy with respect to a conquered Ireland, writing his Treatise of Taxes and Contributions (1679), which evolved into his Several Essays in Political Arithmetick (1699). In the process, Petty developed the key concept, the circular flow of income, that led eventually to national income accounting... It has even been argued that our modern system of national income and product accounts owes its genesis to Lord Keynes' need to illustrate the mechanics of his scheme to enable Britain to pay for World War II' (Neal, 1994).

the same time set the foundation for the international nation-state polity that has since become the norm. As violent rulers began to consolidate their power and organisation, in other words as what we now think of as states began to form, the financial requirements of organised violence rose. And the technology and scale of warfare pushed warmongers to innovate in the techniques of war finance, often quite brutally.[10]

There is a historical argument that explains modern states arising from the behaviour of racketeers involved in organised violence. Rulers were—according to this history—essentially no different from Mafiosi bandits. They sold protection—having first ensured that people needed protecting. Once they had sufficient power they redefined their activities and rewrote their past. Thus these rulers could call the protection money they raised 'tax'; and they could hide their own sordid origins behind the glamorous notion of rule by divine right. But this version of history is sometimes a little overdrawn: in reality more or less established princes or kings, who had ruled with roughly accepted laws for some time, could still introduce new forms of bandit behaviour. German rulers in the early seventeenth century imposed on many towns the formalised *Kontribution*—calibrated by the replacement value of the town's buildings and enforced by threat of setting fire to a town's wooden structures. The 'contribution' developed as the mainstay of seventeenth-century war finance from a merging of earlier traditions of legal levies and occasional *Brandschaltung*, the latter imposed by military leaders without the consent of local authorities. The legendary military commander Wallenstein, who was also the financially savvy centre of a web of lending and borrowing that sustained warfare, was responsible more than anyone for the systematisation of these contributions.[11] There was far more to the longer term development of states and bureaucracies and institutions of 'governance', but this history captures convincingly a central part of the history of institutions that have come to form the basis of political organisation throughout most of the world.

There were also important variations in the ways these rulers funded their military campaigns (both internal and external), variations that affected the longer-term success and competitiveness of the states and the nations they organised. Spain, for example, developed immense ambitions and fought wars both within what is now Spain and much further afield. The kingdoms of Castile and Aragon concocted a coalition of the willing in the late fifteenth century (sealed with the marriage of Ferdinand of Aragon and Isabel of Castile) that enabled a victorious push against the Moorish rulers in Andalusia. Although this campaign helped to consolidate the state of Spain, the terms of the coalition compromised the Castilian rulers' ability to cover the costs of war. For Castile agreed it would not levy taxes on Aragon, Catalonia or Valencia; nor could the central state send troops into these regions. Castilian rulers had, therefore, to scour other sources of funding. They borrowed, on a huge scale. And—describing again that circle of means and ends—they forced huge amounts of silver out of the Americas. There is an argument that this means of war finance, fantastically successful in the shortish term, became a millstone around the neck of longer-term prospects for Spanish success. Because the Spanish state could rely on American silver it did not have to develop awkward political relationships with domestic groups, nor did it have to develop the legal and bureaucratic wherewithal to mobilise domestic financial levies from these groups.* And it was precisely that delicate and difficult balance—between guns, lawyers and money (between a monopoly over violence, a bureaucratic expansion and institutional development, and a political settlement among dominant classes)—that formed the basis for the truly successful state, like Britain.[12]

'From 990 AD onward, major mobilisations for war provided the chief occasions on which states expanded, consolidated, and created new forms of political organisation,' argued Charles Tilly.[13] The more successful states were those that had a growing tax base—which tended to mean, increasingly, those that had a more successful development of capitalism—and those that negotiated the relationship between centralised authority and decentralised interest groups, including capitalists, merchants, peasants and landed nobles, most adroitly. Since war became more and more costly, and because taxation was always a risky strategy, tax revenue tended to be an inadequate source of war finance: access to credit became just as important, if not more so. In the early modern period the state that succeeded best, that had a pioneering capitalist class and a rela-

---

* Castile did have a more modern bureaucracy but did not or could not extend this to other regions. Furthermore, not only did Castile not need to depend on domestic sources of war finance, thanks to its access to gold and silver from foreign sources, but also Castilian rulers destroyed much of the domestic basis for revenue generation. First the *Reconquista*—the successful expulsion of the Muslim states from the south of the Iberian peninsula to north Africa—and then the Inquisition managed to drive out or drive underground Muslim and Jewish merchants who had been the most successful organisers of mercantile activity (and therefore of a tax base) in Iberia.

tively commercialised rural élite, was the English and, eventually, British state. In the fifteenth century England did not, on the face of it, have much of a competitive advantage over France or Spain. However, what it did have in its favour, it made the most of over time. For a start, it had a very early centralised administrative and tax collecting bureaucracy, developed in the earlier wartime experience of the Norman Conquest in 1066. Catastrophic violence is not normally remembered as a part of the development of English gradualism and liberalism, but there is a very strong argument that that later gradualism rested squarely on brutality and warfare. For example, the Wars of the Roses from the 1450s to the 1480s and the Civil War of the 1640s were the crucibles of a political settlement among kings and increasingly commercialised nobles.*

Meanwhile, the English state did need to fund external warfare, but not on the immense scale of the Spanish wars. In the 1530s, for example, Henry VIII first confiscated church land and then, in selling it off, adopted a privatisation programme to fund his failed invasion of France. Tudor monarchs also financed war by pirating silver from Spanish America. One of the other sources of English power was England's relatively good record of repayment on its debts. Internationalised markets were intertwined with this history of the formation of states through violence and its financing. Thus, for example, the Fuggers, the German finance house based in Augsburg, borrowed in Antwerp to help finance Spanish warfare, and used as collateral on these loans expectations of a stock of Spanish American silver.† But as war became more expensive it helped to develop a domestic source of credit instead of only relying on these international networks. Again, England successfully developed

---

* The Wars of the Roses severely weakened the power of the nobility vis-à-vis the central state; later, the Civil War weakened the power of the king to act as an absolute ruler. A classic account of this argument—the importance of violent upheaval in England as the foundation for later gradualism—is in Barrington Moore (1967). Moore also emphasises the significance of the brutality of primitive accumulation later in the development of the industrial revolution, principally through the 'enclosures', by which peasants were forcibly excluded from previously communal land, a measure that was one of the mechanisms that forced poor English families into the wage labour market, having—as Marx put it—separated them from the means of production (see Chapter 6).

† See Tilly (1992). Earlier, the English King Edward I (r. 1272–1307) had mobilised funds loaned by the Riccardi banking family based in Lucca (Italy) to pay for mercenaries equipped with crossbows from Gascony, to back up the construction of imposing castles in Wales in his strategy of containment of Welsh guerrillas.

capital markets that played into the establishment of its national security and international adventures.*

In short, the wars that are associated with the foundation of modern states and some of their key institutions were paid for in a variety of ways. These mechanisms of war finance often involved brutal extraction, appropriation, extortion, theft and piracy. The profits to be made in war attracted and institutionalised, in some periods, specialists in the business of violence. It was only over a lengthy period, and in some countries more effectively than others, that the business of war generated political pressures for 'better governance' and political contracts that paved the way for more democratic management of security and economies.

The American Civil War

For a long time taxation, borrowing, international trade and resource capture have been central to the ability to pay for and conduct warfare, as illustrated above. In some places certain classes or groups, e.g. peasants or rural élites, have fought off the claims of the state. But challenging the central state itself requires resources: this can mean mobilising very similar sources of war finance, including less formalised local taxation and levies, borrowing and resource capture and mobilisation.† All these ways of paying for war, and more modern variations on the themes, have continued to matter to more recent conflicts. One example is the American Civil War, for many commentators the most momentous event in US history and one that imposed dramatic financing demands on its protagonists, demands that the North managed to respond to more successfully than the South. In the North the more developed institutions of capitalist development helped enable the massive war effort, and in turn the war effort and government interventions to pay for the war developed further the institutions of capitalism,

---

* In the same way, from the fourteenth to the early seventeenth century European states trying to expand or simply survive could depend mainly on mercenaries. But as war became a larger undertaking this was not enough—and states had to develop standing national armies, thereby creating another source of institutional and bureaucratic innovation and another source of interest-group pressure.

† In the English Civil War (1643–8) there were similarities between the Royalist and Parliamentarian management of war finance through local taxes and forced loans, but arguably the Royalist administration was more idiosyncratic, unpredictable and personalised by comparison with Cromwell's parliamentarian effort with its beginnings of impersonal committees collecting regular taxes (see Ronald Hutton, 1994).

including capital markets. As one commentator put it: 'Management of Federal debt during and after the Civil War improved the efficiency with which the capital market garnered and allocated investible funds. Lessons learned in "high" finance could then be applied to support the "mundane" expansion of industry, agriculture and transport after 1865.'*

The North began the war in a financial crisis, brought on partly by the lower tariff rates on international trade of recent years and partly by panic and the collapsing credit rating of the administration following the Southern secession. The Union government raised two thirds of its war revenue from loans and just more than 20 per cent of its war needs from taxation. Loan finance through selling government bonds to bankers and taxation through tariffs on trade accounted for part of this story, but the Union administration made far-reaching financial innovations in order to meet the needs of war. First, President Lincoln's Secretary of the Treasury, Salmon P. Chase, pioneered the idea of selling bonds to ordinary people in small denominations and payable in monthly instalments.[†] Further, the government marketed these bonds with urgent, patriotic advertising.[‡] Second, the Union administration introduced the first federal income tax in American history in 1861.

Third, and perhaps most momentous, the Northern government created a national currency, the paper money issued by the Treasury that quickly came to be known as 'greenbacks'. Banks had long worked with paper money but the issuing by government of legal tender fiat money was altogether new, and its introduction was contentious. It was Congressman Elbridge G. Spaulding of New York, as chair of the House subcommittee in charge of drafting emergency legislation, who proposed this bold move, initially, of issuing

* Patrick O'Brien (1988: 59). There was a strong element of 'improvisation', and at times even panic, about the Northern war finance effort: for example, Salmon Chase's efforts to sell long term debt on the New York market at high prices came to little till inflation and military confidence eventually made his prices, by 1863, seem more attractive (see Neal, 1994).
† See McPherson (1990): Chase himself had no financial background and relied especially on the banker Jay Cooke, who was the driving force behind the war bond marketing campaign.
‡ This was to become a huge phenomenon in the First and Second World Wars. The bond notes still trade as memorabilia: Second World War bonds, signed by the War Finance Committee, include a Walt Disney bond. The text—'This is to certify that...is the owner of a War Bond, thereby becoming an investor in this country's fight for human liberty and a contributor in a world struggle to make life free and forever peaceful for all men'—is surrounded by smiling cartoon dwarves, Bambi, Pinocchio, Donald Duck and so on.

$150 million in Treasury notes that would be legal tender: individuals, banks and the government would have to accept US notes as lawful money. Opponents feared an inflationary onslaught if this was allowed to pass. As Spaulding put it: 'The bill before us is a war measure, a *necessary means* of carrying into execution the power granted in the Constitution "to raise and *support* armies"…These are extraordinary times, and extraordinary measures must be resorted to in order to save our Government and preserve our nationality.'* The Legal Tender Act became law in February 1862. There certainly was some inflationary consequence but it was hardly dramatic compared with inflationary war finance in the South or with US war finance experiences during the two twentieth-century world wars. To some extent, inflationary pressure—the excess demand that results when government war needs compete with civilian needs and activities, putting pressure on supply capacities—was soaked up by new tax measures. Again, McPherson puts it pithily:

The Internal Revenue Act of 1862 taxed almost everything but the air northerners breathed. It imposed sin taxes on liquor, tobacco, and playing cards; luxury taxes on carriages, yachts, billiard tables, jewellery, and other expensive items; taxes on patent medicines and newspaper advertisements; licence taxes on almost every conceivable profession or service except the clergy; stamp taxes, taxes on the gross receipts of corporations, banks, insurance companies, and a tax on the dividends or interest they paid to investors; value-added taxes on manufactured goods and processed meats; an inheritance tax; and an income tax. The law also created a Bureau of Internal Revenue, which remained a permanent part of the federal government even though most of these taxes (including the income tax) expired several years after the end of the war. The relationship of the American taxpayer to the government was never the same again.[14]

---

* They were desperate times: the Union defeat at Ball's Bluff in October 1861 and what was increasingly clearly a neurotic aversion to actually fighting on the part of General McClellan led to a loss of confidence in the North that was then compounded by a diplomatic incident when northern forces seized two Southern spies from the British ship *Trent*. Animal spirits in Northern financial markets panicked and there was then a run on the banks. As reserve deposits drained out, the banks responded by suspending payments in specie. This meant the Treasury could no longer pay suppliers, contractors, or soldiers. As McPherson puts it, the 'war economy of one of the world's richest nations threatened to grind to a halt. As Lincoln lamented on January 10, "the bottom is out of the tub. What shall I do?"' (McPherson, 1990: 444). McClellan's brilliance as a trainer of armies and his extraordinary reluctance to take them into action—a reluctance that, arguably, prolonged the war and cost many lives—are well covered in McPherson's and other written accounts of the Civil War; but they are also brilliantly conveyed in Ken Burns's epic documentary film *The American Civil War.*

Confederacy efforts to pay for the war were less successful. Most Southern wealth was tied up in land and slaves; and a cotton embargo (imposed by the North and enforced by its navy) prevented the South from mobilising one of its main assets. The Confederate Congress tried to divert planters' debt to Northern merchants and banks into the war effort, through legislation requiring Confederate citizens to pay into the Treasury the amounts they owed to US citizens, in return for a Confederate bond. But where perhaps $200 million was owed to Northern creditors, this measure only raised about $12 million. Confederate taxation also failed to muster enough revenue. Southerners may have been desperate to hold onto their autonomy and institutions, enough so to back secession and the war, but they were not keen on paying taxes. The pre-war tax burden in the South was very light, and even during the war the Confederate government failed effectively to centralise revenue collection. Thus, when it imposed a property tax it allowed individual states to collect it. However, while South Carolina collected the levy and Texas covered its tax demand by confiscating Northern-owned property, the other Southern states either borrowed the money or printed it in state notes. So the South tried to borrow to pay for the war, issuing bonds, but the take up on these was desperately slow. One innovation was the 'produce loan'—whereby planters could pledge the proceeds from cotton and tobacco and other crops in return for bonds. This too was a disaster. Ultimately, and reluctantly, the South paid for its war by printing money as a way of commanding control over resources. Treasury printed notes were to be redeemed after the war in specie: in other words, the South did not make them legal tender in the way that the North did. Alongside Confederate money printing, Southern states, counties, cities and even private businesses starting issuing notes of their own. The consequence of this approach to war finance was runaway inflation. Inflationary war finance is very common and it works partly as a kind of tax: states issue money to help them meet bills incurred in fighting the war, while private individuals, especially the poor, experience their earnings shrinking in value as prices rise and shortages increase.*

Keynes's How to Pay for the War

In some countries, domestic production for the war effort could also become a source of paying for the war. The greatest intellec-

---

* One example was salt, the only means of preserving meat: the price of salt span out of control while supply was hit by wartime government claims on transport vehicles.

tual analysis of and response to this possibility was Keynes's *How to Pay for the War,* published in 1940. This was a book that grew out of a series of pamphlets that in turn grew out of a number of letters written to *The Times* and papers written for *The Economic Journal.* Keynes developed a strategy to pay for the war out of the extra incomes that would be generated by the huge productive war effort.

The government would have to mobilise extra resources, including, for example, female labour, to keep the economy going and at the same time to produce armaments and ammunition. This immense productive effort and the additional incomes it created would intensify the tension between the demands of war and the claims of private consumption—leading, probably, to a combination of consumer goods shortages and general price inflation. His suggestion for reconciling these competing claims was a scheme of deferred wages. A proportion of pay would be deferred till after the war. In the meantime this would be claimed as loan finance for the government. Keynes expected that after the war there would be an economic depression as the government retreated from the war effort and employment needs were scaled back. At this point, the government would redeem the loans, paying the deferred wages, which would then stimulate enough private consumer demand to divert the recession. Keynes argued this scheme was *necessary*—because the war could not fully be paid for out of taxes or voluntary savings—and *progressive*—because it avoided the regressive consequences of inflationary war finance.

Most wars increase inequality by various means, including the way they are paid for; inflationary war finance, for example, typically hurts the poor especially hard, because they are least able to obtain increases in money income in the face of rising prices. One of the astonishing things in Keynes's plan was his endeavour 'to snatch from the exigency of war positive social improvements'. For the measures envisaged in his scheme embodied 'an advance towards economic equality greater than any which we have made in recent times'.[15] Income earned from the extra effort of wartime would not be dissipated by inflation since it would be held over till after the war and withdrawing income in this scheme from private consumption would lessen inflationary pressure. The rights to deferred consumption after the war would 'be widely distributed amongst all those who are foregoing immediate consumption, instead of being mainly concentrated, as they were last time, in the hands of the capitalist class.'[16] Furthermore, Keynes suggested that, paradoxically, the straitened lifestyles of wartime provided the opportunity to introduce the family allowance for low-income households that, before the war, had been deemed too expensive a social reform. This would only work, Keynes argued, if it were combined with the deferred payments scheme.

Paying for war in late developing countries
— Constraints

Keynes's scheme was the apogee of progressive war finance. Most protagonists in war have not been able to implement such a sophisticated scheme for appropriating resources to fund war, even if they had the political will: their productive forces and financial market instruments are typically not sufficiently developed, their states are less powerful, and/or they lack sufficient political consensus in support of the war effort. Contemporary developing country war finance (and, indeed, advanced capitalist country war finance) has to be set against the historical background of diverse expedients for paying for violent conflict that has been illustrated above. Developing countries generally have a narrower set of options. First, they often have a small tax base from which to raise revenue. Second, although it is also true that most developing country governments traditionally have under-taxed, this does not mean there is a large fiscal slack that can readily be taken in during wartime. The demands of war are only an intensification of the pressing need in all poor countries to mobilise resources to promote capital accumulation, growth and social improvement and there are good reasons, technical and political, why even the potential tax take is not realised.

Further, given that many of the wars in developing countries are to one or another extent 'internal', pitting the government against armed opposition, the politics of taxation are even more constraining. It has been argued that incumbent élites would be happy to have the government raise the tax burden on them in order to defend militarily the status quo;[17] but this is a weak hypothesis. Generally, governments in such conditions of conflict have to negotiate delicate coalitions to remain in power—and this may mean facing a trade-off between raising more tax revenue and securing political backing. Examples range from the Confederacy in the American South to the Sandinista government in Nicaragua, which in trying to maintain a frail coalition with sections of the Nicaraguan middle classes who had also opposed the Somoza dictatorship, found it could not press them too hard with revenue raising demands to pay for the war against the Contras.

Third, financial instruments and markets tend to be less developed in poor countries, and when this is combined with low average incomes it is obvious that there is little scope for paying for the war through capital market innovations. Fourth, war tends to harm the balance of payments both by damaging export production and infrastructure and by raising the demand for imports (including food imports and military hardware). Fifth, unlike the conditions in Britain in the Second World War, very few developing countries now do more than a modest amount of producing their own war effort through manufacturing of arms, uniforms and other provisions. Therefore, there is next to no scope for meeting the demands of war through any deferred payments for the extra wage labour committed to the war effort.

— Inflation

There are only three remedies left: predation and rent finance, inflation, and foreign finance through borrowing or aid. The options open to non-state groups—rebels, freedom fighters, self-determination movements etc.—are even more constrained. The remedy of choice through most of the past three hundred years or so has been inflation. The American, French, Russian and Chinese revolutions were all financed mainly by printing money.* Runaway inflation—caused by money supply policy, excess demand and goods famines—has been a feature of a wide range of violent conflicts since the early twentieth century, including the wars in Angola, Mozambique and Nicaragua, in Zaire/Congo and elsewhere. Inflationary war finance is analogous to rent, at least in terms of the definition of rent as income secured by non-market means. It involves a government (usually but not exclusively) using seigniorage (or the political power to mint money) as a means of appropriating income and resources.

Inflation has often been seen not just as an expedient but also as a weapon of war. This was even more aggressively the case in conflicts involving regimes trying to create socialist societies; for in these cases money itself was seen as a reflection of social relations and class struggle. Rationalising the monetary anarchy of war

* 'Thus the United States came into existence on a full tide not of inflation but of hyper inflation—the kind of inflation that ends only in money becoming worthless' (Galbraith, 1975).

communism during the Russian Civil War of 1918–21, Preobraz-
hensky welcomed the use of the printing press as 'that machine
gun which attacked the bourgeois regime in its rear, namely its
monetary system'.[18]

A good example is Angola after independence in 1975. When
the MPLA came to power it was already engaged in a war that pitted
it against Jonas Savimbi's UNITA and also pitted Cuba and the
Soviet Union against South Africa and the United States, as well as
drawing in other foreign interests. The massive exodus of Portuguese settlers and administrators undermined the tax base available
to the MPLA, especially given the extent to which the Portuguese
had colonised salaried employment in its African 'provinces'. As
another consequence of Portuguese colonial rule, there were extremely few university-educated Angolans at independence; the
MPLA had very little administrative capacity to manage a war economy. Given that the MPLA was also dressed in the full combat gear
of Marxist-Leninist ideology and command economy pretensions,
inflationary war finance was inevitable. Even after the gradual loss
of faith in command economy principles during the 1980s and efforts
to control the money supply through the launch of a new currency,
the Angolan government continued to preside over an inflation-
fuelled war.* This was in spite of its ability to draw both on foreign
aid to prosecute the military effort and on increasing oil revenue.

Meanwhile, although the government imported most of the means
of violence, there was nonetheless some domestic manufacturing
activity stimulated by the needs of provisioning the armed forces.
Being the largest importer of weapons in Africa during some periods (mainly the first half of the 1980s) created a demand, for example, for a local armaments repair workshop industry, the Empresa
de Reparação e Recuperação de Equipamento Militar. There were
also industries in Angola serving both military and civilian needs:
production of flour, sponge cushions (for truck seats), tobacco,
blankets, aluminium dishes, tyres, batteries, shirts, sheets, kitchen
implements, paints, canvas shoes, trousers, beer, soft drinks, metal

---

* The 'growth rate of currency in circulation averaged about 23 per cent annually
from 1977 to 1988. From 1983 through 1988, currency in circulation averaged a 19
per cent annual growth rate, the narrow measure of the money stock (M1) grew at
an average annual rate of 16 per cent, and the broad measure of the money stock
(M2) averaged an annual growth rate of 17 per cent. With prices fixed in official
markets and supplies limited, this growth of the money stock has fuelled inflation
in the parallel market and created extremely large relative price distortions
between the official and parallel markets' (World Bank, 1991: 51).

boards, inner tubes etc. These industries, though, were not a great success. In 1984 95 per cent of total sponge cushion production in Angola was allocated to the military but this still only met 30 per cent of the order that had been put in by the armed forces. The poor performance of domestic industrial production geared fully or substantially to military needs is yet another reminder that the range of interests involved in a major armed conflict is not unitary and coherent, as some seem to think. The armed forces had a strong interest in industrial output plans being fulfilled in the sectors that catered for their needs; however, other interests and decisions undermined the chances of industrial success.[19] Clearly, domestic production for the war economy was not enough to provide any basis for a deferred payments type scheme. And—as elsewhere in hyper-inflationary conditions—when money lost value and meaning, transactions increasingly took place through barter. One alternative currency in the capital during the 1980s was a crate of imported beer cans.

Inflation was what Keynes called a pseudo-remedy for the problem of paying for war. If printing money has been seen as a weapon of war, it is a pseudo-weapon, or worse; for typically, inflationary war finance leads to a loss, rather than a strengthening, of government control. Thus the use of inflation to pay for a war is rather like the unreliable, backfiring 'Angola gun' of the seventeenth century.

US governments at least partly learnt this lesson in successive post-Second World War military engagements in South East Asia. The US-led UN intervention in Korea in the 1950–3 war (intervention began before, the United States having occupied Korea south of the 38th parallel between 1945 and 1948) led to increasingly rapid rates of inflation. Inflation had been running high for the four years leading up to the start of the Korean War in June 1950, a sure sign of social conflict, but during the war price increases reached rates of some 600 per cent. However, when the United States intervened in Vietnam later (in the 1960s) it made determined efforts to stabilise the economy in areas under its control, fearing that inflation of more than 3 per cent a year would generate costly levels of social unrest. Nonetheless, within the United States itself the burden of the Vietnam war contributed—by one estimate—as much as $4bn to the current account deficit in 1967: and large and persistent US balance of payments deficits were the key to the international monetary crisis of 1967/68.[20]

Meanwhile, despite scattered efforts of rebel movements to print money and create their own currencies, most opposition movements do not have the luxury of paying for war by monetary policy. In Afghanistan after 1992, when Mujahideen forces took control of Kabul, there was a progressive fragmentation of state sovereignty. In the multiple conflicts that followed there was a parallel process of minting different currencies by opposing factions. At one stage, for example, there were three different Afghan currencies in circulation. More recently, much of eastern Afghanistan has become a Pakistani rupee zone while Kabul, after the Taliban was toppled, became increasingly a US dollar economy.

— Aid

Many protagonists in wars have relied where possible on foreign aid as a resource, whether or not they can mint their own currency.* This aid takes many forms, financial and otherwise: including military training overseas, direct gifts of or bargain deals on military hardware, providing intelligence, direct and indirect financial support for the war, sending troops to fight, and providing 'non-military' aid that by releasing financial constraints elsewhere enables a government or group to commit other resources to the war effort. Foreign aid in support of warring parties was immense throughout the Cold War and ranged from South African support to Renamo guerrillas in Mozambique and Cuban support for the MPLA government in Angola through covert US aid to the Contras in Nicaragua and Soviet military aid to the Derg regime in Ethiopia. Elsewhere, there was of course massive Soviet assistance to the government in Afghanistan (1979–89), while the US government lent assistance to the Mujahideen—including, as is well known, to Osama bin Laden—directly and, indirectly, through military deals with Pakistan.

War economies and paying for war after the Cold War

Foreign aid to organisations and states fighting wars continues. The most obvious example is US aid to Israel. However, it is generally true that the end of the Cold War has transformed war finance. This was not always a straightforward matter of a sudden cut-off of external financial support. Violent conflict in Afghanistan, for example, was sustained after the end of the Cold War by a shift towards regional financial and other support. Arguably, both governments and rebel movements have to some extent been shoved by circum-

---

* See Skidelsky (2000) on lend-lease aid to Britain and the hard bargain driven by the United States during the Second World War.

stance into paying for war by maximising rent from whatever commodities are available. This is not entirely new—even during the Cold War, for example, there were parties to conflict who generated funding also from this kind of source, including Angolan oil and diamonds. During the Cold War conflict period in Afghanistan the international backers of the Mujahideen, including above all the United States, encouraged the opium trade as what one commentator calls a 'weapon of war' intended not just to provide funds to cover war expenses but also to destabilise Soviet controlled Afghanistan and the Soviet Central Asian republics.[21] Thus the narcotics economy in Central Asia and the Middle East emerged parallel to the massive arms conduit whose main pipeline ran from the United States through Pakistan and the control of the Pakistani intelligence service, the ISI, to the Mujahideen.[22]

Furthermore, there have always been people who have exploited the fact that war itself creates rent: profiteers, speculators, war entrepreneurs. War creates rent because it typically reduces the number of market competitors and increases risk—the combination means the returns to those who take the risk are potentially extremely high. An example from Mozambique illustrates how this can work. There were food shortages in most of the country, including the capital, Maputo, where there was a sizeable middle class, including many foreigners working with aid agencies, NGOs and the government. The roads to South Africa and Swaziland from Maputo were frequently attacked by rebels or sown with landmines. In these conditions there were substantial profits to be made by an entrepreneur who managed to get someone to drive regularly between the capital and the border, so that he could supply individuals in Maputo with meat.

The interests of wartime accumulators and those managing the war effort do not always coincide, though of course they often overlap. Thus transport merchants in Afghanistan profited immensely from the vague boundaries between countries and markets in wartime conditions and, partly because of this, developed close links to the political authorities in Kabul during the Taliban's rule. Nonetheless, the transporters' interests and those of the Taliban did not always match. When profiteers undermined the Taliban's blockade of Hazarajat, by keeping trade routes open, they were working directly against the interests of the Taliban.

What is different in more recent conflicts is that wartime accumulation and profiteering have moved to the forefront of how these wars are paid for and perceived. Rent generating wartime activities are no longer a grubby sideline of violent conflict but have become one of its central features. To a considerable extent this may be because of the waning of Cold War sponsorship, combined with all the constraints on other remedies to paying for war. The ambivalence of the Taliban towards the heroin economy is an excellent example of the complications of war finance, war goals and ideology. Early on in Taliban rule in Afghanistan expediency got the upper hand and poppy production rose rapidly: in Kandahar from 79 tons in 1995 to an estimated 120 tons the following year. In August 1999 Mullah Omar issued a decree that poppy cultivation should be reduced by a third. Another edict passed by the Taliban in July 2000 declared the cultivation of opium poppies as 'un-Islamic' (or *haram*) and enforcement efforts brought production levels down sharply.*

There is another example of this trend in the post-9/11 world of the 'war on terrorism'. Immediately after the al-Qaeda attack on the World Trade Center and the Pentagon there were efforts to tighten regulation and monitoring of international financial flows and to introduce new powers to seize assets. The US and British governments, in particular, sought to persuade banks and other financial intermediaries to collect and pass on more information about their clients and their transactions. This included initiatives to close or regulate more tightly international Money Transfer Networks or MTNs. MTNs are largely informal institutions that grew out of the need of migrants and diasporic communities around the world to remit income back to families, for example the *hawalas* used to transfer money to Somalia and throughout the Middle East. One Somali MTN was closed down because of its alleged use by international terrorist groups. Terrorists do use mechanisms like MTNs to move money from country to country, often mobilising money whose source may well be legal economic activities for end-use purposes that are violent. Also, alongside the vast numbers of quite poor and also very wealthy individuals and families who use

---

* Goodhand (2004: 56). There is some argument over the reasons behind the Taliban's hardening attitude towards poppy cultivation and it seems likely that each of three main reasons (each backed by particular interests within the Taliban) played a part: first, stopping poppy cultivation and exports could be used by the Taliban as a bargaining chip in the relationship with the 'international community'; second, this policy and its enforcement could be used to stockpile opium poppies and so push up the world price—especially in a world market characterised by increasing concentration of production in Afghanistan and Myanmar; and, third, the policy was pushed on religious ideological grounds.

these networks, there are opposition groups or self-determination movements who rely on diasporas for funds for their war effort—for example, Tamils in Sri Lanka. In the post-9/11 era governments challenged by armed oppositions have leapt to have these oppositions declared as 'terrorists' because, for example, of the leverage this gives them in control over their financing, as well as the leeway it gives governments to justify their own violent actions against oppositions. However, there is an argument that the policing response to 9/11 has the effect of driving some MTNs further 'underground' and, by choking off some of the flow of money from diaspora groups, driving armed oppositions into new financing activities including drug production and/or trade.[23]

Globalisation, war finance and institutional innovation

Meanwhile, access to rent is not necessarily used to fund warfare. That is, the fact of available rent does not have to produce an outcome of violence. It can be quite the opposite. William Reno gives an example from Somaliland and Puntland, contrasting their different outcomes with those to the south in what remains of Somalia, with its otherwise very similar conditions. Somalia's recent experience, he argues, shows that not all who exercise coercion do so to maximise personal economic gains. 'Some Somali leaders forego fairly easy predation, while others use violence even where gains are marginal.'[24] Likewise, Reno contrasts violence in the aftermath of state disintegration in Georgia's Abkhazia and South Ossetia with the relative lack of violence in the Georgian regions of Ajaria and Abazhidze and with the curious absence of war in Dagestan and Ingushetia.*

The implication is, quite simply, 'where there's a will there's a way.' Assuming there is not a strong foundation for claims that primary commodity or natural resource abundance is a primary cause of war, it is then clear that the means of paying for war should not be conflated with the causes of war. Whatever the causes of a given war, wars need to be funded somehow. The combination of historical

---

* Dagestan and Ingushetia are ethnically diverse and share borders with Chechnya as well as being targets of numerous provocations by 'ethnic entrepreneurs', yet have managed to sustain a kind of peace even while their neighbours in Chechnya are consumed with violence against Russians and amongst themselves.

trends, economic conditions and the luck of the draw in terms of commodity endowment (and international demand) has meant that recent wars especially have depended on rent-intensive and often illegal market exploitation.

But is it obvious from this that the quality of violent conflict has degenerated? Aside from the fact that the waste and brutality of war is pretty much a constant throughout history, the claim that war has deteriorated turns on this question of war finance and the idea that profiteering rivalry has replaced grand ideological conflict as the source of war. To argue the reverse is almost as plausible. First, the constraints on most organisations involved in wars—especially non-government groups—mean they have to adopt whatever expedients they can to sustain war. Second, for most developing countries until 1989 this meant a dependency on major international powers. For many groups, the end of Cold War regulation has meant a decline in the availability of this source of funding.* They have turned where possible and to a greater extent than before to paying for war by exploiting opportunities in international commodity markets. Governments in Sierra Leone, for example, managed to sustain a war economy at extraordinarily low rates of inflation by their engagement in a war economy characterised by alternative rental activity, including in internationally traded commodities.[25] This success also had the advantage of securing the approval of the IMF and major bilateral donor agencies; the government was, therefore, relieved of some of the pressure from these external sources while also securing access to aid.

Far from confirming the 'marginalisation' of poor or developing countries from the global economy, these are domestically driven forms of integration into that world economy, through diaspora networks and exploitation of world demand for specific goods. Over the longer term, it is possible though far from definite that the accumulation of know-how and wealth in war may, as an unintended consequence, contribute to the formation of capitalist classes compelled to invest in their own economies;† for war finance

---

* As Larry Neal (1994) put it, organisations fighting wars 'prefer to tax rather than borrow, but all prefer to tax foreigners if possible, and then to borrow from foreigners as well.' However, not all groups with a capacity to tax to pay for war do so: one of the most renowned examples is US President Johnson who resisted raising taxes to cover the costs of the Vietnam War; the consequence was accelerating inflation, which was carried over from the US economy to the world economy, feeding into the pressures that brought about the collapse of the post-World War II Bretton Woods system of international payments. Also see Brenner (1998: 118–22).

† Nor is this purely a case of domestic classes resorting to rent-seeking or 'predatory'

methods like these represent a classic case of what Marx called 'primitive accumulation'—that accumulation of capital occurring at the foundation of and as one precondition for later capitalist development. The links between violence and brutality on the one hand, and primitive accumulation and the foundations of capitalist success on the other, are developed in Chapter 6.

The historical overview in this chapter shows that there has been a great variety of techniques of paying for violent conflict. Most of these have been socially regressive—they have hit poorer people hardest, directly or indirectly—and some have been extremely predatory. War finance most often, therefore, adds to the suffering and waste of war. Reaping rents from international commodity markets—for warring parties with little access to aid or to commercial debt markets, with thin financial markets, and with limited capacity to produce their own war matériel—is just the latest addition to this roster of the economic means of war. At the very least, this historical argument suggests there is no reason why recent war finance mechanisms should have a lesser chance than previous mechanisms of generating (unintended) consequences of more progressive change. There may even be processes of innovation at play in contemporary war finance. If there are, the key to their longer term contribution may lie in post-conflict reconstruction policies (see Chapter 7).

Further, these examples of war finance through rent from commodity markets do not show a reaction against globalisation but rather an adroit engagement in international markets. This argument is analogous to that made by Gavin Kitching in *Seeking Social Justice Through Globalisation.*[26] Kitching argues that an unfolding era of global capitalism is an improvement on the era of imperialism—in its consequences for ordinary people worldwide—because it opens up the potential for multiple sources of capitalist development to emerge and because it may encourage both an end to Western liberal guilt and an end to Third World psychological dependency on

activities. After the end of the Cold War the MPLA government in Angola found it harder to get international military aid. In the Bicesse Accord meetings in 1991 the United States, the Soviet Union and Portugal agreed not to supply arms to either the MPLA or UNITA. At the 1994 Lusaka peace negotiations the MPLA and UNITA agreed to a bilateral ceasefire timetable that, among other things, prohibited the purchase of military equipment from external markets. The MPLA government responded by starting up domestic ammunition production. Thus the heavy industry production index for Angola shows a vigorous increase in the second half of the 1990s, surpassing output levels of 1975; but this was almost entirely driven by production of ammunition in the chemicals sub-sector. See Ferreira (2002).

the advanced capitalist countries, both of which represent the legacy of imperialism.

Nonetheless, though not a rebellion against globalisation, much
of the violence in the world may represent the consequences of and
reactions to the failures and choices of government policies, including those policies of wholesale liberalisation and deregulation encouraged by international financial institutions. Many states have
failed to create and allocate rents in ways that generate productive
growth and/or that distribute the benefits sufficiently widely to
secure political legitimacy. Clearly, this is political; it is not remotely
senseless.

One further implication of the argument of this chapter is that
NGOs leading campaigns to boycott 'conflict diamonds' and the
like might be missing the point. Indeed, they might be the well-
meaning equivalent of the ideological romanticism infecting the
'new wars' thesis that contemporary wars are 'not about anything at
all'. This is on top of the fact that most such campaigns—like certifi-
cation schemes in the world small arms trade, like efforts to protect
Fortress Europe (or the United States, or South Africa) against
immigration, and like efforts to police money transfer networks—
only ever have very limited success.* Again, and whether we like it
or not, this suggests the 'where there's a will there's a way' theory
of war.

---

* Not only are these campaigns missing the point about wars and war finance; further, if they were successful they would risk undermining the basic material survival
of large numbers of people who depend on the economies built up around diamond or poppy production etc., without being war profiteers or even predators.
According to some estimates, for example, as many as three or four million
Afghani people depend on poppies for their survival (see Goodhand, 2004).

6

PASSIONATE INTERESTS

The double helix of violent conflict

Angola's history of violence and war confounds many of the recently fashionable explanations of war even as it teases with easy images—Cold War proxy conflict, resource war, ethnic contest. This same history also confirms that features often neglected in explanations of contemporary war do matter: features like a country's specific long-run history, its patterns of production and class formation, the political effects of economic policy and the play of contingency. The quiddity of war in Angola provokes the concern that no general theory of war is possible. The difference between the way UNITA recruited many of its fighters, cooks and porters and the way, for example, the FARC in Colombia or the LTTE in Sri Lanka have attracted volunteers suggests the key to understanding wars lies in accepting a great diversity of forms and origins. The causes and mechanisms of wars are not only multiple: they vary.

These implications of Angolan history support the argument of Chapter 3, that most explanatory models of violent conflict have very limited success. The lessons of Angola chime, too, with other warnings. Historians and anthropologists tend to argue that African, or Latin American, or Asian conflicts cannot simply be forced into analytical categories derived from Western social science or Western history. One commentator argues, for example, that the whole idea of treating violent conflict in Liberia as a 'civil war' is to impose a contorted idea of the conflict, inappropriately projecting onto Liberia an array of international legal norms concerning 'the state' and historical imaginings about European civil wars. There is a risk, too, that squeezing wars like Liberia's into analytical categories like 'civil war' encourages a teleological projection: an assumption that Liberia is simply repeating now what European states

199

underwent hundreds of years ago and, therefore, that the outcomes will doubtless be similar.*

An anthropologist specialising in Algeria makes a related argument: that the persistent failure to take into account the history of
specifically Algerian political traditions has undermined understanding of the violence in Algeria in recent years. Instead, efforts to
explain Algerian conflict trade in lazy economic or cultural deter-
minism, with borrowed argument drawing on analogy (with Egypt,
Sudan, Iran, Afghanistan and so on), or with vague notions of soli-
darity-through-blood ties.[1]

There is, then, a tension between the pursuit of theories that
work across circumstances and geography—theories with their pre-
dilection for overworked analytical categories and for imposing
'unit homogeneity' on apples and pears—and the exploration of
the diverse and unique causes of particular conflicts. Allowing the
coexistence of theory and diversity involves more than mere eclecti-
cism or analytical indecision. It involves a different kind of theory—
specifically, one that cannot claim precise predictive power and
one that is not in hock to probabilistic inference from large-N statistical analysis (the cells of whose comparisons are often filled with
unreliable data and specious precision).

This chapter sketches one model that might help make sense of
diverse violent conflicts. It draws on the discussion and examples in
earlier chapters. It emphasises a spectrum of violence as the appropriate subject of initial inquiry, rather than blocking off different
forms of violence from one another. The model works partly by
metaphor. Specifically, it suggests a kind of 'double helix' that
might describe part of the structure of societies that produce large
amounts of violence. One helical ribbon describes the social and
economic transformation that developing countries are undergoing; the other describes the dynamics and interests of advanced
capitalist countries and enterprises. The space between them could
be seen as the distance of 'lateness' or the productivity gap between
developing and advanced countries. The two ribbons are joined by
'bars' whose definition, in different circumstances, accounts for
much of the variance in incidence and forms of violent conflict.
These connecting bars include those labelled 'commodity markets',

---

* Ellis (2003) makes this case in a discussion of the historical roots of violence in
  Liberia and of the possibility of a technique of historical analysis for all contemporary wars; he cites Feierman's (1993) warning that specific events in Africa cannot
  automatically be assimilated into categories of analysis drawn from Europe, including the construction of European-style states and the growth of capitalism.

'institutions', 'history', 'arms production and exchange', 'techno-logical change', 'ideas, ideals, norms', 'specialists in violence', 're-gional spillover effects', 'IMF and World Bank loan conditionality' and so on.

This, though, is a double helix that moves—to mix metaphors—like a twister. It is propelled by 'transition'—which stands for the immense upheaval of a society's shift from one prevailing and lar-gely accepted form of social, economic, political and institutional organisation to another. And it is propelled by the logic and politics of capitalism in rich countries. Such a transition may be dramati-cally abrupt—taking decades, for example—or it may be protrac-ted over centuries. Figure 7 illustrates this idea and includes some of the bars that bind together advanced capitalism and the period of transition into a potentially violent formation. This model does not fully explain all violence but it does suggest an explanation of part of the structure of most violence and war. Furthermore, the metaphor of the structure of DNA captures a hugely important fea-ture of the spectrum of violence—that is, its immense diversity.

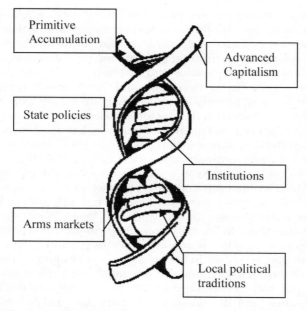

Figure 7. THE DOUBLE HELIX OF VIOLENT CONFLICT

Violence and capitalism

This model emphasises the role of capitalism in the explanation of violent conflict. Clearly this requires some justification. How could the development of capitalism have anything to do with the origins of violent conflict? It may seem an absurd idea. Generally, rich capitalist countries are peaceable, though they may need to shore up a defensive capacity, perhaps against the envy of less fortunate people. This was what Adam Smith and John Stuart Mill expected long ago. They anticipated that economic progress would make countries rich, unwarlike and the objects of envy from the less fortunate and more bellicose. Therefore, as Mill put it, 'assuredly the friends of freedom have a right to employ their own thews and sinews to check the onward flow of barbarism and tyranny.' And the countries that do experience violent conflict appear normally to be those that are backward economically, untouched by the grace of capitalism. Marx also thought war was archaic: one of the ways in which capitalism was superior to anything that had gone before was precisely that it was not a system of perpetual warfare in the literal sense.

Since early in the development of capitalism in England it has been pointed out that the kind of economic relations that capitalism spawned provided a distraction from conflict. Albert Hirschman claimed that political arguments for capitalism turned on a distinction between passions and interests. People are driven by unseemly urges. But the vices that could lead people astray might, it began to be clear, be separable into lesser and greater evils. Greater evils were unmitigated in their awfulness. However, some vices might have less negative consequences. These ideologues of early capitalism characterised money-making as one of these lesser evils. This was itself an extraordinary ideological and ethical shift, and one that was clearly necessary to underpin the evolution of capitalism. For till the seventeenth and eighteenth centuries money-making was typically regarded as avaricious. Now, not only were commerce and the pursuit of wealth reclassified as lesser vices; also, it was argued that these lesser evils—renamed 'interests'—could be enlisted to work against the more pernicious passions.[2] This kind of paradox was very much in keeping with Montesquieu's and Adam Smith's renowned idea that the pursuit of self-interest could lead to a happy social outcome through the operation of the market, specialisation and the division of labour, and the invisible hand mediating supply and demand.[3] As capitalism expanded, drawing a greater and greater proportion of the population into its web of economic compulsions, so it might fairly be expected to take the passions out of society, or at least effectively to suppress them.

Keynes, in the twentieth century, captured this same idea when he wrote: 'Dangerous human proclivities can be canalised into comparatively harmless channels by the existence of opportunity for money-making and private wealth, which, if they cannot be satisfied in this way, may find their outlet in cruelty, the reckless pursuit of personal power and authority, and other forms of self-aggrandizement.'[4] And there is an echo of the argument in Alan Milward's explanation of the curious European success of the post-World War Two period. Contrasting the end of World War Two—with no formal peace treaty—with the failed ending to the First World War in spite of the formal efforts of the Versailles Treaty, Milward argues that the main source of lasting peace and successful post-war reconstruction was the increase in institutionalised transactions among entrepreneurs and governments of European countries. In effect, a rapidly thickening web of commercial relationships and the institutions that underpinned them came to deaden the prospects of renewed violent conflict in the region.*

The idea of pacific capitalism has remained powerful. Particularly in the guise of free trade, laissez-faire ideas, political economists from Cobden and Mill to Keynes have championed the peaceable qualities of capitalism. In 1846 Richard Cobden, champion of the repeal of the Corn Laws in England, identified 'in the Free trade principle that which shall act on the moral world as the principle of gravitation on the universe—drawing men together, thrusting aside the antagonism of race, and creed, and language, and uniting us in the bonds of eternal peace.'[5] Anticipating even more acutely contemporary economic thinking on development and conflict, John Stuart Mill in 1848 wrote: 'Wars, and the destruction they cause, are now usually confined, in almost every country, to those distant and outlying possessions at which it comes into contact with savages.'[6]

The liberal tradition equating free trade with peace and prosperity has carried over into development orthodoxy. The World Trade Organisation, for example, declares that free trade helps to pro-

---

* Milward (1992). The roots of these arguments also lie in liberal arguments that 'the people' or, more narrowly, '*les industrieux*' had a basic interest in peace but were only prevented from exercising this by an older, archaic class of militaristic aristocrats: see Howard (1978).

mote peace: '...sales people are usually reluctant to fight their cus-
tomers...if trade flows smoothly and both sides enjoy a healthy
commercial relationship, political conflict is less likely. What's
more, smoothly flowing trade also helps people all over the world
become better off. People who are more prosperous and contented
are also less likely to fight.'[7] Thomas Friedman reprised these arguments in his popular books on the glories of globalisation, pushing
first the 'Golden Arches Theory of Conflict Prevention' (people in
countries with a large enough middle class to support a McDonald's prefer to avoid war) and then the 'Dell Theory of Conflict Prevention': 'The advent and spread of just-in-time global supply
chains in the flat [*sic*] world are an even greater restraint on
geopolitical adventurism than the more general rising standard of
living that McDonald's symbolised.'[8]

Yet there are also completely contrary arguments about the links
between capitalism and violent conflict. Capitalism needs peace
and stability, yet it also often thrives on war and instability and is typically implanted through violence. Keynes, whose only political
cause before the First World War, as Skidelsky's biography points
out, was free trade, increasingly had his doubts about the pacific
qualities of unregulated capitalism.[9] His later writing contained
different ideas about the economic causes of wars. These ideas
stressed population pressure and 'the competitive struggle for markets'.[10] Keynes's economic theory proposed that the pursuit of full
employment within countries, necessarily violating laissez-faire,
would take the sting out of this competition between countries.
This was the basis, as Turnell argues, on which he developed ideas
for an international economic order—after the Second World War—
that would allow and encourage national full employment policies
and would impose an equitable burden of adjustment on creditor
and debtor nations. Others have argued it was precisely the success
of domestic capitalism in the United States—and the saturation of
the market—that led successive US governments to project power
and to export militarism overseas. More recently, Ellen Meiksins
Wood argues that the Bush doctrine—amounting to a doctrine of
'war without end, in purpose or time'—is a culmination of the
export of 'surplus capitalism' from the United States.*

The liberal, free trade vision of capitalism, not just requiring
peace and stability but positively promoting them, prettifies reality
in two main ways. First, it glosses over the reality of how capitalism

---

* E. M. Wood (2003). This is an argument with roots in early-twentieth-century
  Marxist debates, chiefly in the work of Lenin, Kautsky and Luxemburg.

takes root in a society and how societies have developed into advanced capitalist societies. The beginnings and the effective and progressive development of capitalism are always painful. Even if development is a matter of the opening up of greater freedoms, those freedoms are not only fought for but are often more or less forced on people.* Second, the liberal vision airbrushes the evidence that violence is a habit that even advanced capitalism finds hard to kick. To put this differently: the competitive logic of surplus appropriation drives particular capitalists to profit from cruelty, violence and war; this happens wittingly and unwittingly, on a spectrum that includes outsourcing to cramped sweatshops using child labour as well as the apparently unknowing beneficiaries of Congolese war cited in the UN's panel of experts reports.[11] A different question is whether capitalism as a system contains an inherent and especially violent logic in its mechanisms, making it eternally prone to (perhaps ever intensifying) violence.[†]

The violent beginnings of capitalism

Many explanations of violent conflict, and many visions of 'development', ignore an important stylised fact about economic develop-

---

* For example, a central feature, surely, of economic development has been the absorption of women into the labour market. This is not a freedom identified by Sen (1999) in *Development as Freedom*. However, if it is regarded as a freedom (some freedom of activity and earning, some freedom from the regime of the household, albeit clearly an awkward freedom), then such freedoms clearly emerge through extraordinary conflict and upheaval. There is resistance among men to women working in the wage labour market (dramatically symbolised, despite the uncertainty of unsolved crimes, in the large number of murders of young women in the past decade in Ciudad Juárez on the Mexican/US border in the area of the *maquilas*, the cheap labour assembly factories: see Amnesty International, 2003). Conditions of this freedom are commonly abusive and often physically violent. And while this freedom opens up, often gender discrimination in labour markets endures during industrialisation and may even underpin successful economic development, as it did, for example, in South Korea (see Seguino, 2000).

† Ellen Meiksins Wood, for example, argues: 'I am convinced…that capitalism cannot deliver world peace. It seems to me axiomatic that the expansionary, exploitative and competitive logic of capitalist accumulation in the context of the nation-state system must, in the longer or shorter term, be destabilising and that capitalism—and at the moment its most aggressive and adventurist organising force, the government of the United States—is and will for the foreseeable future remain the greatest threat to world peace' (1995: 265). Meanwhile, some sociologists argue there is a modern impetus towards war—a 'logic of exterminism'—but that the industrialisation of modern war has effectively overwhelmed capitalism and so assumed its own internal logic rather than being driven by the logic of capitalism. See Shaw (2000).

ment. This is that capitalism does not take root without foundational violence. Before any possible violence *of* capitalism, there is conflict and often violence in the ruptures in societies undergoing a transformation *to* capitalism, or at any rate *from* pre-capitalism. Typically, the violence at the foundation of capitalism takes place during a phase of 'primitive accumulation'.

— *A natural evolution of capitalism?*

Before defining primitive accumulation and sketching some examples of the foundational violence of capitalism, it is worth contrasting this stylised fact with the standard orthodox vision of capitalist origins. Many economists tend to assume that capitalism takes shape by a fairly simple and smooth process. Historical arguments along these lines stress the continuity between capitalism and pre-capitalist market exchange and present capitalism largely as a natural growth of commerce. On that basis, modern policy advisers envisage economic development accelerating in a smooth, linear fashion if only governments in poor countries can simply unleash 'market forces', through deregulation and liberalisation of markets. Markets—and the notional invisible hand—will then be able to 'get prices right', resources will accordingly be allocated efficiently, capital will flow in from rich countries and development will proceed nicely.*

This is mistaken. Sweeping liberalisation has not produced great development leaps. Historically, the currently rich economies succeeded by applying policies that were often diametrically contrary to these precepts of laissez-faire.† And the currently rich countries had generally been through staggering upheavals to get onto the tracks of sustained capitalist economic development. The same is true of the group of countries who have most successfully been

---

* Among the assumptions underlying this theory is one that economic activity is characterised by diminishing returns. Given diminishing returns (to capital and labour, as more of each are applied), capital will seek new opportunities for investment, especially where labour is abundant and cheap. Output will then rise in developing countries faster than in already advanced, industrialised economies where returns are dwindling, and incomes per capita in developing countries will converge on those of rich countries. For an excellent analysis of the history of orthodox growth theories and their shortcomings, see Thirlwall (2002).
† See Chang (2002). Thirlwall (2002: 77) tells the development economist Ajit Singh's story of how Nicholas Kaldor at Cambridge taught him three things: 'First, the only way for a country to develop is to industrialise; second, the only way for a country to industrialise is to protect itself; and third, anyone who says otherwise is being dishonest!'

catching up, since the 1960s, with the rich countries, including South Korea and Taiwan and more recently Malaysia, Thailand, Indonesia and then China and India.

The history of capitalism has entailed more than the gradual accretion of market transactions. Economic history also shows that capitalist social and economic organisation is not an eternally 'natural' propensity of humanity, but is a historically specific form of organisation that was resisted by many groups of people before it triumphed. Capitalism—according to this view—imposes compulsions on individuals. Capitalists themselves are compelled, if they are to survive, to reinvest, to innovate, and to compete. Wage workers are compelled to sell their labour in order to survive. They are distinct from serfs, slaves, feudal vassals, colonial *corvée* workers or prison labourers in that they are 'free' to sell their labour to whomever they wish. But they differ from small, independent family farmers and peasants in that they cannot survive without exercising this freedom. This freedom is often, of course, constrained. More viciously, the interlinkage of the labour market with, say, the credit market may mean that a money-lender can force a poor debtor to work on his (probably) or a friend's farm, even if the wage there will be lower than she (quite possibly) can earn on another farm. In this example, the roles of 'extra-economic' force and/or the threat of direct violence in sustaining economic activity and market transactions are clear.[12]

Wage labour is not appealing to families that consider themselves independent and roughly self-sufficient. Capitalist enterprise is also relatively unappealing if the alternative provides wealth drawn from rent (from large landholdings, or from access to other high-rent resources like oil). Therefore, it is legitimate to wonder how it came about that specifically capitalist compulsions, relations and classes emerged to dominate a number of societies. Did independent smallholder farming families or large landowners simply transform themselves, shedding one exo-skeleton and fitting perfectly into a new one, into wageworkers and capitalists? Or was there a contest between these various classes of person and ways of organising economic activity? And where did the capital come from that enabled a self-sustaining process of reinvestment, profit and expansion?

Certainly, capitalism did evolve partly out of a long history of economic change, changes in the division of labour and the extent of markets (the latter particularly as navigational innovations opened up new markets further afield). But this was insufficient.* It took other, more disruptive events to lodge these capitalist ways of organising economic activity and human social relations as predominant over the interests of independent farmers and big landowning aristocrats. Critics of the liberal view have tended to a dramatic style that some take for hyperbole. Marx wrote, contrary to the idea of gradual evolution: 'In actual history it is notorious that conquest, enslavement, robbery, murder, briefly force, play the great part.' And Karl Polanyi wrote of the English enclosure movement (see below) that it was a revolution of the rich against the poor. 'The fabric of society was being disrupted; desolate villages and the ruins of human dwellings testified to the fierceness with which the revolution raged, endangering the defence of the country, wasting its towns, decimating its population, turning its overburdened soil into dust, harassing its people and turning them from decent husbandmen into a mob of beggars and thieves.'[13] But Marx, Polanyi and others had a point. The process of change was spurred on by war, it was influenced by the actions of particular states, and it was driven onward by a vicious displacement of those who got in the way.

— Primitive accumulation

This displacement is often referred to as primitive accumulation, which is a particular form of appropriating an economic surplus. It is coercive and, therefore, by definition conflictual. It involves forcing people off land, expropriating them, and thereby cutting off the option of independence and self-sufficiency. For some, asset accumulation is only primitive accumulation to the extent that it creates a wage labour force where there was not one before, as well as generating the initial surplus that then feeds industrialisation and capitalist reinvestment. This is to define it by its outcome. Other definitions allow for primitive accumulation to include non-market or extra-economic accumulation of wealth that *potentially* drives the transition to capitalism. This potential derives from three sources: first, the way it generates the funds that capitalist development requires to get underway; second, the way it creates a class of wage labourers by undermining people's ability to survive without engaging in wage employment; third, by dint of this wage class, the way it creates a market for the goods that capitalists would produce.

---

* See the debate between Maurice Dobb and Paul Sweezy on this topic (Hilton *et al.*, 1976); the latter's argument has been effectively rebutted more recently by Brenner (1977).

According to this more process-oriented definition, primitive accumulation is a necessary but insufficient precondition for the transition to capitalism.[14]

The classic examples are the period of 'enclosures' in England from the sixteenth to the eighteenth century, the 'clearances' in Scotland and the brutal taking of land and other wealth in English (and other) imperial ventures, for example in Ireland.* The English enclosures, whereby landowners excluded peasant families from what had hitherto been treated as common land, represented the advance of private property rights as an unassailable institution. This is an excellent example of how institutions are not just the solutions to efficiency or transaction cost challenges that many economists think. Even if this efficiency role is part of the eventual function of (many) institutions, it is not their only role: for institutions are the sediment left behind by a political conflict and their form typically reflects a particular arrangement of the relative power of different interest groups. Beneath the form of institutions and legislatures lies 'the forgotten past of real struggles, concealed defeats and victories, and the blood that has dried on the codes', as Foucault put it.[15] It will become clear, below, that the establishment of private property rights for capitalist farmers is still conflictual (especially where the state cannot or will not enforce these rights).

Enclosures were not always violent though they were established by force, and ultimately backed by Enclosure Acts in parliament.† However, enclosure was part of a larger trend towards the concentration of landholdings in the hands of the commercially minded 'improving' farmers. The process pushed the smallest cottagers off the land and shut off their prospects of eking a living by farming or grazing 'common' lands—they were increasingly pushed into the wage labour market, with all its ghastly conditions. Enclosure was a part of this process and the long history of the enclosure movement reflects political struggles in England that were drawn into the tense relationship between the Crown and Parliament, a relationship, of course, that erupted in the civil wars of the 1640s.

One of the major political defences against enclosure was Kett's Rebellion in 1549, in which thousands of peasants were killed. The

---

* I am grateful to Terry Byres for pointing out to me the irony of Scots forced off the land by clearances, sometimes violently, proceeding to North America and themselves dispossessing native Americans, often cruelly.
† On how a legal framework followed and consolidated the early expansion of capitalism and the assertion of private property rights against 'traditional' rights of the peasantry, see Perelman (2000).

defeat of this peasant revolt ushered in what Polanyi calls 'the dicta-torship of the grazier lords'. Indeed, it has been argued that the vio-lent upheavals of the sixteenth and seventeenth centuries, with their political conflict over social and economic change as well as political order and the constitution, and with their civil wars, were the foundation on which England could later establish more grad-ual change.[16]

As the English state increasingly favoured capitalist interests, so it supported the extension of these interests into overseas dominions. An example of the brutality of exporting capitalism through impe-rial expansion was the seventeenth-century colonisation of Ireland. English landlords, backed by the army, not only laid claim to uncul-tivated and empty land but forcibly expropriated land that was lived on and farmed. Just as the triumph of a capitalist money-making mentality needed the ideological and ethical reclassification of erst-while heinous passions as potentially beneficial interests, so colo-nial warfare in the name of capitalism needed an ideological twist to the legitimating doctrine of 'just war'.[17]

As English capitalist empire spread first to Ireland and later far beyond, this was an ethical barrier that had to be broken. As Ellen Meiksins Wood argues, this is what lay behind the legal and moral footwork in Sir John Davies's insistence, in 1610, that the king was morally bound to seize Irish land in the Plantation of Ulster:

…His Majesty is bound in conscience to use all lawful and just courses to reduce his people from barbarism to civility; the neglect whereof hereto-fore hath been laid as an imputation upon the Crown on England. Now civility cannot possibly be planted among them by this mixed plantation of some of the natives and settling of their possessions in a course of Common Law… it stands neither with Christian policy nor conscience to suffer so good and fruitful a country to lie waste like a wilderness, when his Majesty may lawfully dispose it to such persons as will make a civil plantation thereupon.*

When Cromwell embarked, later in the seventeenth century, on an even more vicious settlement of Ireland and aimed at an equitable distribution of Irish land among his soldiers and others, he needed a land survey. In conducting this pioneering survey, William Petty also provided a basis for accounting the value of land and the scope for its improvement.

* Davies himself received 7,500 acres of Ulster land, and the family into which he had married a further 9,000 acres.

— *How market society trapped American family farmers*

Introducing capitalism and its supporting institutions elsewhere has also been conflictual and often violent, though the conflict, the violence and the mechanisms of primitive accumulation have all varied greatly. John Locke argued that the right of property (and the justification for dispossessing American Indians) was secured by dint of the transformation of land into value. If the locals were not as productive as colonial settlers would be, given their experience in English improvement, then forceful colonialism would be just.[18] US economic development relied heavily on both the expropriation and ultimate annihilation of American Indians and the enslavement of Africans.*

The ways in which, over time, northern American farmers were snared by what Polanyi called 'market society' differed substantially from the enclosure process in England. For some time the ease of access to fairly cheap land, through the expropriation of indigenous Americans, allowed the settler society to preserve a system of yeoman farmers. Though these farmers bought and sold in markets, their survival did not depend on it. But this system came under increasing pressure. There were various causes, including the completion of settlement and a rising population, both of which put upward pressure on the price of land. One of the factors that accelerated and concentrated the pressure for change was the disruption of the period of Revolution in the late eighteenth century.†

The Revolution shifted the balance of power between merchants and independent yeoman farming families. Earlier, merchant speculators had invested profits in land in the interior but, so long as the colonial militia could not enforce these speculators' private property rights, smallholder families migrating into the interior successfully squatted on the land. Farmers also won out in battles over tenancy rent, establishing freeholder rights: during the Revolution many landlords—especially sympathisers of the British— were expropriated and their lands redistributed among former tenants. But the balance swung against independent yeoman farmers. State governments requisitioned food, cloth and other supplies from northern farmers. After the war these governments imposed tax hikes to service the public debt accumulated in the war effort. Independent family farmers had also contracted rising debts: as

* See the chapter on 'American Indians and Primitive Accumulation' in Byres (1996: 186–210) and, on slavery in the United States, chapter six of the same book.
† The following account relies especially on Post (1995).

they committed more labour to meeting the demands of the war effort, so they borrowed more and more from store keeper merchants to pay for goods they had previously made for themselves. The post-war period left these farmers indebted and facing a rising tax burden: they were forced to market more and more of their output to hold onto their land and were, therefore, dragged by war, tax and debt into a more exclusive dependence on the market than had been the case before. Meanwhile, urban and small town merchants accumulated wartime profits. Like the war entrepreneurs of present-day Afghanistan, Angola and elsewhere, these were people who exploited the disruption of normal commerce and excelled in smuggling and profiteering. Merchants also soaked up the rapidly issuing paper money and bonds of state governments, and invested in frontier land.

As Charles Post explains, the crisis of independent household production in the northeastern United States 'spawned a major social explosion' in Massachusetts in 1787.[19] From the top down, creditors were calling in debts, and the burden fell increasingly on smallholder farmers. Demands for debt relief and lower land taxes failed to move the Massachusetts General Assembly (now dominated by merchants). Social conflict became violent, with petty harassment escalating into Shay's Rebellion.* Shay's Rebellion is just the largest and best known of a range of conflicts in the region.† There were the Whiskey Rebellion and Fries Uprising in Pennsylvania, the Green Mountain Boys in Vermont and the White Indians of Maine. But the Constitutional Settlement of 1787 created the basis of a central state with effective institutions like a federal army and a tax collection agency. The state, moreover, favoured the political dominance of the merchants.

---

* Daniel Shays, a captain in the Revolutionary war and a Massachusetts farmer, led bands of farmers in raids on debtors' prisons and courthouses and, in January 1787, with 2,000 or so rebels, tried to storm the Springfield arsenal. The rebels failed and were either arrested or dispersed in the following weeks.

† As Thomas Jefferson put it (presaging Eric Wolf's insight, in *Peasant Wars of the Twentieth Century*, that peasant revolts like that led by Zapata in Mexico were tragic affairs in which, effectively, rebels were fighting unwittingly for the overthrow of the traditions and societies they sought to defend): 'I hold it that a little rebellion now and then is a good thing, and as necessary in the political world as storms in the physical. Unsuccessful rebellions, indeed, generally establish the encroachments on the rights of the people which have produced them. An observation of this truth should render honest republican governors so mild in their punishment of rebellions as not to discourage them too much. It is a medicine necessary for the sound health of the government' (see http://www.sjchs-history.org/Shays.html).

— *War as enabling environment*

During the early nineteenth century, these trends were reinforced and expanded into the northwest by state backing for infrastructure expansion (roads, canals and railways), which raised the value of land and the costs to family farmers of establishing their own farms. As in the northeast, waves of speculative investment in land, rising taxes and growing indebtedness all pushed towards the commodification of land and propelled farmers into the clutches of the market. There were, in the 1840s and 1850s in the northwest, no conflicts on the scale of Shay's Rebellion. There were various reasons why, the main one being that the state, by this stage, had a far firmer and more extensive presence and ability to enforce institutional arrangements—through the thickening presence of the federal army, land surveyors, tax collectors and so on. It is important to stress that war in America was not fought *by* capitalism, but the war both altered the balance of interests among social groups and itself accelerated social and economic changes that were to hasten the triumph of capitalism and its 'extra-economic' compulsions. From the perspective of capitalist development, then, war was an enabling environment.

The later, industrial development of capitalism in both England and the United States was also fraught with social conflict, corruption, traumatic disruptions to the lives of the bulk of poor people, and often with violence. Wars were also part of the process of capitalism's spread and development, most obviously the American Civil War. War imposed organisational and financial demands that tended to shore up the power of central states and to accelerate capitalist development. War has also often provided a boost to surplus appropriation and capital accumulation, even as it is utterly against the interests of many capitalists. This makes analogues of contemporary international mining interests thriving on the wartime supply chains of diamonds or coltan, the reconstruction barons benefiting from the war in Iraq in 2003, the so-called private military companies formed by ex-soldiers (e.g. Sandline, Executive Outcomes etc.), modern arms producers and brokers, and the many examples of firms benefiting from violence and war in the earlier history of the advanced capitalist countries, from Farmer and Galton (manufacturers of the Angola Gun) to the German firm of Krupp and beyond.* Far from necessarily being 'development in

* 'Krupp's success with peaceful production was a direct consequence of his military production. If he hadn't made cannon, he wouldn't have become a national insti-

reverse', war and non-war violent conflict have often proven to be an enabling environment for the development of capitalism. This may still be the case, in different ways.

Violent transitions of late development

Other, much later transitions to capitalism around the world have also been as appalling as they have been dramatically transforming. Examples could be taken from many places, to illustrate the diversity of the trauma of this particular, unpredictable, often incomplete transition: the expropriation of land in South Africa and the racial laws that kept labour cheap in mines and industries and that controlled labour mobility; General Franco's use of prison labour in slave conditions to build the infrastructure of Spain's modernisation, including the Guadalquivir canal in Andalusia; the warfare from which an oppressive but reforming South Korean state emerged, and the long years of fierce repression of labour and student dissent in that country's 'miraculous' industrialisation; the expropriation of land and the manipulation of the caste system in Bihar in India; and so on. Even the most sparklingly clean modern societies, technologically advanced, stable and relatively egalitarian, have emerged from histories of violence and struggle. One of the most neglected but extraordinary experiences of 'catching up' was in Finland, which transformed itself from an extremely poor country at independence in 1917 into a highly industrialised society with a renowned progressive public policy. Finland appears as a beacon of stability and calm. Yet Finnish stability is a recent phenomenon, only emerging after the Second World War and the ructions of the first half of the twentieth century: the civil war of 1917/19, the Red and then White terrors unleashed in the aftermath of civil war, an attempted coup in the 1920s by anti-parliamentarians, and the divisions involved in the Continuation War of 1941/4 under a 'co-belligerence' alliance with Nazi Germany, following the defence against Russia in the Winter War of 1939/40.[20]

Much of the rest of the world is trapped in this extended interregnum, where old established institutions have been shaken, twisted, broken or suspended but where there is neither a complete new hierarchy of interests nor a firmly set array of new institutions.

---

tution, and it was the institutionalizing of the Krupps which gave them their supremacy.' (Manchester, 2003: 87, on Alfred Krupp's breakthrough in 1859 in persuading King Friedrich Wilhelm to order his new steel cannon.)

The point about transition in general is that it is by definition a period in which conflict is processed into the production of new institutions.

— Why is transition violent? The war of position

It is not surprising that this intense period of conflict often produces violence. First, the institutional framework that may have regulated violence in the past or that may contain it in the future is unstable or anachronistic: institutions used to resolve certain types of conflict cannot effectively resolve new forms of social conflict. Second, in transition the stakes of conflict are—precisely because of the open-ended features of change and institutional insecurity— more than usually intense. Transition is characterised by a war of position: not in the old military strategic or Gramscian political strategic sense, but in the sense of a scramble for social position in a social structure whose adhesive has not yet set. Third, the social and political conflict during major moments of transition, including a transition that may end up as capitalist, is especially likely to be violent where there are histories of violence and ratchet mechanisms that introduce the means of violence and draw on what Tilly calls 'specialists in violence'.[21] Histories of violence or 'traditions of violence', available to be carried over into transitional or capitalist societies, include Finnish rural knife-fighting, blood feuds, brigandage, lynching, centuries of English ideological admiration of military prowess and centuries of socially accepted spousal violence against women.*

Fourth, the crisis of transition is more likely to be violent if—as is also normal in such protracted moments—there is no credible central authority that can impose a monopoly of the means of and exercise of force, which is common where the fiscal source of the monopoly of violence is weak. Fifth, in the momentous transition at issue the crisis of uncertainty is not just about the viability or rele-

---

* Borkenau (1986: 16) asked, referring to Spain, 'why, at a given moment, old-style Robin Hood brigandage transformed itself into the risings of villages against their owners. The change dates from the [1840s], and is probably connected on the one hand with deterioration of labour conditions and expropriation of communal lands by the aristocracy owing to the change from home consumption to export crops, and, on the other hand, with the creation of the *guardia* in the [1840s]. The "*guardia civil*" is a supremely important element in Spanish politics…it was separate from the population, hated by the masses, and hating them as a natural reaction; and there is no deeper abyss, no more deadly or constant war imaginable, than that waged continually, every day, between the village…and the *guardia*. Anyway, the *guardia* made an end of brigandage. Instead, the state got risings.'

vance of particular institutions, or simply about the fact that power and position are contested. Beyond these, arguably the very principle of power and the placement and constitution of the girders and joists supporting power are uncertain: the characteristics of power are the terms of conflict.* In the shift from feudalism to capitalism, and from medieval royal power to parliamentary democracy, the sources and legitimacy of power as well as its technologies were, violently, under review. So it is that in contemporary developing countries part of social conflict is precisely over what power means: is it vested in 'traditional' authorities, handed down by a genealogy of legend and managed partly through magic; is it vested in the sovereignty of individual dictators or royal dynasties; or is it vested in multi-party procedural democracy and bureaucracy? It is not just that there are fresh vacancies, new positions up for grabs within a social structure, but rather that the structure itself is up for grabs. Sixth, the terms of accumulation and distribution of wealth and the institutions in which these terms are cast are contested. New classes are forming around changing activities and interests; old classes are gripping tight onto accustomed sources of wealth or survival.

The disruption and change work themselves out in a great variety of forms of violent conflict. Thus it may be proposed that a range of violent conflicts—from 'civil war', through mafia-like conflicts, to domestic violence—can be explained within this framework of transition. The management of economic surpluses and inevitable, even if progressive, exploitation is central to this phase of transition. Who can capture surpluses? How do they derive that power and assert that right? What form of surplus appropriation and management will be legitimised? How will this be enforced? What claims will others be able to make on the chief beneficiaries of surplus creation? To the extent that the conflicts over these issues do, then, reflect crises of transition from pre-capitalism, processes of

---

* This argument is derived from Foucault's tracing of the challenge to the power of right and sovereignty that came with the emergence of new ways of being historical, with, essentially, the beginnings of modern politics, which he identifies in seventeenth-century England and a little later in France. Foucault (2003) claims there was a shift from a ternary social order, a pyramidal structure at whose apex sat the king, towards an organisation of societies in binary terms, of victors and vanquished, conquering invaders and subjugated peoples (Normans and Saxons, for example), of royalty and administration versus the nobility. Binary contests gave birth to the notions both of 'nations' and of 'classes' and invested a great part of political conflict over the following centuries with the stamp of racial division. History became, in Foucault's argument, an instrument by which different groups sought to contest their legitimacy.

primitive accumulation are at the heart of much of the violence and war around the world.

— *Primitive accumulation and contemporary violence*

Precisely because the outcome of the political economy of violence and war is often still unclear, various labels have been pinned on this kind of activity: reverse entitlements, asset transfers and accumulation by dispossession. However, to the extent that appropriative struggles generate potentially investible funds and generate potential wage earners dependent on the market for basic consumption goods, then these struggles involve primitive accumulation. In Sudan, for example, David Keen's work showed how targets of raiding warlord incursions were not victimised because of their poverty but rather because of their asset wealth. Sudanese warfare has often involved 'asset transfer', or theft and expropriation of land, livestock and people as labourers. At the same time warfare has displaced large numbers of people.[22] This twin process, of forceful asset accumulation and displacement of people, is exactly what is involved in primitive accumulation.

So it is reasonable, for example, to see the whole phenomenon of internal displacement and international refugees as—in the old formula—the separation of people from their means of production. Violent upheavals in one country often pitch people into labour markets either in the same country or in other countries. Women are often forced to sell sex to secure survival. South African labour markets have for a long time taken advantage of a supply of labour from neighbouring countries, including refugees from warfare. For example, during the 1980s and early 1990s there were many illegal immigrants from Mozambique, effectively refugees from the war there, who were working as wage labourers on commercial farms, as domestic servants in rural areas and in the urban mining and manufacturing sectors.[23] Political upheaval in Zimbabwe has generated a reversal in historical patterns of labour migration as Zimbabweans cross into Mozambique, many in search of work in new agribusinesses in Manica Province. In Western Tanzania in the 1990s, when there were large populations of refugees, there was a widening of the market (e.g. for bananas) and a larger pool of labour: local farmers often hired refugees to work as farm labourers, paying them in food and/or cash.[24]

If the process that creates refugees is analytically related to the depopulation of villages in late medieval English enclosures, then there are also analytical parallels between early English capitalism and the absorption of refugees and internally displaced people (IDPs) into poorly regulated and badly paid wage labour (or un-free labour, as in the case of 'slaves' in Sudan and elsewhere and sex workers throughout much of Europe) and between the English Poor Laws and the reflexes of international relief and immigration policies.[25]

In another example, the sequence of nationalisation, war, and privatisation in Mozambique from the mid-1970s to the mid-1990s proved to be a vector of both dimensions of primitive accumulation: the accumulation of capital assets (especially land) by force and the displacement (through war and villagisation policies) of rural farming families. Following and in a way repeating the earlier Portuguese imperial land grabbing and forced organisation of labour in the Mozambican countryside, this process may be thought of as a post-independence internal colonisation exercise. As with Cromwell's soldiers in Ireland, so it has often been people with military connections who have benefited from the allocation of land in Mozambique.[26] (Chapter 7 develops this example in detail and shows how it accelerated the formation of a class dependent for their survival on wage employment, albeit often seasonal and/or casual.)

Something akin to primitive accumulation is also a feature of the transition to capitalism in Russia. The aspect of primitive accumulation that is the amassing of capital through extra-economic coercion, i.e. generally violence and the credible threat of violence, is present. The labour market dimension might be less clear. However, the transition in Russia has clearly pushed large numbers into poverty and/or the wage labour market. Survival through secure positions in the bureaucracy and through crudely functioning (but still functioning) state social protection systems was no longer viable.* Russian transition has been characterised by extraordinarily concentrated institutional change and uncertainty. A range of interest groups jostled, sometimes brutally, for position—nascent capitalists, resource rentiers, the remnants of a bureaucratic empire, the military and security forces, political entrepreneurs and so on. As social protection collapsed and Russia offered the most dramatic example ever of a collapse in living conditions, violence became a central feature of society. The combination of unemployed specialists in violence (former army members, former members of wrestling sports clubs etc.) with relaxed controls on the distribution of the means of violence gave a clear twist of coercion to the war of position.

* On the staggering statistics of transition in Russia, see Gavin Kitching (1998).

Arguably, over time, the beneficiaries of primitive accumulation needed greater protection of their new investments and began to take an interest in a revival of centralised state authority, while the state began to show signs of an ability to control capital.[27] In other words, according to this argument, in Russia there has been something of a genuine shift from primitive accumulation and the violence of the interregnum towards a more institutionalised framework for the emergence of a capitalist society.

Brazil: a haemophiliac society?

Civil wars, this book has noted, gather under a single label for a given country a range of conflicts fought at different levels of society: they dramatise and organise a plethora of agendas of conflict. In some countries this range of manifestations of violent conflict exists without the casing of a simple category offered by the civil war label. Countries like Brazil, India and South Africa are rife with violence.

To take one example, there is a bewildering kaleidoscope of violence in Brazil. Even here the civil war label hovers with ambiguous categorical relevance. In the late 1980s 'Brazil's largest squatter settlement, the favela of Rocinha in Rio de Janeiro's élite South Zone (Zona Sul) with an estimated population of 150,000 to 200,000, erupted in a show of violence against its middle-class surroundings that the local and national press sensationalistically [*sic*] labelled "a civil war".'[28] Violence, including state violence, has become more intense since the transition to democracy than it was under the military dictatorship.[29] It is not all '*carnival e futebol*'.

— Urban violence, prison violence, police violence

Urban violence is widespread. In May–December 2002 4,534 homicides were registered in Rio. Gang violence has intensified as the drug market has expanded and as the extent of the arms market has grown. In 2003, following a series of incidents, a senior police official in Rio de Janeiro claimed that drug-related violence was out of control: gangs had fought pitched battles with police, they had torched public buses, and in May 2003 one gang sprayed a café full of university students with gunfire, reportedly in retaliation for the police killing of a gang leader.

Data on violent deaths in Brazilian cities—which include deaths from traffic accidents, accidental drowning etc., as well as mortality as a result of intentional violence—show clear patterns relating the incidence of violence to patterns of social and economic structure.

Table 5. DEATHS AND MORTALITY RATES BY EXTERNAL CAUSES*
IN BRAZILIAN CITIES, 1990

State capitals	Deaths	Rate (× 100,000 people)
Fortaleza	935	54.6
Recife	1,360	104.7
Salvador	1,165	56.1
Belo Horizonte	1,388	68.7
Rio de Janeiro	6,322	115.3
São Paulo	9,464	98.1
Curitiba	1,160	88.2
Porto Alegre	1,002	79.3
Goiânia	618	67.0

* 'External causes' is a public health category including traffic and other accidents, suicide,
homicide and other violence.
Source: de Lima and Ximenes (1998).

As the tables below show, in cities like Salvador and Recife young
people are exposed to high risks of violent death. Those who live in
relatively well-off parts of town die more in traffic accidents. Children and adolescents living in poorer areas die more from homicide. Alongside the poverty and higher rates of 'delinquency', the
favelas tend to be characterised by a flimsy apparatus of state institutions like health care, schooling and public protection. What
state presence there is, is often itself vicious and renowned for its
arbitrariedades.

Brazil's urban prisons are notorious sites of violence with brutal
conditions of incarceration and frequent conflicts between inmates
and poorly paid guards. In October 1992 in the largest prison in
South America, the House of Detention in Carandiru in São Paulo,
after a fight between inmates military police killed 111 prisoners.
Nine years later the commanding officer was prosecuted and found

Table 6.1. MORTALITY RATE BY CAUSES AMONG 5–19 YEAR OLDS,
SALVADOR (BAHIA)

Level of social economic welfare	Traffic accidents (× 100,000)	Homicides (× 100,000)
High income/high education	10.6	–
High income/middle education	18.3	9.7
Low income/middle education	12.3	4.1
Low income/low education	12.5	17.8

Source: Macêdo *et al.* (2001).

Table 6.2. MORTALITY BY LEVELS OF LIVING CONDITIONS,
RECIFE 1991

	Stratum 1		Stratum 2		Stratum 3		Stratum 4	
	Number	Rate	Number	Rate	Number	Rate	Number	Rate
Traffic accidents	81	29.1	90	21.3	53	18.2	35	11.5
Suicides	18	6.5	14	3.3	11	3.8	6	1.9
Homicides	84	30.2	214	50.6	159	54.5	114	37.4
Total incl. others	227	81.6	399	94.3	280	96.0	203	66.5

Source: de Lima and Ximenes (1998). Stratum 1 is wealthier, stratum 4 poorer.

guilty of 102 murders. Eighty-five military police were still, in 2002, awaiting trial.

Even more notorious internationally is the murderous vigilante violence against street children. Meanwhile, a book issued by the Brazilian office of UNESCO documents the high and rising incidence of violence in schools and the easy accessibility of guns.[30] Sometimes institutional incentives i.e. how the rules of the game encourage people to behave—are extremely obvious in how they provoke violence. An example is the evidence showing that police rewards schemes put a value on bravery, which in turn appears to have encouraged police in a shoot-to-kill policy that can then be justified in terms of self-defence under fire.[31] Meanwhile, there is evidence of a 'continuum of vigilantism' running from the first unofficial police death squads created by General Kruel in the 1950s, through the use by the military dictatorship of death squads to control dissidence, to the post-dictatorship private death squads, mob lynchings and lone wolf vigilante assassins known as *justiceiros*.[32]

— *Rural violence*

Rural and non-metropolitan Brazil is also violent. The Comissão Pastoral de Terra (the Pastoral Land Commission) issued a report in 1991 detailing a relatively 'good year': fifty-one peasants and rural workers were killed during the year; 383 land conflicts were reported and forty-three conflicts over workers' rights; there were twenty-seven cases of slave labour, allegedly involving a total of 4,883 workers and including young children. In other words, violence often characterises conflicts over both land and labour.[33] Most of the killings took place in the poor northeast of the country, above all in Pará. The Comissão Pastoral de Terra has collected and published data—drawing on primary research and secondary data collection—since 1985. Table 7 gives some idea of the trends, in spite of the obvious fuzziness of the definitions.

For years there have been violent attacks on rubber tappers' movements by police and ranchers in areas where land speculators are slashing the rainforest and so swiping away the tappers' income source. The most famous incident was the assassination in 1988 of Chico Mendes, the leader of a rubber tappers' association in the northern state of Acre.[34] The rubber tapper victims of violence make for just one example of the widespread phenomenon, in recent decades, of violence on the Amazonian frontier, largely pitting rival claimants to land (indigenous people, migrant settlers, speculative landowners, ranchers) against one another in a climate of unevenly enforced institutional property rights and competing economic pressures.[35]

In recent years the landless people's movement, the Movimento Sem Terra (MST), has organised occupations of uncultivated land, challenging the legitimacy of unproductive *latifundistas*, large landowners. For the most part the clashes have not been directly violent, but they have certainly involved violence at times. MST demonstrations, convoys and occupation groups have come under fire from police and from private landowners' militias. The institutionalisation of violence, the way that violence has become one of the rules of the game of social relations in Brazil, is also clear from the widespread phenomenon that Nancy Scheper-Hughes calls 'everyday violence against the poor' in the northeast.[36] What she refers to is the routine, deadening activity of killings and disappearances in towns and rural areas, where the poor are treated effectively as nonexistent.

— Cultures of violence, institutions and accumulation

This aggregation of violence is complex. It is unlikely that it can be understood only in terms of 'cultures of violence', of the comparative advantage of the poor (it is often the rich and powerful that appear in Brazil, as elsewhere, to have a comparative advantage in violence), of state collapse, or of resource greed, though each of these may play a part. Arguably, the panoply of violence is best approached in terms of institutional formation and change, in terms of unsettled relations between groups organised (some more overtly than others) around material interests, and in terms of identity categories that inflect these relations.

The violence outlined here does not describe the whole of Brazil. In many ways Brazil has achieved phenomenal successes in

Table 7. RURAL CONFLICTS IN BRAZIL

	1993	1994	1995	1996	1997	1998	1999	2000	2001	2002
Land conflicts*										
No. of conflicts	361	379	440	653	658	751	870	556	681	743
Assassinations	42	36	39	46	29	38	27	20	29	43
Slave labour										
No. of conflicts	29	28	21	19	17	14	16	21	45	147
Assassinations	0	1	0	4	0	0	0	0	0	0
Labour conflicts**										
No. of conflicts	...	...	...	...	49	56	28	33	25	22
Assassinations	...	...	...	...	1	5		1	...	...
Other***										
No. of conflicts	155	78	93	78	12	279	69	50	129	14
Assassinations	10	10	2	4	0	4	0	0	0	0
Total										
No. of conflicts	545	485	554	750	736	1,100	983	660	880	925
Assassinations	52	47	41	54	30	47	27	21	29	43

* The figure for 2002 combines land conflicts (495), land occupations (184) and encampments (64).

** Labour conflicts include cases of violation of labour legislation and cases of 'over-exploitation', i.e. particularly harsh conditions of labour and unpaid hours of work.

*** Until 1996 this category included labour conflicts; after 1996 it included conflicts during the dry season (collective occupations, roadblocks, pickets etc. demanding food aid, seeds, water etc.), unions, agricultural policy and mines. 2001 figures only include dry season problems. The 2002 total includes dry season conflicts, conflicts over water and mine conflicts.

Source Comissão Pastoral de Terra Documentation Centre, http://www.cptnac.com.br/

its development of capitalism. It was one of the fastest growing economies in the world over the whole period of the twentieth century. However, rapid growth in Brazil has been characterised by staggering inequality, which takes a clear form of 'categorical inequality' largely on racial terms. It is hard to see how this is to be understood other than in terms of the influence of a long history of slavery and colonialism, followed by oligarchic control. Inequality has been a durable feature of Brazil.* Indeed, Brazil has never fully resolved a series of conflicts among groups; the blood has never completely dried in enforceable, accepted and legitimate codes. It is a historically haemophiliac society.

Where institutional uncertainty prevails, the conflict that lies behind the eventual formation of credible and enduring institutional arrangements becomes very clear. In some cases this not only produces violence; violence itself can become institutionalised as a repeated pattern of behaviour that sustains the organisation of relations—between the police and *favela* drug gangs or between prison guards and inmates, between the MST and landlords, between squatters and landowners or rubber tappers and ranchers on the Amazonian frontier, between men and women in the home and often in the workplace. Private property rights, rights to squat or occupy uncultivated land, the rights of prisoners and the rights of the police to use violence, the roughly accepted limits of gang violence (beyond which the military may be called out onto the streets), the rights of street children versus those of vigilantes—these are all constantly being negotiated, tested and refined through repeated conflictual encounters.

Institutional flux and conflict are inevitable, as this chapter has repeatedly stressed, in dramatic transitions. But it is always prolonged and especially pronounced where there is ineffective or indecisive central enforcement of institutions. The reach of the state in the Amazonian frontier regions is often tentative at best. And the state has failed to provide or encourage effective welfare provision, living conditions or economic opportunities in the *favelas*, the peri-urban reserves of historically displaced people (settled in displacement, as it were). *Favela* conditions may encourage poor youths to 'choose' to work in the drugs sector when the returns are typically greater than prevailing minimum wages, though the extent to which they then exercise rational choice in becoming involved in violence, or exercise thereby their comparative advantage, is ques-

---

* See, for example, the graphic data on inequality in Brazil in Sutcliffe (2001).

tionable. Land speculation on the frontier, just like drug business in the *favelas* (partly organised around local market demand and partly around the *entrepôt* business connecting Colombian cocaine with international markets), involves a kind of gloves-off accumulation strategy in conditions of multiple sovereignty: in one case the state, though not always consistently or effectively, legitimises material interests; in another, also ineffectually, it criminalises them. During the long process of negotiating accepted institutions, ultimately political negotiation and social conflict may tame the conflict and remove a good part of the violence, but there is nothing especially predictable about this. Interests, in transition, are clearly passionate; and outcomes are essentially contingent.

Brazilian violence is not simply a form of 'development in reverse', nor a reflection of dualism—a division between backward pre-capitalist classes with a penchant for violence and a more formalising and progressive capitalism. Rather, violence has often been an expression of the ongoing crises of political and economic development.[37] Much of this violent conflict in urban and rural Brazil reflects conflict over the terms of accumulation: violent accumulation on the Amazonian frontier; forceful conflict over the terms of land ownership and labour relations in rural areas; violence emerging in the responses to failed accumulation dynamics, or at any rate staggeringly unequal and limited accumulation strategies, in towns; and violence in the ways that ideology and institutional incentives combine in state (and private) efforts to restrain those responses. A spokeswoman for the Association of Women Workers' Organisations, speaking at a meeting in Santarém in the northern state of Pará in 1999, put it this way: 'Here in the Amazonian interior, we exist between feudalism and a savage emerging capitalism.'[38]

Border wars and property rights in Africa

The institution of private property rights that is critical to capitalism is, again, an institution forged in conflict: it cannot simply be transposed unless there is an appropriate political configuration and an effective enforcement agency to ensure that property rights can serve their more narrow efficiency functions. Property rights claims and resistance to them clearly reflect struggles over the surpluses that may be produced on land: over how these surpluses are to be generated and allocated. At the same time these struggles are over access to and control of labour to produce those surpluses. Two further examples show this process of property rights institutions in political—and violent—negotiation and at the same time confirm the relevance of the idea of the spectrum of violent conflict.

First, in Mozambique establishing the conditions for successful commercial agriculture remains conflictual. There is both a range of material interest groups and a range of collective identity perceptions influencing this process. These include highly differentiated local populations—differentiated, that is, by size of landholding, family size, range of possessions like shoes, radios, zinc roofs, beds, demographic structure, access to the financial contributions of males, levels of education, and access to different kinds of wage employment. Then there are medium-sized farming enterprises run by Mozambicans known as *privados*; larger but long-established commercial plantations, typically managed by foreigners (or white Mozambicans) and often dating to the colonial period; and recent foreign arrivals who have been granted land concessions for commercial agriculture. These latter individuals and groups include South African farmers who, in the wake of the end of apartheid, left South Africa and moved to Mozambique. Some of these South Africans, having failed in one province, have migrated to Manica Province, where the infrastructure and commercial agricultural conditions are better. Manica borders Zimbabwe, and a new category of farmer in Mozambique, especially in Manica but also in other provinces such as Nampula, further north, is the white Zimbabwean farmer who has had his (usually) farm in Zimbabwe seized in the name of redistribution to veterans of the liberation war there.[39] There has also been an influx of Zimbabwean labourers.

The negotiation of secure land tenure conditions among all these groups is fraught. Large and medium-sized commercial farmers—both Mozambican and foreign—are constantly embroiled in social tensions and legal conflicts and land encroachment by local people. These conflicts may involve long-standing claims to land ownership or access rights that clash with recently granted land concessions to large-scale farmers. The conflict can play itself out in different ways: through legal challenges and bureaucratic tangles; through insinuations of the engagement of spirits and curses; and through encroachments on the concession, in the form of grazing animals on the concession land, for example. Elsewhere, recently arrived *boere* farmers in Manica complain that the locals frequently burn their crops and stymie their farm equipment. In another province there are disputes between large farmers—between a long-established plantation company and a more recently arrived sub-sidiary of a major international tobacco firm. This conflict involves using political levers at the national level of policymaking and rule-setting and also efforts to manipulate smaller local farmers over whom the two firms vie for influence. Both firms are involved in outgrower schemes, where they provide inputs and advice to small farmers and in return buy up all the farmers' output, at a price that discounts for the inputs. There is a constant petty conflict of one outgrower scheme trying to buy output from small farmers con-tracted to another outgrower scheme. Most of these conflicts are not overtly violent. They do, however, constrain the behaviour of farmers and can restrict their commitment to new investment in productivity-enhancing practices and equipment. Further, this per-vasive petty conflict, which nonetheless has real economic effects, is only perpetuated by the failure of the central and local state to intervene decisively.

The same kind of conflict happens in parts of rural South Africa, where it can turn genuinely violent. There have been several cases of violent attacks on white commercial farmers in the Orange Free State. There are also many reports of violence on large farms against farm workers.[40] A recent book on the Natal Midlands high-lights the conflict there, through a focus on the killing of the son of one farmer. Jonny Steinberg's *Midlands* tells the story of the many layers of conflict that lie behind this killing.[41] He points out that by early 1997 violent assaults on white farmers were being recorded at an average of three or four a week and that the violence had esca-lated since the end of apartheid. The young farmer in question was killed 'not just figuratively, but quite literally, on the southern mid-lands' racial frontier, the dust road on which he died being a bound-ary between the white-owned commercial farmlands to the west and the derelict common land of a dying black peasantry to the east. Those who murdered him did so in order to push the bound-ary back, a campaign their forebears had begun in the closing years of the nineteenth century, and which their great-grandchildren be-lieved it their destiny, as the generation to witness apartheid's de-mise, to finish.'[42]

Evidently the conflict and the specific killing also evoked a bound-ary between ways of organising economic and social activity and access to land, a boundary between institutions and social relations, as well as a boundary that dramatised social relations and the scope for their renegotiation in the wake of the collapse of apartheid. Institutionally the boundary pitched claims for private property

rights against common access to land: for commercial farms in the
area bordered on the old apartheid era 'homeland' of KwaZulu,
the 'vast expanses of derelict and broken countryside, home to a
former black peasantry that is now for the most part unemployed',
the so-called traditional lands from where white farmers hire
labour and from where people come in the night to steal white-
owned cattle.

Another facet of the accumulation, institutional and relational
conflict is the declaration by white farmers of conservation areas on
unfarmed land. Tenants see this as a kind of enclosure, withholding
a long-standing practice of hunting on uncultivated farmland as
part of their livelihood. As one of Steinberg's informants puts it:
'We are being boxed into our little ghettoes... We will waste away
on our little strips of land.'[43]

Two more factors stand out from Steinberg's narrative. One is a
colonial history that keeps on detonating like a field of landmines
long after the colonial era. Memories, repeated stories, are one
source not only of grievance but also of collective action. These histories include that of the 1904 poll tax introduced specifically to
force people into wage labour on white farms. The second factor
is the influence on a conflictual situation of local specialists in
violence. The white farmers who organise self-defence watches, vigilante patrols and private militias talk in the idiom of warfare
learned from the time some of them (and their employees) spent
in the South African Defence Force or in other security agencies. In
the local black settlement, an influence of violence has trickled in
from a range of sources: individuals with experience in Umkhonto
we Sizwe (MK—the ANC's armed wing), with experience of the
township violence of the last decades of apartheid, or with experience of the war fought in the 1980s and early 1990s between the
ANC and Inkatha in Natal.

These are just two examples of the increasingly widespread conflicts—some violent, some non-violent, some an important part of
the processes leading to warfare—over land, labour and accumulation throughout Sub-Saharan Africa. Pauline Peters, reviewing the
evidence of this phenomenon, argues convincingly that these conflicts reveal deepening social differentiation 'and, though this differentiation takes many forms—including youth against elders, men
against women, ethnic and religious confrontations—these also reveal new social divisions that, in sum, can be seen as class formation.'[*]

* Peters (2004: 279). Woodhouse *et al.* (2000) also discuss the various processes that
they argue amount to 'African enclosures'.

A particularly sharp example is Somalia, where the violent conflict of the 1990s was both a period when conflict over land in areas like the fertile Jubba valley in the south intensified and a product of earlier 'processes of land occupation and expropriation by the Somali state and its governing élites', combined with demographic change and shifting market conditions.[44] Institutionally, one of the mechanisms supporting particular interests in this contest over the terms of accumulation was the 1975 Land Law, which made it easier for 'those with privileged access to the mechanisms of registration' to secure titles to land that had been previously been used by local farmers.*

Local transition in a global context

Ernest Gellner argued that the whole point about any transition was that the past became virtually irrelevant: to approach the problem of transition through history is impossible because everything is new and different.[45] Yet if there is a history of transitions, then perhaps a historical perspective is feasible. Thus far, this chapter has argued that capitalism since its inception has instigated a transition elsewhere; that this has in some cases become a transition to capitalism but that 'the end' of the transition is not always clear; and that the interregnum of this period has always been conflictual and violent in one way or another. Violence is the norm in development. As Gavin Kitching puts it, no major structural change has ever been smooth, peaceable and democratic; and industrialisation, as much as imperial conquest, has been for most people a repugnant experience of having immense changes forced on them that were initiated by other people.[46] If this is so, contemporary poor countries, characterised by the transitional traits of institutional and structural flux and violence, can be seen from this same perspective. Violence is not just an aberration, a virus that afflicts societies, it is a part of potential development. Nor is violence only a throwback.

---

* Besteman (1996: 11–12), cited in Peters (2004: 297). Although these examples are recent, the struggles over land and labour and the terms and forms of accumulation that they reflect have been going on for some time in various parts of Africa. An excellent example is described in Frederick Cooper's analysis of social conflicts and their diverging political outcomes in Zanzibar and parts of the Kenyan coast in the late colonial and early post-colonial period. Central to the drawn out conflicts over clove production in Zanzibar and cashew cultivation in Kenya was the failure of the state effectively and unambiguously to intervene to back one particular set of class interests and accumulation institutions. See Cooper (1980).

Further, the perspective adopted here allows for the treatment of violence across the spectrum of forms that was proposed in earlier chapters. Nonetheless, to return to Gellner's point, the contemporary transition (where the *from* remains clearer than the *to*) in many countries is partly a transition without a past; it is different from previous transitions since the advent of capitalism, by dint of the increasing 'lateness' of the transition. These interests of advanced capitalism take the form of direct market involvement—through commodities and capital flows. And they take the indirect form of industrialised countries 'kicking away the ladder', that is, making it difficult for developing countries to utilise the protective, state interventionist policies on which, without any empirical doubt, advanced country wealth was itself based. Thus the second helical strand that this chapter looks at, in the structure underlying violence and war, concerns the interests of the richer economies. These interests can themselves be passionate. Far from tempering the passions and cooling conflict in developing countries, the presence of advanced capitalist interests (in the form of investments, commodities supply and demand, and political pressure through the corporate and diplomatic arms of rich country nation-states, as well as through arms exports and other military goods and services) can aggravate violence.

The novelty of contemporary transition needs some qualification: for it is also true that every transition since England's industrial revolution has been characterised by the intense pressures of 'catching up', and by Gerschenkron's tension between the promise of industrialisation and its benefits and the obstacles in the way of securing those benefits.[47] Most countries have simultaneously faced the related challenges of state formation and the development of an 'imagined community' of the nation. Arguably, though, while the particular national challenges vary (in some countries, for example, there are greater social preconditions for nationalism than in others), the international context continues to evolve. The international division of labour is more highly refined now than it was a hundred years ago, and while the international extent of the market has also grown low and middle income countries face more and more intense competition from other suppliers of primary commodities and basic manufactures. The technological gap between the most advanced and the least industrialised economies in the world is greater than ever, as is the span of incomes per head across countries. The logic of capitalism has expanded beyond the boundaries of the nation-states that, nonetheless, capitalism still requires in order to guarantee its largely preferred conditions of predictability.

Also, the ideological and political conditions within which a given national transition evolves differ. Largely through the mechanisms of debt management and the apparatus of aid, the community of international creditors exercises extraordinary control to micro-manage the economic policy of national debtor governments, typically insisting on measures that open economies up to international markets. These factors combine with an ideological denial of the significance of capitalist class formation; for many developing country governments and also the international financial institutions (principally the IMF and World Bank) either deny the existence of substantial capitalist interests and a class of wage labourers or appear to have no understanding of how to promote the development of these groups.* Further, the effects of colonial rule vary but often include the way that collective identities below the level of the nation are shaped—the classic example being the colonial impact on the Tutsi/Hutu relationship and its historiography in Rwanda and Burundi.[48]

Finally, if the fact that developing countries exist in a world shaped by the power of a hegemon is not new, it is true that the characteristics of that power have changed. Overlapping with late European colonial rule and then taking over after the decolonisation of European empires, the United States has exercised an imperial hold over much of the world, especially since the end of the Second World War. It is still probably far too early definitively to assess the form and implications of the Bush doctrine—the set of bold imperialist policies developed in the United States by a clique including Paul Wolfowitz, Richard Perle and Donald Rumsfeld.† However, for a long time the United States has had a historically spectacular military-industrial prowess and an international penchant for military and political intervention that rather belies the image of an isolationist, somewhat gauche world power. Military and intelligence interventions since the Second World War included

---

* The whole 'discourse' of civil society has glossed over the historical role of trade unions as perhaps the most effective civil society organisation in economic development. Meanwhile, there has been a prevailing notion that capitalists will spontaneously 'emerge', rather than needing massive support from their national states.

† 'This is total war. We are fighting a variety of enemies. There are lots of them out there. All this talk about first we are going to do Afghanistan, then we will do Iraq, then we take a look around and see how things stand. This is entirely the wrong way to go about it... If we just let our vision of the world go forth, and embrace it entirely, and we don't try to piece together clever diplomacy, but just wage a total war...our children will sing great songs about us years from now': Richard Perle, in E. M. Wood (2003: 151).

Greece from 1947 to the early 1950s and again in the 1960s and early 1970s; Korea from 1945 to 1953; Germany in the 1950s; Guatemala in the early 1950s; Indonesia, Syria, Italy and the Philippines also in the 1950s; Vietnam; Congo in the early 1960s; Brazil; Chile; Iraq in the 1970s; Angola, Afghanistan and Nicaragua in the 1970s and 1980s; and on and on.[49]

The ideology of American power has always justified interventions overseas very much in terms of John Stuart Mill's phrase quoted early in this chapter: that 'the friends of freedom have a right to employ their own thews and sinews to check the onward flow of barbarism and tyranny.' However, there is plenty of evidence that the projection of American power around the world has been more than self-defensive. The dissimulation that surrounded the US entry into conflict in Vietnam only came to light because of a leak by someone who had, till his conscience was disturbed, been the epitome of American establishment values.[50] Similarly, the former US military officer Andrew Bacevich is no anti-American radical but argues that US expansionism exists outside the particular logic of the Cold War. Bacevich's argument is that US expansionism is largely a function not of self-defence but of internal political and economic tensions.[51] For him the internal key lies in an American missionary ideology, sometimes called liberal internationalism, sometimes international economic interdependence, and nowadays normally 'globalisation', but always involving the zealous advance of US business across the world. *Le défi americain*, as a rallying cry to European industrial revival once called it, is an enduring and truly global experience faced by most people in one way or another. US imperialism has acquired a new impetus since the end of the Cold War.[52]

In parallel with the push for greater and greater economic openness (through the management of financial crises and through the institutional development of the WTO), the US has since the Cold War 'embarked on nearly four dozen military interventions...as opposed to only 16 during the entire period of the Cold War'.[53] These military interventions have been accompanied by an expansion in the bureaucracy of American empire. Thus the staffs of the European, Central and Pacific Commands each exceed the size of the Executive Office of the President, while their budgets expanded significantly during the 1990s. For others, American expansionism has deeper roots in the management of internal economic tensions. One starting point was the 1949 US recession, a period of union militancy that was also the background against which the defence budget surged. Military Keynesianism, and specifically its justification in the intervention in Korea, helped resolve economic and domestic political tensions. As Dean Acheson put it: 'Korea saved us.'[54]

The historical transition that is commonly captured by the label of development is one, then, that is inseparable from its international context and from international influences. There are various mechanisms or ways in which this international dimension can aggravate the conflicts at the heart of this transition, in some cases becoming integral to these conflicts turning violent. These mechanisms vary in kind: some are incidental; some involve the indirect effects of policies; some are more direct and conscious influences. Before outlining some of these mechanisms in the abstract and by example, there are two caveats. First, there are conflicts that are very much expressions of internal, domestic tensions and that are rather more indirectly linked to the world economy, overseas capital, or American imperial power than others. Second, often the role of the international is to aggravate rather than principally to cause a given conflict. Nonetheless, there are times when it simply does not make sense to sustain a causal distinction between 'internal' and 'external'.

If foreign agribusiness takes up a concession in a low-income agrarian country, this may intensify already existing tension locally over appropriate property rights institutions, especially where the state is politically ambivalent on these issues. This may happen even where there is good reason to believe, as is often the case, that the foreign company will provide more wage employment opportunities to poor rural people and in better conditions than local farmers can. This situation involves no interest on the part of the foreign enterprise in provoking instability. Another possibility, however, is where foreign capital has an interest in conflict and instability. If conflict shakes up existing rights to assets like land or mineral deposits, encouraging conflict or the violent exclusion of some local interests may open new ownership and investment opportunities. This can happen where violent conflict is already underway (and thus may help prolong conflict) or where such conflict has still not set in. The Angolagate scandal, involving a range of individual business interests, major oil corporations and French state officials, is one example already discussed in Chapter 5. Other examples include mining interests in Congo and in Papua New Guinea, and competition between fruit multinationals in the Somali banana sector.

— Financial flows

Just as late medieval wars individually do not make much sense
without an appreciation of the way international capital flows were
organised at the time, so access to international finance is a substantial factor in contemporary wars. Financial flows may run through
mechanisms such as the *hawalas*—informal international money
transfer networks that, for example, feed remittance money back
from diasporas to country-of-origin families. Finance may also flow
through more formal capital markets. Thus the Angolan government has been able to sustain its war effort partly through the arms-
length commercial transactions involved in oil-backed loans. Meanwhile, the changing technology of the global oil industry and the
entry of new oil companies from Asia allow a government like that
of Angola to diversify its sources of finance. Finance can flow
through overt or covert state mechanisms of support for governments or rebels. And finance can help fund wars through aid fungibility, that is, when aid money given to a country ostensibly for one
purpose releases the financial burden on the country so that it can
more easily also pursue other objectives, including military expenditure. Thus the biggest recipient of US aid (including military and
non-military aid) is Israel and there is no question but that this aid
facilitates the Israeli war economy. In another example, mentioned
earlier in this book, critics argue that British government aid to
Uganda has effectively made it easier for the Ugandan government
to pursue its war aims in Congo. In other words, financial markets
can play an incidental role and direct financial payments or loans
can play a direct one in stoking conflict.

— Commodities

Violence and war, and institutional conflict, are often organised
around markets for commodities that are powerfully international.
In this sense, with or without any nefarious direct interest of overseas individuals, corporations or states in conflict, the conflict
cannot be understood other than in terms of this plaiting of developing country transition and the wider world economy. Greed,
grievance and other subjective motives and emotions doubtless figure powerfully; but they can only figure so significantly because of
the more structural conditions of change involved. The commodity
markets in question are legion. Shifting social relations, political
jostling and institutional tensions around cloves, coffee cultivation,
finance and export have defined violent conflict in Zanzibar, Angola,

Costa Rica, El Salvador, Guatemala and Rwanda. Cocaine has been central to conflict in Colombia and to violence in Brazil and Jamaica, as has heroin in Afghanistan. Despite the significance of these drugs, it would be absurd to say that cocaine or heroin caused civil war in Colombia or war in Afghanistan. Oil and diamonds have shaped and partly defined the longevity and scale of war in Angola and Sierra Leone. Columbite-tantalite, or coltan, has been part of the focus of war in the eastern Kivu districts of Congo and of the quasi-state building in the area by the Rwandan government and military. Elsewhere, in Burma, Liberia, Indonesia and so on, other commodities have mattered—like precious stones and timber.

Chapter 3 discussed the extent to which the preponderance of these primary commodities may or may not be a powerful cause or predictor of the incidence of 'civil war'. The point here is simply to show how international commodity markets are an important dimension of contemporary violence and war, just as wool exports encouraged English sixteenth-century landlords to lay claim to common land through 'enclosure': effectively Polanyi's dictatorship of the grazier lords was the equivalent of the power of contemporary warlords tied into export markets.

— Policy

Next, the policies that developing and debtor countries are strongly encouraged to adopt in the management of their economies may have a secondary, aggravating effect on the local dynamics of conflict. This point can be overdone: there is a long and slightly tiresome tradition of blaming virtually everything unfortunate in developing countries on structural adjustment programmes designed by the IMF and the World Bank. Despite the very significant shortcomings of these programmes, which are extremely poor guides to how to promote capitalist development, there is, for example, really no convincing evidence that structural adjustment 'causes' war.[55] Nonetheless, it can be argued that structural adjustment-type policies can add to and stir up situations that are already highly conflictual. Further, historically for primitive accumulation to give a transitional impetus to dynamic capitalist development, it has required a variety of state interventions. The spread of neo-liberal policies that restrict the scope for states to attempt these experiments in intervention is liable to be one factor allowing for less dynamic, less effectively transitional forms of accumulation.

Two examples are Rwanda and the former Yugoslavia.[56] In neither case did structural adjustment cause genocide or civil war. In both cases there was a long pre-history to the nightmare of the 1990s. Government policy was a central part of this longer historical build-up. In the case of the former Yugoslavia, this history involved economic and administrative reforms from the 1960s onwards, which had the effect of undermining the coherence of the federal nation, weakening the overall economy, and creating incentives for ethno-nationalist politicians. Yugoslavia's descent into warfare had been a gradual one before, but at the end of the 1980s it became steeper. But as this descent became sheer the IMF and World Bank imposed steep debt repayment terms that undermined the credibility and room for manoeuvre of the last federal government.

When the strictures of democracy, consumer pressure groups, shareholder opinion and legal constraints are not too binding some business enterprises are at least tempted by the returns that may be won from conditions of war. Resort to essentially non-capitalist labour relations, and the use of force, represents a tic that from time to time afflicts capitalist enterprise. An old example is that mentioned in Chapter 1—when vanguard activities of capitalist expansion in the reconstruction era of the post-bellum southern US states (in the late nineteenth century) benefited from the convict lease system, obtaining what was close to slave labour from prisons for work in the turpentine industry and in infrastructure construction. This was repeated when the Nationalist government in Spain after the Civil War used political prison labour in infrastructure projects.* The point is that some capitalists, though part of a progressive system, are drawn to coercion and tempted by conditions of violence and war. Again, doing away with the analytical instinct to treat capitalism as a sentient being, this is hardly surprising: capitalism itself has no morality—and cannot be expected to have one. However, the organisation and logic of capitalism do mean that, contrary to earlier hopes, economic activity in this system does not always allow for a clean distinction between the passions and the more moderate interests.

— Arms

Lastly, the ready availability of arms operates as a ratchet effect on political conflict. Since the Angola Gun and before, weapons have embodied the intersection of countries at radically different stages

---

* Cf. Krupps's use of wartime forced labour (Manchester, 2003) and Japanese use of colonial labour.

of development, they have promoted conflict, and the organisation of arms markets has helped shape them. Technological development can dovetail nicely with the demographics and sociology of wars and with the way in which collective action problems are often resolved. Thus most people in most wars nowadays are killed or wounded by small arms rather than by advanced weapons platforms or aerial bombardment.[57] And these true weapons of mass destruction are so designed, nowadays, that they facilitate the conduct of war by children—automatic rifles and shoulder-mounted mortars can easily be carried by kids. Structural change in a range of economies through privatisation and in the wake of the collapse of communism has led to a proliferation of arms producing and exporting nations and to fierce competition for overseas markets. Although there are plentiful small arms coming from Turkey, Bulgaria and the Ukraine, and indeed from Pakistan, it is still the case that the biggest arms producers are major OECD economies like the United States, Britain and France. And in these countries the politics of arms manufacture and exports belies the veneer of laissez-faire policy.

One form of state support for arms exports in recent years has been the use of government export credit agencies. Peter Evans argues that 'a rough estimate suggests that aid and trade credits for military goods and services provided by supplier states now exceed $10 billion annually.'[58] Government supplied export finance for arms deals is especially significant for sales to countries with least credit worthiness, i.e. developing countries. The United States provides roughly $3.5 billion a year in grants and loans to purchasing countries to facilitate sales of US military goods and services. In one estimate for Britain, while military exports accounted for about 2 per cent of total visible exports (in 1997–2001) they absorbed roughly 30 per cent of Export Credit Guarantee Department (ECGD) support.[59] And more than one third of guarantees made by the French export credit agency COFACE are for arms. In one example that has become well known, the South African government agreed to buy more than $1 billion worth of fighter planes with export credit support from the British and Swedish governments.*

Meanwhile, since the end of the Cold War the private security firm sector has flourished, often with clear links to national governments in states where they are based. Thus while on the one hand governments socialise the risk of private sector arms deals by offer-

* For explanations and details on export credit agencies see www.eca-watch.org.

ing export credit financial guarantees, on the other these governments privatise some features of their foreign policy and its attendant
risks. One example is International Charter Incorporated of Ore-
gon (ICI), partly managed by former US Special Forces operatives
and contracted by the US government in the late 1990s to conduct
operations in Sierra Leone, Liberia and Haiti. The International
Consortium of Investigative Journalists (ICIJ) argues that ICI's
operations in Sierra Leone, for example, were part of the pursuit of
US interest in protecting the stability of Nigeria.[60] Evidence of a
trend was reflected in reports that the stock of publicly traded security firms increased in value at twice the rate of the Dow Jones average during the 1990s.

There is an argument that contemporary wars are the product of
a shift in the world economy in recent decades: where once the
world economy was expansive and inclusionary, it has contracted
and become exclusionary. Developing countries, left out of the
world economy, fall apart and reassemble in warfare and illiberal
political complexes and institutions. This chapter has argued that
something close to the opposite is true: that the integration of developing countries into the world economy is central to an understanding of violence and war; and that the development transition
(a transition in which there may be consumption goods and other
benefits on the horizon but in which there is no necessary end in
sight), which is itself conflictual and typically violent, often takes on
a particular intensity by dint of this integration.

This chapter, thus far, has tried to portray the idea of the foundational violence of capitalist development as common rather than
the perverse phenomenon many continue to imagine it to be.
Primitive accumulation is, analytically, one way into this idea. Primitive accumulation is the precursor of capitalism: but it is not bound
to produce capitalism. In other words, if primitive accumulation
provides the sharp increase in the basic capital that may then be
reinvested and built upon through capitalist mechanisms of production and exchange, and if it prises ordinary rural people away
from the means of their self-sustenance, there is no guarantee that
the crudity of primitive accumulation will be followed by its easy
transformation into dynamic capitalism that produces growing
wealth and generates improving material conditions for those whose
work creates surpluses. The same is true of the broader transitional
trauma discussed in this chapter. The outcome depends on whether
the interests of capitalists win out over those of other interest
groups. Marx quipped: 'This primitive accumulation plays in Politi-

cal Economy about the same part as original sin in theology.' And he contrasts this with the amnesia of political economy, in 'the tender annals' of which 'the idyllic reigns from time immemorial'.*

Because of the multiple and often conflicting interests within developing (as in any other) countries, linear developmental outcomes cannot be pleasantly predicted. Struggles over the rights to accumulate and over the terms of accumulation necessarily produce resistance from both those who most obviously lose out and those who might be rivals for accumulation rights. This can mean the drama of accumulation and the conflict and violence that go with it do not always fit a clear functional dynamic. For example, the coercive land occupations in Zimbabwe in the early twenty-first century in one way look like primitive accumulation: they involve a violent dispossession of landowners and a reallocation of rights to ownership of assets, with state support. In another way, though, they would seem to reverse the logic of primitive accumulation. An earlier bout of primitive accumulation had through colonialism generated a dynamic, export-oriented commercial farming sector that was white owned and relied on a large labour force. This had also provided the basis for manufacturing investment and development, partly, indeed, fostered during the Ian Smith regime to diversify in the face of international sanctions. After years of mismanagement and economic stagnation, Robert Mugabe's regime turned on this farming sector partly as a source of patronage for supporters. In doing so, the regime damaged the productive forces that had been built up within the sector and displaced an existing wage labour force. This can only seem, as Rob Davies argues, to be destructive accumulation.[61] At least, this is what it looks like as it unfolds. Another variant of the accumulation drama of transitional societies is Bangladesh, where it has been argued that there is a continual process of 'churning', whereby land and other assets are claimed by some people, appropriated by others, then again reallocated forcefully.[62] This churning of assets is made possible by a context of institutional uncertainty. Its outcome is to stifle the potential for a shift of gear out of primitive accumulation towards a

---

* Marx, *Capital*, vol. I. For another perspective on the foundational violence of modern liberal democracy, see Michael Mann (1999). Girard (1996) argues that all social orders rest on foundational violence; and that this is rooted in competitive identification, or mimesis. Political and economic history has plenty of examples of mimesis and mimetic appropriation and resistance: e.g. Japanese 'reverse engineering', rich countries 'kicking away the ladder' of trade protection, Gerschenkron's identification of mechanisms of 'catching up', and the modular spread of nationalism.

more progressive organisation of assets, production, and economic development.

Ratchets of violence

The argument presented in this chapter is not meant fully to explain all contemporary violence and war. What it does claim is to explain part of the underlying structure of most such violence and war. It is also argued that this section of the structure needs to be addressed more fully and explicitly than is typically the case by students of violence and war and by policy makers and donor agencies. Beyond this, there are many factors necessary to turn social conflict into violence. And there are many factors that help determine the difference between forms of violent social conflict—the variety of Brazilian violence, for example, or the rural conflict between Naxalite groups and landlord armies in Bihar in India, genocidal paroxysms in Bosnia-Hercegovina or Rwanda, or protracted war in Colombia or Sudan. What follows is a brief list of some of the relevant factors.

Perhaps most important, the power and policies of states are central to the source and form of violent conflict. Often contemporary wars are to a large degree part of the process of state formation, that is, of the acquisition of credible centralised power over a society and the development of the state as itself a site of political contest. This process is certainly neither linear nor guaranteed to end in the emergence of successful liberal democratic states. And while the relationship between violence and state formation is centuries old and rife with precedent, it varies over time and across countries in its forms and outcomes. Where the central state is relatively powerful, but still might not have a genuine monopoly on the legitimate use of force, arguably there is a greater tendency for violent social and political conflict to take forms other than 'civil war': the fragmented conflicts of Brazil, India and South Africa. An unusual case is Colombia, which combines a comparatively evolved state (and a strong record of sustained economic growth) with a protracted civil war as well as non-war violence. Charles Tilly, in one of the few analytical exercises in distinguishing the determinants of different forms of collective violence, relates types of violence to a matrix of 'governmental capacity' and degree of democracy.* This

* 'State capacity' is a misleading term: it has entered the lexicon of development aid and policy chiefly as a technical concept; however, it is not possible to treat capacity

model allows for distinctions between collective violence in Iran
('high-capacity undemocratic'), Somalia and Congo ('low-capacity
undemocratic'), Germany and Japan ('high-capacity democratic')
and Belgium and Jamaica ('low-capacity democratic'). Partly, this
model interacts with the discussion in this chapter of transitional
conflict; for Tilly argues that the salience of violence (the extent to
which violence dominates social relations) increases when '(a) participants in political interaction are themselves specialists in violence, (b) uncertainty about an interaction's outcome increases,
(c) stakes of the outcome for the parties increase, and (d) third
parties to which the participants have stable relations are absent.
Activation and suppression of different political identities (i.e., of
bundled boundaries, stories, and social relations) directly affect
conditions (a) to (d). But the ease of activation and suppression of
various political identities depends in turn on the regime's array of
prescribed, tolerated, and forbidden performances.'[63] These conditions correspond rather closely to those that characterise institutional, political and economic transition under the influence of
international capitalism.

State power, for example in terms of the degree of monopolisation of force in society by the armed forces and police, clearly
affects the scope for large-scale coordinated violence. A range of
state policies, moreover, shapes the agenda of social and political
conflict. Tax policies have often provoked conflict—violent or otherwise. A government's management of rural policy can also provoke
or contain conflict: the villagisation policies (and poorly managed
state farm investments) in Ethiopia and Mozambique, among other
places, were central to the origins of violent opposition to governments; persistent state policies favouring particular interests in the
coffee sectors of Costa Rica, Guatemala and El Salvador, and preju-
diced against the interests of others, were central to wars in all three
countries in the twentieth century.

The flip side of provocative policy is the coordination of violence. Collective action challenges are genuine—neither gangland
violence in Johannesburg and Rio de Janeiro, nor civil war in
Colombia or Angola, nor suicide missions in Sri Lanka or Iraq are
possible without some mechanism for overcoming the common
resistance to collective action. However, what the examples in this
book have shown is that there is no single mechanism for resolving

---

independently of politics—the political will to achieve or enforce policies and
rules, and the political source of capacity, e.g. through taxation.

collective action or coordination problems. Instead, there are diverse ways of tackling the problems. UNITA and the MPLA in Angola might have depended for the most part on coercive recruitment, often of children, for military service and logistical support, and to a far lesser extent in most people's cases on direct material benefits, but in El Salvador and Colombia there has been little direct material reward to combatants and at the same time high levels of voluntary recruitment, sometimes—as Chapter 3 pointed out—in the face of extraordinarily off-putting conditions, from a rational choice perspective at least. In Angola, Mozambique and Somalia ethnicity did not play a leading role in coordinating rebellion, though it clearly played some part, and probably more so in Angola. However, in Rwanda and Burundi, as in the former Yugoslavia, the politicisation of ethnicity—what Tilly calls the activation of collective identity boundaries—has been the central mechanism of coordination. In most of these cases, and elsewhere too, collective action is also facilitated by the absorption into the grander social conflict of local level rivalries and petty tensions and intimate agendas of social conflict (between generations, between men and women, and so on). Even for particular forms of violence that appear similar, like suicide missions in different conflicts, there is in fact a striking diversity in the development and organisation of the phenomenon.[64]

Collective action does not spring fully formed from social structure. Typically, and especially in cases where collective action becomes violent, it emerges from a protracted political mobilisation and internal organisational debate. Chapter 4 showed how the nascent nationalist movements in exile from Angola in the 1950s and early 1960s fretted over whether or not to take up arms and how hard they each had to work to mobilise support among populations in many ways not prepared for nationalist political imaginings.[65] Another example is the background to the uprising in Chiapas in southern Mexico. The Chiapas example shows neatly the interaction of state power and policy with institutional change, activated collective identity boundaries and political mobilisation, as well as the 'resource' of political traditions going back to the revolutionary imagery of Villa and Zapata in the twentieth century.

Part of the first communiqué of the leader of the Ejército Zapatista de Liberación Nacional (EZLN), Subcomandante Marcos, on New Year's Day 1994 read:

We are the product of five hundred years of struggle: first against slavery, then in the War of Independence against Spain led by the Insurgents, then in order to avoid being absorbed by United States expansionism, then to be able to promulgate our Constitution and expel French imperialism from our soil. Then the dictatorship of Porfirio Diaz denied us the just application of the Laws of Reform and the people rebelled, forging their own leaders. Villa and Zapata rose up, poor men like us, who have been denied the most elemental instruction, in order thus to use us as cannon fodder and loot the wealth of our country without any care for the fact that we are dying of hunger and curable diseases; without any care for the fact that we have nothing, absolutely nothing; no roof worthy of the name, nor land, nor work, nor health, nor food, nor education; without the right to elect our authorities freely and democratically; without independence from foreigners, without peace or justice for ourselves and for our children. Today, we say ENOUGH![66]

Rhetoric is rhetoric and does not capture fully the actual sources of conflict; but it works for a reason. Chiapas provides one fifth of the country's electricity and a third of its coffee production; yet about 30 per cent of the state's 3.2 million people are illiterate and half have no running water. Alcoholism is rampant, as are parasitic diseases among children. Per capita GDP was 43 per cent below the national average in the early 1990s and literacy was 24 per cent below the average. On top of these characteristics, three policy developments were especially important to the build-up to the uprising. First, in 1974 a government decree gave control over a vast expanse of common land to seventy families: the effect was that of primitive accumulation all over again, depriving huge numbers of peasant families of room for extensive expansion into the jungle. Second, more recently President Salinas had amended Article 27 of the Constitution so that *ejidos*, communally owned farms, could be sold. One implication of this was that if crop failure drove farmers into defaulting on loans, their land could be claimed and traded in the market. Third, when the international coffee market crashed in 1989, Salinas refrained from subsidising producer prices. This was a blow to the coffee farmers who produced the bulk of the country's output and who had previously expanded production in response to government exhortation and incentives.

However, there was no natural causal line from these structural and policy factors making violent uprising inevitable. Instead, the uprising was only possible as the product of a long history of political mobilisation and debate, developing strong ideologies and giving voice to social protest, and typically led by urban outsiders such as church organisations or marginalised urban middle-class intellectuals. On the one hand liberation theologians like Bishop Samuel Ruiz generated political voice among the Mayan Indians in

Chiapas, while on the other a loose collection of agrarian activists was also at work from the 1960s onwards, many of them (like the Naxalites in India) defining themselves as Maoist. By the time Subcomandante Marcos had arrived on the scene in the mid-1980s the joint efforts of the Church (sections of it) and secular radicals had created a distinctive political mentality in the region that had finally locked on to local Mayan culture. Still this did not mean armed rebellion was a dead certainty. There were protracted conflicts between reformists and those more hopeful for the prospects of armed uprising.

Other dimensions of the cause of violence and of variations across the spectrum of violence in development include not just the degree of democracy but also moments of democratisation, and the role of spillovers across national boundaries. Further, although this book has argued that the principal sources of violent conflict lie in the structural, relational and institutional tensions of particular transitions, the fact of violent conflict can sometimes partly be attributed to the influence of 'modular' ideologies of rebellion. One example would be the way the Cuban Revolution influenced political mobilisation in Central and South America.[67] Another would be the circulation of ideologies and practices of violence among some radical Muslim organisations in recent years, dramatised in the events of 9/11, bombings in Jakarta and Bali and elsewhere, and the volunteer 'specialists in violence' migrating to fight in Bosnia or Chechnya. Certainly, the flow of violence internationally is partly an 'ideas' transfer, but to regard this as independent of relations, structure and transitional crisis is surely wrong.

These are just some of the relevant factors. Each of these and others too need far more detailed attention. Some, like the institutional change implied by 'democratisation', have received abundant attention elsewhere. If they are not discussed in detail here that does not mean they deserve short shrift in general. However, the main objective of this chapter, indeed of this book, has been to stress how they are plaited into a particular set of issues in the origin of violence across the spectrum, a set of issues that do not receive sufficient analytical attention in general and that crystallise round conflict over the terms of accumulation. The following chapter takes up the implications of the analysis in this one for the current era of 'post-conflict reconstruction'.

7

THE GREAT POST-CONFLICT MAKEOVER FANTASY

The onset of peace is a threat to development. After the major international wars of the twentieth century this threat was especially clear, twice, in Germany. But there are echoes of the punitive impulses towards Germany after the two world wars in the shared values and conventional wisdoms foisted on contemporary 'post-conflict' societies, whether they have concluded their own peace, had a peace brokered by international intervention, or been invaded and liberated by international powers.

Contemporary post-conflict threats to development have three main sources. First, post-conflict reconstruction and peace building exercises are not technical projects but are sharply political. Developmental prospects depend on what coalition of political forces succeeds in dominating the peace and whether this coalition does or does not promote a potentially progressive capitalist expansion. Second, the developmental outcomes of peace settlements depend on whether economic policy is a product of ideological fantasy or of a realistic acknowledgement of particular economies and of historical experience. Third, the post-conflict moniker itself can be misleading. Such societies are typically characterised by continuing conflict and often by violence: there is often a transformation of violence from large-scale warfare to other types of violence. At worst, ongoing conflict and violence prefigure a return to war.[1] This chapter focuses chiefly on the fantasies underpinning the current era of reconstruction. It begins, though, by introducing some historical experiences that may be relevant to thinking about contemporary post-conflict reconstruction.

Punitive peace initiatives: from Versailles
to the Morgenthau Plan

After the First World War the Treaty of Versailles imposed a punitive peace on Germany, with destabilising consequences. Keynes
famously vented his disappointment with this treaty in *The Economic
Consequences of the Peace*, calling the settlement a Carthaginian
Peace. Keynes's complaint was against the French, for wanting to
weaken, shrink and destroy Germany; with Lloyd George and the
British delegation to Versailles, for pushing the huge reparations
demands made by the Treaty; and with the Americans, for a lack of
financial imagination. There were two related problems with the
peace deal, aside from the schemes to fragment the country. First,
Keynes thought the reparations demanded of Germany were
unpayable. Second, one reason for a commitment to excessive reparations demands was the failure to tackle constructively the debts
among the Allies who had fought against Germany. Keynes thought
these should be cancelled; that Germany should be asked to pay
realistic, and substantially smaller, reparations; and that France
should have a claim on a larger share of those reparations while
Britain should give up all rights to them. 'If we aim deliberately at
the impoverishment of Central Europe, vengeance, I dare predict,
will not limp,' Keynes argued.[2]

   Later, Keynes's American sparring partner in the Bretton Woods
Conference that conceived the IMF and the World Bank (the International Bank for Reconstruction and Development or IBRD),
Harry White, had a hand in the second twentieth-century post-conflict threat to German development. The US Secretary of State,
Henry Morgenthau, loathed Germany and exerted considerable
influence over President Truman. The Morgenthau Plan, hatched
towards the end of the war, was a scheme explicitly to restrict the
scope for Germany's industrial renewal. If Germany could be
reduced to a pastoral ideal of smallholder farming then the country would not, it was thought, be able ever again to pose a security
threat to the rest of Europe and the wider world. The scheme set
out two principal objectives: to destroy industrial capacity, chiefly in
the Ruhr valley; and, by cancelling the institution of primogeni-
ture, to break up German agriculture into myriad farm shards.*

---

* 'On their aeroplane journey to London on 6 August, White pulled from his brief-
case a State Department paper on German reparations, which "envisaged the eventual reintegration of Germany into the world economy". The fiercely anti-German
Morgenthau was aghast, and this gave White his chance to press an alternative

Although the plan was adopted as policy, it was soon abandoned, partly as a result of the conflicts between the Treasury and State Departments.

The Morgenthau Plan and its abandonment reflected the policy tussle within the United States that eventually, and far from inevitably, paved the way for the adoption of the Marshall Plan and US insistence that European states should forge a political union. Marshall aid, massive in scale, came mainly in grants rather than loans, though not without the strings of conditionality. This programme for the reconstruction of Europe, which bypassed the World Bank (itself providing too little aid, too slowly, in the opinion of Marshall Plan supporters), reflected both American magnanimity and American self-interest.

Germany's revival—and possibly wider post-World War Two reconstruction and peace—survived French intentions as well as the Morgenthau scheme. Some French politicians tried hard to prevent German recovery and expansion. Early post-war French manoeuvring focused on achieving French security by reducing and splitting Germany. If Germany could be fragmented and if the resources of the Ruhr (especially its steel industry) could be internationalised, then perhaps a lasting peace, and French pre-eminence, might be secured. Meanwhile, the French government sought to promote France's own reconstruction through the expansionist Monnet Plan. However, once French negotiators acknowledged they would not get British or US backing, they swung rapidly towards a different security strategy, this time one that involved forging very close ties to a larger, resuscitated Germany.

---

scheme. At a conference of American officials in Redrice, Hampshire, on 12 August, Morgenthau outlined a plan for destroying Germany's capacity to wage war in the future. Its industries would be eliminated, it would be broken up into little bits, and it would be converted into an agricultural territory. Destruction of German industry would enable Britain to take over Germany's export trade. Now it was the State Department's turn to be aghast. When Penrose from the American Embassy pointed out that Germany's population was too big to be supported by agriculture, Morgenthau replied easily that any excess could be dumped in North Africa.' (Skidelsky, 2000: 362) Penrose himself remembered first hearing about the plan: 'As we lounged on the grass Mr. Morgenthau in brief, simple terms expounded his views on what to do with Germany... The only hope was to cripple Germany economically and deprive her for as long as possible of the power to take aggressive action again. The way to accomplish this was to destroy German industries and convert Germany into a pastoral country...' Penrose (1953: 245–6) Roosevelt repudiated the Morgenthau Plan but still conflict among the Treasury and the State and War Departments confused policy.

European reconstruction after the Second World War

The history of European reconstruction and Marshall Plan aid after the Second World War is voluminous and still contested. It is far from obvious that the amounts and timing of Marshall aid were really the key to successful reconstruction and the translation of physical restoration after the war into a sustained economic boom. However, to summarise briefly some of the main arguments made by one of the leading historians of this period will be useful. After the First World War there was a major international peace settlement, but the peace failed. After the next World War there was no conclusive peace settlement, yet the peace within Western Europe held and the region passed from reconstruction to sustained boom. Alan Milward argues that the key to this success was the development of intricate economic and institutional interdependences among European countries. The ties that bound economies together—through infrastructure, the European payments union, provisions for the production and trade in steel, and trade in other goods and services—not only produced the fretwork of expansion but also knit these countries together more peaceably.[3]

But there was more to successful reconstruction and expansion. First, there were *diverse* policies and institutional developments among European countries. Some, like the Benelux countries, were keener on free trade, others less so. Some, including France and Britain, promoted nationalisation. This institutional diversity was an extremely significant feature of reconstruction. Nonetheless, second, there were certain common features of national reconstruction policy. Most European countries emphasised the expansion of exports—partly because they were all driven by a shortage of dollars to cover imports. Thus, even if they differed in their degree of commitment to laissez-faire trade policy, these governments did commit to trade expansion: the two should not be confused, though they often are.

Third, governments in Western Europe tended to be expansionist in their policies. One of the main reasons was political: after the insecurities of the inter-war period and the destruction of the war itself the only source of legitimacy for European governments was a commitment to full employment. This typically involved relatively high levels of government spending. Reconstruction and the boom that followed was not a purely public sector led phenomenon. Private sector investment boomed too. However, there is good evidence to suggest this private sector dynamism depended on the stimulus of public spending.* Overall, as Mark Mazower puts it, there spread through much of Western Europe after the Second World War a dominant 'ideology of growth'.

Fourth, to secure growth governments retained or applied state controls over financial markets, by contrast with the current post-conflict reflex of rapid liberalisation of financial and other markets. This was true in Europe and elsewhere.

Japan directed credit to priority sectors through the state-owned Reconstruction Finance Bank: in 1949 this institution was responsible for one-third of lending to industry. Underlying such control is a strategy to allocate meagre post-war savings (together with Marshall Aid) to sectors identified as priorities by planners, which implies credit rationing for non-priority sectors. Countries that did not receive Marshall Aid—for example Finland—financed post-war reconstruction mostly out of domestic savings, and accordingly used a number of state controls over the banking system and flow of funds to achieve this.[4]

Reconstruction is the continuation of war by other means: America after the Civil War

The fantasies of institutional universalism that are common nowadays spread an idea that reconstruction, and development, are simply technical feats. Yet reconstruction is a form of revolution from above. The history of post-war Europe during the twentieth century drives home the point that reconstruction is a highly charged political moment.[†] This is just as obvious in every other example, starting

---

* A widespread commitment to full or high employment was given greater priority over price stability and deficit containment policies. Thus, as Maddison argues, the keys to the sustained boom that evolved out of post-war reconstruction were, especially, 'managed liberalism in international trade' and the success of government spending in 'nurturing a buoyancy of demand which…kept the economies within a zone of high employment.' (Maddison, 1991: 167–77) Also, on the way that demand management—backed by trade unions and government intervention—was essential to fostering sustained recovery and growth, see Marglin and Schor (eds) (1990). Hogan (1987: 431) similarly argues that the key to the Marshall Plan was that copious aid, backed by a 'New Deal synthesis', enabled fragile European coalitions 'to operate within a range of political choice that precluded vigorously deflationary policies, promised higher living standards, and thus closed the door to extremist elements on the Left and the Right.'

† This was not just because of the conflict over what to do with Germany. Most of the massive population movements during and in the wake of the war were to be permanent: the main reason was that 'after the inter-war era's unsatisfactory experience with minorities in the new nation-states, people were being moved in order to

with post-Civil War America. The actual content of reconstruction then was fiercely contested. At one moment the possibility of radical change was possible, and was sought by some, but soon the opening began to close. The overall outcome was a formal shift in the content of the American idea of freedom, and a realignment of interests that allowed for profound continuities, in the American South, with the antebellum era.[5]

The political struggle over reconstruction is illustrated by the fate of the Radical Republican group. This group—led by Thaddeus Stevens—pushed a populism that was both aggressive and idealistic. 'The foundation of their institutions both political, municipal, and social *must* be broken up and *re-laid,* or all our blood and treasure have been spent in vain. This can only be done by treating and holding them as a conquered people,' wrote Stevens in a speech in 1865.[6]

The programme of Free Soil radicals and abolitionists attracted support from Northern manufacturers and railway interests as well, till at its peak the Radical Republican movement made for a concerted drive to rebuild the South in the image of the North, with its 'free speech, free toil, schoolhouses, and ballot boxes'. Yet, as Barrington Moore put it and as others have also shown, the brief revolutionary flash represented by the Radical Republicans 'sputtered and went out in a mire of corruption'. This version of a punitive but progressive peace failed to prevail. The Radicals were unable to introduce plantation confiscation into the reconstruction acts of 1867. The possibility of genuine land redistribution in the South proved unpalatable even for many Northern interests and was ultimately politically unfeasible. One of the main outcomes of the struggle over Reconstruction was a shift from slavery through experimentation with wage labour to a large-scale adoption of sharecropping.*

---

consolidate political boundaries' (Mazower, 1999: 217). In Eastern Europe many minorities were virtually eliminated in post-war population transfer agreements—more than seven million Poles, Czechs, Slovaks, Ukrainians and Balts were evicted and resettled.

* During Presidential Reconstruction (1865–7) when President Andrew Johnson gave the South freedom of movement to define reconstruction, Southern states enacted the Black Codes, denying blacks equality before the law and political rights, and imposing mandatory year-long labour contracts. They overdid it: Northern Republicans struggled with Johnson and succeeded in forcing through the enactment of laws and constitutional amendments that 'redrew the boundaries of citizenship and expanded the definition of freedom' (Foner, 1998: 104).

Political struggles to revive white supremacy were intense. They were also violent. Post-war violence in the South was widespread. The lynching, hanging, drowning, and shooting of blacks but also of scalawags and carpetbaggers, for example by the Ku Klux Kan during the 1870s, helped stifle the experiment in Southern democracy.* In North Carolina shortly after the war, it was said, 'they govern...by the pistol and the rifle.' The ex-slave H. Adams claimed that 'over 2,000 coloured people' were murdered in 1865 around Shreveport, Louisiana. If true, that figure would of course be above the 'civil war threshold' of 1,000 deaths a year, and although these were not strictly speaking battle-deaths the level of violence undermines the clarity of the 'post-conflict' category. Beatings and shootings were common in Texas, where the Northern army appeared reluctant to intervene. The Texas Freedmen's Bureau collected records that show the 'reasons' for some of the thousand or so murders of blacks by whites between 1865 and 1868: one didn't remove his hat when passing a white person; one wouldn't give up his whisky flask; one white man simply wanted to 'thin out the niggers'; and so on.[7] The wave of violence and intimidation, particularly between 1868 and 1871, effectively spoiled the democratic process in state and presidential elections and was one of the main factors in bringing Reconstruction to a miserable end. It prefigured nicely the 'free and fair' but profoundly compromised elections in more recent post-conflict societies like Bosnia and Hercegovina, Haiti, Cambodia or Iraq.

There are still arguments over the longer-run economic implications of the war. Post-war economic recovery and expansion was highly uneven, even within the South. However, it is fairly clear that growth, diversification, industrialisation and urbanisation all accelerated in the South after the war, though with something of a lag so that industrialisation really took off in the 1880s. But this economic development was from a very low base and it was not enough to prevent the South remaining economically backward, compared to Northern states, well into the twentieth century. The destruction

---

* A scalawag was what Southerners called a Southerner who supported Northern government and Reconstruction reforms; carpetbaggers were the Northerners who came south to make money in the post-conflict period (many of them travelled about with their goods in rucksacks and holdalls made out of carpet material). The Ku Klux Klan—which described itself as an organisation of 'chivalry, humanity, mercy and patriotism'—was only the most famous of a range of paramilitary groups that had widespread Southern popular support and were the violent wing of the political pressure to unravel Reconstruction: other groups included the Knights of the White Camellia and the White Brotherhood.

caused by the war itself was one constraint on development. Another was the decline in international demand (and the proliferation in competitive sources of supply) for cotton, a commodity that continued to be important to the South in spite of diversification. A third constraint was the institutional mess that shaped post-emancipation agriculture.[8] Emancipation and Union were key features of the peace settlement. But that settlement ultimately resolved itself into the reversal of democratisation in Southern states and the substitution of a stifling set of rural institutions for slavery. The dominant institutional form was sharecropping, which was interlinked with credit markets that largely excluded blacks and poor white farmers. These were the conditions in which the potential for expansion in the South was held in check. In other words, the particular peace in the United States inhibited the development of Southern society and its economy.

Railway track in the South expanded dramatically: from 819 miles in 1865 to 1,404 in 1866, 2,541 in 1867, and more than 6,500 by 1871. Textile production doubled between 1865 and 1866 and then rose again by more than 50 per cent by 1869. Yet by 1880 the values of Southern farms and livestock were still well below their values in 1860 on the eve of the war. The post-war boom was partly driven by wartime economic stimuli rather than simply reconstruction injections or policies. There had been dramatic technological innovations during the war, in the clothing and machinery industries as well as elsewhere. For example, the universal milling machine had first been designed to drill holes in gun parts but evolved to be able to cut all kinds of metal shapes and was sold to makers of cutlery, hardware, locks, locomotives, and so on. This had its echo in the post-war boom after the Second World War, which owed a lot to technological advance in the United States during the war.

A second feature of the American boom after the Civil War was that, as Robert Heilbroner put it, 'many of the fortunes that would power post-war expansion had their origins in the war itself.' Some of these wartime fortunes were, frankly, ill gotten. A congressional committee investigating army procurement contracts found that suppliers had provided tents for the troops that were so flimsy that soldiers said they could keep dry better by sleeping outside them than in. Foodstuffs suppliers were found to have sold the army coffee that was a mix of roasted peas, liquorice and a smidgeon of actual coffee grounds. Not for the last time did the special market conditions of wartime stimulate unscrupulous but highly effective accumulation.*

---

* During 2004 US accountability agencies were starting to ask questions of some of

Third, post-war expansion owed a lot to a government whose policies were determinedly pro-business and pro-industry, including the imposition of high trade tariffs and support for agriculture and agro-industry through grants to railway companies and attractive land lease terms.[9] Meanwhile, uneven economic growth in the South was led by intensification of cotton farming, and high labour demand for cotton growing led to a wave of immigration to the region. Processing industries expanded too, around the cotton economy and chiefly in cotton manufacturing and in fertiliser production; and growth was largely underpinned by substantial investments in infrastructure (canals and railways, the telegraph etc.) and by a far more active government than the region had experienced before the war. As with the 'ideology of growth' after the Second World War, there was a 'gospel of prosperity' spreading through the South after the Civil War and many reckoned the legitimacy of the Reconstruction state depended on expansion and diversification. A vibrant Republic would 'spring up in the track of the railroad as inevitably, as surely as grass and flowers follow in the spring', said one Tennessee scalawag.[10] There was some diversification and there was infrastructural expansion, but the gospel of prosperity was undermined by widespread corruption, e.g. the diversion to private pockets of monies meant for railway grants, by mounting state debts, and ultimately by the political settlement that buried Reconstruction and shaped the longer term peace.

The modern era of reconstruction

The pastoral idyll dreamt up for Germany by Harry White and Henry Morgenthau and, for a while, by French post-war politicians is mirrored in the standard development strategy that influences most contemporary post-conflict reconstruction experiences, though based on different motivations.* Development, like it or not, means

---

the major corporate winners of the war in Iraq. Corpwatch (www.corpwatch.org), for example, cited an Associated Press report that Pentagon auditors had criticised Halliburton's estimating, spending and subcontracting procedures and that the Justice Department was investigating allegations of overcharges, bribes and kickbacks. Halliburton had won some $2bn in contracts in 2003 for rebuilding Iraq. Another group, Public Citizen, forwarded information to the Department of Defence suggesting that Bechtel had failed in its contractual mandate to reconstruct essential water delivery and sewage disposal in Iraq.

* See Reinert's (2003) distinction between two ideal types of economic policy in terms of the contrast between Marshall Plans and Morgenthau Plans (p. 455).

industrialisation and, in poorer countries, the spread of capitalism. Orthodox development policy is designed with no apparent understanding of either. Instead, the laissez-faire ideology of some and the populist pipe dreams of others merge with the direct interests of yet other people and organisations to produce the contorted policy package of 'structural adjustment', 'market liberalisation', privatisation and support (through provision of seeds and tools and the concoction of 'micro-credit schemes') for smallholder family farming and self-employment promotion.[11] The effect is to threaten prospects of economic development.

The principal mechanism through which this package comes to be encouraged in developing countries is debt. Debt brings a country to the donors and lenders of 'the development community', and loans are made enthusiastically but on condition the recipient country shows it has 'shared values' in common with the lender, which boil down to some display of multi-party democracy, promises to control corruption and, above all, an eagerness to adopt market deregulation. Conflict affected countries typically have not benefited from debt relief schemes like the Heavily Indebted Poor Country (HIPC) initiative; and international indebtedness has usually increased after wars rather than shrinking or being cancelled.*

* In Nicaragua the debt: GDP ratio rose from 500 per cent in 1987–9 to 600 per cent in the post-conflict period of 1992–4, while over the same period the ratio of actual debt service payments to earnings from exports rose from 9 per cent to 39 per cent. In Mozambique the debt:GDP ratio rose from 351 per cent to 385 per cent between the two years before the peace agreement of 1992 and 1994; while in Ethiopia this ratio increased from 43 per cent in 1988 to 78 per cent in 1993, after the end of the war. In Mozambique and Nicaragua interest payments on external debt, as a share of total government expenditure, also were on average higher in the five or so years *after* war than they were during the war (see Brück *et al.*, 2000). The *Financial Times* (10 March 2001) reported that Nicaragua and Honduras had received only a fraction of the debt relief they qualified for under HIPC terms: the IMF had not contributed a cent to debt reduction, insisting that all creditors provide proportionate debt forgiveness, even though it was harder for some of these creditors to do so—for example, the Central American Integration Bank, the *FT* argued, would go bust if it wrote off debts. In 1995 the IMF lent $45 million to Bosnia through a new post-conflict credit window. The loan was heralded as underpinning a new beginning. 'But its purpose was simply to allow the Bosnian government to repay a bridge loan from the Dutch government, which in turn had been used to repay Bosnia's assessed share of the former Yugoslavia's arrears to the IMF. Old Yugoslavian debt was thus transformed into new Bosnian debt'. (Boyce, 2002: 1041) Nonetheless, there are exceptions to this trend and dramatic debt write-offs in the aftermath of war or political crisis have happened—e.g. in Germany in 1953 and in Indonesia in 1970. In 2003–4 France, Germany and Russia resisted pressure for forgiveness of Iraqi debt, while the US administration wanted a more radical write-off.

Development policies often are foisted on borrowing countries, but there are plenty of interests within those countries that support these policies. Some people within debtor countries are trained in the discourse of orthodox economics and regard the policies as simply self-evident truths. Others are less interested in the niceties of economic theory but are drawn more by the political and material advantages of adopting these 'efficient' policies.[12] Obviously this does not happen exclusively in countries emerging from armed conflict: it is a far more general predicament of late development. However, the post-conflict moment throws the wider development issue into especially clear relief.

Economists commonly project a fantasy of perfectly competitive markets onto the real world, where it becomes a benchmark against which actual market institutions and behaviour look 'distorted'. Equally, political scientists, political economists and international financial institutions regularly project a fantasy of liberal states benignly providing basic services and public goods. Set against reality, this becomes a benchmark of 'good governance' and, in an extraordinary twist of self-deception, 'shared values'. Where states fall short, the fantasy is often displaced on to decentralised, local government structures. These common fantasies show a remarkable lack of historical memory and contemporary understanding. They are never more common than at the beginning of so-called 'post-conflict' moments.*

The projection of these fantasies is often justified by the claim that a country emerging from war is a 'blank slate'.† Reconstruction officials in Afghanistan in 2003 talked of an 'institutional vacuum' and, if they were American, often referred to post-invasion, post-Taliban Afghanistan as 'ground zero'. Another paper on Afghanistan produced in Washington says that from 'the Soviet invasion in 1979 to the fall of the Taliban in November 2001, development in

---

* As in Ferguson's (1990) discussion of development discourse and the interventions organised around it, these fantasies have real effects and typically project 'a representation of economic and social life which denies "politics"…everywhere whisking political realities out of sight' (pp. xiv–xv).

† On the 'international community's' assumption of a *terra nullius* in East Timor, see Chopra (2002). But two qualifications to this point are: there have been differences among aid agencies, e.g. in Afghanistan, in the degree to which they treated the country after war as a blank slate; and, beyond just naivety or poor analysis, the temptation to treat a country as a blank slate can be driven by institutional logic, for example institutional dogmas, personalities and pressures to disburse overriding sensitivity to local and historical realities. (Thanks to Jonathan Goodhand for his suggestion of this comment on the back of Afghan experience.)

Afghanistan had ceased, turning many Afghans into wards of the international community.'[13] This captures well the idea of war as 'development in reverse', and clearly in Afghanistan war and policy combined especially destructively. It captures less well the highly sophisticated *hawala* system of money transfer, including foreign exchange and counterfeit currency transactions. Nor does the idea that development ceased take into account the complexity of the war economy, analytically divided by some into the overlapping categories of war economy, adaptive economy and coping economy.*

Meanwhile, one paper quotes a World Bank official arguing that in the 'extreme void' of a post-conflict moment institution building is easier.† A UNDP document talks of the need to 'create task forces to compensate for the weakness or near institutional vacuum' in Angola. And an Amnesty International background note on Iraq in 2003 claims the 'collapse of the Iraqi government created a political and institutional vacuum.' Post-conflict reconstruction policies may reflect the wider paradigms of development policy thinking but they are often regarded as a virgin terrain onto which, as David Moore put it, utopian capitalist intellectuals shift to engage in a form of extensive cultivation.[14]

In this context a standard model of reconstruction has emerged in recent years. In the past they did things differently. The idea of breaking Germany up was not particularly unusual. A common pol-

* See, for example, Collinson (ed.) (2003) and Goodhand (2004). Blank slate imagery is not a new phenomenon: the phrase '*stunde null*'—Zero Hour—was widely used in Germany to describe the country's predicament in 1945. But *stunde null* had three different meanings: one was an end to Nazism and war; one was simply the devastation of the country; and the third, more problematic meaning, was that of starting over, 'unfettered by the recent past'—'Germany had, in a strange and painful way, become a blank slate' (Harris, 1996: 39).
† Collier and Pradhan argue: 'The period of transition to peace is a particularly suitable time for radical policy reform.' (1994: 133) See also Haughton (1998: 20). There are exceptions: one project document for Afghanistan states: 'It is important to work with the grain of existing institutional arrangements. Afghanistan is not an institutional tabula rasa—the weaknesses in the public sector institutional arrangements do not amount to a blank slate. Many elements of the central planning model that had been imposed on Afghanistan by the Soviet Union remain in place. There are basic laws and procedures that were functioning during the period of the late President Daoud, during Soviet occupation, during the *mujahideen* period and even under the Taliban. Some administrative functions continued to be performed and many mid-level and lower-level cadre government employees have remained in their jobs. However great the need for a fresh start, these existing institutional realities must be worked with.' The blank slate image remains an ideological reflex, but there has been some learning within international organisations: see, e.g., Lonnberg (2002).

icy of the great powers was to split up a war-torn country or to absorb it into a larger political entity. Nowadays, though, the policy is to rebuild a nation-state in the self-image of the Western liberal state. Indeed, the reconstruction model is one indication of how important the state remains to an era of globalisation, even if these states are limited in what they can do. 'Peacebuilding', one person wrote, 'is in effect an enormous experiment in social engineering—an experiment that involves transplanting Western models of social, political, and economic organisation into war-shattered states in order to control civil conflict: in other words, pacification through political and economic liberalisation.'[15]

The accretion of lessons from previous experiences has led to the development of a bewilderingly complex post-conflict reconstruction model. Reconstruction prescriptions 'are becoming so complicated that they defy implementation', argues Marina Ottoway, who identifies the following components in the prevalent model of state reconstruction after violent conflict:

Security: disarmament, demobilisation and reintegration (DDR) programmes, and comprehensive 'security sector' reforms touching on armed forces, police and intelligence services as well as customs agents, defence ministries, finance ministries, budget offices, audit offices and the judiciary;

Political reform: rapid moves to introduce democratic institutions, new electoral laws and electoral institutions, constitutional change, parliamentary capacity building, financing and training of civil society organisations, development and (independent) repositioning of the judiciary, and other provisions for governance and accountability;

Economic reconstruction and reform: relief to the war-affected population and support to returning internally displaced people and refugees quickly combined with or followed by macroeconomic stabilisation reforms, and 'an almost endless array of reforms, concerning everything from the banking system to the commercial codes, which will [sic] eventually make it possible for the country to become a viable economic entity'.[16]

Often this model means a country has to pass rapidly through a 'triple transition': from war to peace, from authoritarian one-party rule to multi-party democracy, and from state management of the economy to free market liberalism.

The package rests on assumptions that are not always well founded. Norma Kriger, for example, argues that security reforms rest on Western assumptions about the link between demobilisation and development rather than on recent and longer-run historical experiences, and that these assumptions fail to account for the political risks of massive demobilisation.* The political transition rests on the 'democratic civil peace' thesis. This is the corollary of the larger democratic peace thesis that concerns relations between countries, which holds that democracies do not go to war with one another. If the same is true within countries, i.e. that democracies are more peaceable than other polities, then democratisation might be a 'method for peace'. Thus since the end of the Cold War democratisation has been a driving force of international policy and ideology.† Finally, of course, the economic transition is based on the elaborate foundations of neo-classical economic theory—it is not based on any accurate reading of how countries historically have succeeded in industrialising and moving out of poverty.[17]

The array of prescriptions for the post-conflict reconstruction makeover has been applied increasingly since the end of the Cold War. The World Bank increased the volume of lending to post-conflict countries by 800 per cent between 1980 and 1998. The big increase was in the early 1990s, as can be seen in Figure 8. In 1998 post-conflict lending accounted for 16 per cent of the total lending commitments of the International Bank for Reconstruction and Development and International Development Association: in the Europe and Central Asia region and in the Middle East and North Africa post-conflict lending made up nearly half of World Bank lending commitments.

---

* Norma Kriger (2003): the 'presumption that full or partial demobilisation is essential for peace-building has more to do with analysts' beliefs about the relationship between demilitarisation and development than with past and recent experiences' (p. 21). These experiences include the victors in the Napoleonic wars, who did not impose demobilisation on defeated enemy forces because they feared the demobilised men would engage in banditry and threaten the stability of the restored monarchy whose rule they wanted to support; and Nigeria and Uganda, where the cost of supporting a large army after civil war was reckoned to be worthwhile given the anticipated political risks of rapid demobilisation.

† There is a large literature on the democratic peace thesis and on democratisation since the end of the Cold War. Quantitative studies regularly find evidence of the democratic peace thesis in relations between countries. Dissenters include Gowa (2000), who distinguishes historical periods and, as a result, finds the international relations version of the democratic peace thesis holds only during the Cold War and argues, therefore, that it is a rather weak foundation for theory and policy in a post-Cold War era no longer characterised by the bipolar world order of that period. Snyder (2000) is especially clear on the risks of overenthusiastic and rapid democratisation.

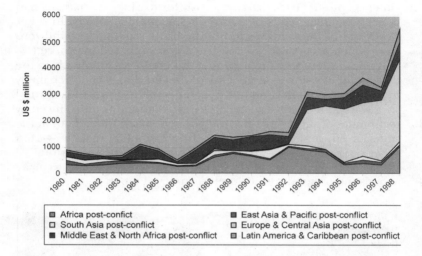

Figure 8. WORLD BANK RECONSTRUCTION LENDING
Source: World Bank (1998).

To establish a clear picture of this trend is extremely difficult. There is no internationally agreed definition of what constitutes 'post-conflict reconstruction' aid. It is not clear whether this would include all projects in a conflict-affected country or only those activities specifically linked to problems incurred as a direct result of conflict, such as the reintegration of demobilised soldiers or of returning refugees or the repair of war-damaged infrastructure. Nor is it clear when the 'post-conflict' moment actually begins. For these reasons, aid organisations like the IMF, the World Bank and the OECD Development Assistance Committee (DAC) do not clearly categorise lending and grants in reconstruction terms.

Fantasy and reality in war and peace in Mozambique

According to the liberal interpretation, war in rural areas drives people—if not into exile or displacement—into a 'retreat into subsistence'.[18] Meanwhile, there is some acknowledgement of a group of economic beneficiaries of wartime—warlords, war entrepreneurs, speculators and so on; but these tend to be treated as an unsavoury indication of the perversity of war and little more. After a war the rural economy is easily conceived of as simply undone by violence, pushed back to its most basic form. This in turn is taken to mean a homogeneous peasantry or smallholder society. In other words, this is the rural version of the blank slate, the ground zero from which post-conflict reconstruction is supposed to proceed.

It is important to emphasise that this conforms absolutely to the development vision at large. One of the few things on which many in the 'development community' agree is this mythical idea of rural society in poor countries. An empirical assumption (reproduced by techniques of surveying the rural poor) is mixed with a faith in the superior efficiency of small farms. In post-conflict societies—as in other poor countries—what is recommended is not a re-pastoralisation *à la* Morgenthau but (using the magic of the market) to make an existing pastoral society less insecure and more 'sustainable'.

BUILDING THE FUTURE
Source: postcard, Public Information Bureau, Mozambique.

Arguably, this whole vision and its post-conflict projection need inverting. Rural societies in most poor countries are obviously characterised by substantial and increasing social differentiation, a process that involves the evolution of wage labour markets rather than just the evenly shared expansion of smallholder production for the market. Moreover, war often *accelerates* differentiation and, in so doing, reproduces some of the patterns common to historical experiences of capitalist transition. By failing to account for the reality and its shaping during war, the post-conflict makeover fantasy passes up opportunities to encourage a progressive turn in the dynamics of change and avoids the chance to determine policies that can clarify realistic escape routes from poverty.

The history and policy experience of Mozambique illustrate this argument. In many ways the Frelimo party that took power at independence in 1975 pioneered the blank slate fantasy in Mozambique. Theirs too was a *tabula rasa* vision. Frelimo came to power with a modernising ambition and a strong belief in the power of the state to galvanise rapid development through economic planning and the expansion of state-run economic activities. The first president, Samora Machel, declared the country would secure 'victory over underdevelopment in ten years!' An ambitious political and economic project was given extra urgency by the evacuation of the country and many of its commercial enterprises by Portuguese colonists. The party's nationalisation plans had, for example, to be implemented faster and more sweepingly, despite extreme shortages of experienced managers.

Frelimo's vision of the future was built on embarrassment. The party's Marxist-Leninist ideology, and the defeat in internal conflict of people seen as backward thinking, petty bourgeois African nationalists, made the party more than uncomfortable with ideas of 'tradition' in the countryside. Frelimo's first leader, Eduardo Mondlane, wrote in 1968, during the liberation war: 'The traditional political structure was in reality destroyed by the Portuguese… Frelimo is busy organising new political structures there where there did not exist any political tradition…the structures of the past have vanished forever. Frelimo must fill the void with new structures.'[19]

Frelimo viewed the rural population as largely composed of a homogeneous population of subsistence farming peasants. These peasants should be encouraged to form producer cooperatives and to move to rationally organised communal villages. However, this undifferentiated mass of subsistence farmers could not be a progressive foundation of rapid development. Instead, the state, which took over colonial plantations, would provide, over time, the base of rural development. Massive investment in state farms would create the demand for labour necessary to transform the peasantry into a proletariat. Labour would be drawn from the communal villages.

Frelimo's notions of the rural population were fanciful. There was no developmental ground zero. The countryside was richly variegated, socially, and had grown increasingly so. Rural people could not just be described as smallholder subsistence households. Colonialism had, as it did throughout Africa, provoked social and economic change, instigating processes of capitalist development even as it sought to curb them. The simple implication, for the argument of this chapter, is that in Mozambique there had been profound rural change that had, among other things, resulted in the expansion of wage labour as a critical feature of many people's 'livelihoods' and survival.[20]

Much of the investment that was skewed towards the state farms was wasted by a haemorrhage of inefficiency and unrealistic policy. But hopes were increasingly dashed, too, by the escalating war against Renamo rebels. Renamo was a creation of Rhodesian intelligence services before Zimbabwean independence, and then later was adopted enthusiastically by the apartheid government in South Africa. Despite this 'proxy war' dimension, Mozambique's war took root within the country. A lot of Renamo's recruits were kidnapped and brutalised to prepare them for guerrilla warfare. But increasingly Renamo attracted at least tacit support, especially in central and northern areas of the country, from people disaffected by Frelimo's contempt for local beliefs and practices and by Frelimo's abject miscalculations.

The war had varying effects across the country. In some areas Renamo subjected the population to a campaign of more or less unmitigated destruction. Elsewhere it controlled rural areas and fed itself on them by levying food taxes and exacting labour tributes, or in other words organising slave labour. Many of these areas were already among the poorer parts of the countryside. They did not feature in Frelimo's plans for state farms or communal villages and they had lost most of the opportunities for seasonal labour migration that had been available in the colonial period. Where Frelimo's hopes were concentrated, the party focused its military protection. In these areas—near state farms and communal villages—and in the interstices between Frelimo or Renamo control, the rural differentiation that had been underway during colonialism accelerated.

Despite ferocious warfare, the destruction of health posts, schools and anything smacking of the presence of the state, despite the night-time raids on villages, the abduction, murder, rape and torture, and despite the roads pitted by landmines and lined with truck carcasses, this was no vacuum. For most people, one of the most immediate effects of government policy and war was a 'goods famine': there was an acute shortage of basic consumer goods like soap and matches or batteries and building materials, and inputs for agriculture like fertiliser. State plantations and the army competed to secure scarce goods, to entice workers, and to feed soldiers.[21] Anyone who could produce an agricultural surplus, or anyone else with some economic edge—people with access to the remittances of migrant labourers in neighbouring countries, skilled workers on the state farms, those with some connections to the party or to the profiteers of the parallel markets or *candongas*—could manage to survive and even expand their activities and to attract extremely cheap labour. Anyone without these kinds of advantage would desperately seek wage work if there were any prospect at all of buying food or other goods. As one of the people who conducted rural research in Mozambique during the war put it: 'Far from retreating into a subsistence economy, therefore, the war and crisis heightened the need for the poorer peasantry to sell their labour to obtain cash to buy food and other rural wage goods.'[22]

The state farms and army were not the only ones keeping this situation alive. There were others who were caught up by and helped propel the momentum of a war economy. These included a few Portuguese colonists who, for one reason or another, had decided to stay put at independence; former employees of large colonial plantations who used saved earnings and accumulated skills to hold onto some form of agricultural production; and Tiny Rowland's multinational Lonrho, which stayed on, hired a private army to protect its tomato and cotton farms, and made smart deals with both the army and Renamo rebels. Then there were the people who ran the gauntlet of risk to drive imported consumer goods from South Africa and Swaziland to the capital city, Maputo, or the Asian origin Mozambican traders who resuscitated rural trade in parts of the country, with their own small private militias.[23]

War raises risk but also, because risk and difficulties deter most people, it may reduce competition in markets and raise potential

SEIMPOL

SOCIEDADE DE EXPORTAÇÃO & IMPORTAÇÃO, LDA.

```
S E I M P O L
T R A D I N G C O M P A N Y
E X P O R T / I M P O R T
```

FILET/FILETE BEEF	7,00 USD/KG	28,30 R
RAMP STEAKY	6,80 USD/KG	17,04 R
SILVER SIDE/CARNE PARA ASSAR	6,20 USD/KG	19,43 R
TIBONE STEAKY	6,60 USD/KG	19,14 R
BEEF SAUSICHES	9,50 USD/KG	26,00 R
LEG OF LAMB/PERNA DE CARNEIRO	8,00 USD/KG	23,20 R
MINCEL MEAT/CARNE MOIDA	7,00 USD/KG	20,30 R
RIB CHOPS/COSTELETAS DE OVELHA	7,70 USD/KG	22,33 R
PORK FILET/FILETE DE PORCO	7,50 USD/KG	21,17 R
NECK OF LAMB/SHANDER/PESCOÇO DE CARNEIRO	7,70 USD/KG	22,40 R
FRENCH POLAND/POLANDE DE VACA	5,20 USD/KG	18,85 R
BACOM	4,00 USD/KG	11,60 R
RIB PORK/COSCOLETAS DE PORCO	6,30 USD/KG	18,27 R
SAUSICHES LAMB COOKTAIL/	9,00 USD/KG	26,00 R
SAUSICHES LAMB BEEF COOKTAIL	9,00 USD/KG	26,00 R
LEG IMPALA	7,80 USD/KG	22,62 R
CHOPS IMPALA	7,70 USD/KG	22,33 R
RIPS IMPALA	7,60 USD/KG	22,14 R
ROLLED-SILON	9,00 USD/KG	23,39 R
BEEF-STROGONOFF	8,70 USD/KG	25,23 R
CHICKEN FILETS	5,20 USD/KG	15,80 R
GOUDA LOAT	9,80 USD/KG	28,42 R
ROUND GOUDA	9,50 USD/KG	26,00 R
SAUDUNCH HAM	7,00 USD/KG	20,30 R
LANGE SALAMI	19,00 USD/KG	55,01 R
CHIKEN/FRANGO	5,00 USD/KG	14,90 R

EACH ORDER IS DELIVERED IN YOUR HOUSE
ENTREGAMOS NA SUA CASA ENCOMENDA
THANK YOU VERY MUCH

Rua Major Teixeira Pinto n.° 10 — Telef. 733130 — MAPUTO

SUPPLYING THE CITY: WAR ENTREPRENEURIALISM IN MAPUTO,
1992

returns, especially because there is no effective regulation of the ensuing monopoly conditions. These are the conditions of market structure that propel people organising endeavours like the supply of bacon and burgers to the Maputo élite and to the foreign aid workers living there. They are the same market conditions that kept some agriculture going, where farmers could supply food to the army or to the rebels and hope to evade surveillance or capture by the other side (or supply both). Over time, there were also increasing conflicts over control of land during the war; gradually, and increasingly with state support, former settlers and senior party and military officials secured relatively large tracts of land. As O'Laughlin put it, 'the war resolved their labour recruitment problems.'[24] Thus war in Mozambique propelled a crude change that forced many people, where possible at all, to look for wage employment despite its awful conditions and paltry remuneration, and that allowed some others to do relatively well out of it. This was a kind of capitalist change. But it was what Mark Chingono called a 'vicious market fundamentalism'.[25]

Post-war land grabbing alongside continued indigence further stimulated socio-economic differentiation and, in some cases, has begun to increase the demand for wage labour. However, this time the whole apparatus of international post-conflict reconstruction, led by the IMF and the World Bank, was organised around the vision of free market development and a homogeneous rural society. As Wuyts argues, this version cast rural people as a mass of small-holder families naturally eager to join the market but constrained simply by the distorted noise of imperfect market signals caused by state intervention.[26] Instead of villagisation and state farms, the potential of the rural economy would be unleashed by market liberalisation backed by schemes to improve smallholders' access to 'micro-credit' to encourage them to engage in self-employment or 'micro-enterprise' activities. The realities of Mozambican rural economic history were—once again—smothered by this vision. The blank slate prevailed. Wage labour, for example, was believed not to exist in the countryside—or to exist only for a small 'labour aristocracy'. In other words, rural labour markets were thought to be irrelevant to poverty reduction in post-war Mozambique.*

---

* It 'will be very difficult to use wage labour markets as a policy tool to alleviate poverty' (Tschirley and Benfica, 2001: 338). A myopic attention to the smallholder as market-oriented producer—in post-conflict as in other societies—is defined clearly by the standard techniques of collecting information on poverty and well-

This rural vision of the basis for post-conflict reconstruction was only one part of a large fantasy. Now that there was 'peace', the state could be pared down to a small entity charged only with creating an 'enabling environment' for private sector activity. Post-conflict reconstruction in Mozambique involved the typical 'triple transition'— security sector reform, political reform and democratisation, and economic reform. In other words it involved a double demobilisation: demobilisation of the army and Renamo guerrillas accompanied an economic demobilisation as the state shed its commitment to mobilise resources for development. This latter demobilisation was achieved by privatisation and liberalisation, with very mixed results. The recklessness of post-conflict experiments was reflected in what was the largest privatisation programme in sub-Saharan Africa in the 1990s. The political innocence of the liberal policy and governance fantasy meshed neatly with the passionate interests of domestic groups. Consequently, the privatisation programme acted partly as a mechanism for corrupt accumulation and asset stripping, but was not backed by an industrial policy of the kind that has always been necessary genuinely to nurture structural change in poor economies.

The rural vision and the overall projection of an ideological fantasy came together most sharply in the World Bank's now infamous treatment of Mozambique's cashew sector, in what amounted to post-conflict economic destruction.[27] In the 1960s and early 1970s Mozambique was the largest supplier of cashew nuts in the world. After independence the government tried to build the processing industry. The main plank of the policy was the ban on exports of raw nuts, which otherwise would be exported to India. But this industrial protection policy came to mean very little in a context of hopeless macroeconomic policy management, and worsening war.

---

being in rural areas. Living Standards Measurement Surveys are carried out to assess the extent and distribution of poverty. A key feature is to survey a sample of the population on the principle of random sampling and to follow a set pattern of questions that concentrates, for example, on a respondent's 'main activity'. This is inappropriate in rural areas that are characterised, first, by dramatically uneven dynamics and, second, by the multiple activities that poor rural people typically engage in to survive. In Mozambique there is both older research (e.g. O'Laughlin, 1996) and new evidence (Sender, Oya and Cramer, 2006) showing a much greater significance for rural labour markets in the lives of very poor Mozambicans, and showing how much of this rural reality is missed by the standard sampling and survey methodologies.

The factories where the cashews were roasted, shelled and packed fell into disrepair, managers could not access inputs, power cuts affected productivity and the quality of the kernels deteriorated.

To compete on the world market for processed cashew nuts a firm needs to produce a high proportion of 'whole white nuts'. Instead, too much of the Mozambican product was broken and scorched from being over-roasted or from the raw nuts being handled badly, which tends to raise the moisture content and then lead to burning. Meanwhile, during the war farmers were more and more isolated and had little incentive or support to look after their cashew trees or plant new ones as the old ones aged or grew diseased.

After the end of the war the World Bank came up with its own vision for the cashew sector, taken straight from undergraduate microeconomic theory. The Bank insisted on privatisation of factories and on rapid liberalisation of cashew trade. The ban on raw nut exports had already been replaced by an export tax, designed to have the same effect, but this tax was now to be slashed. The Bank expected some industrial collapse and employment loss in the factories, but the projected benefits would far outstrip this transitional cost. Liberalising foreign and domestic trade in cashews would lead to sharp increases in the farm-gate price paid to rural cashew growers. Since it was assumed that all cashew production was carried out on a million or so undifferentiated smallholder plots, each with a few trees, the benefits of this price increase would be substantial for poverty reduction across the country. This price signal would stimulate new planting, better care for trees (cleaning around the base of the tree, pruning, and spraying with insecticide) and, therefore, over time a substantial income increase for small farmers. The ensuing widespread improvement in rural incomes would stimulate the beginnings of a manufacturing industry making the more modest (and unspecified) consumer goods for which there was to be domestic rural demand. Meanwhile, a flexible labour market would nicely re-allocate to new jobs those people made redundant as the cashew processing factories closed.

Sure enough, thousands of people lost their jobs in urban cashew processing factories—in towns like Xai-Xai and Nacala. The benefits of the reform—on the best assumptions—were paltry. The price of Mozambican raw cashews did rise moderately, which underpinned this calculation. But the price has collapsed in recent years—partly because of world competition, as India has pushed to increase its own production, as Tanzania's cashew sector has expanded, and as new producers like Vietnam have aggressively promoted their cashew production and exports.[28] Mozambican cashews have also suffered from the spread of oidium, a fungal disease that interferes with a tree's ability to produce a large crop of good quality fruit and nuts. A number of projects have been started, to spread awareness of the benefits of pruning properly and spraying with fungicide. But there has been no dramatic expansion in planting new trees or new varieties, or of the careful cultivation of existing, ageing trees. On any meaningful gauge, cashew policy in Mozambique since the mid-1990s has failed. The policy promoted in the interests of post-conflict reconstruction and economic efficiency amounted to wiping the slate clean.

There were many flaws in the theoretical model applied by the World Bank to the cashew sector in Mozambique, a model whose implementation was staggeringly naïve. Above all, the Playmobil economics of the World Bank in this instance involved abstracting from political interest and conflict. On the one hand the government did not have the political configuration that would result in a concerted push to ensure that liberalisation had the best possible results. On the other the government also had no effective political foundation for pushing much of an alternative, for example, a revised and more effective industrial promotion of cashew processing. The cashew sector has fallen down a crevice of political paralysis and policy indecision. Any effective policy would have had to begin from acknowledging the interest groups ranged against each other, as a basis for working out how to build a more constructive political settlement among farmers, traders and processors. In the end the main group to benefit has been, probably, the traders and middlemen who organise rural collection of cashews and their export, unprocessed, to India. Even this group would benefit further from a more dynamic growth of cashew tree planting and a widespread tree care improvement.

Mozambique is generally deemed one of the most obvious success cases of modern post-conflict reconstruction, perhaps the single greatest success story. The cashew experience, though, suggests it might not be entirely straightforward to work out what are the appropriate criteria of success or failure. War ended in Mozambique and peace has held for more than a decade. There is no obviously serious threat to that peace. Democratic multi-party elections, nationally and locally, have been held at intervals since the peace settlement. A disarmament and demobilisation programme was carried out, and over several years the majority of the landmines sown in fields and on roads and footpaths have been removed. Bridges have been repaired and roads rebuilt, especially effectively in the south. Renamo has changed from a band of atrocious rebels into some ramshackle kind of political party. Most people's lives are better than during the years of warfare.

The war was so hellish in Mozambique that nobody would want to quibble with this transformation. A lasting peace should be celebrated, not scoffed at. But that does not mean there is no justification for questioning the post-conflict makeover. Formally, it is difficult to know against what counterfactual the experience might be assessed. The criteria of success are typically taken to be simply the implementation of the key symbolic targets of reconstruction programmes—holding elections, carrying out demobilisation, liberalising the economy. These criteria are, as Norma Kriger argues, abstract, externally designed and subjective. They can often act as a decoy, diverting attention from the politics of reconstruction, reform and reconciliation, in which post-conflict reconstruction reflects the continuation of war by other means.*

But from another angle, Mozambique is a more corrupt place than it used to be: it is a gangster democracy characterised by sharp inequalities; it was revealed by the elections in 2004 to be a one-party democracy; girls are commonly abused in schools and women throughout the countryside experience male violence as well as restricted access to education and labour markets; parts of the country are awash with cheap firearms; elections have been manipulated, the opposition party is incapable of mobilising its potential support and presenting any constructive alternative and appears to be more interested in enjoying the spoils of political position; the country's best known journalist, Carlos Cardoso, was assassinated and a bank manager was also killed, hurled down the stairwell of the central bank—both these murders were linked to efforts to stop information about high level corruption leaking into the public

---

* In Kriger's (2003) Zimbabwe case-study, the peace settlement of 1980 'set the stage for subsequent violent conflict and ...veterans' programs were characterised by a central political dynamic in which the ruling party and its liberation war veterans collaborated to establish power and privilege in ways that built a violent and extractive political order' (p. 5). The two main episodes of violence were the repression in Matabeleland in the early 1980s and the appropriation of white-owned farms (and the expulsion of many of their wage workers and attacks on many other rural Africans) since early 2000. For an account of the background and course of the Matabeleland conflict, see Alexander *et al.* (2000).

domain.* And economic policies have failed to make anything like the inroads they could into reducing the widespread and extreme indigence in the countryside. The country has gone from an unrealistic dream of development by self-reliance to being fantastically dependent on foreign aid. The post-conflict makeover was shoddy: the foundation is cracked, the gloss is a little garish and the highlights cannot hide the blotches and pustules.†

Fantasies of economic perfection pushed up against raw power and passionate interests more generally in the post-conflict privatisation programme in Mozambique, as elsewhere. The Frelimo government had already been privatising some state owned enterprises during the later years of the war, but in the 1990s the momentum and strategy of privatisation were taken over by external advisers, making privatisation one of the many conditions for continued foreign loans and advertising it as virtually a panacea for economic ills. Privatisation would unleash pent up entrepreneurial panache, it would spread ownership among Mozambicans, it would generate superior efficiency and it would underpin economic growth. A privatisation policy was necessary in Mozambique. But the programme of the 1990s proved to be more snake oil than panacea.²⁹

One way of assessing this privatisation process is as a trajectory of accumulation by a class of people, an inchoate national bourgeoisie, across the span of war and peace, nationalisation and privatisation. From this perspective two things become clearer. First, the war does not make sense simply as 'development in reverse'. Second, when the post-conflict makeover fantasists hijacked post-war policy the signals on the tracks of development were switched. A class that accumulated assets during war and in the war-to-peace transition was effectively routed towards becoming the kind of rentier class that aid agencies and economists loathe—in an economic policy version of the 'blowback' phenomenon.

---

* In November 2000, when Cardoso was killed, Mozambique was 'reeling from the bloodiest scenes since the peace accord of 1992'. (Fauvet and Mosse, 2003: 1) Renamo had staged nationwide demonstrations against the December 1999 elections that it claimed were rigged. In some northern towns there were clashes between Renamo and the police: some forty people died. There were reprisals. In Montepuez (Cabo Delgado province), at least eighty-three people died of asphyxiation in an overcrowded police cell. The Carter Centre reported that the elections in December 2004 were neither free nor transparent: 'Postelection statement on Mozambique Elections, Jan 26th, 2005' (www.cartercenter.org).
† As Paris (2004: 145) puts it: 'Mozambique offers only qualified support for the Wilsonian hypothesis of peace-through-liberalization in countries that have just experienced civil wars.'

During the war, party officials, military officers, and sundry war-time entrepreneurs began to manoeuvre themselves into a position of relative wealth and power, through corruption and the extraction of a 'war tax'. Once privatisation began, in the political conditions of war, some of them moved early to lay claim to assets like land with commercial potential.* After the war, these were people with the assets and connections to take advantage of privatisation. Even where state enterprises were sold to foreign investors, there were Mozambicans who either formed companies to run joint ventures with these investors or took up seats on the boards of enterprises that retained a state stake. To a large extent, the state took control of assets through nationalisation and then influenced their allocation through privatisation: it created and managed the allocation of rent.

Policy makers and donors were uninterested, though, in how the new private sector might be regulated and how it might be nurtured—other than through a war on red tape.† Arguably, this undermined the prospects for the class of beneficiaries of the nationalisation-privatisation cycle to develop into a truly dynamic capitalist class. This lack of interest, combined with macroeconomic policies that made borrowing capital extremely costly, that opened up capital markets, and that opened up consumer markets to import competition across the board, shaped incentives to enterprise owners. The incentive mix made it easier and more attractive to strip and sell assets and to speculate, or to shift funds into oppor-

* During and after the war Frelimo sought also to modernise the army and hoped that the sale of public assets to retired officers at subsidised prices would help to 'reintegrate' them into civilian life and to avoid political trouble. Later on, because war veterans often had fewer resources than some of the new post-war business class, the government selected some enterprises and shares for direct sale to veterans outside the framework of public tenders. The state effectively subsidised privatisation: many buyers delayed payments indefinitely or paid by instalment, while inflation eroded the value of any eventual payment—by early 1996, Mozambican buyers had paid only $9 million of the $52 million owed to the state. This was, though, an inefficient subsidy: it was not tied to any performance criteria or to a strategic selection of beneficiaries on grounds of promoting comparative or competitive advantages. See Cramer (2001).
† Car boot sale privatisation reduces the scope for post-conflict states to develop the fiscal base on which they might build some legitimacy and authority, while bolstering the power of a minority who do not necessarily have a commitment to economic efficiency, development, or peace. Boyce (2002: 1042) discusses the privatisation of Aluminum Mostar in Bosnia and Hercegovina to hardline Bosnian Croat political leaders—which the British ambassador to Bosnia described as 'criminal'.

272   *The Great Post-Conflict Makeover Fantasy*

tunities for quick returns, and harder to commit to long-term productive investment risks. These were the circumstances in which corruption scandals over bad debts proliferated. For where regulatory institutions are weak, regulatory capture by private and political interests is not unusual. In post-conflict countries it is common, for example, for 'private banks to be owned by powerful political actors, including...former warlords'.*

Meanwhile, rural policy in the war to peace transition has kept the growth of the rural economy and increases in poor people's incomes below a realistically possible rate of expansion. Mozambique's economy is not at all without dynamism. It does have highly uneven patterns of growth and change. However, the momentum of development has been skewed—'distorted', to use a favourite word of economic theory—by the appliance of dogma; and policies have failed to maximise the scope for post-conflict recovery to reduce poverty.†

Reconstruction is the continuation of war by other means: Iraq

'US and Iraqi institutions have systematically lost and the insurgency gained momentum as living conditions failed to improve. Economic hard-

---

* Addison *et al.* (2001b): 'In Cambodia some 33 private banks were licensed to operate during the transition from war to peace in the 1990s. Of these, only 12 are considered to be "legitimate" by industry observers. The others do not offer the usual retail banking services, but are reported to serve the interests of groups reportedly engaged in money laundering, drug trafficking, illegal logging, and other illicit activities. The National Bank of Cambodia (NBC) also had its own agenda in multiplying the number of banks despite its weak regulatory capacity since there are numerous official and informal fees and fines associated with the licensing of a bank.'

† As Addison argues, over-enthusiastic financial market liberalisation without adequate institutional development has led to the kind of banking crisis that an extremely poor country emerging from years of devastating warfare cannot afford. Writing of the bad debt and corruption crises at the Banco Comercial de Moçambique and at the Austral bank, he argues: 'The high fiscal cost of resolving bank crises takes public money from much-needed development spending and social spending. As part shareholder in BCM and Austral, the Government of Mozambique faces a bill of at least US$80 million (to be raised by issuing treasury bonds), and possibly more if the banks' private shareholders cannot meet their share of the recapitalisation... Mozambique's domestic debt was in decline prior to the banks' failure, but is now expected to rise from MT 15 billion to MT 196 billion. As a country still reconstructing from war, and one in which 69 per cent of the population is poor, Mozambique can ill afford the fiscal burden of bank crisis' (Addison *et al.*, 2001b).

ship and violence...feed on each other: heightened popular dissatisfaction and unemployment swell insurgent ranks and the growing insurgency further hampers development.'[30]

In Iraq too the period since the US government declared the war over was one in which the 'peace' that prevailed threatened prospects for development. Did the threat come from destructive imperialist impulses (defensive or otherwise)? Or did it come from the projection of a neoliberal fantasy of democratic liberty, market efficiency and good governance best practice? In post-war reconstruction in Iraq the themes introduced in this chapter combine. Reconstruction policy may well be propelled both by a desire to break a potentially dangerous regional power in the Middle East and by a mirage of harmonious development in the wake of liberation.* It is too soon to make much of a claim about this—especially since, as with the origins of the Marshall Plan and the fate of the Morgenthau Plan, foreign designs on Iraq are partly a product of ongoing internal debate within the United States and its coalition partners.† 'Turf battles between the State Department and the Pentagon were a major problem', claimed the International Crisis Group, 'leading to delays in the disbursement of funds and to repeated changes in staff at the expense of experience and know-how.'[31]

However, a few features of the first reconstruction year are worth highlighting. The lack of a plan for post-conflict reconstruction (and the casting aside of what pre-war planning there had been) and the rapid purge of the Baath party combined with rapid disbandment of the army all suggest a fantasy at play in the Coalition of the Willing. So too does the evidence of an expectation of radical market reform. The Coalition Provisional Authority (CPA) took little notice even of the joint World Bank and UN agencies' assessment of Iraq's post-war needs.‡ Meanwhile, wishful programming

---

* 'Iraq is not a political blank slate, to be transformed at American will into a democratic, secular, pluralist, and federal state' argue Ottoway and Yaphe (2003).
† For a historical overview of evolving thought on the meaning of reconstruction and on tensions within the United States over its appropriate role in international reconstructions, see Williams (2004).
‡ International Crisis Group (2003) cites the case of agriculture, where the World Bank/UN joint assessment found it would be necessary to maintain the supply of (subsidised) input supplies—fertilisers and pesticides—to protect against a reduction in farm production, fearing that otherwise there would be agricultural involution, a surge in unemployment, and a large increase in the food import requirement. As the ICG report puts it: 'The CPA did not implement this recommendation' (p. 5).

for a dramatic privatisation programme (which quickly ran aground, as argued below) confirmed a disregard for reality. Kenneth Pollock, writing in *Foreign Affairs*, took an optimistic line on American-led reconstruction efforts in Iraq but pointed out some of the sources of worry. First:

The United States must fundamentally reorient its security strategy. To date, U.S. forces have concentrated on chasing insurgents and protecting themselves. Although not unimportant, these pale in comparison with the need to provide basic security for the Iraqi people. Today, the fear of common crime and attacks committed by those who seek to undermine the course of the reconstruction are the single greatest impediments to Iraq's economic and political reconstruction.

Second, economic reconstruction was held in check partly by US policy. Indeed, the failure to provide basic security was one of the main reasons for this, since this insecurity 'makes the ordinary flow of goods and personnel across the country difficult, raises production costs, and cripples investment'.* Insecurity is partly a function of the fact that the war and overthrow of Saddam Hussein—followed by rapid 'de-Baathification' and disbandment of the army—threw as many as a million young men (mostly) onto the streets, who only knew how to use a gun or a shovel. This is despite the fact that there is now abundant evidence from around the world that releasing 'specialists in violence', as Charles Tilly calls them, into the social ether is one of the main reasons for the prevalence of non-war violence in many countries. 'We used to fear one man, Saddam Hussein, and we all knew where he was', said an Iraqi construction sector businessman in an interview with *The Financial Times* in June 2003. 'Now there are a thousand Saddams out there and we don't know who they are.'

Economic revival was also hampered by the fact that in a year of reconstruction the Coalition had 'not corrected shortages of electricity, clean water, and gasoline, to name only the most pressing' of basic services.† A further confirmation that the US government

---

* Mustafa Tabra, son of the founder of the Saad Tabra Trading Company, which makes building materials in Baghdad, told a reporter: 'If I have to take half a million dollars across town how am I going to do it? The Americans have said I can't carry a gun, but are they going to protect me? Of course not' ('Iraqi businessmen face uncertain future', *Financial Times*, 9 June 2003).

† 'Little major public construction work has occurred; factories by and large are deserted, and a number of industrial estates have become rubbish dumps. Nor has

seemed to believe in 'reconstruction lite' is that, in Pollock's argument, the reconstruction effort is woefully understaffed.

This is true on the security side, where there simply are not enough U.S. and Coalition infantry to provide security for the Iraqi people, and the Iraqi security forces are not yet ready to do the job. It is true in the political and economic realms too, where the CPA is so short-staffed that it has virtually no presence outside of Baghdad and as a result, numerous aspects of reconstruction are suffering. And it is also true in terms of the numbers of civil affairs personnel in the field working with the Iraqis.

A director-general in the Ministry of Electricity in Iraq contrasted Coalition reconstruction with reconstruction after the 1991 Gulf War: 'The main difference is that back then, we had a state. Everyone worked 24 hours a day, non-stop. We got very high wages from the government; they were throwing money at us.'[32]

The US-led Coalition authority believed—as is typical of reconstruction efforts everywhere nowadays—that privatisation is a panacea for post-conflict economic ills. And yet, as Pollock argues, this policy in Iraq might have as many liabilities as benefits. Nationalisation is a long-standing policy in Iraq with a heritage stretching back beyond Saddam Hussein into a field of economic nationalism and state-led development. Although many state owned industries are inefficient and there may well be grounds for a privatisation programme—as in Mozambique—rapid and sweeping privatisation may be economically inefficient and politically stupid. The coalition administration and the interim authority to be introduced in mid-2004 did not have the legitimacy to proceed with this policy; it is a policy that would doubtless spew further thousands of workers out of the labour market into an uncertain economy; and it could well reallocate state assets to beneficiaries of Saddam Hussein's regime if they are the only nationals capable of buying up these assets (aside from allocating them to US and other foreign companies).[33] Rapid privatisation was the plan. The CPA ended up ditching it in the face of opposition and other constraints, and instead

---

damaged infrastructure, including roads and bridges, been significantly repaired. Iraq only recently matched its pre-war power generation... Due in part to power cuts, in part to the April 2003 looting, water treatment facilities operate at levels below those prior to the conflict' (International Crisis Group, 2003: 2). For a comparison of the successful reconstruction of Germany during occupation after the end of World War II and the failure of the occupation and reconstruction effort in Iraq, see Barnett (2005).

shifted to a purely ad hoc approach and 'failed to devise an alternative approach that might have revived ailing state companies so they could be used to find temporary jobs for the unemployed'.[34]

Conclusions and implications

Post-conflict experiences in Mozambique and Iraq, as well as in Europe after the two World Wars and in the United States after its civil war, show that reconstruction never takes place in a political vacuum. Many of the passionate interests that both helped generate war and emerged during war continue to shape political conflict after a peace settlement. As war settles into politics it often shows its hand in violence.* And war becomes part of the legitimating discourse of peace.†

We still know little about real existing post-conflict reconstruction experiences. One reason for this is the reliance on shallow evaluation criteria. If demobilisation is completed the whole thing is declared a success. If elections are roughly 'free and fair' then democratisation is working as a method of peace-building. Just how shallow these judgements can be is shown in the case of Haiti. In 1994 the Clinton administration sent in—having secured a UN mandate—20,000 US troops to restore democracy: at any rate, to restore the elected leader, Jean-Baptiste Aristide, to power. Over the next few years Clinton's secretary of state, Madeleine Albright, repeatedly declared the democratisation policy in Haiti a success. And yet Haiti lurched from crisis to crisis, wavering in a constitutional limbo, failing by most measures to meet the requirements of a democracy.[35] Meanwhile, the city slums like Cité de Soleil—the largest in the country—became increasingly violent and subordinate to local gang power as well as awash with weapons.[36]

---

* In El Salvador, homicide rates after the war were higher than wartime violent deaths. Violent deaths also increased in Brazil after the mid-1980s, when violence regulated post-authoritarian political and social relations to extraordinary degrees.
† Kriger (2003: 191) argues, for example, that the politics of pensions for war veterans in Zimbabwe showed a dynamic of simultaneous conflict and cooperation as 'party and veterans manipulate each other, using violence and intimidation and a war discourse, to advance their respective agendas.' Meanwhile, more recently party backers have often supported 'party youth who call themselves war veterans, though they are obviously too young to have fought in the war. The purpose is twofold: first, to legitimate their activities, such as land occupations, as part of a new war for economic liberation, and second, to capitalise on the prevailing fear ex-combatants still invoke among civilians' (p. 192).

Another reason why so little is really known about post-conflict reconstruction is that the debates are driven by a search for a single model rather than by an acceptance of diverse possible ways of managing the challenges of the war to peace transition. Generals are notoriously prone to preparing to fight previous battles. International post-conflict reconstruction programmes are too often about making a previous peace. Hence the lessons of the last exercise in intervention accumulate into an unmanageable burden of best practice demands on post-war states.

The historical evidence supports a view that there are diverse, but not unlimited, economic policy packages that may underpin economic recovery and longer term expansion. Just as the causes of war are not just multiple but different, so successful post-conflict reconstruction is likely to vary in its characteristics and influences. This historical record certainly does not support the argument that there is a single and obvious post-conflict reconstruction policy solution and that this is the current economic orthodoxy. But the record does suggest that for economic development to achieve some progressive momentum in the wake of violent conflicts, and for the violence of war to peter out rather than mutate into pervasive post-war violence, a powerful central state is necessary, not the flimsy decentralising and enabling bureaucracy of the post-conflict reconstruction makeover fantasy. 'It appears', wrote the authors of a summary of a conference on Afghanistan, 'questionable whether a "light state" can deliver reconstruction under the conditions of extreme state frailty now prevailing in Afghanistan.'*

But a powerful state is not sufficient. The great intangible problem—if the developmental implications of a violent conflict are to be converted into a longer term developmental momentum—is how to identify and encourage the conditions under which that state is dominated by political and economic coalitions that encourage an equivalent to the 'gospel of prosperity' that Republican Recon-

* See Putzel *et al.* (2003). For an argument that effective reconstruction in Afghanistan requires a greater commitment to a strong centralised state with the ability to enforce a monopoly of violence, see Cramer and Goodhand (2003). In late 2004 the central state clearly still had no monopoly of violence. 'If all had gone according to plan, almost a quarter of the estimated 100,000 Afghan militia loyal to regional warlords would have been disarmed by now, well on the way to the Kabul government's goal of having 27,000 of them demobilised by next month's Afghan presidential election. With just over two weeks to go until polling day, however, the number that have beaten their AK-47s into ploughshares is, officials admit, highly disappointing: a paltry 9,272' ('Gun law still rules for Afghan warlords', *Financial Times*, 24 September 2004).

struction leaders preached in the postbellum South in the United States of the 1860s, or of the 'ideology of growth' that swelled up beneath policy making in Western Europe after the Second World War. This is a problem that the international financial institutions and the governments of the major international powers do not appear to be thinking creatively about in contemporary reconstruction interventions.

CONCLUSION

Between the liberal interpretation of war and the romance of redemptive violence

Violence is destructive; it constrains, it devastates, and it undoes. This is why Hannah Arendt wrote that violence is always about the destruction of the old, it is never about the construction of the new. Yet the conflicts and activities in which violence is involved are not always purely destructive. In destroying, violence can also keep things in place; it can even set in motion change and the construction of the new. Since violence is a way of relating between people— as is sometimes said, a form of communication—then violence that keeps people in place has different effects on different people: some it keeps in place by repression and restraint, others by securing their privileges. Violence interacts with political and economic interests and relations to change the course of those relations and interests; it can produce institutional changes, amendments to the rules of the game. In retrospect, many changes that come to be seen as progressive have their origins in social conflicts that have taken a violent turn. This is a paradox of violence and war: violence destroys but is also often associated with social creativity. And this paradox is the source of many of the problems in understanding violence.

One way to resolve the paradox would be to emphasise the destructive force of violence, and then either to deny the association with progressive change or to insist, reasonably, that such change could surely be achieved without violence. This is the liberal reflex. Another resolution would come from being seduced by the creativity of violence and then either to belittle or glorify the suffering and destruction that comes with it. Yet the record of romantic visions of redemptive violence over the past hundred years and more, in fascist, socialist, nihilist, Islamist and other guises, has been calamitous.*

---

* For an illustration of the very modern themes of romantic violence through a selection of biographies (T. E. Lawrence, Ernst Jünger, Marinetti and the Futurists, and others) see Pfaff (2004). Roy (2004) draws out the links between Islamic fun-

These two perspectives confront each other directly, politically and violently in the early twenty-first century, in the opposition between utopian terrorism and the furiously defensive rhetoric of politicians claiming the liberal tradition in the West. What is difficult is to steer between these reflexes: to insist on the possibility of progressive change without violence while not denying that violent conflicts, when they happen, can, but do not always, have progressive consequences. At the very least, violence often produces change, in social relations and institutions; at most, those changes may be 'developmental'.

This book has taken issue especially with the liberal interpretation of wars. This is largely because this interpretation, which took shape during the Enlightenment, but which has even older antecedents, continues to be the main influence on contemporary explanations of violence and war in poor countries. Moreover, its influence is not merely intellectual; it suits political interests. However, these interests are not quite the same as those served by its earlier proponents; for many of the philosophers, economists and pamphleteers who shaped the classic formulations of the liberal interpretation of war—people like Kant, Montesquieu, Condorcet, Adam Smith and Tom Paine—were driven by a project of liberation from the political clasp of various coalitions of royalty, feudal aristocrats and military castes.

In this spirit of opposition and hope, ideas that had circulated for a long time began to take a firmer grip of the intellectual imagination. According to the emerging view, war was unnatural: the natural condition of society was peace. Therefore, war was something caused by a distortion of this natural, rational order. There were two main sources of distortion: political and economic. First, war was caused by the narrow vested interests of militaristic élites. They were able, through their power and through control of information, to sustain the misunderstandings on which wars are founded. Second, mercantilism, barriers to market entry and the general lack of free trade also interfered with people's ability to pursue their natural inclination to peaceful intercourse. The solutions to war, which were also means of changing the political order, were straightforward in principle. In the language of the twenty-first century, these solutions were to democratise and to encourage free

---

damentalist terrorists and the Western traditions of romantic radical violence, for example, in the 1960s.

trade, a project of political and economic liberalisation. The other dimension of the liberal interpretation of war was the assumption that war was always exclusively negative in its economic consequences.

This interpretation of war has an honourable history but is unsuitable as a guide to understanding and responding to the violence and war prevalent in developing countries integrated in various ways into the world economy. Hence, to replace it involves a challenge both to the liberal interpretation of violence and to the liberal view of development.

Adam Smith wrote that little else was required 'to carry a state to the highest degree of opulence from the lowest barbarism, but peace, easy taxes, and a tolerable administration of justice'.[1] For a latecomer to industrialisation and a modern economy, sustaining economic expansion and relieving indigence through production, employment and safety nets, this is not a straightforward proposition. The content of justice is being wrought through social and political conflicts. The fiscal base is thin and elusive, too much so for the challenge of development and also for the tolerable administration of justice, and is itself a source of political struggle. Peace is precisely the problem: it is not something that can just be wished forth. And as this book has shown, for first movers as well as latecomers, actually an important part of development, or of the conditions that help propel it, has emerged in conditions very different from those of peace, easy taxes and a tolerable administration of justice. War, and non-war violence, have often provided an enabling environment for the accumulation of wealth, social organisation and institutional and technical change that feed development. And often, in many ways, development has been an unintended consequence of violent conflict.

There are other weaknesses in the liberal interpretation of war and development. First, while early proponents were genuine believers in free trade, many contemporary political groups and organisations propounding a liberal view of war are tinged with double standards. Advice to developing countries to liberalise their trade regimes indiscriminately is combined with Western, creditor country protectionism. More important, though, the historical record of capitalist expansion and catching up shows clearly that successful industrialisation does not rest, initially at least, on free trade. While protectionism is often wasteful and stultifying, protectionist policy has been a keystone in the economic development of Britain, the United States, Germany, Japan, South Korea, China and other countries.

Second, the liberal interpretation of war is an inappropriate way of understanding wars and developing country violence. It ignores the character of war economies and the history of development. It has lost its innocence. Modern societies have not sloughed off violence and outgrown it, and modern liberal democratic, capitalist societies clearly have foundations of brutality. The liberal conscience has repeatedly been compromised by the realities of war, as the historian Michael Howard showed.[2] Further, while narrow vested interests play a large role in the movement towards war and in the development of violent means of protecting turf or securing resources, the problem of violence is far from exclusively a problem of the narrow vested interests of an entrenched élite. Violence and war easily become sources of meaning, serve a variety of 'functions', enable the pursuit of various agendas of political and social conflict, and provide employment and/or material sustenance to a large number of people, many of them far from élite.

Third, the history of wars within and between countries and the recent history of the political economy of wars in Africa and elsewhere show that wars are not typically exclusively negative in their economic consequences. War is not simply development in reverse. Rather, wars combine destruction with change; they provoke social, institutional and sometimes technical adjustments, some of which have the potential to contribute to longer-term accumulation.

Adopting a siege mentality in immigration policy or a war on terror, and treating collective violence in 'civil wars' as barbaric while justifying torture in the cause of Operation Freedom, cannot fully hold at bay the connections between violence in poor countries and actions taken in and by rich countries. These connections are in many ways the dark side of the interconnectedness celebrated in paeans to globalisation. The connections of violence, the sustained dialogue of violence, has involved various mechanisms, including: the consequences of US (and other rich country) policies in nurturing Mujahideen groups in Afghanistan and Saddam Hussein's regime in Iraq; the barely controllable consequences of international arms trade and its regulation; economic policies naively foisted on poor countries; and the political policies of shoring up militaristic, élite-controlled governments in some countries while propounding a liberal rhetoric of good governance globally.

In contemporary versions of the liberal interpretation of war there has been, as Mark Duffield in particular has emphasised, a merger of security and development.[3] One product of this merger is the shibboleth that there can be no development without peace and vice versa. The drone of this formula captures an incomplete truth; this book has explored the domain where the formula lacks meaning. An implication of the security/development merger is that economic growth brings peace, straightforwardly. Again, this suits some of the assumptions of liberal economics that growth is linear, efficient and uncomplicated in its benefits. The truth is full of contradictions, though. It has often seemed—for example, in much of Europe since the end of the Second World War—that growth does bring peace. However, if it does, this might be not just a function of the cooperative functions of free trade or the diversionary functions of taking care of business (Keynes's idea of channelling the passions towards the more mundane and peaceable business of making money). Rather, the mechanisms may have more to do with the spread and effects of wage employment, the expansion and effectiveness of the state, the development of institutions for exercising 'voice' and for renegotiating the terms of accumulation and distribution.

These mechanisms are not functionally inevitable but vary according to the content and trajectory of political and intellectual contests. Nonetheless, in many countries rapid growth over a sustained period of time has not snuffed out violence. In countries like Brazil rapid growth and diversification have certainly removed large-scale war but have been compatible with continued institutional mess, unresolved extremes of accumulation and poverty and widespread violence. And the glibness of the idea that growth ends violence is also belied by the interest of some capitalists in benefiting from violence on various scales—arms production and brokerage etc. All this suggests that if growth is to bring peace, it requires regulation, a state capable of making effective interventions both to stimulate growth and to shape its social and political character, and a set of institutions allowing for political voice and conflict.

A stupid thing?

This book has, in part, been forced out of a protracted chewing over of that piece of dialogue, in a story of Sciascia's, which gives it its title.* Of course civil war, all war and all violence are stupid. But civil war, or more broadly violence in developing countries, is not irrational or pointless. Contemporary violent conflicts are not eruptions of meaninglessness; nor are they outbursts of (savage or

* See quotation at the beginning of the Introduction.

barbarian) backwardness. Violence all too often makes sense. To make sense, though, does not mean to fit a single and rigid model of rationality, whether narrowly economic or otherwise. Violence makes sense to different people in different ways in varied contexts; and it may make different kinds of sense to one person or group at the same time, that is, different rationales and meanings are not necessarily exclusive. This is as true of suicide bombing recruits and organisers as it is of the participants in political violence and wars around the world.

Violence also makes sense as a form of communication, often where other means of communication have broken down. That may be terrible but it is not stupid. This is especially the case if the communication generates understanding. Understanding in violent communication is itself varied. Where MPLA and UNITA soldiers collude in operating diamond mining in adjacent sections of the mines in the middle of war, they have established one form of understanding: violence between them has also produced a form of non-violent communication. Elsewhere, violence in El Salvador might have escalated in a series of provocative statements but ultimately established limits to the extent of exploitation in Salvadoran society. Ultimately, the communication of violence may almost always tend to produce some kind of peace as understanding. This is very like St Augustine's idea: war always tends towards peace of some kind.[4] One difficulty is that communication through violence, even if it generates peace, fosters an evolving linguistic register of violence. Again, El Salvador is a good example. War ended in peace. But the violence of war has broken up, in peace, into multiple smaller vicious communications.

Sciascia also raises the question of whether some forms of violent conflict make more sense than others. For the person in the story, a civil war is better than a war between countries. The idea of a civil war categorically distinct from an inter-state war is not always convincing—and the war Sciascia was writing about, the Spanish Civil War, was both an internal, civil war and a salvo in the international conflict that resolved itself into the Second World War. The idea of an honourable class war is also difficult to sustain now. Nonetheless, the possibility of distinguishing between good wars and bad wars is still a tempting notion.* And class is far more relevant to

---

* Consider the renewed debate over the legacy of John Brown, the American anti-slavery activist hanged in 1859 after being arrested after his assault on the Harper's Ferry arsenal. James McPherson ('Days of Wrath', *New York Review of Books*, vol. LII,

understanding contemporary violent conflicts in many parts of the
world than is typically acknowledged. This is not to say that these
wars pit against each other categorically enclosed groups explicitly
identifying themselves as distinct 'classes'. But to the extent that
wars and non-war violence are bound up with the transition to, and
trajectories of, competitive capitalist economic organisation, contemporary violent conflicts are very much phenomena of class.

The disturbance of previously prevailing class structures and relations generates great social uncertainty. It is obviously conflictual.
Positions in a society—that regulate access to resources, opportunities and so on—are not set. There is conflict in the very forming of
classes and in the establishment of relations between them. For
example, if a capitalist class is to emerge in developing countries it
will need to secure private property rights where there will before
have been other ways of organising access to land or water or other
assets. To secure private property rights excludes others. Where
one group of people is engaged in securing exclusive rights to mine
gemstones, farm land or establish tourist game parks and another
group is by dint of this becoming excluded, there is a process of
class formation underway. And where there is conflict in the process, that conflict is at least partly 'class conflict'. In Somalia, where
the conflict is not typically regarded as a class war, the evidence is
precisely that much of the violence, for example where it erupted
in the Lower Jubba Valley, was vented in a context of an uncertain
shuffling of the institutions and relations of the management of the
economy.

The world economy, and its politics, integrate latecomer societies. In this way, there is obviously a class element to the international dimensions of contemporary conflicts too. Again, this is not a
simple contest between capital and labour. But some capitalist
interests clearly benefit from and stoke violent conflict, others are
ambivalent, and others are plainly disadvantaged by ongoing vio-

no. 8, May 12, 2005, pp. 14–17) reviews recent contributions on John Brown and
on the question of whether he can be considered a hero in the wake of Osama bin
Laden, Timothy McVeigh and an assortment of bombings of abortion clinics and
the assassination of an abortion doctor. This is an especially awkward judgement to
make given that some of these (McVeigh after the Oklahoma bombing and at least
one of the anti-abortion activists convicted of bombing a clinic) explicitly invoked
John Brown's example of political violence. The judgement turns on what criteria
are used to deem violence 'good' or 'bad' and, perhaps more difficult still, on who
can be the appropriate arbiter of such judgements, when many perpetrators of violence claim to be engaged in violence in pursuit of the good, in pursuit of peace.

lence. If people are working in violent and barely remunerated
conditions to produce the diamonds or heroin poppies or oil or
coltan or cashew nuts or other internationally traded goods that are
part of 'commodity chains' organised internationally, then there is
a class relation between these people and those who draw profits
along the local, national, regional and international links of this
chain, whether the particular form of production is a cause of a
larger conflict, a means of reproducing it (of sustaining the conversation), or a profitable by-product discovered during the conflict.

These and other class dimensions of violence do not develop pre-
dictably from the structure of society. The poor treatment of farm
workers by large landowners in El Salvador was an important feature of the political processes that led to war in the 1980s and many
of these farm workers volunteered to join the FMLN rebels. But
many did not. Further, in many conflicts it is far from rare for people to kill others very like them, socially—not the demon other of
a different, threatening or exploiting class, not even the demon
other of a different ethnic group. Killing the people you really
hate does not have to mean a peasant killing a large landowner, or
a *garimpeiro* miner killing a rentier warlord. It often means killing
a marginally wealthier neighbour or getting one's own back on
someone.

Economics without reductionism

If this book stresses the economic, or political economy, dimensions
of much of the violence and war that takes place in developing
countries, is the argument really any different from the narrowly
economic theories of violent conflict that it criticises? The answer
turns in part on the difference between an argument highlighting
primitive accumulation and one highlighting the rational choice
making individual of neo-classical economic theory. The neo-classical economic story says that wars in developing countries are caused by the conditions within which private individual material
incentives to fight are greater than incentives not to fight: conditions where utility is maximised by conflict not cooperation. The
primitive accumulation story also says that economic issues are central to the explanation of wars and violence. And primitive accumulation very definitely involves individuals.

However, first, the accumulation analysis is primarily an explanation of wars and violence in terms of the turmoil of conditions of
transition: social conflict over terms of accumulation—which forms

can be pursued, what range of people will benefit, what will be the terms and forms of distribution. Thus, second, it is more about the causes within which a variety of motivations exist and it therefore allows for a complex set of motivations rather than a single driving kind. Third, specific histories and social patterns of meaning matter. Politics therefore matters too. And though individual motives are important, they are not the only key to joining conflicts; nor are these motivations restricted to individualist material direct returns. Indeed, in this approach, which may appear to give primacy to economics, economics is not a separate dimension from others. This is precisely why, for example, greed and grievance are inseparable rather than the discrete variables that some have pretended they could be.

This book has argued that the study of war and violence in developing countries helps illuminate the broader subject of development and the shortcomings of traditional techniques for analysing it. A related argument was made by the IMF's Raghuram Rajan: 'One problem with relying on models that are within a few standard deviations of the complete markets model to guide policy in poor countries is that solutions may seem far easier than they actually are.' And again: 'A better starting point for analysis than a world with only minor blemishes may be a world where nothing is enforceable, property and individual rights are totally insecure, and the enforcement apparatus for every contract must be derived from first principles.'[5] The difficulty here is the swing from one extreme—a utopian benchmark of perfect competition—to another—a dystopian, Hobbesian anarchy; i.e. from one unreality to another. The study of violence and war in developing countries, and the study of development, need to proceed by means of a political economy rooted in actual historical experiences. This book has tried to show some of the kinds of experiences that need to be taken into account.

Policy matters

Wars start for many reasons. Violence is various in its causes, functions and meanings. But this book has argued that there are family resemblances among wars—and many examples of non-war violence—in developing countries. These are mainly visible in features revealing related experiences of societal transition. These features are defined by varieties in the way these countries have dealt with the institutional management of accumulation and dis-

tribution, nationally, regionally and in the integration into the
world economy.

Violence and war have been common experiences of transition
since the very early origins and spread of capitalism. However, this
book does not argue that war is inevitable. It does not argue that
the developmental benefits associated with war are so commonplace and overwhelming that we should 'give war a chance'. The
challenge is always to secure social and economic transformations,
inevitably conflictual experiences, while minimising the devastation involved. And where conflict has become violent the challenge
is not just to minimise its damage but to maximise any potential for
positive change that might arise in the course of that conflict.

The implications are that the prevalent policy mix of the late
twentieth and early twenty-first century is not the most appropriate
to tackling these challenges. This is partly because this mix relies
complacently on the assumptions of the liberal interpretation of
war and on the equally inappropriate liberal (and, of late, neo-liberal) interpretation of development.

Thought to be appropriate ways of preventing war from breaking
out and to be sensible ways of proceeding during post-conflict reconstruction periods, especially when combined with rapid movement towards multi-party elections, the following and other tenets
constitute the orthodox policy package for development: the blan-
ket recommendation that developing countries liberalise their
trade regimes and that there should be a reciprocal removal of
trade tariffs and other barriers to trade in rich and poor countries;
the lingering convictions that a minimal state is the most effective
foundation for a rapidly developing economy; disapproval of anything smacking of industrial policy in a developing country; rural
development policies based on a populist imagining of myriad smallholder family farmers successfully engaged in micro-enterprise and
benefiting from evenly rising incomes. These are often combined
with initiatives to impose sanctions on 'conflict diamonds', or to
suggest modest improvements to OECD code-of-conduct guide-
lines on multinational company practices so as to encourage less
egregious profiting from violent conflict in poor countries.

Perhaps, though, policy makers need to develop a broader range
of possible interventions. There are two alternatives, for example,
to the mild slap on the hand offered in the reports of the UN Panel
of Experts on illegal mineral exploitation in Congo. One is for UN
member states, especially the members of the Security Council, to
make more credible threats and to regulate more effectively those

corporations that profit from violence and war. The other is to develop more effective incentives for companies that are compromised by their involvement in the violent politics of developing country transitions, to encourage them to make a positive contribution to the ability of such countries to generate a sustained rise in investment over the longer term and in sectors generating employment and export revenue.

Meanwhile, this book has also shown, in its discussion of primitive accumulation and its links to development and in its discussion of post-conflict reconstruction, how a state that has the independence and wit to intervene effectively in the interests of structural change is crucial both to development and to more peaceable development. Particular policy choices in some countries, combined with the pressure internationally since the beginning of the 1980s to minimise the role of the state, have in many places shifted incentive structures so that accumulation has taken a turn for the primitive. Where that has happened, and where it is associated with violence and with warfare, the policy challenge for states and for international advisers, e.g. in post-conflict reconstruction programmes, is to twist the dynamics of accumulation to more constructive ends.

NOTES

Introduction

1. Sciascia (1988: 189).
2. See the Uppsala Conflict Data Program (www.pcr.uu.se) and Chapter 3 of SIPRI (2004).
3. World Bank (2003: 97).
4. The World Bank created a Post-Conflict Unit in 1997 but through the late 1990s was increasingly 'mainstreaming' research and development activities on conflict; in 2001 its executive directors approved Operational Policy/Bank Procedures 2.30, 'Development Cooperation and Conflict'; and the Post-Conflict Unit was renamed the Conflict Prevention and Reconstruction Unit. Government aid agencies have institutionalised conflict analysis: for example, the UK's Department for International Development (DfID) created CHAD, the Conflict and Humanitarian Affairs Department, as well as instigating 'conflict in development' analytical initiatives; and in 2002 USAID established its Office of Conflict Management and Mitigation in the Bureau for Democracy, Conflict, and Humanitarian Assistance. Among NGOs, International Alert was founded in 1985 to 'address the root causes of violence and to contribute to the just and peaceful transformation of violent internal conflict'; INCORE (International Conflict Research) was founded in 1993 as a joint project of the United Nations University and the University of Ulster; Conciliation Resources (an international service for conflict prevention and resolution) was founded in 1994; and the International Crisis Group was founded in 1995.
5. These passages are taken from Clausewitz (1976: 89). There is quite a history to the interpretation of this 'remarkable trinity'. Arguments turn on how far the trinity captures the distinction among social classes—the people, the army, and the government—and how far it is really a division among societal forces—inherent violence and hatred, talent and creativity, and means/ends rational policy making. A useful discussion of the different approaches, concluding with an argument for the relevance of analysing war in terms of 'rationality, non-rationality, and irrationality', is in Villacres and Bassford (1995). On Clausewitz, see Gallie (1978) and Howard (2002).
6. The quotations from the Einstein-Freud correspondence are found in Nathan and Norden (eds) (1960: 186–203); and may also be found at: http://www.idst.vt.edu/modernworld/d/Einstein.html.

7. Sebald's examples include the inner logic of the Nazi concentration camps (recalled in an essay on Jean Améry, the Austrian Auschwitz survivor) and the bombing of Dresden and other German cities by the Allies towards the end of the Second World War. Sebald emphasises the tragedy of economic logic, in which 'so much intelligence, capital and labour went into the planning of destruction that, under the pressure of all the accumulated potential, it had to happen in the end' Sebald (2003: 65).
8. Taussig (2004).
9. Ibid.
10. The particular wars referred to in the phrase were the American Civil War and the South African Wars: Alexander and Halpern (2004: 17).
11. Maier (1996: 15).

Chapter 1 *Violence, Memory and Progress*
1. The most comprehensive history of this encounter is given in Miller (1988): see especially p. 118.
2. Miller (1988: 153–4; see also 229–32 on slave export trends in the eighteenth and early nineteenth century).
3. 'An official check of the trade guns stocked in Luanda in 1759 revealed that 200 of the 4,000 on hand, or only 5 percent, met the government's standards of military reliability' (Miller, 1988: 88).
4. S. Galton, quoted in W. A. Richards (1980: 44, note 4). On the import of firearms into West Central Africa see also Inikori (1977). David Ricardo was born seventeen years after the Lisbon earthquake: he was born in London, into a Sephardic Jewish family originally from Portugal (his parents had migrated from the Netherlands to England shortly before his birth).
5. Quoted in Richards (1980: 53).
6. Both quotes are cited in Inikori (1977).
7. Quoted in Richards (1980: 55).
8. See Pythian (2000).
9. Ibid.
10. Human Rights Watch (1994).
11. Global Witness (2002).
12. Pythian (2002).
13. Foucault (2003).
14. Smith (1982: 508–12).
15. See also Roxborough (1999).
16. Nairn (1998).
17. Goldhagen (1996).
18. This is a literary analogue of the economic historian Gerschenkron's (1962) discussion of the tension among all latecomers following the industrial revolution in England.
19. African Rights (1995).
20. Kolko (1994: 426).

21. 'The wickedness and awesome cruelty of a crushed and humiliated people', *The Independent*, 12 September 2001.
22. Kaplan (1994).
23. A variant is Olson's (1991) distinction between roving bandits (who pillage wantonly and move on) and stationary bandits (who realise they need to cultivate some legitimacy and to limit their predation if they are to survive themselves). Olson's schema is evolutionary: over time roving bandits become stationary bandits and realise the political benefits of reciprocating, generating gradual democratic pressures. While roving banditry is as rational as other forms of power and politics, this approach still puts a distance between liberal democracy and violence by suggesting that the former have evolved from the latter.
24. Benjamin (1969: 256).
25. Human Rights Watch (2004a).
26. Rose (2004).
27. In Hobsbawm (1998).
28. Rawson (2001: 279).
29. Swift (1985: 318–19).
30. Rawson (2001).
31. Chang (2002).
32. Howard (2001).
33. See, e.g., McPherson (1996: 74).
34. See Hobsbawm (1969: 48–9).
35. World Bank (2003).
36. Hampshire (2000).
37. See Hanssen (2000).
38. These quotes are cited in Mazower (1999).
39. Shaw (2000).
40. Vogel (1996).
41. This US transition is debated, partly because of the way it snagged on the institution of share-cropping instead of a clear shift from slavery to free wage labour. See, e.g., Byres (1996); and also Chapter 7, below.
42. For a comparative study of convict labour in Birmingham, Alabama and in Kimberley, South Africa's first industrial city, in the late nineteenth and early twentieth centuries, see Worger (2004).
43. Lichtenstein (1996: xvii).
44. Ibid.: 195.
45. Murdoch (2003).
46. Bloch (1962).

Chapter 2 *Categories, Trends and Evidence of Violent Conflict*

1. Holsti (1996).
2. For a survey of these and other datasets and their nuances, see Wallensteen (2002). For COW, see: http://webapp.icpsr.umich.edu/cocoon/ICPSR-STUDY/09905.xml; for Uppsala data see: http://www.pcr.uu.se/research/UCDP/UCDP_toplevel.htm; for AKUF see www.akuf.de.

3. Fukuyama (1992).
4. Carnegie Commission on Preventing Deadly Conflict (1997).
5. Fearon and Laitin (2003).
6. Cavalli-Sforza (2001).
7. Ibid.: 29.
8. Ibid.
9. Sambanis (2002: 14–15).
10. Sambanis (2002).
11. de Waal (1997).
12. Contributors to the Correlates of War have over time, and over different versions of the database, redefined its coding rules and reclassified many extra-systemic wars as civil wars (Sambanis, 2002); shifts within the coding rules of COW have not always been tracked assiduously by others drawing on COW for their own quantitative analyses.
13. Anderson (2005: 4) cites estimates of thirty-two European settlers killed, together with less than 200 British army and police and more than 1,800 African civilians murdered by Mau Mau guerrillas. Officially, 12,000 Mau Mau rebels died in combat but, summarising the research on this, Anderson argues the number is likely more than 20,000.
14. http://www.onwar.com/aced/data/india/ireland1968.htm; Hancock (1998).
15. Sambanis (2002).
16. See, for example, Marchal and Messiant (2002).
17. Gibson (1983).
18. Orwell (2000); see also Borkenau (1986).
19. Mazower (1999).
20. Hobsbawm (2002).
21. de Witte (2001).
22. Guevara (2001).
23. On the rebranding of mercenaries as private military corporations see FCO (2002).
24. Breman (1993; 1996).
25. According to press estimates, more than 2,000 Muslims were killed in riots in Gujarat in 2000. Human Rights Watch (1996) cited estimates that more than 1,700 died in anti-Muslim violence in Gujarat and Maharashtra in December 1992/January 1993 (events that followed the destruction of the Ayodhya mosque and ensuing protests) and also point out that there are other, higher estimates; these figures leave aside the huge numbers of rapes of Muslim women in the same waves of communal violence.
26. See Human Rights Watch (2002b) on Gujarat.
27. Kohli (1990).
28. Estimates of Iraqi battlefield casualties in the First Gulf War vary massively, from an initial US official estimate of some 100,000 down to

25,000, and as low as Heidenrich's (1993) estimate of 1,500 Iraqi soldiers killed.

29. Enzensberger (1994).
30. Kaldor (1999).
31. See, for example, le Billon's (2001) distinction of resource wars in
    terms of whether resources are characterised by 'point' or 'dispersed'
    production.
32. For a critique of the new war category see Kalyvas (2000b).
33. Guevara (2001: 67).
34. Guevara (2001: 90).
35. The quotes in this paragraph are from McPherson (1990).
36. On Renamo see: Vines (1996), Clarence-Smith (1989), Geffray (1990),
    Minter (1994), Hanlon (1986).
37. Murray *et al.* (2002).
38. Jewkes and Abrahams (2000).
39. See Barclay and Tavares (2002) available through the website: www.
    homeoffice.gov.uk/rds/hosbpubs1.html. See also the Seventh United
    Nations Survey of Crime Trends and Operations of Criminal Justice
    Systems (www.undcp.org/odccp/crime_cicp_survey_seventh.html).
40. Murray *et al.* (2002).
41. Brockett (1992: 169).
42. Enzensberger (1994: 19).
43. World Health Organisation (2002: 7–11 and Statistical Annex).
44. Tilly (2000: 12–20).
45. Ibid.: 15.
46. For example, in Alesina and Perotti (1996).
47. Anderson (1998).

Chapter 3 *Deviant Conditions*

1. Huntington (1998).
2. See, e.g., Mitchell *et al.* (1999).
3. *La Stampa*, 7 December 2001 (also available on the World Bank
   website).
4. Krueger and Maleckova (2002).
5. Bloch (1954: 194–5).
6. Tolstoy (1982: 716).
7. Nordstrom (1997) argues against a pervasive 'taming of violence', in
   which violence is fetishised and banished to the outer margins of
   human life: 'we have erased the actual fact of violence in the very act of
   accounting for it' (p. 17).
8. On contrasting perspectives on evidence in different disciplines, see
   Richards (2005).
9. Reno (2003).
10. Suganami (1996).
11. Eckstein (1980).
12. Gurr (1970).

13. Gilligan (2000a; 2000b).
14. Tilly (1978).
15. Tilly (2000).
16. Ibid.: 1.
17. Huntington (1998).
18. Keegan in the *Daily Telegraph*, 15 April 1993, quoted in Mazower (1999: xiv; and 1995). The idea suggested that anthropologists are the only people who understand ethnicity and its central causal role in contemporary conflict. However, most anthropologists do not have an essentialist understanding of ethnicity.
19. See Mann, M. (1999).
20. Hobsbawm (1998: 340).
21. Canetti (1962: 166–7).
22. Bernard of Clairvaux (1957–75: 412). This passage is discussed in Pranger (2003).
23. See Didion (2000; 2003).
24. Huntington (1998: 28). Huntington suggests the post-Cold War world is characterised by 'seven or eight major civilizations' (p. 21): his map (pp. 26–27) locates nine—Western, Latin American, African, Islamic, Sinic, Hindu, Orthodox, Buddhist and Japanese.
25. Hassan (2001) cited in Ricolfi (2005).
26. Anderson (1983).
27. See Schierup (1992; 1993).
28. Schetter (2002).
29. Ibid.: 12.
30. Plato, quoted in Cowell (1995: 21).
31. Montaigne (1981: 119).
32. Nafziger and Auvinen (2002: 155).
33. This and the following figure are reproduced from Cramer (2003).
34. Braeckman (1996), Maton (1994) and Storey (2000). For further discussion see Cramer (2003).
35. Tilly (1999).
36. Ibid.: 225.
37. Ibid.
38. Kaplan (1994).
39. Cited in Fairhead (2000).
40. See Starr (1991).
41. André and Platteau (1998).
42. Girard (1977; 1996).
43. Hirschman (1995) makes this distinction in analysing social conflict.
44. Ehrenreich (1997: 122).
45. Kalyvas (2000a).
46. Swift (1985: 308).
47. For a critical discussion of Dutch Disease see Rowthorn and Wells (1987).
48. Soysa (2000).

49. Ross (1999).
50. Di John (2002)
51. Fithen and Richards (2005: 122).
52. Cramer and Weeks (2002).
53. Keynes (1937: 241).
54. Hirshleifer (1994).
55. Hirshleifer (1988).
56. Nonetheless, some variables (e.g. inequality) play rather different roles in different versions of the models.
57. Collier (2000).
58. Levi (1986: 60).
59. On Greece see Eudes (1972); on the Korean War see Halliday and Cumings (1988).
60. Hassan's study involving interviews with nearly 250 militants and associates involved with the Palestinian cause is cited in Krueger and Maleckova (2002).
61. Klein (1997).
62. Sebald (2003: 157). See also Bizot (2004), Taussig (2004).
63. Marchal and Messiant (2001; 2002).

Chapter 4 *Angola and the Theory of War*

1. Another end-date is 4 April 2002, when UNITA generals and the MPLA signed a ceasefire.
2. Guimarães (2001: 52).
3. See Wheeler and Pelissier (1971: 191), Marcum (1969: 15).
4. For accounts of the battle see Maier (1996) and Fauvet and Mosse (2003).
5. See Maier (1996) and Anstee (1996).
6. Buijtenhuijs (2000).
7. See Global Witness (2002: 17).
8. See Tvedten (1997).
9. Human Rights Watch (2004b).
10. Heywood (1998).
11. See Messiant (1998) and Birmingham (1992).
12. See Minter's (1994) account of this.
13. On Nito Alves's attempted coup, see Messiant (1998).
14. Reno (2000: 231–2).
15. On parliamentarians' capture of rent in the English Civil Wars, see Edwards (2000).
16. Ferreira (2002: 253–4).
17. Messiant (1998: 154).
18. See SIPRI website: www.sipri.org.
19. Minter (1994: 154).
20. A literal example was the reported involvement of President dos Santos's daughter in a new diamond enterprise.
21. See especially Dietrich's account in Cilliers and Dietrich (2000).

22. Hodges (2001: 137).
23. IMF (1999).
24. For this argument on the timing of military turning points in Angola see Frynas and Wood (2002); on cotton prices and major turning points in the American Civil War see Brown and Burdekin (2000).
25. Messiant (2001).
26. Hodges (2001: 133).
27. Cited in Hodges (2001). For 2003 UNICEF estimates the under-five mortality rate to be 260/1,000 live births: http://www.unicef.org/info-bycountry/angola_502.html.
28. See, particularly, Marcum (1969).
29. Malaquias (2000: 95–105).
30. Messiant (1998: 144).
31. In the ten provinces beyond those obviously controlled by the two main parties, in the 1992 elections, the MPLA won 77 per cent of the parliamentary vote and 72 per cent of the presidential vote.
32. The Jaga were 'militarised bands of cannibalistic marauders' operating from the late sixteenth century onwards (Heywood, 1998).
33. At least one eminent historian of Angola agrees that many urban Angolans do not really see themselves as Africans.
34. Maier (1996).
35. To reinforce this see, for example, the particular personality and career of Jonas Savimbi, or the complex individual political histories of leading MPLA characters like Agostinho Neto, Nito Alves, José Eduardo dos Santos.
36. A parallel in economic analysis is the debate between Bhaduri (1986) and Stiglitz (1986) on choice versus coercion in rural economic behaviour.
37. See Miller (1988) and Clarence-Smith (1985).
38. On Sierra Leone see, e.g., Keen (2002).

Chapter 5 *How to Pay for a War*

1. Lévy (2004: 3). A certain type of conflict is becoming more common, Lévy argues, wars that 'have seemingly let go of the cord that tied them to the Universal' (pp. 3–4). This meaninglessness and its conflicts produces an 'adversity that has become illegible' (p. 5). See also pp. 123–56.
2. Hobsbawm (1998: 348).
3. Retort (2005).
4. Duffield (2001).
5. See http://www.american.edu/TED/gumarab.htm.
6. On coltan, but also particularly on the regional and global dimensions of conflict commodity supply chains, see Pugh, Cooper and Goodhand (2004: 26–30). See also Moyroud and Katunga in Lind and Sturman (eds) (2002); Jackson (2003).
7. See Amsden (1997).
8. Hirshleifer (1994: 4).

9. 'It was very largely because war, for the ruling classes, remained an almost automatic activity, part of the natural order of things, that wars for territory, inheritance and allegiance, sharpened by religious differences, continued well into the seventeenth century' (Howard, 2001: 13).
10. See Howard (2001); Tilly (1985).
11. On war finance during the Thirty Years War (1618–48) and on the careers of Wallenstein and other seventeenth-century warlords-cum-war entrepreneurs see Redlich (1959; 1994). On the earlier mercenary career of John Hawkwood, the Englishman who terrorised and extorted money from northern Italian city states in the fourteenth century, see Saunders (2004).
12. For an exposition of the 'Lawyers, guns and money' state-formation argument see Schwartz (1994).
13. Tilly (1992: 70). Tilly is the best known proponent of this kind of argument about the formation of European states and their similarity to organised crime: see also Tilly (1985).
14. McPherson (1990: 447–8).
15. Keynes (1940: preface, quotes from iii and iii–iv respectively).
16. Keynes (1940: 10–11).
17. Collier and Hoeffler (1996).
18. See Dobb (1966).
19. For these details see Ferreira (2002).
20. See Makinen (1971); and Dudley and Passell (1969): both reprinted in Larry Neal (ed.), *War Finance*, vol. 3.
21. See Cooley (1999: 131).
22. Lumpe (2000).
23. Fitzgerald (2003) makes this case.
24. Reno (2003).
25. Keen (2005: 167).
26. Kitching (2001).

Chapter 6 *Passionate Interests*

1. Roberts (2003).
2. As Hirschman (1977) explains, this idea—of some classes of vice tempering or counteracting other, more worrying vices—has a long heritage going back to St Augustine.
3. In Montesquieu the paradox had more to do with statecraft and politics than with the market. Rothschild (2002) argues that Smith's use of the idea of the invisible hand was ironic, by contrast with the earnest use of the image by twentieth-century economists.
4. Quoted in Hirschman (1977).
5. Quoted in Turnell (2002: 4).
6. Ibid.
7. Quoted in Turnell (2002: 5).
8. Friedman in *The Guardian*, 21 April 2005. See Friedman (2005).
9. Skidelsky (1992; 1994); Turnell (2002).

10. Keynes, *Collected Works VII*: 381–2, quoted in Turnell (2002: 8). See also Skidelsky (1994: 477).
11. UN Security Council (2002; 2003).
12. On interlinked markets and forced commerce see Bharadwaj (1985).
13. Polanyi (1944: 35).
14. Byres (2004).
15. Foucault (2003: 269–70).
16. See Moore (1967).
17. E. M. Wood (2003). See also Howard (1978: 17–18), who quotes Thomas More's *Utopia*, whose residents include as a just war the case in which a people 'possess land that they leave idle and uncultivated and refuse the use and occupancy of it to others who according to the law of nature ought to be supported from it.'
18. E. M. Wood (2003).
19. On this agrarian transformation in the northern United States see Post (1995).
20. On Finland's history of violence in the *longue durée*, see Ylikangas *et al.* (2001).
21. Tilly (2003).
22. Keen (1994).
23. Sender (2002).
24. Whitaker (1999).
25. Harding (2000) on immigration in Europe. Sender, Cramer and Oya on refugees and labour markets in Africa (2005).
26. Chingono (1996); Castel-Branco and Cramer (2003); Pitcher (2002).
27. This is the argument proposed by Volkov (2002). That this process is far from even or functionally smooth is obvious from the political struggles over the legitimacy of property rights in post-Soviet Russia, as evident in the example of the battle between Putin's government and Mikhail Khodorkovsky, founder of the oil company Yukos.
28. Leeds (1996).
29. Koonings (1999).
30. Abramovay and Rua (2002).
31. See Caldeira (2000), Macaulay (2002).
32. Huggins (2000).
33. For example, Pereira (1997) discusses violence against union leaders and members in the coastal sugar growing region of the north eastern state of Pernambuco.
34. The assassin was the son of a local landlord and member of the UDR, the landowners association; father and son were arrested but, after the national and international clamour faded, escaped from jail. See Huggins (2000).
35. See, e.g., Alston *et al.* (1997).
36. Scheper-Hughes (1992).
37. On nineteenth-century political change and violence see Bieber (1999).
38. www.oxfam.org.uk/policy/gender/99mar/399braz.htm.

39. See Hanlon (2003).
40. South African Human Rights Commission (2003).
41. Steinberg (2002).
42. Steinberg (2002: viii–ix).
43. Steinberg (2002: 227).
44. Besteman (1996: ix), cited in Peters (2004: 297).
45. See Gellner (1964).
46. Kitching (2001).
47. Gerschenkron (1962).
48. See, for example, Lemarchand (1996); Mamdani (2001); Pottier (2002).
49. One encyclopaedia of intervention is Blum (2003).
50. Ellsberg (2003).
51. Bacevich (2002).
52. Servan-Schreiber (1967).
53. Gowan (2003).
54. Ibid.
55. Cramer and Weeks (2002).
56. On Rwanda see Storey (1999) and Chossudovsky (1995); on Yugoslavia see Blackburn (1993) and Schierup (1992; 1993).
57. Lumpe (2000).
58. Evans (2003).
59. Ann Feltham (Campaign Against Arms Trade), Presentation to NGO seminar on export credit reform, House of Commons, London, 23 May 2002.
60. Peterson (2002).
61. See Davies (2005).
62. Khan (2004a).
63. Tilly (2003: 51).
64. Gambetta (2005).
65. More generally, see Hroch (2000).
66. Cited in Guillermoprieto (1995), on which the discussion of Chiapas principally draws.
67. See Grenier (1996).

Chapter 7 *The Great Post-Conflict Makeover Fantasy*

1. See Darby (2001). Peace settlements themselves, in certain conditions, can help bring about new wars: see Hughes and Seligmann (2002).
2. Keynes (1971: 170).
3. Milward (1984).
4. Addison *et al.* (2001a).
5. On the non-linear, contested history of the meaning of freedom in the United States see Foner (1998).
6. Cited in Moore (1967: 144).
7. Foner (1988).
8. See O'Brien (1988).
9. Heilbroner (1977).

10. Cited in Foner (1988).
11. On 'neo-populist pipe dreams' see Byres (1979).
12. On the domestic impetus for privatisation in Mozambique, both during and after war, see Castel-Branco and Cramer (2003). More broadly, see Hibou (1999).
13. Carlin (2003).
14. Moore (2000).
15. Quoted in Ottoway (2003).
16. Ibid.: 250–1.
17. See also Paris's (2004) argument that institutional development needs to precede liberalisation in the war to peace transition.
18. See, e.g., Azam *et al.* (1994).
19. Translated from the quotation in Cahen (1988).
20. O'Laughlin (1996).
21. Wuyts (2003).
22. Ibid.: 147.
23. On this wartime effort to revive rural trade see Pitcher (2002).
24. O'Laughlin (1996: 32).
25. Chingono (1996).
26. Wuyts (2003).
27. Cramer (1999); McMillan *et al.* (2002); and *International Herald Tribune*, October 2000.
28. While world prices have declined, the share of the border price that farmers receive has not risen as high as expected because of ongoing oligopolistic arrangements in rural trading: see Pitcher (2002: 229).
29. Cramer (2001); Pitcher (2002).
30. International Crisis Group (2004).
31. Ibid.: 9.
32. Quoted in *The Financial Times*, 'Unrest grows over rebuilding Iraq', 24 June 2003.
33. Pollock (2004).
34. International Crisis Group (2003: i).
35. See Mobbek (2000).
36. See also Farmer (2004) and subsequent exchanges on Haiti in the letters page of the *London Review of Books*.

Conclusions

1. From a lecture in 1755, quoted in Jones (2004).
2. Howard (1978).
3. Duffield (2001).
4. See St Augustine, *City of God*, Book 19, Chapter 12.
5. Rajan (2004: 57).

BIBLIOGRAPHY

Abdullah, Ibrahim and Patrick Muana, 'The Revolutionary United Front of Sierra Leone' in Christopher Clapham (ed.), *African Guerrillas*, Oxford and Bloomington: James Currey and Indiana University Press, 1998.

Abramovay, Miriam and Maria das Graças Rua, *Violence in Schools*, Brasilia: UNESCO, 2002.

Addison, Tony, 'Rebuilding Post-Conflict Africa: Reconstruction and Reform, The Nexus Between Economic Management and the Restoration of Social Capital in Southern Africa', Cape Town: World Bank/Centre for Conflict Resolution, 11–13 October 1998.

———, Alemayehu Geda, Philippe Le Billon and S. Mansoob Murshed, *Financial Reconstruction in Conflict and 'Post-Conflict' Economies*, Discussion Paper no. 2001/90, Helsinki: UNU/WIDER, 2001b.

Addison, Tony, Philippe le Billon and Murshed Mansoob, *Finance in Conflict and Reconstruction*, Discussion Paper no. 2001/44, Helsinki: UNU/WIDER, 2001a.

African Rights, *Rwanda: Death, Despair and Defiance*, London: African Rights, 1995.

Aijmer, Goran and Gus Abbink (eds), *The Meanings of Violence: A Cross-Cultural Perspective*, Oxford: Berg, 2000.

Alesina, A. and R. Perotti, 'Income Distribution, Political Instability, and Investment', *European Economic Review*, 40, 6 (1996), 1203–28.

Alexander, Jocelyn, JoAnn McGregor and Terence Ranger, *Violence and Memory: One Hundred Years in the 'Dark Forests' of Matabeleland*, Oxford, Portsmouth, NH, Cape Town and Harare: James Currey, Heinemann, David Philip and Weaver Press, 2000.

Alexander, Peter and Rick Halpern, 'Introduction: Comparing Race and Labour in South Africa and the United States', *Journal of Southern African Studies*, 30, 1 (2004).

All Party Parliamentary Group for Angola, *Impressions and Recommendations on a Visit to Angola, 3–10 May, 2003*, London, 2003.

Allan, J. A., 'Hydro-Peace in the Middle East: Why No Water Wars? A Case Study of the Jordan River Basin', *SAIS Review*, XXII, 2 (summer–fall 2002), 255–72.

Alston, L. J., G. D. Libecap and B. Mueller, 'Violence and the Development of Property Rights to Land in the Brazilian Amazon' in John Drobak and John Nye (eds), *Frontiers of the New Institutional Economics*, Academic Press, 1997.

Amnesty International, *Report 41/027/2003*, 2003.

Amsden, Alice, 'Editorial: Bringing Production Back in—Understanding Government's Economic Role in Late Industrialization', *World Development*, 25, 4 (1997), 469–80.

———, *The Rise of 'The Rest': Challenges to the West from Late-Industrializing Economies*, New York: Oxford University Press, 2001.

Anderson, Benedict, *Imagined Communities: On the Origin and Spread of Nationalism*, London: Verso, 1983.

———, 'Murder and Progress in Modern Siam' in *The Spectre of Comparisons: Nationalism, Southeast Asia and the World*, London: Verso, 1998.

Anderson, David, *Histories of the Hanged: Britain's Dirty War in Kenya and the End of Empire*, London: Weidenfeld and Nicolson, 2005.

André, Catherine and Jean-Philippe Platteau, 'Land Relations Under Unbearable Stress: Rwanda Caught in the Malthusian Trap', *Journal of Economic Behaviour and Organization*, 34, 1 (1998), 1–47.

Anstee, Margaret, *Orphan of the Cold War: The Inside Story of the Angolan Peace Process*, New York: St Martin's Press, 1996.

Arendt, Hannah, *Eichmann in Jerusalem: A Report on the Banality of Evil*, London: Faber, 1963.

Azam, J. P., D. Bevan, P. Collier, S. Dercon, J. Gunning and S. Pradhan, *Some Economic Consequences of the Transition from Civil War to Peace*, Working Paper no. 1392, Washington, DC: World Bank, 1994.

Bacevich, Andrew, *American Empire: The Realities and Consequences of US Diplomacy*, Cambridge, MA: Harvard University Press, 2002.

Barclay, Gordon and Cynthia Tavares, *International Comparisons of Criminal Justice Statistics 2000*, Home Office Research Development and Statistics, 05, London: Home Office, 2002 (12 July).

———, *International Comparisons of Criminal Justice Statistics 2001*, Home Office Research Development and Statistics Directorate, London: Home Office, 2003.

Barnett, Corelli, *Post-Conflict Civil Affairs: Comparing War's End in Iraq and in Germany*, London: Foreign Policy Centre, 2005.

Baudrillard, Jean, *The Gulf War Did Not Take Place*, Bloomington: Indiana University Press, 1995.

Baumann, Zygmunt, 'The Uniqueness and Normality of the Holocaust' in Catherine Besteman (ed.), *Violence: A Reader*, Basingstoke: Macmillan, 2002, 67–96.

Benjamin, Walter, *Illuminations*, New York: Schocken Books, 1969.

Bernard of Clairvaux, 'De Consideratione II, 1–3' in *Sancti Bernardi Opera*, vol. V, edited by C. H. Talbot and J. H. M. Rochais, J. Leclercq, Rome: Editiones Cistercienses, 1957–75, 411–13.

Besteman, C., 'Local Land Use Strategies and Outsider Politics: Title Registration in the Middle Jubba Valley' in C. Besteman and L. V. Cassanelli (eds), *The Struggle for Land in Southern Somalia: The War Behind the War*, Boulder, CO: Westview, 1996.

————, *Unraveling Somalia: Race, Violence, and the Legacy of Slavery*, Philadelphia, PA: University of Pennsylvania Press, 1999.

Bhaduri, A., 'Forced Commerce and Agrarian Growth', *World Development*, 14, 2 (1986), 267–72.

Bharadwaj, Krishna, 'A View on Commercialisation in Indian Agriculture and the Development of Capitalism', *Journal of Peasant Studies*, 12, 4 (July 1985), 7–23.

Bieber, Judy, *Power, Patronage and Political Violence: State Building on a Brazilian Frontier, 1822–1889*, Lincoln: University of Nebraska Press, 1999.

Birmingham, David, *Frontline Nationalism in Angola and Mozambique*, London and Trenton, NJ: James Currey and Africa World Press, 1992.

Bizot, François, *The Gate*, London: Vintage, 2004.

Blackburn, R., 'The Break-Up of Yugoslavia and the Fate of Bosnia', *New Left Review*, 1/199 (May–June 1993), 100–19.

Bloch, Marc, *The Historian's Craft*, Manchester University Press, 1954.

————, *Feudal Society*, vol. I: *The Growth of Ties of Dependence*, London: Routledge and Kegan Paul, 1962.

Blum, William, *Killing Hope: US Military and CIA Interventions Since World War II*, London: Zed Books, 2003.

Bollet, Alfred J, *Civil War Medicine: Challenges and Triumphs*, Tucson, AZ: Galen Press, 2001.

Borkenau, Franz, *The Spanish Cockpit: An Eyewitness Account of the Political and Social Conflicts of the Spanish Civil War*, London and Sydney: Pluto, 1986.

Boyce, James, 'Aid Conditionality as a Tool for Peacebuilding: Opportunities and Constraints', *Development and Change*, 33, 5 (2002), 1025–48.

Braeckman, C., *Terreur africaine. Burundi, Rwanda, Zaïre: les racines de la violence*, Paris: Fayard, 1996.

Brandolini, A. and A. B. Atkinson, 'Promise and Pitfalls in the Use of "Secondary" Data-Sets: Income Inequality in OECD Countries as a Case Study', *Journal of Economic Literature*, 39, 3 (2001), 771–99.

Breman, Jan, 'Anti-Muslim Pogrom in Surat', *Economic and Political Weekly*, 17 April 1993, 737–41.

————, *Footloose Labour: Working in India's Informal Economy*, Cambridge University Press, 1996.

Brenner, Robert, 'The Origins of Capitalist Development: A Critique of Neo-Smithian Marxism', *New Left Review*, 104 (1977).

————, 'Uneven Development and the Long Downturn: The Advanced Capitalist Economies from Boom to Stagnation, 1950–1998', *New Left Review*, 229 (1998), 1–264.

Brockett, C., 'Measuring Political Violence and Land Inequality in Central America', *American Political Science Review*, 86, 1 (1992), 169–76.

Brown, William Jr and Richard Burdekin, 'Turning Points in the US Civil War: A British Perspective', *Journal of Economic History*, March 2000.

Browning, Christopher, *Ordinary Men: Reserve Police Battalion 101 and the Final Solution in Poland*, London: Penguin, 2001.

Brück, Tilman, Valpy Fitzgerald and Arturo Grigsby, 'Enhancing the Private Sector Contribution to Post-War Recovery in Poor Countries', Working Paper no. 45(1), Oxford: Queen Elizabeth House, 2000.

Buijtenhuijs, Robert, 'Peasant Wars in Africa: Gone with the Wind?' in D. Bryceson, C. Kay and J. Mooij (eds), *Disappearing Peasantries? Rural Labour in Africa, Asia and Latin America*, London: IT Publishers, 2000.

Byres, T. J., 'Of Neo-Populist Pipe Dreams: Daedalus in the Third World and the Myth of Urban Bias', *Journal of Peasant Studies*, 6, 2 (1979), 210–44.

———, *Capitalism from Above and Capitalism from Below: An Essay in Comparative Political Economy*, Basingstoke: Macmillan, 1996.

———, 'Neoliberalism and Primitive Accumulation in LDCs' in Alfredo Saad-Filho and Deborah Johnston (eds), *Neoliberalism: A Critical Reader*, London: Pluto, 2004.

Cahen, Michel, 'La crise du nationalisme', *Politique Africaine*, 29 (March 1988), 2–13.

Caldeira, Teresa, *City of Walls: Crime, Segregation, and Citizenship in São Paulo*, Berkeley and Los Angeles, CA: University of California Press, 2000.

Callinicos, Alex, *The New Mandarins of American Power*, Cambridge: Polity, 2003.

Canetti, Elias, *Crowds and Power*, London: Gollancz, 1962.

Carballo, M. and S. Solby, 'HIV/AIDS, Conflict and Reconstruction in Sub-Saharan Africa', paper presented at the Conference on Preventing and Coping with HIV/AIDS in Post-Conflict Societies: Gender Based Lessons from Sub-Saharan Africa, 2001.

Carlin, Ann, *Rush to Reengagement in Afghanistan: The IFI's Post-Conflict Agenda*, Washington, DC: Bank Information Centre, 2003.

Carnegie Commission on Preventing Deadly Conflict, *Preventing Deadly Conflict: The Final Report*, Washington, DC: The Commission, 1997.

Castel-Branco, Carlos and Christopher Cramer with Degol Hailu, 'Privatization and Economic Strategy in Mozambique' in Tony Addison (ed.), *From Conflict to Recovery in Africa*, Oxford University Press, 2003, 155–70.

Catholic Commission for Justice and Peace, *Breaking the Silence: A Report on the Disturbances in Matabeleland and the Midlands*, Harare: Catholic Commission for Justice and Peace, 1997.

Cavalli-Sforza, Luigi Luca, *Genes, Peoples and Languages*, London: Penguin, 2001.

Chandan, Suba and Alok Kumar Gupta, 'India: Caste Violence and Class in Bihar: The Ranvir Sena' in Paul van Tongeren, Monique Mekenkamp and Hans van de Veen (eds), *Searching for Peace in Central and South Asia*, Boulder, CO: Lynne Rienner, 2002.

Chang, Ha-Joon, *The Political Economy of Industrial Policy*, Basingstoke: Macmillan, 1993.

———, *Kicking Away the Ladder: Development Strategy in Historical Perspective*, London: Anthem, 2002.

Chingono, Mark, *The State, Violence and Development: The Political Economy of War in Mozambique, 1975–1992*, Aldershot: Avebury, 1996.

Chopra, Jarat, 'Building State Failure in East Timor', *Development and Change*, 33, 5 (2002), 979–1000.

Chossudovsky, M., 'IMF-World Bank Policies and the Rwandan Holocaust', *Third World Network Features*, 24 January 1995.

Cilliers, Jackie and Christian Dietrich (eds), *Angola's War Economy: The Role of Oil and Diamonds*, Pretoria: Institute for Security Studies, 2000.

Clarence-Smith, W. G., 'Class Structure and Class Struggles in Angola in the 1970s', *Journal of Southern African Studies*, 7, 1 (October 1980), 109–26.

———, *The Third Portuguese Empire, 1825–1975: A Study in Economic Imperialism*, Manchester University Press, 1985.

———, 'Review Essay', *Southern African Review of Books*, 8 (April–May 1989).

Clausewitz, Carl von, *On War*, translated by Michael Howard and Peter Paret, Princeton University Press, 1976.

Cohn, Carol, 'Sex and Death in the Rational World of Defence Intellectuals' in Nancy Scheper-Huges and Philippe Bourgois (eds), *Violence in War and Peace: An Anthology*, Oxford: Blackwell, 2004.

Collier, Paul, 'Doing Well Out of War: An Economic Perspective' in Mats Berdal and David Malone (eds), *Greed and Grievance: Economic Agendas in Civil Wars*, London and Boulder, CO: IDRC/Lynne Rienner, 2000.

——— and Anke Hoeffler, 'On the Economic Causes of Civil War', mimeo, Oxford: Centre for the Study of African Economies, 1996.

———, 'Conflicts' in Björn Lomborg (ed.), *Global Crises, Global Solutions*, Cambridge University Press, 2004, 129–56.

Collier, Paul and Sanjay Pradhan, 'Economic Consequences of the Ugandan Transition to Peace' in D. Bevan, J-P. Azam and P. Collier (eds), *Some Economic Consequences of the Transition from Civil War to Peace*, Policy Research WP 1392, Washington, DC: World Bank, 1994, 119–33.

Collinson, Sarah, *Power, Livelihoods and Conflict: Case Studies in Political Economy Analysis for Humanitarian Action*, Humanitarian Policy Group Report no. 13, London: ODI, 2003.

Cooley, John, *Unholy Wars: Afghanistan, America and International Terrorism*, London: Pluto, 1999.

Cooper, F., *From Slaves to Squatters: Plantation Labor and Agriculture in Zanzibar and Coastal Kenya, 1890–1925*, London and New Haven, CT: Yale University Press, 1980.

Cowell, F., *Measuring Inequality*, London: Prentice-Hall/Harvester Wheatsheaf, 1995.

Cramer, Christopher, 'Can Africa Industrialize by Processing Primary Commodities? The Case of Mozambican Cashew Nuts', *World Development*, 27, 7 (1999), 1247–66.

———, 'Privatisation and Adjustment in Mozambique: A Hospital Pass?' *Journal of Southern African Studies*, 27, 1 (2001), 79–104.

———, 'Homo Economicus Goes to War: Methodological Individualism, Rational Choice, and the Political Economy of War', *World Development*, 30, 11 (2002), 1845–64.

———, 'Does Inequality Cause Conflict?' *Journal of International Development*, 15 (2003), 397–412.

———, *Conflict and the Very Poorest, Issues Paper,* London: DFID, 2004.

——— and Jonathan Goodhand, 'Try Again, Fail Again, Fail Better? War, the State and the "Post-Conflict" Challenge in Afghanistan' in Jennifer Milliken (ed.), *State Failure, Collapse and Reconstruction,* Oxford: Blackwell, 2003, 131–56.

——— and John Weeks, 'Macroecononomic Stabilization and Structural Adjustment' in E. Wayne Nafziger and Raimo Vayrynen (eds), *The Prevention of Humanitarian Emergencies,* Basingstoke: Palgrave/UNU WIDER, 2002.

Cumings, Bruce, 'The Origins and Development of the Northeast Asian Political Economy: Industrial Sectors, Product Cycles, and Political Consequences' in Frederick Deyo (ed.), *The Political Economy of the New Asian Industrialism,* Ithaca, NY: Cornell University Press, 1984, 44–83.

Darby, John, *The Effects of Violence on Peace Processes,* Washington, DC: United States Institute of Peace Press, 2001.

Davies, Rob, 'Memories of Underdevelopment: A Personal Interpretation of Zimbabwe's Economic Decline' in Brian Raftopoulous and Tyrone Savage (eds), *Injustice and Political Reconciliation,* Cape Town: Institute for Justice and Reconciliation, 2005.

de Lima, Maria Luiza C. and Ricardo Ximenes, 'Violência e Morte: Diferenciais Da Mortalidade por Causas Externas No Espaço Urbano Do Recife, 1991' [Violence and Death: Differentials in Mortality from External Causes in Recife, Pernambuco, Brazil, 1991], *Caderna Saúde Pública,* 14, 4 (October–December 1998), 829–40.

de Waal, Alex, *Famine Crimes: Politics and the Disaster Relief Industry in Africa,* Oxford: James Currey, 1997.

de Witte, Ludo, *The Assassination of Lumumba,* London: Verso, 2001.

Deaton, Angus, 'Saving in Developing Countries: Theory and Review', *World Bank Economic Review,* Supplement: Proceedings of the World Bank Annual Conference on Development Economics (1989), 61–96.

Deininger, Klaus and Lynn Squire, 'A New Data Set for Measuring Inequality', *World Bank Economic Review,* 10 (1996), 565–91.

del Castillo, Graciana, 'Post-Conflict Reconstruction and the Challenge to International Organizations: The Case of El Salvador', *World Development,* 29, 12 (2001), 1967–85.

Di John, Jonathan, 'Mineral Resource Abundance and Violent Political Conflict: A Critical Assessment of the Rentier State Model', Crisis States Programme, Working Paper, London: DESTIN/LSE, 2002.

———, 'Mineral Resource Rents, Rent-Seeking and State Capacity in a Late Developer: The Political Economy of Industrial Policy in Venezuela, 1920–1998', PhD Thesis, Economics and Politics, Cambridge University, 2004a.

———, *The Political Economy of Economic Liberalization in Venezuela,* Working Paper no. 46, http://www.crisisstates.com/Publications/wp/working.htm, June 2004b.

Didion, Joan, 'God's Country', *New York Review of Books,* 2 November 2000.

————, 'Mr. Bush and the Divine', *New York Review of Books*, 6 November 2003.

Dobb, Maurice, *Soviet Economic Development Since 1917*, London: Routledge, 1966.

Doner, Richard F., Bryan K. Ritchie and Dan Slater, 'Systemic Vulnerability and the Origins of Development States: Northeast and Southeast Asia in Comparative Perspective', *International Organization*, 59, 2 (spring 2005).

Dudley, Leonard and Peter Passell, 'The War in Vietnam and the United States Balance of Payments', *Review of Economics and Statistics*, 50, 4 (1969), 437–42.

Duffield, Mark, *Global Governance and the New Wars: The Merging of Security and Development*, London: Zed Books, 2001.

Dugard, Jackie, *From Low-Intensity War to Mafia War: Taxi Violence in South Africa (1987–2000)*, Johannesburg: Centre for the Study of Violence and Reconciliation, 2001.

Eckstein, H., 'Theoretical Approaches to Explaining Collective Violence' in T. R. Gurr (ed.), *Handbook of Political Conflict*, New York: Free Press, 1980, 135–67.

Edwards, Peter, *Dealing in Death: The Arms Trade and the British Civil Wars, 1638–52*, Stroud: Sutton, 2000.

Ehrenreich, Barbara, *Blood Rites: Origins and History of the Passions of War*, London: Virago, 1997.

Ellis, Stephen, *Civil War in Liberia: Generalizing from a Case Study*, Leiden: Afrikastudiecentrum, 2003.

Ellsberg, Daniel, *Secrets: A Memoir of Vietnam and the Pentagon Papers*, London: Penguin, 2003.

Eltringham, Nigel, *Accounting for Horror: Post-Genocide Debates in Rwanda*, London: Pluto, 2004.

Enzensberger, Hans Magnus, *Civil War*, London: Granta, 1994.

Eudes, Dominique, *The Kapetanios: Partisans and Civil War in Greece, 1943–49*, London: New Left Books, 1972.

Evans, Peter C., 'Appendix 13E. The Financing Factor in Arms Sales: The Role of Official Export Credits and Guarantees' in *SIPRI Yearbook 2003: Armaments, Disarmament and International Security*, Oxford University Press, 2003.

Fairhead, James, 'The Conflict Over Natural and Environmental Resources' in F. Stewart, R. Vayrynen and E. Wayne Nafziger (eds), *War, Hunger, and Displacement volume I: The Origins of Humanitarian Emergencies—War and Displacement in Developing Countries*, Oxford University Press, 2000.

Farmer, Paul, 'Who Removed Aristide?', *London Review of Books*, 26, 8 (15 April 2004).

Fauvet, Paul and Marcelo Mosse, *Carlos Cardoso: Telling the Truth in Mozambique*, Cape Town: Double Storey, 2003.

Fearon, James and David Laitin, 'Ethnicity, Insurgency, and Civil War', *American Political Science Review*, 97, 1 (2003), 75–90.

Feierman, Stephen, 'African Histories and the Dissolution of World History' in V. Y. Mudimbe, R. H. Bates and J. O'Barr (eds), *Africa and the Disciplines: The Contributions of Research in Africa to the Social Sciences and Humanities*, University of Chicago Press, 1993.

Ferguson, James, *The Anti-Politics Machine: 'Development', Depoliticization, and Bureaucratic Power in Lesotho*, Cambridge University Press, 1990.

Ferreira, Manuel Ennes, 'Angola: Civil War and the Manufacturing Industry, 1975–1999' in Jurgen Brauer and J. Paul Dunne (eds), *Arming the South: The Economics of Military Expenditure, Arms Production and Arms Trade in Developing Countries*, Basingstoke: Palgrave, 2002.

Fithen, Caspar and Paul Richards, 'Making War, Crafting Peace: Militia Solidarities and Demobilisation in Sierra Leone' in Paul Richards (ed.), *No Peace No War: An Anthropology of Contemporary Armed Conflicts*, Oxford: James Currey, 2005, 117–36.

Fitzgerald, E. V. K., 'Global Financial Information, Compliance Incentives and Conflict Funding', Working Paper no. 96, Oxford: Queen Elizabeth House, 2003.

Foner, Eric, *Reconstruction: America's Unfinished Revolution, 1863–77*, New York: Harper and Row, 1988.

———, *The Story of American Freedom*, London: Pimlico, 1998.

Foote, Christopher, William Block, Keith Crane and Simon Gray, 'Economic Policy and Prospects in Iraq', *Journal of Economic Perspectives*, 18, 3 (summer 2004), 47–70.

Foreign and Commonwealth Office (FCO), *Green Paper HC577*, 2002.

Foucault, Michel, *Society Must be Defended*, London: Allen Lane/Penguin, 2003.

Friedman, Thomas, *The World is Flat: Brief History of the Globalized World in the 21st Century*, London: Allen Lane, 2005.

Frynas, Jedrzej George and Geoffrey Wood, 'The Liberal View of the Trade-Peace Relationship Re-Considered: Oil and Conflict in Angola', Vereinigung von Afrikanisten in Deutschland conference, 2002.

Fukuyama, Francis, *The End of History and the Last Man*, London: Penguin, 1992.

Galbraith, J. K., *Money: Whence It Came, Where It Went*, London: Deutsch, 1975.

Gallie, W. B., *Philosophers of War and Peace*, Cambridge University Press, 1978.

Gambetta, Diego, *The Sicilian Mafia: The Business of Protection*, Harvard University Press, 1996.

——— (ed.), *Making Sense of Suicide Missions*, Oxford University Press, 2005.

Geffray, Christian, *Le cause des armes au Mozambique: Anthropologie d'une Guerre Civile*, Paris: Karthala, 1990.

Gellner, Ernest, *Thought and Change*, London: Weidenfeld and Nicolson, 1964.

Gerschenkron, Alexander, *Economic Backwardness in Historical Perspective: A Book of Essays*, Cambridge, MA: Belknap, 1962.

Gibson, Ian, *The Assassination of Federico Garcia Lorca*, London: Penguin, 1983.

Gilligan, James, 'Violence in Public Health and Preventive Medicine', *Lancet*, 355 (2000a), 1802–12.

———, *Violence: Reflections on Our Deadliest Epidemic*, London: Jessica Kingsley, 2000b.

Girard, René, *Violence and the Sacred*, Baltimore, MD: Johns Hopkins University Press, 1977.

———, 'Mimesis and Violence' in J. G. Williams (ed.), *The Girard Reader*, New York: The Crossroad Publishing Company, 1996.

Glaser, Clive, *Bo Tsotsi: The Youth Gangs of Soweto, 1935–1976*, Portsmouth: Heinemann, 2000.

Gleditsch, Nils Petter, 'Armed Conflict and the Environment: A Critique of the Literature', *Journal of Peace Research*, 35, 3 (1998), 381–400.

——— and Peter Wallensteen, 'Armed Conflict 1946–2001: A New Dataset', *Journal of Peace Research*, 39, 5 (2002), 615–37.

Global Witness, *All the President's Men: The Devastating Story of Oil and Banking in Angola's Privatised War*, London: Global Witness, 2002.

Goldhagen, Daniel Jonah, *Hitler's Willing Executioners: Ordinary Germans and the Holocaust*, New York: Little, Brown, 1996.

Goodhand, Jonathan, 'Afghanistan in Central Asia' in Michael Pugh and Neil Cooper (eds), *War Economies in a Regional Context: Challenges of Transformation*, Boulder, CO: Lynne Rienner, 2004, 45–90.

Goody, Jack, 'How Ethnic is Ethnic Cleansing?', *New Left Review*, 7, Jan–Feb 2001.

Gowa, Joanne, *Ballots and Bullets: The Elusive Democratic Peace*, Princeton University Press, 2000.

Gowan, Peter, 'Review', *New Left Review*, 21, May/June 2003.

Grenier, Yvon, 'From Causes to Causers: The Etiology of Salvadoran Internal War Revisited', *Journal of Conflict Studies*, fall 1996, 26–43.

Guevara, Ernesto 'Che', *The African Dream: The Diaries of the Revolutionary War in the Congo*, London: Harvill Press, 2001.

Guillermoprieto, A., 'The Shadow War', *New York Review of Books*, 42, 4 (2 March 1995).

Guimarães, Fernando Andresen, *The Origins of the Angolan Civil War: Foreign Intervention and Domestic Political Conflict*, Basingstoke: Macmillan, 2001.

Gurr, T. R., *Why Men Rebel*, Princeton University Press, 1970.

———, Monty G. Marshall and Deepa Khosla, *Peace and Conflict 2001: A Global Survey of Armed Conflicts, Self-Determination Movements, and Democracy*, College Park, MD: University of Maryland, Center for International Development and Conflict Management (CIDCM), 2002.

Halliday, John and Bruce Cumings, *Korea: The Unknown War*, London: Viking/Penguin, 1988.

Hampshire, Stuart, *Justice is Conflict*, Princeton University Press, 2000.

Hancock, Landon, *Northern Ireland: Troubles Brewing*, Background paper, CAIN Web Service, 1998, http://cain.ulst.ac.uk/othelem.

Hanlon, Joseph, *Beggar Your Neighbours: Apartheid Power in Southern Africa*, London: James Currey and Catholic Institute of International Relations, 1986.

———, 'Renewed Land Debate and the 'Cargo Cult' in Mozambique', *Journal of Southern African Studies*, 30, 3 (September 2003), 603–25.

Hanssen, Beatrice, *Critique of Violence: Between Postmodernism and Critical Theory*, London: Routledge, 2000.

Harding, Jeremy, *The Uninvited: Refugees at the Rich Man's Gate*, London: Profile, 2000.

Hardt, Michael and Antonio Negri (2005), *Multitude: War and Democracy in the Age of Empire*, London: Hamish Hamilton.

Harris, James, 'A Critical View of "Stunde Null" in Comparative Historical Perspective: 1865, 1945, 1990' in Norbert Frizsch and Jurgen Martschukat (eds), *Different Restorations: Reconstruction and 'Wiederaufbau' in the United States and Germany, 1865, 1945, 1990*, Providence, RI: Berghahn Books, 1996.

Harvey, David, *The New Imperialism*, Oxford University Press, 2003.

Hassan, N., 'An Arsenal of Believers: Talking to the Human Bombs', *New Yorker*, 22 November 2001.

Haughton, Jonathan, *The Reconstruction of War-Torn Economies*, Harvard Institute for International Development (HIID), 1998.

Heidenrich, John G., 'The Gulf War: How Many Iraqis Dead?', *Foreign Policy*, 90 (spring 1993).

Heilbroner, Robert, *The Economic Transformation of America*, New York: Harcourt Brace Jovanovich, 1977.

Heimer, Franz Wilhelm, *The Decolonization Conflict in Angola, 1974–76: An Essay in Political Sociology*, Geneva: Institut Universitaire des Hautes Études Internationales, 1979.

Hemingway, Ernest, *Hemingway on War*, New York: Scribner, 2003.

———, 'Notes on the Next War: A Serious Topical Letter (*Esquire*, September 1935)' in *Hemingway on War*, edited by S. Hemingway, New York: Scribner, 2004, 301–6.

Herodotus, *The Histories*, London: Penguin, 2003.

Heywood, Linda M., 'Towards an Understanding of Modern Political Ideology in Africa: the Case of the Ovimbundu of Angola', *Journal of Modern African Studies*, 36, 1 (1998), 139–67.

———, *Contested Power in Angola, 1840s to the Present*, Rochester, NY: Rochester University Press, 2000.

Hibou, Béatrice, 'The "Social Capital" of the State as Forger, or the Exercise of Economic Intelligence' in Stephen Ellis, Béatrice Hibou and Jean-François Bayart (eds), *The Criminalization of the State in Africa*, Oxford: James Currey, 1999.

Hilton, R. (ed.), *The Transition from Feudalism to Capitalism*, London: New Left Books, 1976.

Hirsch, Fred, *Social Limits to Growth*, Harvard University Press, 1976.

Hirschman, Albert O., *The Passions and the Interests: Political Arguments for Capitalism Before its Triumph*, Princeton University Press, 1977.

———, 'The Changing Tolerance for Income Inequality in the Course of Economic Development' in A. O. Hirschman (ed.), *Essays in Trespassing: Economics to Politics and Beyond*, Cambridge University Press, 1981.

———, 'Social Conflicts as Pillars of Democratic Market Societies' in A. O. Hirschman (ed.), *A Propensity to Self-Subversion*, Harvard University Press, 1995.

Hirshleifer, Jack, 'The Bioeconomic Causes of War', *Managerial and Decision Economics*, 19 (1988), 457–66.

———, 'The Dark Side of the Force', *Economic Inquiry*, 32 (1994), 1–10.

Hobsbawm, Eric, *Industry and Empire*, London: Penguin, 1969.

———, *Age of Extremes: The Short History of the Twentieth Century, 1914–1991*, London: Michael Joseph, 1994.

———, *On History*, London: Abacus, 1998.

———, 'War and Peace in the 20th Century', *London Review of Books*, 21 February 2002.

Hochschild, Adam, *King Leopold's Ghost: A Story of Greed, Terror and Heroism in Colonial Africa*, London: Macmillan, 1999.

Hodges, Tony, *Angola from Afro-Stalinism to Petro-Diamond Capitalism*, Oxford and Bloomington: James Currey and Indiana University Press, 2001.

Hogan, Michael J., *The Marshall Plan: America, Britain, and the Reconstruction of Western Europe, 1947–1952*, Cambridge University Press, 1987.

Holsti, Kalevi, *The State, War, and the State of War*, Cambridge University Press, 1996.

Howard, Michael, *War and the Liberal Conscience*, New Brunswick, NJ: Rutgers University Press, 1978.

———, *The Invention of Peace*, London: Profile, 2001.

———, *Clausewitz: A Very Short Introduction*, Oxford University Press, 2002.

Howson, Gerald, *Arms for Spain: The Untold Story of the Spanish Civil War*, London: John Murray, 1998.

Hroch, Miroslav, *Social Preconditions of National Revival in Europe*, New York: Columbia University Press, 2000.

Huff, Daryll, *How to Lie with Statistics*, Harmondsworth: Penguin, 1973.

Huggins, Martha, 'Modernity and Devolution: The Making of Death Squads in Modern Brazil' in B. Campbell and A. Brenner (eds), *Death Squads in Global Perspective: Murder with Deniability*, New York: St Martin's Press, 2000.

Hughes, Matthew and Matthew Seligmann, *Does Peace Lead to War? Peace Settlements and Conflict in the Modern Age*, Thrupp: Sutton, 2002.

Human Rights Watch, *Rural Violence in Brazil*, New York: Human Rights Watch, 1991.

———, *Angola: Arms Trade and Violations of the Laws of War Since the 1992 Elections*, New York: Human Rights Watch, 1994.

———, 'India: Communal Violence and the Denial of Justice', *Human Rights Watch*, 8, 2(c) (1996).

———, *Broken People*, New York: Human Rights Watch, 1999.

———, *The War Within the War: Sexual Violence Against Women and Girls in Eastern Congo*, New York, Washington, DC and London: Human Rights Watch, 2002a.

———, '"We Have No Orders To Save You": State Participation and Complicity in Communal Violence in Gujarat', *Human Rights Watch*, 14, 3(c) (2002b).

———, *Forgotten Fighters: Child Soldiers in Angola*, New York: Human Rights Watch, 2003.

———, *'Enduring Freedom': Abuses by US Forces in Afghanistan*, Washington, DC: Human Rights Watch, 2004a.

———, *Some Transparency, No Accountability: The Use of Oil Revenue in Angola and its Impact on Human Rights*, New York: Human Rights Watch, 2004b.

Human Security Centre (2005), *Human Security Report 2005: War and Peace in the 21ˢᵗ Century*, University of British Columbia, Oxford and New York: OUP.

Huntington, Samuel P., *The Clash of Civilizations and the Remaking of World Order*, London: Simon Schuster, 1998.

Hutton, Ronald, 'The Royalist War Effort 1642–46' in Larry Neal (ed.), *War Finance*, vol. I, *War From Antiquity to Artillery*, Aldershot and Brookfield, VT: Edward Elgar, 1994.

IMF, *Staff Country Report 99/25*, Washington, DC: IMF, 1999.

Inikori, J. E., 'The Import of Firearms Into West Africa 1750–1807: A Quantitative Analysis', *Journal of African History*, XVIII, 3 (1977), 339–68.

International Crisis Group, *The Kivus: The Forgotten Crucible of the Congo Conflict*, Africa Report no. 56, Washington, DC: International Crisis Group, 2003.

———, *Reconstructing Iraq*, Amman, Baghdad and Brussels: International Crisis Group, 2004.

Jackson, Stephen, *Fortunes of War: The Coltan Trade in the Kivus*, Overseas Development Institute (ODI), Background research for HPG Report 13, London: ODI, 2003.

Jameson, Frederick, 'Postmodernism and Consumer Society' in Hal Foster (ed.), *The Anti-Aesthetic: Essays on Postmodern Culture*, Seattle, WA: Bay Press, 1983, 111–25.

Jayawardena, Kumari, *Ethnic and Class Conflicts in Sri Lanka: Some Aspects of Sinhala Buddhist Consciousness*, Dehiwala: Centre for Social Analysis, 1986.

Jewkes, Rachel and N. Abrahams, *Violence Against Women in South Africa: Rape and Sexual Coercion*, Pretoria: Crime Prevention Research Resources Centre, 2000.

Kaldor, Mary, *New and Old Wars: Organized Violence in a Global Era*, Cambridge University Press, 1999.

Kalyvas, Stathis, *The Logic of Violence in Civil War,* http://www.duke.edu/web/licep/1/kalyvas/kalyvaspaper.pdf, March 2000a.

——, '"New" and "Old" Civil Wars: A Valid Distinction?', *World Politics,* 54, 1 (2000b), 99–118.

Kang, Seonjou and James Meernik, 'Determinants of Post-Conflict Economic Assistance', *Journal of Peace Research,* 41, 2 (2004), 149–66.

Kaplan, Robert D., 'The Coming Anarchy', *Atlantic Monthly,* February 1994.

Keen, David, *The Benefits of Famine: A Political Economy of Famine and Relief in Southwestern Sudan, 1983–1989,* Princeton University Press, 1994.

——, *'Since I Am a Dog, Beware My Fangs': Beyond a 'Rational Violence' Framework in the Sierra Leonian War,* Crisis States Programme Working Paper, 14, London: London School of Economics, 2002.

——, *Conflict and Collusion in Sierra Leone,* Oxford: James Currey, 2005.

Kentridge, Matthew, *An Unofficial War: Inside the Conflict in Pietermaritzburg,* Cape Town: David Philip, 1990.

Keynes, J. M., 'The General Theory of Unemployment', *Quarterly Journal of Economics,* 51, 2 (1937).

——, *How To Pay for the War: A Radical Plan for the Chancellor of the Exchequer,* London: Macmillan, 1940.

——, *The Economic Consequences of the Peace: The Collected Writings of John Maynard Keynes,* vol. II, London: Macmillan and Cambridge University Press, 1971 (1st edition 1919).

Khan, Mushtaq, 'Power, Property Rights, and the Issue of Land Reform: A General Case Illustrated with Reference to Bangladesh', *Journal of Agrarian Change,* 4, 1 (2004a).

——, 'State Failure in Developing Countries and Strategies of Institutional Reform' in Bertil Tungodden, Nick Stern and Ivar Kolstad (eds), *Towards Pro-Poor Policies: Aid Institutions and Globalization,* proceedings of World Bank's Annual Bank Conference on Development Economics, 2002, Oxford University Press and World Bank, 2004b, 165–96.

—— and K. S. Jomo, *Rents, Rent-Seeking, and Economic Development: Theory and the Asian Evidence,* Cambridge University Press, 2000.

King, Gary and Christopher J. L. Murray, 'Rethinking Human Security', *Political Science Quarterly,* 116, 4 (2001–2).

Kitching, Gavin, 'The Development of Agrarian Capitalism in Russia, 1991–97: Some Observations from Fieldwork', *Journal of Peasant Studies,* 26, 1 (1998), 43–81.

——, *Seeking Social Justice Through Globalization: Escaping a Nationalist Perspective,* University Park, PA: Pennsylvania State University Press, 2001.

Klein, Melanie, 'Envy and Gratitude (1957)' in *Envy and Gratitude and Other Works 1946–1963,* London: Vintage, 1997, 176–235.

Koestler, Arthur, *Dialogue with Death,* London: Macmillan, 1983 (1942).

Kohli, Atul, *Democracy and Discontent: India's Growing Crisis of Governability,* Cambridge University Press, 1990.

Kolakowski, Leszek, *Modernity on Endless Trial,* University of Chicago Press, 1990.

Kolko, Gabriel, *Century of War: Politics, Conflicts, and Society Since 1914*, New York: The New Press, 1994.

Koonings, Kees and Dirk Kruijt (eds), *Societies of Fear: The Legacy of Civil War, Violence and Terror in Latin America*, London: Zed Books, 1999.

Kotze, J. C., *In Their Shoes: Understanding Black South Africans Through Their Experiences of Life*, Kenwyn: Juta, 1993.

Kriger, Norma, *Zimbabwe's Guerrilla War: Peasant Voices*, Cambridge University Press, 1991.

———, *Guerrilla Veterans in Post-War Zimbabwe*, Cambridge University Press, 2003.

Krueger, Alan and Jitka Maleckova, 'Education, Poverty and Terrorism: Is There a Causal Connection?', Annual Bank Conference on Development Economics, World Bank, April 2002.

le Billon, Philippe, 'The Political Ecology of War: Natural Resources and Armed Conflict', *Political Geography*, 20, 5 (2001), 561–84.

Leach, Fiona, Vivian Fiscian, Esme Kadzamira, Eve Lemani and Pamela Machakanya, *An Investigative Study of the Abuse of Girls in African Schools*, Educational Papers, 54, London: DFID, 2003.

Leeds, Elizabeth, 'Cocaine and Parallel Politics in the Brazilian Urban Periphery', *Latin American Research Review*, 31, 3 (1996), 47–83.

Lemarchand, René, *Burundi: Ethnic Conflict and Genocide*, Cambridge University Press, 1996.

Levi, Primo, *The Periodic Table*, London: Abacus, 1986.

Lévy, Bernard-Henri, *War, Evil and the End of History*, London: Duckworth, 2004.

Lichtenstein, Alex, *Twice the Work of Free Labour: The Political Economy of Convict Labour in the New South*, London and New York: Verso, 1996.

Lind, Jeremy and Kathryn Sturman (eds), *Scarcity and Surfeit: The Ecology of Africa's Conflicts*, African Centre for Technology Studies and Institute for Security Studies, Pretoria: ISS, 2002.

Lindqvist, Sven, *Exterminate all the Brutes*, London: Granta, 1992.

Lonnberg, Åke, *Restoring and Transforming Payments and Banking Systems in Post-Conflict Economies*, Washington, DC: IMF, 2002.

Lumpe, Laura (ed.), *Running Guns: The Global Black Market in Small Arms*, Norwegian Initiative on Small Arms Transfers, London: Zed Books, 2000.

Macaulay, Fiona, 'Political and Institutional Challenges of Reforming the Brazilian Prison System', Working Paper CBS-31-02, Oxford: Centre for Brazilian Studies, 2002.

Macêdo, Adriana, Jairnilson Silva Paim, Ligia Maria Vieira da Silva and Maria Conceição Nascimento Costa, 'Desigualdades Sociais e Mortes Violentas em Crianças e Adolescente da Cidade do Salvador', *Bahia Análise e Dados*, 10, 4 (2001), 115–21.

Macmillan, Ross and Rosemary Gartner, 'When She Brings Home the Bacon: Labour Force Participation and the Risk of Spousal Violence Against Women', *Journal of Marriage and the Family*, 61 (1999), 947–58.

Maddison, Angus, *Dynamic Forces in Capitalist Development: A Long-Run Comparative View*, Oxford University Press, 1991.

Maier, Karl, *Angola: Promises and Lies*, London: Serif, 1996.

Makinen, G. E., 'Economic Stabilization in Wartime: A Comparative Case Study of Korea and Vietnam', *Journal of Political Economy*, 79, 6 (1971), 1216–43.

Malaquias, Assis, 'Ethnicity and Conflict in Angola: Prospects for Reconciliation' in Jakkie Cilliers and Christian Dietrich (eds), *Angola's War Economy: The Role of Oil and Diamonds*, Pretoria: Institute for Security Studies, 2000, 95–113.

Mamdani, Mahmood, *When Victims Become Killers: Colonialism, Nativism and the Genocide in Rwanda*, Oxford: James Currey, 2001.

Manchester, William, *The Arms of Krupp*, Boston, MA, New York and London: Back Bay Books, Little, Brown, 2003.

Mann, Michael, 'The Dark Side of Democracy: The Modern Tradition of Ethnic and Political Cleansing', *New Left Review*, 235 (1999).

Mann, Thomas, *Doctor Faustus*, London: Vintage, 1999.

Marchal, Roland and Christine Messiant, 'Une lecture symptomale de quelques théorisations récentes des guerres civiles', Paris: CERI, 6 March 2001.

———, 'De l'avidité des rebelles. L'analyse économique de la guerre civile selon Paul Collier', *Critique Internationale*, 16 (July 2002).

Marcum, John, *The Angolan Revolution*, vol. I: *Anatomy of an Explosion, 1950–1962*, Cambridge, MA: MIT Press, 1969.

Marglin, Angus and J. Schor (eds), *The Golden Age of Capitalism: Reinterpreting the Postwar Experience*, Oxford: Clarendon Press, 1990.

Marshall, Monty G. and Ted Robert Gurr, *Peace and Conflict 2003: A Global Survey of Armed Conflicts, Self-Determination Movements, and Democracy*, College Park, MD: University of Maryland, Center for International Development and Conflict Management (CIDCM), 2003.

Marx, Karl, *Capital*, vol. I, 4th edition, Harmondsworth: Penguin/New Left Review, 1976.

Maton, J., 'Développement économique et social au Rwanda entre 1980 et 1993: le dixième decile en face de l'Apocalypse', Université de Gand: Faculté des Sciences Economiques, 1994.

Matovu, J. and F. Stewart, 'Uganda: the Social and Economic Costs of Conflict' in F. Stewart, E. V. K. Fitzgerald *et al.*, *War and Underdevelopment*, vol. 2, Oxford University Press, 2001.

Mazower, Mark, *Ethnicity and War in the Balkans*, National Humanities Center, http://www.nhc.rtp.nc.us:8080/publications/hongkong/mazower.htm#N_2_, 1995 (Accessed 11 March 2005).

———, *Dark Continent: Europe's Twentieth Century*, London: Penguin, 1999.

———, *The Balkans: A Short History*, London: Weidenfeld and Nicholson, 2000.

McMillan, Margaret, Dani Rodrik and Karen Horn, *When Economic Reform Goes Wrong: Cashews in Mozambique*, NBER, Working Paper 9117, Cambridge, MA: National Bureau of Economic Research, 2002.

McPherson, James M., *Battle Cry of Freedom: The American Civil War*, London: Penguin, 1990.

———, *Drawn with the Sword: Reflections on the American Civil War*, Oxford University Press, 1996.

Messiant, Christine, 'Angola: The Challenge of Statehood' in David Birmingham and Phyllis Martin (eds), *History of Central Africa: The Contemporary Years, Since 1960*, London and New York: Longman, 1998.

———, 'The Eduardo Dos Santos Foundation: Or, How Angola's Regime is Taking Over Civil Society', *African Affairs*, 100 (2001), 287–309.

Miller, Joseph C., *Way of Death: Merchant Capitalism and the Angolan Slave Trade, 1730–1830*, London: James Currey, 1988.

Milward, Alan S., *The Economic Effects of the Two World Wars on Britain*, Basingstoke: Macmillan, 1984.

———, *The Reconstruction of Western Europe 1945–51*, London: Routledge, 1992.

Minter, William, *Apartheid's Contras and the Roots of War: An Inquiry in the Modern History of Southern Africa*, London: Zed Books, 1994.

Mitchell, Sara McLaughlin, Scott Gates and Havard Hegre, 'Evolution in Democracy-War Dynamics', *Journal of Conflict Resolution*, 43, 6 (1999), 771–92.

Mobbek, Eirin, 'Enforcement of Democracy in Haiti', Political Science Association UK 50th Annual Conference, London, 10–13 April 2000.

Montaigne, Michel de, 'On Cannibals' in *Essays*, London: Penguin, 1981.

Moore, Barrington Jr, *Social Origins of Dictatorship and Democracy: Lord and Peasant in the Making of the Modern World*, London: Penguin, 1967.

Moore, David, 'Levelling the Playing Fields and Embedding Illusions: "Post-Conflict" Discourse and the Neo-Liberal "Development" Agenda', *Review of African Political Economy*, 83 (2000), 11–28.

Moser, C. and A. Winton, *Violence in the Central American Region: Towards an Integrated Framework for Violence Reduction*, London: ODI, 2002.

Murdoch, Iris, *Metaphysics as a Guide to Morals*, London: Vintage, 2003.

Murray, C. J. L. and G. King, 'Armed Conflict as a Public Health Problem', *British Medical Journal*, 321 (9 February 2002), 346–9.

Nafziger, E. W. and J. Auvinen, 'Economic Development, Inequality, War, and State Violence', *World Development*, 30, 2 (2002), 153–63.

———, *Economic Development, Inequality, and War: Humanitarian Emergencies in Developing Countries*, Basingstoke: Macmillan, 2003.

Nairn, Tom, 'Reflections on Nationalist Disasters', *New Left Review*, 230 (1998), 145–52.

Nathan, Otto and Heinz Norden (eds), *Einstein on Peace*, New York: Schocken Books, 1960.

Neal, Larry, 'Introduction' in Larry Neal (ed.), *War Finance*, Aldershot: Edward Elgar, 1994.

Netz, Reviel, 'Barbed Wire: A History', *London Review of Books*, 20 July 2000.

Nordstrom, Carolyn, *A Different Kind of War Story*, Philadelphia, PA: University of Pennsylvania Press, 1997.

O'Brien, Patrick, *The Economic Effects of the American Civil War*, Basingstoke: Macmillan, 1988.

O'Laughlin, Bridget, 'Through a Divided Glass: Dualism, Class and the Agrarian Question in Mozambique', *Journal of Peasant Studies*, 23, 4 (1996), 1–39.

Olson, Mancur, 'Autocracy, Democracy and Prosperity' in R. J. Zeckhauser (ed.), *Strategy and Choice*, Cambridge, MA: MIT Press, 1991, 131–57.

Orwell, George, *Homage to Catalonia*, London: Penguin, 2000.

Ottoway, Marina, 'Rebuilding State Institutions in Collapsed States' in Jennifer Milliken (ed.), *State Failure, Collapse and Reconstruction*, Oxford: Blackwell, 2003, 245–66.

——— and Judith Yaphe, *Political Reconstruction in Iraq: A Reality Check*, Carnegie Endowment for International Peace, http://www.ceip.org/files/pdf/IraqBrief.Ottaway.pdf, March 2003.

Paris, Roland, *At War's End: Building Peace After Civil Conflict*, Cambridge University Press, 2004.

Penrose, E., *Economic Planning for the Peace*, Princeton University Press, 1953.

Pereira, Anthony W., 'The Crisis of Developmentalism and the Rural Labour Movement in North East Brazil' in C. M. Vilas, D. Chalmers and K. R. Hite (eds), *The New Politics of Inequality in Latin America: Rethinking Participation and Representation*, Oxford University Press, 1997.

Perelman, Michael, *The Invention of Capitalism: Classical Political Economy and the Secret History of Primitive Accumulation*, Durham, NC: Duke University Press, 2000.

Peters, Pauline, 'Inequality and Social Conflict Over Land in Africa', *Journal of Agrarian Change*, 4, 3 (2004), 269–314.

Peters, Rudolph, *Jihad in Classical and Modern Islam*, Princeton, NJ: Markus Wiener, 1996.

Peterson, Laura, 'Privatizing Combat, the New World Order' in *Making a Killing: The Business of War*, http://www.publicintegrity.org/bow/report.aspx?aid=148, 28 October 2002.

Pfaff, William, *The Bullet's Song: Romantic Violence and Utopia*, New York: Simon and Schuster, 2004.

Pfetsch, Frank and Christoph Rohloff, 'KOSIMO: A Databank on Political Conflict', *Journal of Peace Research*, 37, 3 (2000), 379–89.

Pitcher, M. Anne, *Transforming Mozambique: The Politics of Privatization, 1975–2000*, Cambridge University Press, 2002.

Polanyi, Karl, *The Great Transformation: The Political and Economic Origins of Our Time*, Boston: Beacon Press, 1944.

Pollock, Kenneth, *After Saddam: Assessing the Reconstruction of Iraq, Author's Update*, http://www.foreignaffairs.org, January 2004.

Porto, João Gomes and Imogen Parsons, *Sustaining the Peace in Angola: An Overview of Current Demobilisation, Disarmament and Reintegration*, Bonn International Centre for Conversion, 2003.

Post, Charles, 'The Agrarian Origins of US Capitalism: The Transformation of the Northern Countryside Before the Civil War', *Journal of Peasant Studies*, 22, 3 (1995), 389–445.

Pottier, Johan, *Re-Imagining Rwanda*, Cambridge University Press, 2002.

Pranger, M. B., 'Monastic Cruelty' in M. B. Pranger (ed.), *The Artificiality of Christianity*, Stanford University Press, 2003, 39–58.

Pugh, Michael and Neil Cooper with Jonathan Goodhand, *War Economies in a Regional Context: Challenges of Transformation*, Boulder, CO: Lynne Rienner, 2004.

Putzel, James, Conrad Schetter, Stefanie Elbern and Bettina Woll, 'Report of the Symposium: State Reconstruction and International Engagement in Afghanistan', London: Centre for Development Research (University of Bonn) and Crisis States Programme, LSE, 30 May–1 June 2003.

Pythian, Mark, *The Politics of British Arms Sales Since 1964*, Manchester University Press, 2000.

Rahman, Aminur, 'Micro-Credit Initiatives for Equitable and Sustainable Development: Who Pays?', *World Development*, 27, 1 (1999), 67–82.

Rajan, Raghuram, 'Assume Anarchy? Why an Orthodox Economic Model May not be the Best Guide for Policy', *Finance and Development*, September 2004, 56–7.

Rawson, Claude, *God, Gulliver, and Genocide: Barbarism and the European Imagination, 1492–1945*, Oxford University Press, 2001.

Redlich, Fritz, 'Contributions in the Thirty Year War', *Economic History Review*, XII, 1 (1959), 247–54.

———, 'The Business of the Military Enterpriser, Part II: Finances' in Larry Neal (ed.), *War Finance*, vol. III, Aldershot: Edward Elgar, 1994.

Reinert, Eric S., 'Increasing Poverty in a Globalized World: Marshall Plans and Morgenthau Plans as Mechanisms of Polarization of World Incomes' in Ha-Joon Chang (ed.), *Rethinking Development Economics*, London: Anthem, 2003, 453–78.

Reno, William, 'The Real (War) Economy of Angola' in Jakkie Cilliers and Christian Dietrich (eds), *Angola's War Economy: The Role of Oil and Diamonds*, Pretoria: Institute for Security Studies, 2000, 219–35.

———, 'Resources and the Future of Violent Conflict in Sierra Leone', unpublished mimeo from a workshop held in London and organised by Queen Elizabeth House, Oxford, 2002.

———, *Somalia and Survival in the Shadow of the Global Economy*, Working Paper no. 100, Oxford: Queen Elizabeth House, 2003.

Retort, 'Blood for Oil?' *London Review of Books*, 27, 8 (21 April 2005).

Richards, Paul, *Fighting for the Rainforest: War, Youth and Resources in Sierra Leone*, Oxford: James Currey, 1996.

——— (ed.), *No Peace No War: An Anthology of Contemporary Armed Conflicts*, Oxford and Athens, OH: James Currey and Ohio University Press, 2005.

Richards, W. A., 'The Import of Firearms Into West Africa in the Eighteenth Century', *Journal of African History*, 21, 1 (1980), 43–59.

Ricolfi, Luca, 'Palestinians, 1981–2003' in Diego Gambetta (ed.), *Making Sense of Suicide Missions*, Oxford University Press, 2005, 77–129.

Roberts, Hugh, *From Segmentarity to Opacity: On Gellner and Bourdieu, or Why Algerian Politics Have Eluded Theoretical Analysis and Vice Versa*, Crisis States Programme, Working Paper no. 19, London: DESTIN/LSE, 2003.

Roberts, L., R. Lafta, R. Garfield, J. Khudairi and G. Burnham, 'Mortality Before and After the 2003 Invasion of Iraq: Cluster Sample Survey', *The Lancet*, 364, 9445 (30 October 2004).

Robin, Corey, 'Liberalism at Bay, Conservatism at Play: Fear in the Contemporary Imagination', *Social Research*, 71, 4 (winter 2004).

Robinson, Joan, *Economic Philosophy*, London: Watts, 1962.

Rose, David, *Guantanamo: America's War on Human Rights*, London: Faber and Faber, 2004.

Ross, Michael, 'The Political Economy of the Resource Curse', *World Politics*, 51, 2 (1999), 297–322.

Rothschild, Emma, *Economic Sentiments: Adam Smith, Condorcet, and the Enlightenment*, Harvard University Press, 2002.

Rowthorn, Bob and John Wells, *De-Industrialization and Foreign Trade*, Cambridge University Press, 1987.

Roxborough, Angus, 'The Persistence of War as a Sociological Problem', *International Sociology*, 14 (1999), 491–500.

Roy, Olivier, *Globalized Islam: The Search for a New Ummah*, London: Hurst, 2004.

Said, Mohammed El Sayed, 'Islam and Social Conflict' in Mary Kaldor and Basker Vashee (eds), *Restructuring the Global Military Sector*, vol. I, London and Washington: Pinter, 1997, 78–107.

Sambanis, Nicholas, 'Partitions as a Solution to Ethnic War: An Empirical Critique of the Theoretical Literature', *World Politics*, 52 (2000).

———, 'Defining and Measuring Civil War: Conceptual and Empirical Complexities', Yale University, Department of Political Science, May 2002.

Sanín, Francisco Gutiérrez, *Criminal Rebels? A Discussion of War and Criminality from the Colombian Experience*, Crisis States Programme, Working Paper no. 27, London: LSE/DESTIN, 2003.

Sarkees, Meredith R., 'The Correlates of War Data on War: An Update to 1997', *Conflict Management and Peace Science*, 18, 1 (2000), 123–44.

Saunders, Frances Stonor, *Hawkwood: Diabolical Englishman*, London: Faber and Faber, 2004.

Scheper-Hughes, Nancy, *Death Without Weeping: The Violence of Everyday Life in Brazil*, Berkeley: University of California Press, 1992.

——— and Philippe Bourgois (eds), *Violence in War and Peace: An Anthology*, Malden, MA and Oxford: Blackwell, 2004.

Schetter, Conrad, 'Misunderstanding Ethnicity in the Afghan Conflict', *ISIM Newsletter*, September 2002.

Schierup, Carl-Ulrich, 'Quasi-Proletarians and a Patriarchal Bureaucracy: Aspects of Yugoslavia's Re-Peripheralisation', *Soviet Studies*, 44, 1 (1992), 79–99.

——, 'Prelude to the Inferno: Economic Disintegration and the Political Fragmentation of Yugoslavia', *Balkan Forum*, 1, 8 (1993), 89–120.

Schwartz, Herman, *States Versus Markets: History, Geography, and the Development of the International Political Economy*, New York: St Martin's Press, 1994.

Sciascia, Leonardo, *Sicilian Uncles*, London: Carcanet, 1988.

Sebald, W. G, *The Rings of Saturn*, London: Harvill Press, 1998.

——, *On the Natural History of Destruction*, London: Penguin, 2003.

Seguino, Stephanie, 'Gender Inequality and Economic Growth: A Cross-Country Analysis', *World Development*, 28, 7 (2000), 1211–30.

Sen, Amartya, *Development as Freedom*, Oxford University Press, 1999.

Sender, John, 'Women's Struggles to Escape Poverty in Rural South Africa', *Journal of Agrarian Change*, 2, 1 (2002), 1–49.

——, Christopher Cramer and Carlos Oya, *Unequal Prospects: Disparities in the Quantity and Quality of Labour Supplies in Sub-Saharan Africa*, SOAS Department of Economics Working Paper, 145, London: SOAS, 2005.

——, 'Women Working for Wages: Putting Flesh on the Bones of a Rural Labour Market Survey in Mozambique', *Journal of Southern African Studies*, 32 (forthcoming, 2006).

Servan-Schreiber, Jean-Jacques, *Le défi américain*, Paris: Denoël, 1967.

Seventh United Nations Survey on Crime Trends and the Operations of Criminal Justice Systems (1998–2000) http://www.unodc.org/unodc/crime_cicp_survey_seventh.html.

Shaw, Martin, 'The Contemporary Mode of Warfare? Mary Kaldor's Theory of New Wars', *Review of International Political Economy*, 7 (2000), 171–80.

——, *War and Genocide*, Cambridge: Polity, 2003.

Shuler, S. R. *et al.*, 'Men's Violence Against Women in Rural Bangladesh: Undermined or Exacerbated by Micro-Credit Programs?', Population Association of America Annual Meetings, Washington, DC, 1997.

Silberschmidt, Margarethe, *'Women Forget That Men Are the Masters': Gender Antagonism and Socio-Economic Change in Kisii District, Kenya*, Uppsala: Nordiska Afrikainstitutet, 1999.

SIPRI, *SIPRI Yearbook 2004*, Stockholm International Peace Research Institute, Oxford University Press, 2004.

Skidelsky, Robert, *John Maynard Keynes*, vol. I: *Hopes Betrayed, 1883–1920*, London: Papermac, 1992.

——, *John Maynard Keynes*, vol. II: *The Economist as Saviour, 1920–1937*, London: Macmillan, 1994.

——, *John Maynard Keynes*, vol. III: *Fighting for Britain, 1937–1946*, London: Macmillan, 2000.

Smith, Adam, *The Wealth of Nations*, Harmondsworth: Penguin, 1982.

Snyder, Jack, *From Voting to Violence: Democratization and Nationalist Conflict*, New York: Norton, 2000.

South African Human Rights Commission, *Final Report of the Inquiry Into Human Rights Violations in Farming Communities*, Pretoria: SAHRC, 2003.

Soysa, Indra de, 'The Resource Curse: Are Civil Wars Driven by Rapacity or Paucity?' in Mats Berdal and David Malone (eds), *Greed and Grievance: Economic Agendas in Civil Wars*, Boulder, CO: IDRC/Lynne Rienner, 2000.

Srinivasan, T. N., *Growth, Poverty Reduction and Inequality*, http://www.worldbank.org/abcde/eu_2000/pdffiles/srinivasan.pdf, June 2000.

Starr, Joyce, 'Water Wars', *Foreign Policy*, 82 (spring 1991), 17–36.

Stedman Jones, Gareth, *An End to Poverty? A Historical Debate*, London: Profile, 2004.

Steinberg, Jonny, *Midlands*, Johannesburg and Cape Town: Jonathan Ball, 2002.

Steiner, George, *In Bluebeard's Castle: Some Notes Towards the Redefinition of Culture*, Yale University Press, 1974.

Stewart, Frances, *Crisis Prevention: Tackling Horizontal Inequalities*, Working Paper no. 33, Oxford: Queen Elizabeth House, 2000.

Stiglitz, Joseph, 'The New Development Economics', *World Development*, 14, 2 (1986), 257–65.

Stiles, T. J., *Jesse James: Last Rebel of the Civil War*, London: Pimlico, 2004.

Storey, A., 'Economics and Ethnic Conflict: Structural Adjustment in Rwanda', *Development Policy Review*, 17, 1 (March 1999), 43–63.

————, 'The World Bank's Discursive Construction of Rwanda: Poverty, Inequality and the Role of the State', Working Paper Series no. 1, School of Sociology and Social Policy, Queen's University Belfast, 2000.

Suganami, Hidemi, *On the Causes of War*, Oxford: Clarendon Press, 1996.

Sutcliffe, Bob, *100 Ways of Seeing an Unequal World*, London: Zed Books, 2001.

Swift, Jonathan, *Gulliver's Travels*, London: Penguin, 1985.

Székely, M. and M. Hilgert, *What's Behind the Inequality We Measure: An Investigation Using Latin American Data*, IBRD, Working Paper 409, Washington, DC: World Bank, 1999.

Taussig, Michael, 'Culture of Terror—Space of Death: Roger Casement's Putumayo Report and the Explanation of Torture' in Nancy Scheper-Hughes and Philippe Bourgois (eds), *Violence in War and Peace: An Anthology*, Malden, MA and Oxford: Blackwell, 2004, 39–53.

Thirlwall, A. P., *The Nature of Economic Growth: An Alternative Framework for Understanding the Performance of Nations*, Cheltenham: Edward Elgar, 2002.

Tilly, Charles, *From Mobilization to Revolution*, Reading, MA: Addison-Wesley, 1978.

————, 'War Making and State Making as Organized Crime' in Dietrich Rueschemeyer, Peter Evans and Theda Skocpol (eds), *Bringing the State Back In*, Cambridge University Press, 1985.

————, *Coercion, Capital and European States, AD990–1992*, Cambridge: Blackwell, 1992.

————, *Durable Inequality*, Berkeley, CA: University of California Press, 1999.

————, 'Introduction: Violence Viewed and Reviewed', *Social Theory*, 67, 3 (fall 2000).

————, *The Politics of Collective Violence*, Cambridge University Press, 2003.

Todorov, Tzvetan, *The Fragility of Goodness: Why Bulgaria's Jews Survived the Holocaust*, London: Weidenfeld and Nicolson, 2001.

Tolstoy, Leo, *War and Peace*, London: Penguin, 1982.

Tschirley, David L. and Rui Benfica, 'Smallholder Agriculture, Wage Labour and Rural Poverty Alleviation in Land Abundant Areas of Africa: Evidence from Mozambique', *Journal of Modern African Studies*, 39, 2 (2001), 333–58.

Turnell, Sean, *Keynes, Economics and War: A Liberal Dose of Realism*, Macquarie Economics Research Papers, 7/2002, Macquarie University, 2002.

Turton, David, 'War and Ethnicity: Global Connections and Local Violence in North East Africa and Former Yugoslavia', *Oxford Development Studies*, 25, 1 (1997), 77–94.

Tvedten, Inge, *Angola: Struggle for Peace and Reconstruction*, Boulder, CO: Westview, 1997.

UN Security Council, *Report of the Panel of Experts on the Illegal Exploitation of Natural Resources and Other Forms of Wealth of the Democratic Republic of the Congo*, New York: UN Security Council, 2002.

————, *Final Report of the Panel of Experts in the Illegal Exploitation of Natural Resources and Other Forms of Wealth of the Democratic Republic of the Congo*, New York: UN Security Council, 2003.

Villacres, E. J. and C. Bassford, 'Reclaiming the Clausewitzian Trinity', *Parameters, the Journal of the US Army War College*, autumn 1995.

Vines, Alex, *Renamo: From Terrorism to Democracy in Mozambique*, York, Amsterdam and London: Centre for Southern African Studies (York), Eduardo Mondlane Foundation and James Currey, 1996.

Vogel, Jeffrey, 'The Tragedy of History', *New Left Review*, 1, 220 (1996).

Volkov, Vadim, *Violent Entrepreneurs: The Use of Force in the Making of Russian Capitalism*, Ithaca, NY: Cornell University Press, 2002.

Vonnegut, Kurt, *Slaughterhouse 5*, London: Jonathan Cape, 1970.

Wallensteen, Peter, *Understanding Conflict Resolution: War, Peace and the Global System*, London, Thousand Oaks, CA and New Delhi: Sage, 2002.

Wheeler, Douglas and René Pélissier, *Angola*, London: Pall Mall Press, 1971.

Whitaker, B. E., *Changing Opportunities: Refugees and Host Communities in Western Tanzania*, New Issues in Refugee Research Working Paper, 11, Geneva: UNHCR, 1999.

Williams, Andrew, 'Post-Conflict Reconstruction Before the Marshall Plan', Making Peace Work, Helsinki: UNU/WIDER, 4–5 June 2004.

Wolf, Eric, *Peasant Wars of the Twentieth Century*, New York: Harper and Row, 1969.

Wong, J. W., *Deadly Dreams: Opium and the Arrow War (1856–1860) in China*, Cambridge University Press, 1998.

324 Bibliography

Woo-Cumings, Meredith, 'National Security and the Rise of the Developmental State in South Korea and Taiwan' in Henry Rowen (ed.), *Behind East Asian Growth*, New York: Routledge, 1998, 319–40.

Wood, Elisabeth J., *Insurgent Collective Action and Civil War in El Salvador*, Cambridge University Press, 2003.

Wood, Ellen Meiksins, 'Capitalism and Human Emancipation: Race, Gender and Democracy' in E. W. Wood (ed.), *Democracy Against Capitalism*, Cambridge University Press, 1995.

———, *Empire of Capital*, London and New York: Verso, 2003.

——— and Neal Wood, *A Trumpet of Sedition: Political Theory and the Rise of Capitalism, 1509–1688*, London: Pluto, 1997.

Woodhouse, Philip, Henry Bernstein and David Hulme, *African Enclosures? The Social Dynamics of Wetlands in Drylands*, Oxford, Trenton, NJ, Cape Town and Nairobi: James Currey, Africa World Press, David Philip and EEP, 2000.

Worger, William H., 'Convict Labour, Industrialists and the State in the US South and South Africa, 1870–1930', *Journal of Southern African Studies*, 30, 1 (March 2004), 63–86.

World Bank, *Angola: An Introductory Economic Review*, Washington, DC: World Bank, 1991.

———, *Breaking the Conflict Trap: Civil War and Development Policy*, Washington, DC: World Bank, 2003.

World Health Organisation, *World Report on Violence and Health*, Geneva: WHO, 2002.

———, *World Report on Violence and Health*, Geneva: WHO, 2003.

Wright, Eric Olin, 'The Metatheoretical Foundations of Charles Tilly's Durable Inequality' in *Panel on Charles Tilly's Durable Inequality*, Social Science History Conference, Chicago, 20–23 November 1999.

Wuyts, Marc, 'The Agrarian Question in Mozambique's Transition and Reconstruction' in Tony Addison (ed.), *From Conflict to Recovery in Africa*, Oxford University Press, 2003, 141–54.

Yashar, Deborah, *Demanding Democracy: Reform and Reaction in Costa Rica and Guatemala, 1870s–1950s*, Stanford University Press, 1997.

Ylikangas, Heikki, Petri Karonen and Martti Lehti, *Five Centuries of Violence in Finland and the Baltic Area*, Columbus, OH: Ohio State University Press, 2001.

Young, Tom and Margaret Hall, *Confronting Leviathan*, London: Hurst, 1997.

Zeitoun, Mark, 'The Conflict vs. Cooperation Paradox: Fighting Over or Sharing of Palestinian-Israeli Groundwater?', King's College London, Department of Geography, 2004.

INDEX

aerial bombing 29, 83
Afghanistan 70, 88, 106–7, 173,
 192–4, 235, 255–6, 277
agriculture, *see* rural economies
 and societies
aid 192, 234, 258–9
AKUF project 53
al-Qaeda 88
Algeria 41, 62, 100, 140, 141
All African Peoples Conference 140
Amazonia 98, 222, 224, 225
American Indians 108, 211
ANC (South Africa) 228
Anderson, Benedict 86
Angola 11–12, 14, 15–22, 104n, 119,
 121, 139–69, 173–4, 190–1, 199,
 233, 234, 242, 256, 284
Angola Farm 45–6
'Angola Gun' 18–20, 21, 149, 191,
 213, 236
anti-Semitism 26, 28–9
Arendt, Hannah 26, 41–2, 43n, 279
arms (trade) 4, 6n, 12, 15, 17–21,
 145, 148–150, 156, 193, 197n,
 198, 213, 219, 236–7
Arrow War 6, 38–39

Bakongo 141, 152, 162, 163, 164
Bangladesh 113, 239
Barbarism 32–37, 42–43, 47, 87,
 100, 137, 202, 210, 232, 281,
Belgium 69
Benjamin, Walter 43–4
Bernard of Clairvaux, St 101
Bihar 72–3, 83, 214, 240
Birmingham 18–19
Bloch, Marc 48, 91–2

bond issues 184, 186
Bosnia 36n, 82, 99–100, 254n, 271n
BP 159–60
Brazil 1, 12, 16, 65, 73–4, 98, 108,
 111, 219–25, 276n
Britain 6, 18–21, 23, 29, 36, 38–9,
 42n, 63, 68, 88, 119, 181–3, 209–
 11, 234, 235, 237
Browning, Christopher 26–7
Bulgaria 26n
Burundi 231, 242
Bush, George W. 6, 89, 101, 123n,
 231

Caetano, Marcello 142
Cambodia 6, 60, 272n
Canetti, Elias 100–1
capitalism 13, 24, 36–9, 147–8, 181,
 196–8, 201–19, 222–40, 285–6
Casement, Sir Roger 47
cashew nuts 175, 266–8
Catholic Church 101, 113, 243–4
Cavalli-Sforza, Luigi 57–8
Chechnya 62, 94, 195n
Chiapas 242–4
child soldiers 164–5, 237, 242
China 6, 38–9
CIA 78
civil war, definition of 61–86
Clausewitz, Carl von 3–4, 5, 26, 53
Coalition Provisional Authority
 (Iraq) 273–6
Cobden, Richard 39, 203
cocaine 173, 225, 235
coffee 152, 163, 243
Cold War 11–12, 67–8, 51, 77, 78–9,
 100, 128, 146, 193, 196, 232

Collier, Paul 129, 135, 256
Colombia 9, 73, 132–3, 173, 225, 235, 240
coltan (columbite-tantalite) 34n, 69, 175
commodity trades 77–8, 121–3, 160, 157, 172–6, 234–5; *see also individual commodities*
Congo, Democratic Republic of/ ex-Belgian Congo/Zaire 12, 34, 68–70, 78–9, 119, 121, 152, 175, 205, 234, 235, 288–9
Congo Free State 34, 47
Conrad, Joseph 34, 47
Continuum of violence 11–13, 49, 74, 84–86
Correlates of War (COW) project 53, 59
corruption 159–60, 177, 269–70
cotton 152, 158, 252, 253
Creoles (Angolan) 151, 159, 163, 164, 167
Crusades 101
Cuba 139, 141, 142, 154, 244
Cuito Cuanavale 142
Cyprus 60

Dalits 72–3
debt (of developing countries) 254
Defence Systems and Equipment international trade fair 21
democratisation 244, 257–8, 268, 269, 276
diamonds 144, 145n, 149–57, 173–5, 198, 284
dos Santos, José Eduardo 143
'Dutch Disease' 119–20

Eckstein, H. 95–7
economic aspects and explanations of conflict 40–1, 114–38, 170–98, 200–44
Ehrenreich, Barbara 117–18
Eichmann, Adolf 26, 41
Einstein, Albert 4–5
El Salvador 9, 284, 286

ELF (ethno-linguistic fractionalisation) index 104–6, 127, 129–30, 137
enclosures 208, 209–10, 235
environmental questions and war 114–16
Enzensberger, Hans Magnus 76–7, 85
Ethiopia 61, 105
ethnicity 99, 102–3, 104–8, 161–4, 242
European post-war reconstruction 203, 248–9, 278, 283
Executive Outcomes 154

famine 16, 61, 116
Fanon, Frantz 41, 140
FARC (Colombia) 9, 132–3
Farmer and Galton 18–20
favelas 219–20, 224–5
financing of wars 170–98
Finland 21, 214, 248
FNLA (Angola) 139–42, 152, 161
forced labour 45–6, 152
Foucault, Michel 28n, 42, 44, 176, 216n
France 36n, 62, 100, 108, 148, 233, 237, 247
Franco, Francisco 214
Frelimo 80–1, 261–3
Freud, Sigmund 4–5
Fuggers 182
Fukuyama, Francis 54

Gellner, Ernest 229–30
Georgia 195
Germany 25–9, 36n, 179–80, 182, 245–7, 256
Gilligan, James 96
Girard, René 117, 118
globalisation 31, 76, 78, 197–8, 204, 257
Goldhagen, Daniel 25–6
Goody, Jack 100
Greece 131–2
Guevara, Che 69, 78–9